LEADING PENNSYLVANIA INTO THE 21st CENTURY:

Policy Strategies for the Future

Edited By
DON E. EBERLY

The Commonwealth Foundation for Public Policy Alternatives

LEADING PENNSYLVANIA
INTO THE
21st CENTURY:

Policy Strategies
for the Future

Edited By
DON E. EBERLY

Library of Congress Catalog Card Number: 90-80890

ISBN 0-9626032-0-1

Cover by Rinker Graphics
Illustration by Harry L. Rinker, Jr.

Table of Contents

Acknowledgments

This anthology was conceived at the very first meeting of The Commonwealth Foundation Board of Directors. I am particularly grateful to the Foundation's Board for the counsel and encouragement that was offered from the inception of this project to its completion. Special appreciation goes to Commonwealth Foundation Co-Founder and Board Chairman Alex McKenna for his unflagging confidence in the simple belief that men and women, if determined enough, can bring about lasting change in the public policy arena. His vision is a constant source of inspiration.

I also want to recognize with deep appreciation the many grant-making foundations, corporations and individuals whose generous financial support makes the work of the Foundation possible.

I am indebted to each of the distinguished authors whose work is included in the following pages and to the dozens of leading academics across the Commonwealth who contributed advice, and gave the Foundation the benefit of their extensive experience in policy areas.

Thanks goes to Commonwealth Foundation staff members Yvonne Eshelman, Clifford Frick, Paula Gekas, and Kevin Harley, for applying their skills to see this project's fulfillment.

Finally, special recognition and thanks are in order for Foundation research assistant Keith Basehore who provided invaluable editorial assistance in transforming these manuscripts into a well-organized book.

Don Eberly

Contributors

JAMES H. BROUSSARD is Chairman of the Department of History and Political Science at Lebanon Valley College. He is also Director of Citizens Against Higher Taxes and was one of the leaders against the 1989 tax reform referendum in Pennsylvania. Broussard holds an A.B. from Harvard College and a Ph.D. from Duke University.

PATRICIA A. CRAWFORD is Director of Public Information for the Pittsburgh Public Schools. She has several published articles in educational journals and general interest magazines. Crawford earned her M.S. in Communications at Temple University.

EDWARD DONLEY serves as Chairman of the Executive Committee of the Board of Air Products and Chemicals, Inc. He was Chairman of the Business-Higher Education Forum of the American Council on Education from 1986 to 1988. Donley earned a Bachelor of Mechanical Engineering degree at Lawrence Institute of Technology.

WILLIAM A. DONOHUE is Chairman of the Department of Sociology at LaRoche College and an Adjunct Scholar at The Heritage Foundation. He has recently authored *The New Freedom: Individualism and Collectivism in the Social Lives of Americans*. Donohue has a B.A. and Ph.D. from New York University.

WILLIAM C. DUNKELBERG serves as Dean of the School of Business and Management and Professor of Economics at Temple University. He is also Chief Economist for the National Federation of Independent Business and a leading national authority on small business. Dunkelberg received an M.A. and Ph.D. in Economics from the University of Michigan.

DON E. EBERLY is President and Co-Founder of The Commonwealth Foundation, and previously was Deputy Director of the Office of Public Liaison for The White House. While in Washington, he was also Executive Director of the House Republican Study Committee. Eberly earned an M.A. at George Washington University and an M.P.A. at Harvard University.

GEORGE J. EVANS, Jr. is presently serving the Iaccoca Institute at Lehigh University as the IBM Executive in Residence. He has also been Director of Information Systems and Administration for the IBM World Trade Americas Group. Evans holds a B.S. from Duke University and an M.S. in Mathematics from Harvard University.

PETER J. FERRARA is Director of the Cato Institute Center for

Entitlement Alternatives and an Associate Professor of Law at the George Mason University School of Law. He is a former Senior Staff Member of The White House Office of Policy Development. Ferrara received an A.B. from Harvard College and a J.D. from Harvard Law School.

CHARLES R. GEROW is an adjunct faculty member of Messiah College and a practicing attorney. In addition, he has extensive consulting experience and previously served as President of Pennsylvanians for Effective Government. Gerow earned a B.A. at Messiah College and a J.D. at Villanova University School of Law.

W. WILSON GOODE is Mayor of the City of Philadelphia. Prior to being elected Mayor in 1983, he was the City's Managing Director and once held the position of Chairman of the Pennsylvania Public Utility Commission. Mayor Goode graduated from the University of Pennsylvania's Wharton School with a Master's Degree in Governmental Administration.

CHARLES E. GREENAWALT, II is an Adjunct Professor of Political Science at Millersville University. He also serves as director of a policy research staff for the Pennsylvania State Senate. Greenawalt holds both an M.A. and Ph.D. from the University of Virginia.

KEVIN F. HARLEY serves as Legislative Liaison and Research Associate for The Commonwealth Foundation. He is also a former Legislative Research Analyst in the Pennsylvania House of Representatives. Harley received a B.A. in Political Science from Millersville University.

EUGENE W. HICKOK, JR. is Assistant Professor of Political Science at Dickinson College and an Adjunct Professor of Law at Dickinson School of Law. He served as Special Assistant in the Office of Legal Counsel at the U.S. Department of Justice from 1986-1987. Hickok has an M.A. and a Ph.D. in Government from the University of Virginia.

JOSEPH HORTON is Dean of the School of Management at the University of Scranton. He has also been President of the North American Economics and Finance Association and Vice-President of the Eastern Economic Association. Horton received a B.A. from New Mexico State University and a Ph.D. from Southern Methodist University.

ROBERT V. IOSUE is President of York College. He is also a U.S. Department of Education appointee to the Congressional Advisory Committee on Student Financial Aid. Iosue holds an M.A. from Columbia University and a Ph.D. in Mathematics from Adelphi University.

MARY ELLEN KIRBY is coordinator of Parent/Community Involvement for the Pittsburgh public schools. She is responsible for Pittsburgh magnet program recruitment and formerly taught English at the University of Pittsburgh. Kirby earned her M.A. at Columbia University.

JORDAN P. KRAUSS is a private consultant and former Executive Deputy Director of the Pennsylvania Governor's Cabinet Committee on Economic Development. Krauss is the author of several major policy documents including *Enterprise Development Area Program* and *A Housing Policy for Pennsylvania*.

MICHAEL D. LaGREGA is Professor of Engineering at Bucknell University and a Program Director for Environmental Resources Management, Inc. He is the former Director of Hazardous Waste Planning for the Pennsylvania Department of Environmental Resources. LaGrega received both an M.S. and Ph.D. in Environmental Engineering from Syracuse University.

ANDREW S. McELWAINE serves as Director of Congressional Affairs for the Institute of Scrap Recycling Industries, Inc. Previously, he was Legislative Counsel to Senator John Heinz and as Senator Heinz' Staff Director on the Senate Governmental Affairs Committee. He holds a J.D. from Duke University.

HAROLD D. MILLER is Associate Dean of the School of Urban and Public Affairs at Carnegie Mellon University. From 1980 to 1986, he served first as Deputy Director and then Director of the Pennsylvania Governor's Office of Policy Development. Miller has an M.S. in Public Management and Policy from Carnegie Mellon University.

NEVIN J. MINDLIN is Minority Staff Director of the Pennsylvania House of Representatives Labor Relations Committee. He is responsible for managing the research operations of the committee along with performing analysis of major legislative policy issues. Mindlin earned an M.A. in Government at Lehigh University.

DANIEL S. NAGIN is Professor of Management at the School of Urban and Public Affairs, Carnegie Mellon University. He was Deputy Secretary of Fiscal Policy and Analysis in the Pennsylvania Department of Revenue from 1981 to 1986. Nagin received his M.S. and Ph.D. from Carnegie Mellon University.

KANT RAO is Associate Professor of Business Administration at The Pennsylvania State University. He has been Deputy Budget Secretary for the Commonwealth of Pennsylvania and Associate Deputy Secretary for the Pennsylvania Department of

Transportation. Rao holds a Ph.D. in Management Science from Pennsylvania State University.

CAROLE A. RUBLEY is a Regulatory Analyst at Environmental Resources Management, Inc. She is a member of the Pennsylvania Solid Waste Advisory Committee and is involved with designing and presenting seminars on solid waste issues. Rubley has an M.S. in Environmental Health from West Chester University.

JAMES I. SCHEINER is President and Chief Operating Officer of Stoner Associates, Inc. He served in the Governor's Cabinet as Secretary of the Pennsylvania Department of Revenue from 1983-1987 and as Deputy Secretary of Transportation from 1979-1983. Scheiner earned a B.S. at the United States Military Academy and an M.P.A. at Princeton University.

KEVIN C. SONTHEIMER is Chairman of the Department of Economics and Director of the Economic Policy Institute at the University of Pittsburgh. He has previously been on the faculty of the Virginia Polytechnic Institute and Macalester College. Sontheimer holds an M.A. from Pennsylvania State University and a Ph.D. from the University of Minnesota.

JOHN A. SPARKS is Professor of Business Administration at Grove City College. He is President of the Public Policy Education Fund, and is also a member of the law firm of Bogaty, McEwen and Sparks, P.C. Sparks received an A.B. from Grove City College and a J.D. from the University of Michigan Law School.

BRADY M. STROH is presently the Senior Partner of Decision Support Services and Contractor for Delta Development Group, Inc. Stroh has experience in demographic analysis and local planning. He has a Master's Degree in Urban and Regional Planning from Pennsylvania State University.

ANTHONY R. TOMAZINIS is Professor of City and Regional Planning at the University of Pennsylvania. He has pioneered work in the privatization of public sector delivery systems in both the United States and the Third World. Tomazinis earned his Ph.D. at the University of Pennsylvania.

RICHARD C. WALLACE, JR. is Superintendent of Schools in the Pittsburgh Public School District. He is also an Adjunct Professor at the University of Pittsburgh Graduate School of Education. Wallace received both his Master's and Doctorate degrees from Boston College.

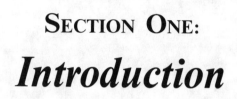

SECTION ONE:

Introduction

CHAPTER ONE

FACING GLOBAL CHANGE THROUGH BOLD POLICIES AND VISIONARY LEADERSHIP
By Don E. Eberly

Pennsylvanians, like all Americans, are facing momentous changes at a dizzying pace. Pollster George Gallup has described the profound shifts underway just beneath the surface of American society as "a great historical tidal wave — a set of monumental political, social and economic impulses, which are carrying us relentlessly toward a rendezvous with the future."[1]

If the next century is, as futurists tell us, about job-threatening competition in global markets, and an information-based economy with constant technological innovation, the 21st century has already arrived. What perhaps hasn't arrived is a commensurate change in our national thinking. Living in an integrated global village will require "thinking globally, acting locally." As John Naisbitt, author of the best-seller *Megatrends*, has said: "the problem is our thinking, our attitudes and consequently our decision-making have not caught up with the reality of things. We act on assumptions that are out of date."[2]

In the pages that follow, The Commonwealth Foundation is offering to help Pennsylvania's leaders think about the future, and to better understand how changing global realities are affecting the lives of our people. The authors that have contributed to this work are pleased to present a range of ideas that might help reinvigorate Pennsylvania's policy process and help ensure that the state remains competitive and strong.

Pennsylvania: Past, Present and Future

As Pennsylvania collectively focuses on the new century just over the horizon, contrasts will inevitably be drawn between Pennsylvania's current position relative to her glorious past and uncertain future. The images that emerge are mixed.

At the turn of the last century, Pennsylvania had 32 seats (which peaked at 36 in 1921) in the U.S. Congress, making it one of the most powerful states in the Union. Today, the number is down to 23, and it is about to lose two or three more to the sunbelt.

As we entered the 20th century, one third of the nation's population farmed. By the turn of the 21st century, less than 3% of the population will produce 120% of the nation's food needs, which will be fewer people than are currently employed by universities.

One hundred years ago, Pennsylvania worried about finding jobs for the millions of immigrants moving into our urban centers. Today, the worry is over a shortage of skilled workers, as America's industrial age gives way to an economy in which only 9% of Americans work in factories.

Pennsylvania will always have a lot going for it, and if properly managed, the enduring qualities of its land, people and enterprises will continue to produce renewal and growth. The state possesses major assets in its rich agriculture, strong and diverse small business sector and top ranked universities. Nature has strategically granted it easy access to large regional markets, and endowed it with an abundance of mineral resources and a natural beauty that attracts tourists from far and wide.

But there are continuing signs that, if not properly lead by bold policies and visionary leadership, Pennsylvania may face decline into second rate status. In addition to lost political clout through the shifting of Congressional seats to the west and south, significant percentages of Pennsylvania's most gifted university graduates are choosing to pursue opportunity elsewhere.

Although the work ethic remains strong, large percentages of the state's work force is aging, is underskilled, or is locked in poverty. Pennsylvania has the second highest percentage of senior citizens (15.2% of its population) of any state in the country. It is home to a sizable urban underclass that is wracked by crime, drugs and joblessness. The state ranks third in illiteracy and 48th in the number of its high school graduates who go on to college.

Perhaps the state's greatest handicap is not its problems, but its approach to them, which is often rooted in old ideas and old political alliances. Pennsylvania is not a state that is known for its innovation and openness to change. Left unaltered, these social and political traits may only compound the state's economic decline, for while Pennsylvania has its own unique problems, it is also, like every other state, caught in the currents of major national and international trends. America is quickly shifting from a self-sufficient national economy, to an interdependent global economy in which the U.S. is far less dominant, production is shared, and economic activity is heavily influenced by international capital flows.

This will inevitably result in a global division of labor which results in the transfer of traditional labor-intensive manufacturing, long the economic bedrock of the industrial northeast, to the third world. Today, our manufacturers must compete with labor forces paid as little as one-tenth of what American workers earn. To expand economically, advanced nations will have no alternative but turn to those fields which require more advanced skills — service industries and those which create, manage and distribute information.

The Global Economy, The Information Age and the Restructuring of American Business

The economic shifts and social change produced today by the microelectronic revolution are far more profound in their consequences for American society than such previous breakthroughs as steam power, electricity, or the combustion engine.

According to leading management guru Peter Drucker, of all the major shifts underway in American society, the biggest and most consequential, by far, is the shift to the information-based economy in all developed countries. Drucker has described the society we're moving into as a "knowledge society," where the vast majority of us will ultimately be "knowledge workers" who manage great volumes of information, and who are required to continuously adapt in order to stay ahead. With scientific knowledge doubling every ten to fifteen years, the generation currently entering the work force may be forced to change careers as often as three times.

For a state like Pennsylvania with heavy manufacturing interests, these global shifts will mean continuing disruption. In many of our communities where, for decades, one generation has followed another into manufacturing jobs, the social center of gravity is now shifting to service and information careers. In the 21st century, the passport to good jobs and career opportunities in these communities will be a good education and the pursuit of continuous learning as a matter of habit and life-style.

With this transformation will come unprecedented entre-preneurial opportunity for individuals who prepare. As individ-ual skills and entrepreneurship become the engine of growth, the concentrated power of large centralized institutions — corporations and labor unions, in particular — will be weakened and dispersed. Since 1980, America's 500 largest companies have lost almost three million jobs, while small businesses — those with one hundred employees or fewer — have created ten million.[3] According to Forbes, start-up companies have created over 14 million jobs since 1980.[4] The number of Americans who run businesses or work for them-selves now equals the number who belong to unions. In Penn-sylvania, virtually all new jobs today are being created by this small business sector.

Many Pennsylvanians will continue to owe their jobs to large publicly held companies. But to preserve these jobs and survive in the face of global competition, big business will be forced to make unprecedented commitments to innovation. Surveys of corporate CEO's indicate that more time than ever before is being spent by executives on coping with international competi-tion. In 1960, only 20% of goods produced in the U.S. were in active competition with foreign products; by the 1980's a full 70% were. In 1970, imports accounted for 9% of all goods pur-chased by Americans; just ten years later, they accounted for 22%.[5]

But fostering a climate of innovation that produces great re-search and product breakthroughs requires a long-term vision. Corporate America has come under increasing attack for its short-term perspective. John Naisbitt has openly blamed American business managers for our nation's economic de-cline. He said their preoccupation "with short-term results and quantitative measurements" were responsible for the neglect of the necessary investment and innovations needed to create wealth.[6] He specifically blamed the incentives built into corporate salary and bonus deals that sacrificed long-term growth for short-term profits.

In companies large and small, short-term thinking must give way to long-term strategies that are long on research and invest-ment, and short on immediate gratification. As one corporate leader put it:

In a world awash in low-wage labor, our future rests
upon our ability to make research breakthroughs in
the laboratory, to translate those breakthroughs into
new products and processes, and to manufacture the
results using the kind of technological sophistication
and skilled labor that is still rare in developing nations. In a nutshell, our future rests upon our ability
to innovate.

Innovating and rethinking old assumptions will be central to
Pennsylvania's long term prosperity. As the world shrinks even
farther in the 1990's and beyond, as distance evaporates as a
limiting social and economic factor, as communication replaces transportation as the primary mode of human interaction, and trade is driven by information and capitol, old
policies and outmoded thinking will have to be replaced. When
the global economy allows U.S. firms to trade stock in Hong
Kong or Tokyo, and move production offshore to South America
or Eastern Europe, the physical boundaries of states and
nations become irrelevant. Social progress becomes determined instead by such intangible barriers as attitudes, ideas and
values.

It seems absurd in the extreme, for example, that in the face of
a national trend toward home-based entrepreneurship, the
Pennsylvania Legislature would watch approvingly as industrial homework is banned and thousands of jobs are instantly
transferred to Asia. By the turn of the 21st century, as many as
one in every five workers may be employed out of the home, yet
Pennsylvania chooses the path of clutching to old ideas rather
than embracing new economic realities and opportunities.

To prevent the erosion of economic opportunity, Pennsylvania policy makers will need to examine all current policies
and programs in light of what will be required for the Commonwealth to meet the challenges of a global economy.

The Changing Federal System: Each State For Itself

As states struggle to preserve their competitive footing, they
will be forced to get by with less support from Washington.
Naisbitt has said that the most important governments in
America are state and local. Once ridiculed as public policy

backwaters lacking in professionalism and vision, states are increasingly becoming the "laboratories of democracy," supplying creative new ideas and pulling a larger share of the nation's fiscal load.

The decisions of state governments will be more important than ever in determining the economic destinies of the respective states and, in turn, the nation. Since the 1950's, state and local governments have been consuming a growing share of the nation's economic output (now 15% of GNP) and a larger portion of total national expenditures (now 27% of total national spending). The result is that high tax states may find their economies producing less growth, their business climates worsening, and their tax bases shrinking.

The trend of shifting the fiscal burden to states, produced in large part by persistent federal deficits, is expected to continue well into the future. This trend will undoubtedly place northeast industrial states with aging populations and large urban centers such as Pennsylvania at a greater disadvantage, which makes the need for creative cost-cutting and policy innovation within such states all the more compelling.

The experience of recent years suggests that northeast states can prosper if they develop aggressive leadership, and direct that leadership toward reinvigorating the economy through tax reduction, getting tough with wasteful government, and boosting the role of the private sector. Effective state-level leadership will not only supply clear-headed fiscal prudence, it will be called upon to cajole and browbeat recalcitrant political forces into action.

Pennsylvania can become a laboratory of growth and opportunity for the world to admire, but only if its leaders have an understanding of the present, a clear vision for the future, and a strategy for how to get there. The state does not distinguish itself, for example, when it numbers itself among only a handful of states who have done nothing to reform product liability laws which are destroying product innovation and development. Pennsylvania must put failed economics, outdated politics and short-sighted interests behind.

Rethinking What Government Does and How It Does It

One of the disadvantages of modern interest group politics is that government does what it does more on the basis of interest group pressures than on rational strategies or sound economics. Government services and programs are delivered almost entirely on the basis of political, not economic, principles. New programs are spun off, not because cost benefit ratios suggest they are a wise public investment, but because interest groups supporting action are stronger than those opposing it. The result: pressing problems are rarely effectively addressed, but they always serve as a pretext for more bureaucracy, the hiring of more program consultants, the letting of more contracts, and the creation of more patronage posts. In the end, interest groups are satisfied, politicians are rewarded, and the economic climate becomes more enervated.

During earlier periods when government faced rapid revenue expansion and limited global competition, the consequences might have been minimal. But in the world of today, where billions in capital cross sovereign state and national boundaries in a matter of seconds, carrying with it productive capacity and jobs, state and local governments will increasingly pay a high price as their economies sputter under the load of heavy bureaucracy, senseless regulation, and tax overload. Former Colorado Governor Richard Lamm has said it very well:

> We are sailing into a new world of public policy: a world as strange as Columbus discovered. It is a world where infinite governmental demands have run straight into finite resources.[7]

He added that most of our institutional memories and political culture come out the 1960's and 1970's when the U.S. had the industrial world's highest productivity growth rate and was doubling its wealth every 30 to 40 years. Today we have the lowest rate of productivity growth in the industrial world, and it now takes approximately 130 years to double our national wealth.

Lamm argues that the next governmental revolution will be a revolution of helping Americans "adjust to the realization that the economy of the country cannot carry the expectations we have built up in our citizens." He says, if we are to meet public needs, governments — federal and state — will have to "rethink what they do and how they do it."[8]

Policy makers in the future will have to reconcile the public's contradictory demands. On the one hand, people want solutions. They want cities and towns that are well managed, police and prison systems that protect, schools that teach, and roads and infrastructure that get us safely and efficiently where we want to go. Our citizens at the same time want their trash cheaply and efficiently removed and their environment protected from the waste overload, all with strong decisive action.

On the other hand, they don't always want government solutions. The American people simultaneously want to "do more to help the poor" but they don't want more government programs, and certainly don't want higher taxes. This is true for many other categories of government. The criminal justice system, for example, will come under increasing pressure to respond to the competing demands of the public to both get criminals off the street and to find ways to house them without busting the budget.

Under this new paradigm, which is essentially liberal in its goals while conservative in means, government may simply be called upon to be the catalyst — providing the leadership and organizing the solutions through means other than costly and direct government intervention. More and more, the public can't be fooled: they know the difference between political leadership and political posturing that brings ineffective solutions.

Before paying the price, the people want to know there is some certainty of the program working. They're unlikely to tolerate the creation of more programs like CETA, which spent $85 billion dollars over its 15 year history on dubious job-creating activity before finally being abolished. Government today must cease to be the employment agency. It must become a provider of vital services on a lean, no thrills basis, and rely as extensively as possible on the private sector.

Education: The Coming Revolution

If there is one American institution that cries out for radical reform, and will probably get it in the coming decades, it is the public school system. At the very time when literacy skills are most important to America's advancement, the American educational system is turning out a grossly inferior product. One University of Texas study showed that only 40% of American adults can read and write well enough to cope with rudimentary job related writing requirements like completing a job application or government forms. It seems absurd, in the face of this astonishing failure, that anyone would blame America's declining economic status on "unfair competition from abroad."

The business community is slowly awakening to the basic fact that maintaining a competitive advantage in the information age may depend more on what is happening in the classroom than what is happening in the halls of Congress on such vital issues as trade, regulatory or tax policies, as important as those policies are. The burden of closing the learning deficit is already falling to business. According to the Carnegie Foundation for the Advancement of Teaching, U.S. companies are currently spending upwards of $40 billion a year to deliver education to about eight million workers.[9] And if current trends continue, the costs to corporate America of this on-the-job education will soon exceed the $60 billion that colleges and universities spend annually on post-secondary education.

Contributing to the alarm is the growing sense that, as far as American education is concerned, the more things change, the more they stay the same. In fact, in many respects schools have become worse. The status quo, having failed to produce any discernible progress, will increasingly be seen as the culprit. Every wave of "reform" in the recent past has produced schools that are even more politicized, more unionized, and more buffeted about by pressure groups that have narrow, not broad public interests, foremost in mind.

Educational reforms in the 1990's will go well beyond the mere tinkering that was adopted in the 1980's. The public will demand broader parental input, greater school output, and higher accountability across the board. The fact is that no American institution, public or private, has enjoyed such a low level of accountability for actual results. Where conventional education reformers may have miscalculated is in mistaking the people's strong support for the public education with boundless patience in waiting for results.

The American people are slowly realizing that legislatures have adopted just about every costly "reform" the education establishment has proposed, particularly since the President's Education Commission in 1983 warned of a rising tide of mediocrity which placed the entire nation at risk, and none of it has worked. All of the factors the experts told us would improve education — better teacher pupil ratios, higher expenditures, and more generous teacher salaries — have been addressed, and they appear to be having virtually no measurable effect on educational quality.

It is a traditional American impulse to assume that good things can be bought. Put enough money in, and results will follow. Yet, in the field of education, this impulse may have contributed to a postponement of real change. The American educational system is clearly not lacking in money. National expenditures per pupil have more than tripled since 1950, ballooning by 83% (in real terms) since 1970 alone. And our spending more per-pupil has long been at or near the top of all industrial nations.

What have we received for this money-equals-quality reform? Virtually no change in SAT scores. SAT scores dropped 90 points between 1963 and 1981, and today remain more than 75 points below their highwater mark. A comparison of the best math students in 11 nations, including many nations with which the U.S. has to compete economically, shows that American students came in dead last in calculus and algebra. Another recent study conducted by the Educational Testing Service found that American 13 year-olds perform worse in science and math than students in all of the other countries tested. South Korea's students achieved levels four times higher than that of American students. Pennsylvania ranks eighth in per pupil expenditures, but is 20 points below the national average in SAT scores.

Not surprisingly, the debate over education reform is focusing less on money and more on the way we organize education in America. David Kearn, Chairman of the Xerox Corporation and coauthor of the recent book on public education entitled *Winning the Brain Race* has described today's public education system as "a failed monopoly — bureaucratic, rigid and in unsteady control of dissatisfied captive markets."[10]

The fact is the current system is obsolete. How is it, many are asking, that as we approach the 21st century, we have an educational system that was designed, not in the 20th century, not even in the industrial age, but in the agrarian age when 80% of the people graduated and went off to perform roughly the same tasks for an entire lifetime?

Increasingly, states are coping with educational decline and parental dissatisfaction by adopting far reaching reforms. Gone is the policy of centralization and standardization.

Coming in its place is a set of policies broadly described as "public schools of choice," which introduce parental choice, creative entrepreneurship within schools, and competition among school districts. Administrators are encouraged to run schools like companies, with everyone involved in the learning process viewing themselves as innovators and entrepreneurs who are forced to maintain happy customers through superior products.

Cities: Reversing the Downward Spiral

With two major metropolitan centers, and dozens of smaller cities, many of them facing declining tax bases and disintegrating infrastructures, Pennsylvania will have to come to grips with its urban development problems in the 21st century. With a less responsive federal government transferring more urban expenses to the states, urban and rural constituencies throughout Pennsylvania will ultimately discover that they have a shared interest in alleviating urban decay.

It is now almost universally recognized that large new programs from Washington are only not forthcoming, but even if they were to arrive, they would probably fail to solve many of the most acute problems. Polls show that even the neediest residents in places like Philadelphia and Pittsburgh doubt that solutions out of Washington or Harrisburg would make much of a difference.

As Peter Drucker has pointed out, no one need expect the arrival any time soon of a bold new scheme such as a "New Deal," "Fair Deal," or "Great Society." Such comprehensive, top-down strategies are now viewed as costly failures which inspire little confidence or enthusiasm, even as slogans in the political marketplace. The policies of the future will substitute "bottoms-up," community-based ideas which emphasize empowering people by creating opportunity rather than redistributing income, and which harness the private sector through such initiatives as enterprise zones and partnerships with the private and volunteer sectors.

While the interests of disadvantaged Americans may have been well served during the 1970's and 1980's through the expansion of legal protection against discrimination, the elevation of low income people in the future will increasingly require economic strategies, ridding neighborhoods of crime, improving education, and rebuilding destroyed neighborhood institutions like the family, churches and volunteer networks. Studies show that one of the greatest threats to low-income neighborhoods today is crime. Rampant inner city violence and theft serves as perhaps the heaviest "tax" on minority businesses, property owners, and individuals who want nothing more than to move freely about their neighborhoods.

One of the key ingredients of upward mobility during earlier periods was mobility. When jobs moved, people moved with them. Yet today the poor are becoming less and less mobile, and more are locked into pockets of despair where conditions of poverty become self-perpetuating, while middle class and the working poor move out.

Tragically, today the composition of cities is changing to the detriment of poor people. According to the Census Bureau, 57% of all Blacks and 49% of Hispanics live in the central cities. But about 75% of all new jobs are in the suburbs, according to the Bureau of Labor Statistics. Philadelphia lost more than 350,000 people and 200,000 jobs since 1966, leaving behind a tax base which depends very heavily on the poor themselves.

When the producers of wealth, even city managers and people who make their living caring for the poor migrate to the suburbs, the needy are starved of the socialization that previous generations of poor people received from economically mixed neighborhoods. A growing commentary has focused on the behavioral and attitudinal traits of individuals who have been raised in the underclass, isolated from middle class role models. The result: children having children, gangs substituting for families, young males channeling entrepreneurial abilities into thriving drug businesses, and behavioral traits that are increasingly outside the American mainstream.

The Convergence of Economic and Social Issues

Periods of rapid economic change in the past have usually been accompanied by deep social upheaval, and this is certainly true today. Perhaps like never before, the social and economic problems of the late 20th century have intersected to produce a society which is at once absorbed with fears of external economic threat and bogged down in internal social malaise.

Many of the underlying stresses in post-industrial America are social, not economic, but they produce economic consequences. One nationally recognized economist recently lamented the "death of economics," citing as evidence the fact that many leading newspapers now dwell on crime, AIDS, educational decline, drugs, teen pregnancy, and other social ills rather than on such standard economic fare as monetary policy and federal deficits.

In reality, this new focus on social concerns is perhaps a more honest way of examining our nation's underlying fiscal and economic problems. Whether it is lost productivity due to domestic conflict and drug and alcohol abuse, or federal deficits spurred on by mounting social welfare costs, many of today's economic problems are rooted in changing individual behavior and social mores. According to one study, for example, the stress alone produced by rapid social change costs the American economy around $150 billion per year in lowered productivity, absenteeism and spiraling medical costs.[11]

Another social trend with potentially dire economic consequences for a nation hoping to expand and compete economically is the so-called "birth dearth." Between 1965 and 1980, the U.S birth rate plummeted. Total births in the U.S dropped from 72.5 million during the postwar baby-boom years to 56.6 million in the baby-bust generation. Not only will demand for housing and other basic consumer goods decline, but the labor shortage may deepen.

Social disease will continue to play a major role in driving up costs and driving down the ranks of qualified workers. In the early 1990's, approximately 54,000 Americans will be dying of AIDS each year, more than the annual road casualty toll of 50,000 people today, and more than the casualties of the entire Vietnam War.[12] By 1991, AIDS-related medical bills could total as much as $14 billion annually. When lost productivity is thrown in, annual costs will exceed $66 billion.[13] When coupled with a birth rate that is well below the replacement rate, increasing numbers of analysts are worried about the growing impact of the loss of workers on productivity. Biology becomes destiny.

The Economic Impact of Changing Social Values

As society braces for a long competitive struggle, its greatest

asset or liability will be its human capital. The workforce of
tomorrow will be a place where cognitive and character qualities will substitute for manual labor. Such a society will require,
as one leading economist put it: "human creative power, a
highly educated work force, organizational talent, the ability to
choose, the ability to adapt." [14] The question, then, becomes
whether we are replenishing society with individuals who
possess the necessary skills and aptitude to prevent decline.

Perhaps the most disconcerting social indicator concerns our
nation's children. Societies with a long-term perspective have
always placed their highest priority on children, sacrificing
rewards today for the betterment of the next generation tomorrow, selflessly passing on the basic aptitudes, ethics and
habits of democratic life.

As the "me" decade draws to a close, more are coming to the
conclusion that today's society may be collectively engaged in a
reverse Robin Hood scheme, living well today off of assets
borrowed from future generations.

The current generation has been particularly ungenerous
towards its children. Greater numbers of children are born out
of wedlock than ever before. Tens of thousands face early
handicaps like fetal alcohol syndrome, nutrition deficiencies
and increasingly the AIDS virus. Every year, 2.5 million children are physically or sexually abused. One in five lives in poverty; one in every four with a single parent. Ten million are
classified as "latch key" kids. Since 1950, the suicide rate for
young people aged 15-24 tripled, becoming in 1984 the second
leading cause of death for that age group.[15] The institutional
care of youth in foster care, psychiatric institutions, and juvenile detention centers skyrocketed throughout the eighties.

Today's values are oriented overwhelmingly towards achieving material goals. Ironically, while 76% of all college freshman,
according to one study, have ranked "being very well off financially" as their top personal goal, most young adults are less
equipped to avail themselves of the opportunity than their
predecessors.[16] The tragedy is that while America has produced
more economic opportunity than ever dreamed of previously,
with quality jobs going unfilled, millions of American youth are
missing out entirely because adults have failed them.

As more people conclude that our children have become an
expendable commodity and calls for action increase, a growing
debate will focus on private versus public responsibilities for

children. How far can the government go in playing parent, or even enforcing parental responsibilities among adults, particularly indigent adults?

Some will fault cutbacks in federal programs, or a lack of commitment to imaginative new public initiatives. However, if government is the solution, it is hard to imagine what degree of government intervention would be needed to deal effectively with the problems of teen pregnancy, truancy and delinquency, high school drop out, and drugs. The emotional and cognitive development of children has more to do with the voluntary decisions of adults than the inaction of government.

Family Disintegration and Poverty

Perhaps the most fundamental of all social ailments is the continuing and growing problem of family disintegration and non-formation. The importance of the family preservation is not, as many have come to assume, a tenet of western morality alone, somehow divorced from purely pragmatic considerations. Moreover, it was Confucious, not Moses, Jesus, or Plato who emphasized that family breakup would bring about the unraveling of the social fabric. Not coincidentally, many of the Asian countries that are giving U.S. industries the run for their economic lives, are traditional cultures which place a heavy emphasis of family strength and parental authority over children.

Although behavioral science research has consistently warned of the consequences, particularly for young children, of family disruption, America now leads the world in several categories, including the rate of teen pregnancy and the number of marriages terminated in divorce. More than 15 million kids are now living in single parent families, and, according to the Census Bureau, by the mid 1990's, 50% of all children will have spent at least some time between the age of 1 and 18 living with just one parent.

The income inequities created by this family disruption for women and children is severe. Today, family breakup is the leading cause of poverty in America. Since the early seventies, there has been a sevenfold increase in single parent families and half of these families live at or near the poverty level. Sixty percent of all new poverty in America today is created by the formation of single parent families.

The result is that every public and private institution in America — the day care system, public schools, universities, social agencies, the juvenile justice system, police, private charities, and employers — are all forced to adjust to, and compensate for the one private institution — the family — which had long been counted on to produce character and competence in people.

Although business leaders typically view these societal issues as outside of their range of interests or concerns, private businesses will increasingly bear the greatest burden for them. The economic costs to the nation in underskilled and maladjusted workers, lost economic output, and social welfare costs is simply staggering. State and local governments spend billions through our health and welfare system dealing with spouse and child abuse, juvenile delinquency, educational decline and poverty.

Business interests would be well served by joining with other cultural forces to reinforce the family. It is the one cost-effective social agency, which, if strengthened, could produce a new generation of well adjusted workers at no cost to anyone, and great savings for everyone.

Conclusion

Expert opinion is divided on whether America is simply going through massive change and readjustment, or whether she is staggering towards decline. Perhaps, as Paul Kennedy argues in *The Rise and Fall of Great Nations*, world leadership is too great a burden for any one nation to endure for long; that the passing of economic supremacy and world leadership is only natural, even desirable.

On the other hand, there is plenty of evidence to suggest that America remains a highly resilient society that is still capable of facing its challenges with sober-minded realism and tough action. Marvin Cetron and Owen Davies, writing in *American Renaissance* see an America at the turn of the next century which has fundamentally come to grips with its educational decline, has strengthened its middle class, retooled its industry and reformed its institutions. The key is that America will put itself on a "war footing," not for the purpose of suppressing foreign aggressors, but to defeat internal threats, particularly educational mediocrity. According to Cetron and Davies, America in the 1990s will "at long last recognize in debt, drugs, AIDS and illiteracy the fabled moral equivalent of war and achieve the consensus that has so long eluded them."[17]

What is certain about the future is that leadership at all levels of society will be perhaps the most critical ingredient for achieving progress. But leaders must lead. They must take risks and confront the status quo. Political leadership, particularly at the state level, will be called upon to develop visionary agendas and to muster the political will to adopt them.

This book is offered in the hope that policymakers will consider these and other ideas to ensure that Pennsylvania will be a strong, competitive state in the 21st century. With enlightened community and political leadership, Pennsylvania will be a state whose proud heritage is preserved and whose economy is a magnet for growth and expanded opportunity for generations to come.

CHAPTER TWO

PENNSYLVANIA: A STATE IN TRANSITION
By Brady M. Stroh

EDITOR'S SUMMARY

Pennsylvania is culturally and demographically diverse. If America was the great melting pot of the world, Pennsylvania was the great melting pot of the nation. Most of the immigrants were German, Scottish, Irish, English, Welsh, Italian, Polish, and Swedish.

Drastic changes in immigration patterns have occurred in the past fifty years. Immigration has shifted from mainly European to Asian and Latin American. For example, from 1940 to 1970 the number of Italian and Polish born residents fell 55% and 70% respectively, while the number of Latin American immigrants increased by 23% and Asians increased their ranks by 135%.

Stagnation in population growth has accompanied immigration pattern changes. From 1790 until 1910, Pennsylvania increased its population by at least 20% every ten years. More recently, in the 1970's, the population inched up by only 0.5%. Extremely modest ten year growth rates of less than 2% are anticipated until, at least, the year 2000.

Pennsylvania's population is aging. Due to advances in medicine, people are living much longer than 100 years ago. In 1880, only 3.9% of the population was age 65 or older but by 1980, nearly 13% of all persons in the Commonwealth were 65 or older.

Another important population change is the birth rate decline. The baby boom of the post-World War II era has given way to fewer and fewer live births. The birth peak in the Commonwealth was in 1957 when 254,997 babies were born, but by 1980, the number of live births had declined to 148,004.

Pennsylvania's economy has undergone significant changes during the past 200 years. As early as 1750, Philadelphia was considered the industrial hub of the colonies and continued to be the nation's most important industrial center well into the 20th century. However, beginning in the 1950's, Pennsylvania's industrial supremacy began to falter.

Manufacturing in Pennsylvania has given way to the service industry. In 1950, over 35% of the workforce was employed in manufacturing but by the 1980 census this number had dropped to 26.5%. Meanwhile, the portion of the workforce employed in services has risen from under 8% in 1950 to close to 30% today.

Above all, the most significant demographic change in Pennsylvania involves regional diversity. Growth has been concentrated in the Commonwealth's south and east. Many of the other areas of the state offer inexpensive land for development and an eager workforce. The challenge now is to convince business and industry to move into these areas.

Brady M. Stroh is presently the Senior Partner of Decision Support Services and a Consultant with Delta Development Group, Inc.

They came to Pennsylvania in search of trade routes to India and the Far East. They were the Dutch and the Dutch East India Company escorted by the English navigator Henry Hudson and his ship, the Half Moon. What they discovered was not a passage way to the distant riches of India but, instead, a land that itself innocently flaunted vast natural wealth — navigable inland waterways, fertile river valleys, hardwood forests, abundant wildlife for furs and skins and Native Americans with whom to trade. It was 1609 and they stayed, not to conquer or settle, but simply to establish and protect their commercial interests.

For thirty years the Dutch monopolized the trading activity between Europe and the Delaware Bay region. But soon others began to arrive. By 1626 the Swedes and the Swedish South Company had found their way to the region, breaking the Dutch monopoly. Their interests too were trade and commerce. But rather than coming to simply protect and defend, they settled new communities and developed the land — first at New Sweden near present day Wilmington, later to the more defensible Tinicum Island and eventually to Upland, the site of present day Chester.

From its earliest pre-colonial beginnings the fuel that fed Pennsylvania's growth was the desire of people of diverse nationalities and cultures to trade goods and skills with one another in order to better their economic situation. Their spirit of entrepreneurship and independence established a societal drive that propelled Pennsylvania and the nation from colonization and revolution to industrialization, consumerism and global economic interdependence. The economic journey from 1609 to 1990 has been extremely difficult and at times excruciatingly painful — civil war, depression, world wars and military conflicts. Nevertheless, the spirit today is as strong as it was then, indeed maybe stronger.

But Pennsylvania is a land founded on a base much broader than the selfish pursuit of wealth and fortune. It more properly and traditionally symbolizes the fruit of a quest for spiritual and intellectual liberty. For it was the compulsion to escape the tyranny of the Anglican Church and the British Crown, not economic gain, that drove William Penn and his Quaker followers to Chester in 1682 to begin the "Holy Experiment."

Pennsylvania's past reflects the powerful will of a culturally and demographically diverse people to protect and promote their deeply held principles of spiritual independence, intellectual freedom, social well being and economic prosperity. The nature and importance of these ideals have changed through time and will continue to evolve into the 21st century. But it is these ever changing values that challenge us, as a society, in mapping our future. How many of us are there? How old are we? How rich or poor are we? How educated are we? How do we make our living? Where have we come from? Where are we going? What do we want for ourselves and for others? To solve the problems facing us in the 21st century we must responsibly ponder and act on these questions.

The Infant State Grows

By 1681, when William Penn was granted a charter for the first 28 million acres of land that was to become Pennsylvania, only about 500 persons had established their homes and communities there. They were the original Swedish, Dutch and English settlers and while a few of these early Pennsylvanians made their fortune exporting furs, skins and tobacco to the mother land, most of them scratched out meager lives as subsistence farmers. In a sense, these first 500 were the forward scouts who cleared the land and established the first urban centers in Pennsylvania to which the later arriving masses would gravitate.

The great migration to Pennsylvania, which began soon after the founding of Philadelphia in 1682, continued for over 200 years, well into the 1900's. In the 19 years from 1681 to 1700, the population of the colony increased from 500 to over 20,000. By 1720 there were 50,000 Pennsylvanians, and sometime around 1740 the population hit the 100,000 mark. When the first constitutionally mandated U.S. census was taken in 1790 the official population of the Commonwealth was recorded at 434,373. In just over 100 years Pennsylvania had grown from a small band of Swedish, Dutch and English traders and subsistence farmers, to a culturally and economically diverse society of almost one half million.

Population growth accelerated dramatically in the early 1700's when German and Scotch-Irish immigrants began to pour into Pennsylvania, rapidly settling areas west of Philadelphia and reaching the Susquehanna River by 1729. Soon after, they moved northward into the Wyoming Valley and continued still further west and south to the Cumberland Valley and beyond, following the ridges and valleys of the Appalachian chain into Maryland and Virginia. Second tier urban centers were established and quickly populated — Lancaster growing to nearly 3,800 by 1773 and Reading and York both reaching populations of over 2,000 by 1790. Meanwhile, Philadelphia continued its rapid expansion as Pennsylvania's center of trade, commerce, industry, finance and culture, growing from about 4,400 in 1700 to well over 42,000 by 1790.

Traditionally, we view the economy of Pennsylvania and the nation as a progression from early settlement hunting-gathering and subsistence farming, to agriculture, to mining and manufacturing and finally to, as many call it, the "post industrial" service economy. Pennsylvania was, however, manufacturing-oriented well before the generally acknowledged start of the Industrial Revolution around 1820. As early as 1750, Philadelphia was considered the industrial hub of the colonies and continued to be the nation's most important industrial center well into the 20th century. Export trade also began early in Pennsylvania with Philadelphia being the port of departure for goods bound for England, Southern Europe and the West Indies.

By the mid-1800's, the Industrial Revolution was in full swing in Pennsylvania and with it came the insatiable demand for workers of all sorts — miners, railroaders, oilmen, textile workers and steel workers to name just a few. The great industrial engine that formed the Commonwealth's keystone economy was winding up, fueled by its bountiful natural resources and a labor force imbued with the desire to make a better life no matter what the cost. Thus began the great demographic transformation of Pennsylvania. Farmers left the land and the countryside and migrant laborers left Europe to become factory workers in Philadelphia and Pittsburgh, miners in the Wyoming Valley, loggers in Williamsport, oilmen in Bradford and quarrymen in the Lehigh Valley.

They came from Germany and Poland, Ireland and Wales and began the flow of immigrants that continues to this day. They came to build ships and locomotives, to make cement, to mine coal, to produce oil, to build the railroad, ship goods and produce myriad household convenience items. They came to flee political and religious repression to be sure but they also came to earn money in hopes of returning home. Some did, in fact, return to the old country but most stayed and settled. If America was the great melting pot of the world, Pennsylvania was the great melting pot of the nation, both industrially and demographically and despite occasional recessions and depressions, Pennsylvania led the nation to global industrial supremacy for well over 100 years.

In 1820, of the over 137,000 persons in the eastern Pennsylvania work force, nearly 34% were employed in manufacturing. In the less industrialized western portion of the Commonwealth about 20% worked in manufacturing, while only about 14% of all workers held industrial jobs. By 1860, 28% of all employed persons statewide were industrial workers laboring in 415 different industrial categories at over 22,000 separate establishments. In 1860, 13,389 persons were making boots and shoes; 29,777 mined anthracite and bituminous coal; 17,770 produced iron bars, rails and pig iron; and 14,007 manufactured various cotton goods. By 1900 the number of industrial establishments had swelled to over 52,000.

The industrial beast's voracious hunger for labor fed mercilessly on the farm population. In 1820 over 80% of employed persons were farmers. But by 1860 that number had dropped to below 30% and by 1920 less than 20% of the Commonwealth's labor force worked on farms. The acute farm labor shortage that resulted in turn, fueled the beast even more by creating a demand for machines that could replace the lost labor. But migration from the farm only partially satisfied the growing demand and the labor that agriculture could not supply, Europe and Great Britain did. In 1860, 15% of Pennsylvania's 2,906,215 residents were foreign born and by 1910 nearly 19% were born outside of the United States. Most of the immigrants were German, Scottish, Irish, English, Welsh, Italian, Polish, and Swedish.

While most of Pennsylvania's industries generated steady growth for hundreds of communities well into the mid-1900's, a few had more volatile and colorful demographic effects. The mining industry and, to a greater extent, the oil and gas business provided Pennsylvania with its share of gaudy boom towns which later left only their ghostly remains. The most famous of these, an oil town called Pithole, is interestingly described by E. Willard Miller in his book, *Pennsylvania — Keystone to Progress*:

> Amidst the drilling, Pithole evolved as one of the most striking 'mushroom cities' in the history of the

American oil industry. On May 24, 1865 there was one
building under construction. When Pithole was incorporated as a borough on September 30, 1865, the population was estimated from 12,000 to 15,000 and the
land valued at fifty million dollars...

Pithole had the appearance of a gigantic city of
shreds and patches, not a brick or stone house in it.
The odor of new lumber, fresh paint, and pungent petroleum was everywhere. Hotels, saloons, drinking and
gambling dens, brothels, and boardinghouses were
built by the score...

The rapid growth of Pithole had astounded the
world, but its decline was even more fantastic. The first
shock to the speculative bubble came late in August
1865, when the wells on the Holmden farm stopped
flowing...

When oil production declined, the town was abandoned in a few months. The Danford House, built for
$50,000 and subleased for $14,000, was sold in 1868 for
$16 and torn down for kindling wood. Although
Pithole was the epitome of oildom's boomtowns,
scores of other ghost towns marked the once reckless
exploitation of a great resource in western Pennsylvania.

Growing Pains

From its infancy in the 17th century, through childhood and
adolescence in the 18th and 19th centuries to its entry into young
adulthood in the 20th, Pennsylvania has matured on high
spirits, high energy and optimism. But the social and economic
obstacles it had to overcome were not unlike the issues it faces
today as a wiser but still energetic and optimistic middle-ager.
We tend to view the problems of the '80's and '90's as somehow
alien to our past — and in many ways they are. But the issues that
badger us today are fundamentally the same as those overcome
by our ancestors...

- In health, our AIDS was their smallpox, diphtheria
  and tuberculosis;
- In welfare, our homeless were their urban tenement
  dwellers;

- In labor, our shortage of service workers was their shortage of mill hands;
- In education, our dropouts were their children of the mines and factories;
- In the environment, our solid waste were their belching smoke stacks;
- In transportation, our deteriorating roads were their mud paths;
- In migration, our flight from the rust belt was their flight from the farm.

But while we gain solace from the fact that our ancestors faced many of the same challenges that we do, we are perplexed to find that today's problems defy simple solutions. They spring forth from a population that is larger and more culturally, socially and economically diverse than ever before and they demand more innovative and technically complex strategies to address them. Nevertheless, we persistently search for elegantly simple solutions and try to transform our problems into opportunities.

In order to be realistic in our approach to the issues of our day, however, we must understand the "people statistics," or demography of our state. For it is the collective impact of these people that creates our difficulties but, more importantly, it is their collective spirit that provides our greatest hope for a just and prosperous 21st century.

If dramatic population growth and industrial expansion was the signature of the 1800's and early 1900's, demographic, economic, and cultural differentiation and complexity has been the mark of the past 50 years. Immigration patterns, for example, have exhibited a major shift from mainly European to Asian and Latin American. The number of English born residents fell 36% in the 30 years from 1940 to 1970. The number of German born fell 45%, Italian born declined 55% and Polish born residents slipped 70%. The number of Mexicans, on the other hand, increased 23% and Asians increased their ranks by 135%.

Most dramatically, the number of "other Americans," primarily Latinos, increased astronomically between 1940 and 1970. The Cuban population in Pennsylvania, which was negligible before 1960, grew to over 3,400 by 1970 due to the Castro revolution in the late 1950's. In the early 1980's another influx of Cubans arrived in Pennsylvania during a second refugee wave swelling the Cuban and Latin American populations even more. Other Latins, primarily Puerto Rican-Americans, have also poured in seeking Pennsylvania jobs and its benevolent public assistance programs. The result was an increase in the Spanish speaking populations — both foreign born and American born — from an estimated 15,000 to 20,000 in 1960 to 153,961 by 1980. Of these, 91,802 were Puerto Rican-American, 19,355 were Mexican, 5,600 were Cuban and 37,204 were of various other Central and South American nationalities.

Nearly as impactful as the Latino influx has been the migration of Southeast Asians. During the mid-1970's Pennsylvania became the resettlement home of a large number of Vietnamese, Cambodian and Laotian refugees who were fleeing the political and economic persecutions of their new governments. Their massive migration and subsequent offspring swelled the Asian/Pacific Islander segment of the Commonwealth's population from just over 14,000 in 1960 to 64,379 by 1980. While most of the Asian/Pacific Islander population has remained in the major metropolitan areas of the Commonwealth, small enclaves have developed throughout the hinterlands giving rise to the almost ubiquitous "Oriental" restaurant. Today many of the larger Pennsylvania municipalities have at least one Oriental restaurant that competes with the usual complement of Italian-American and local ethnic establishments.

More significant than the blend of nationalities that make up Pennsylvania is the African-American population of well over one million. Pennsylvania's role in the Civil War and the freeing of African-American persons from the bondage of slavery was so great that a commentary here would not do the topic justice. Nevertheless, during the deepest, darkest days of slavery, Pennsylvania too was responsible for the confinement of a few thousand African-Americans — a time that we should not try to forget but should keep in perspective as we move ahead toward the 21st century.

During and after the Civil War, Pennsylvania provided African-Americans with a haven from the continuing repression they experienced in the South. By 1880, 85,535 blacks had migrated to the Commonwealth. By 1890, the 100,000 mark was broken and sometime during the early to mid 1940's one-half million African-Americans resided here, taking jobs in factories, service industries and agriculture. In addition to the resident population, many more blacks came to Pennsylvania each year as migrant farm laborers to help with the annual fruit and vegetable harvest.

By 1980, 8.8% of the total population of Pennsylvania was African-American. But as has been the case with the Hispanic and much of the Asian population, the growth in the black population has been essentially an urban phenomena. In 1980, 12.4% of the urban population was black while only 0.8% of the rural population was. Even more than an urban phenomena, the story of the black Pennsylvanian is a center city story, much in contrast with the rural black scenes of the South. Over 27% of the 2.9 million persons living in Pennsylvania's central city areas in 1980 were black while only 4.5% of the 4.1 million persons living in the urban fringe areas were.

Just as the racial and cultural milieu has evolved during the Commonwealth's history, so has the age distribution of the population. We begin with the obvious. Because of advances in medicine, health care practices, technology and life styles, people are living longer, healthier lives today than they did 100 years ago. In 1980, only 3.9% of the population was age 65 or older and in 1930 still only 5.3% of the population was in this category. By 1980, however, nearly 13% of all persons in the Commonwealth were 65 or older. As individuals this trend is exciting. We can now retire at age 65 with the soothing feeling that we have a excellent chance of living another two decades in relatively good health. As a society, however, we are apprehensive about this trend and nervously ask ourselves...Who will care for the elderly? Who will pay for their support? What will they do to occupy their time? Where will they spend their money? How will they affect the political balance?

Another pivotal demographic phenomena of the past forty years is the famous "baby boom" — that procreative surge of activity that began after World War II as men and women were delivered from the bondage of the great war machine to the freedom and optimism of the post-war years. In 1940, persons under five years of age made up 7.3% of Pennsylvania's population. A total of 165,456 live births were recorded that year. By 1950, 9.8% of the population was under five years old and 221,635 live births were recorded. Near the peak of the boom in 1960, 10.5% of all Pennsylvanians were under five and the live birth rate checked in at 241,099 deliveries. The actual live birth peak in Pennsylvania was in 1957 when 254,997 babies were born. During the mid-1960's the boom began to cool down and the birth rate began a steady decline which bottomed out in 1976. Only 148,004 Pennsylvania babies were born that year and by 1980 only 6.3% of the population was under five years old.

Adulthood in the 21st Century

The most important demographic trend in Pennsylvania over the past fifty years, however, has been the leveling off of population growth. From the first U.S. census in 1790 until 1910, Pennsylvania increased its population by at least 20% every ten years. Three decades during the mid and late 1800's even experienced growth rates of over 30%. But during the decade of the First World War, things began to change. From 1910 to 1920 the Commonwealth grew by only 13.8% and by 1950, even with the baby-boom in full swing, the ten year increase had dwindled to 6%. In the ten years from 1970 to 1980 the population inched up by only 0.5% and it has been estimated by the Pennsylvania State Data Center that the number of people living in Pennsylvania actually fell slightly between 1975 and 1980. While actual population declines are not expected to continue, extremely modest ten year growth rates of less than 2% are anticipated until, at least, the year 2000.

The alarms were sounded in business and industry, in labor and in politics. Had Pennsylvania, the healthy, vibrant, middle-aged adult of the 1940's and 1950's begun an early and rapid aging process during the 1960's and 1970's? Or was it entering still another natural and positive phase of maturation? Were 200 years of European immigration, rapid growth, industrial expansion and burgeoning commerce being replaced by stagnation, economic decline, cultural confusion and out-migration? Or were we simply experiencing a healthy but uncomfortable course correction?

As we enter the last decade of this century we continue to ponder these questions, both philosophically and practically. Over the past 20 years, Pennsylvania has struggled, along with the rest of the nation, in coming to grips with the effects of domestic and global homogenization. We are used to being unique. We saw ourselves as Europeans in a new world, who were busily building a state and a nation and producing products needed by the rest of the world. We became addictively enamored with the ability of our productive capacity to inspire awe at home and around the world. In many ways we viewed ourselves as the king of the economic mountain.

But we are no longer just European, no longer just urban or rural, no longer the only ones who can efficiently produce. We are black, white, Hispanic and Asian as well as European. We are suburban and urban fringe as well as rural and center city. The Gulf States, Alaska, and the North Sea help produce the oil we discovered near Titusville; the Midwest and High Plains states help us to mine coal; Japan helps us with steel production; and the South gives us a hand in the production of all kinds of manufactured goods. In a sense, the rest of the world has finally caught up to Pennsylvania. Our job as a Commonwealth, then, is not to worry so much about what we are doing wrong but to try and do better what we have always done well — innovate, adapt, produce, maintain high standards and move forward.

This is not to say that the road ahead will be smooth and straight. It has never been. There are many obstacles to clear in the years leading us into the 21st century and beyond. Some of these are political, many are economic and others are strictly social. None of the obstacles will be removed, though, without a keen sensitivity to the demographic realities that lie ahead. The chapters of this book examine specific issues that are critical to Pennsylvania's success in the 21st century, each from the unique perspective of its author. The common thread in all of these issues, however, is that they are ultimately people issues. With this in mind let us briefly consider the most important demographic issues that will confront us through the 1990's.

Regional Diversity: The demographic character of the Commonwealth varies tremendously from place to place. The racial issues of West Philadelphia are the problems of another world to people living in Orangeville (Columbia County) where everyone is white. The economic stagnation and out-migration that frustrate residents of the anthracite mining town of Kulpmont (Northumberland County) is hardly an issue in affluent Upper Merion Township (Montgomery County). The financial security and well being of the elderly is more of a problem in Homestead (Allegheny County), where 24% of the residents are 65 or older, than it is in Northampton Township (Bucks County), where under 5% of the population fall into this group.

Aging War Babies: The post-war baby boomers, whether they

like it or not, are becoming middle-aged adults. The youngest
ones are rapidly approaching their thirtieth birthday and the
oldest ones are already into their forties. For the next quarter of a
century this group of over 3 million Pennsylvanians will essentially run the state. They will be its political leaders, its corporate
executives, its hospital administrators, its inventors and its
teachers. They will possess the money and power to purchase
products and services, from homes to cars to bowling balls and
bikes, in volumes never before experienced. They will be the
largest contributors to the Social Security fund — but they had
better be, because by 2010 they could begin to tap it dry.

This group's demand for services will challenge both private
and public providers. Most of the boomers, for example, now
have families and children of their own who need to be cared for.
Since in many of these families both mother and father work to
pay the household bills and in many others a single parent is in
charge, a heavy demand for child day care has developed and
will continue for many years.

On the supply side, the massive labor force offered by the
baby-boomers will shrink dramatically over the next 20 years
creating potentially severe labor shortages. These shortages are
already being experienced in low-paying service jobs and entry
level clerical and computer positions. In many sectors of the
economy the glut of workers that marked the 1970's and early
1980's is gradually being replaced by a dearth of trained
labor.

Single Moms: Along with the coming of age of the baby
boomers has come a sharp rise in the number of female-headed,
single-parent families and various non-family living arrangements. It is estimated by the Pennsylvania State Data Center
that the number of white children living in female-headed
households rose from 6.3% in 1970 to 13.5% in 1985. Even more
significantly, the number of black children living in this type of
family increased from 32% in 1970 to 63% in 1985.

While some single-parent, female-headed families are doing
just fine economically, the majority are experiencing hardships
to a degree generally not known to traditional two-parent families. Even though both parents in many two-parent families
work outside the home, creating a need for child care, this need
is nearly universal among single-parent families. The single
parent, however, has the added disadvantage of usually having

only one source of income. Concerns about child care, education and health care are particularly acute with this group of Pennsylvanians.

Women in the Work Force: The need for traditional families to have both parents at work, the female-headed household and the increasing number of women who prefer to remain single into their thirties and forties, have precipitated the entrance of large numbers of women into the workforce. It has been estimated that in 1985 about 60% of Pennsylvania's women between the ages of 16 and 64 were working outside the home. They continue to enter the traditionally female careers of teaching, nursing and administrative support, but they are also working their way into previously male-dominated positions as managers, executives, lawyers, heavy machine operators and airline pilots. While Pennsylvania has accepted and welcomed women into the workforce, much remains to be done in the areas of pay differentials, benefits and accommodation of maternal duties.

New Jobs For a New Age: Whether they are male or female, the types of jobs Pennsylvanians now hold are much different than they were in the past. Just as we left the farm during the Industrial Revolution to work in the factories, we are well along in our conversion from manufacturing to service providing. In 1950 over 35% of the civilian work force was employed in manufacturing but by the 1980 census, this number had dropped to 26.5%. The portion of the work force employed in professional services, meanwhile, has risen from under 8% in 1950 to over 20% in 1980.

The pessimist looks at these figures and worries about the number of industrial jobs we are losing to the Japanese and the Sun Belt. The optimist, while not totally at ease with the loss of manufacturing jobs, is encouraged by the diversification that he sees developing in the Commonwealth's economy. From the optimist's perspective, we appear to be in the process of building a broader-based economy. The process has been and will probably continue to be difficult. But when we have made it through we hope to find ourselves insulated from the fickleness of specific industries. We hope that when the demand for steel slumps, the demand for computer hardware and consumer products will boom, and that when the demand for these eventually cool off, new competitive advantages in steel production and other primary industries will soften the blow. If the industrial jobs do not return, all is not lost. Wholesaling, retailing, and myriad service businesses will be there to replace them.

But we must heed the pessimist too, for while service jobs of all sorts have been born and we are beginning to see the return of some industries from the Sun Belt, many labor and social issues need to be addressed. Can the industrial worker in his or her fifties be effectively retrained to compete for the new jobs on the block? Does the young, inner-city black or Hispanic person have the skills to land a job as a computer programmer or even as a data entry clerk? Can the inner city black or Hispanic afford to acquire these skills? Can the single mother in Johnstown or Dubois house and feed her three school-aged children by working at Dunkin Donuts or is she better off staying home and taking public assistance? These are the challenges leading us to the 21st century.

A Mobile Society: The people of Pennsylvania want their leaders to adopt creative public policies that address the issues that the Commonwealth faces, but it is not in their character to simply sit and wait for change. The primitive instincts that drive us to fight or flight are as strong today as they were during our hunting and gathering days. We can either fight to bring about the changes that need to be made or we can, as herdsmen, move on to new locales of perceived, if not real opportunity. Over the past few decades, many Pennsylvanians have opted for migration, either from one part of the state to another or out of Pennsylvania entirely.

We lost over 200,000 persons to other states between 1980 and 1987. Many that we lost were elderly moving to the gentler climates of Florida and the Sun Belt. Many others were young adults, themselves seeking the sun but also in search of employment and careers in Texas, California, Maryland and Virginia. Pennsylvania is not alone though. Other so-called "rust belt" states including New York, Ohio and West Virginia join us in net out-migration and interestingly, Pennsylvania experiences a net in-migration from one of these states, New York. We should keep in mind, however, that when we speak of population losses to other states the numbers are expressed in terms of net migration. While over 24,000 Pennsylvanians move to Florida each year, for instance, about 12,000 Floridians migrate back to Pennsylvania.

In addition to moving from one state to another, Pennsylvanians continue to migrate from county to county within the Commonwealth. The great shift from the farm and rural areas to the city in the 1800's and early to mid 1900's gradually evolved into a migration from both of these areas to the suburbs. The flight from the central cities of Philadelphia, Pittsburgh, Harrisburg and others in the 1960's and 1970's, caused mainly by race relations and economic conditions, seemed to feed on itself giving rise to fears of irreversible urban decay and an exodus to the hinterlands.

Fortunately, the predictions of doom and gloom for the cities have not come to pass. Make no mistake, the problems of Pennsylvania's large urban areas are real and severe. But, we are beginning to see encouraging signs that the decline has bottomed out. Investment and real estate development in downtown areas, enterprise zone establishment, minority business openings and a quiet and modest but definite "return to the city" spirit are slowly but surely reversing the trend of the past 20 years.

The central cities are showing us positive signs, but even more significant for Pennsylvania is the rapid expansion of the metropolitan areas that surround those cities. The great East Coast megalopolis that runs from Washington D.C. through Philadelphia and on to Boston is annexing much of southcentral and southeastern Pennsylvania. Southern York County is becoming a bedroom community for Baltimore commuters. Corporate office complexes, manufacturers, residential subdivisions and shopping centers are eating up valuable farmland from Chester to Lancaster and the Harrisburg and Allentown/Bethlehem metropolitan areas are emerging as major satellite centers of business and commerce. Even the rural counties of Wayne, Pike and Monroe in the northeastern part of the state are feeling pressure from the megalopolis as second home owners and courageous commuters invade from Northern New Jersey and the New York metropolitan area.

The migratory trend in the nation is generally south and west, but in Pennsylvania the trend is to the south and east. North and west of the valley and ridge section of the Commonwealth nearly every county experienced net out-migration during the 1980's. But with the exception of Philadelphia County, most of the counties south and east of the North Branch of the Susquehanna River showed net in-migration. The concentration of

economic activity and population growth around the Commonwealth's southeastern metropolitan areas will generate enormous opportunity into the 21st century. It will, however, also
bring with it many problems: transportation, social services,
education, health care, crime and other issues will demand our
resources and attention in the coming years. The scenario in
much of the rest of the state is quite different. Idyllic small towns
with inexpensive land for development and an eager workforce
will try to convince business and industry to move into their
areas to provide jobs and prop up eroding tax bases. Many of
these areas have enormous economic potential and can offer
good schools, open space, low crime rates and a generally high
quality of life. But they will face intense competition from
Pittsburgh and southeastern Pennsylvania.

Pennsylvania faces a paradox as the 21st century draws near.
The complexity and fluidity of our people create a multitude of
problems that are often difficult to define, let alone solve. Yet it
is precisely our demographic diversity and our willingness to
move from place to place that make us creative and resilient and
allow us to turn those problems into opportunities. In the years
ahead we must anticipate the future and devise public policy
strategies that take into account who we are and who we will be.
If we are getting older, how can we make old age more pleasant
and secure? If we are white and black and Hispanic and Asian,
how can we build a Commonwealth that taps our individual
strengths and is compassionate to our weaknesses? If we are
rural and suburban and metropolitan, how can we complement
each others' abilities and resources? We are all Pennsylvanians
— all different, ever changing and ever-moving but common in
our desire to make Pennsylvania a more just and prosperous
home in the 21st century. By understanding ourselves we will
gain the knowledge we need to make it happen.

SECTION TWO:
Education

CHAPTER THREE

PENNSYLVANIA EDUCATION FOR THE 1990's: THE NEED FOR CHOICE AND SUBSTANCE

By John A. Sparks

EDITOR'S SUMMARY

National test trends and assessments show that U.S. students are not performing up to the academic standards of twenty-five years ago. From 1963 to 1981 the average total score of those tested for the SAT fell more than 90 points. Other nationally administered tests show a similar decrease in the mean score of students taking the tests.

The general public is concerned about the educational trends in their local school districts. A September 1989 Gallup Poll on the subject of American public education shows that when those polled were asked to grade the public schools in their own communities, approximately 57% gave the schools a "C" "D" or "F". Only 8% gave public schools an "A".

Educational quality in Pennsylvania has suffered as well. The average SAT scores for 1989 place Commonwealth students 17 to 18 points below the national average. In order to counter this trend, specific reforms need to be undertaken in the Commonwealth's educational system.

Four major public school "standards approach" reforms were accomplished in Pennsylvania during the 1980's. These reforms included increases in high school graduation requirements, the addition of continuing professional development requirements, the mandating of standardized certification testing for new teachers, and the requirement of TELS tests for remedial students.

However, the "standards approach" reforms have not produced fundamental changes in the Commonwealth's educational system. For meaningful change to occur, schools of choice need to be introduced statewide in Pennsylvania. The justification for increasing choice in schooling comes from combining economic and educational theory.

Schools of choice have several advantages. Students who have chosen a school will have enhanced motivation for making the most of the choice. Likewise, individual schools and their staffs have more direct incentives to give careful attention to the quality of educational services since the schools would no longer have "captive" enrollments. The availability of the transfer option will keep schools responsive to parental concerns.

A system of expanded choice would encourage parental involvement. Parents are more likely to support a school that they considered rather than one that was decided for them by the location of their residence. Individual schools in the Commonwealth should be free to respond to educational demand with the least interference from the state or the district, consonant with certain minimal curriculum requirements.

John A. Sparks is Professor of Business Administration at Grove City College and President of Public Policy Education Fund, Inc.

In this age of instantly manufactured crises, does the condition of Pennsylvania elementary and secondary education dictate the need for more "fine tuning" of an essentially sound system, or are conditions such that more fundamental measures are advisable? Is the Commonwealth similar to or different from other states which have suffered the decline of educational quality?

The National Results — SAT's and Standardized Tests

First, national test trends and assessments agree that U.S. students are not performing up to the academic standards of twenty-five years ago. Probably the best publicized evidence of decline is the scores of students taking the Scholastic Aptitude Test (SAT) distributed and administered by the College Board and the Educational Testing Service of Princeton, New Jersey. From 1963 to 1981 the average total score of those tested fell more than 90 points.[1] The "verbal" portion of the score fell approximately 50 points and the "math" portion dropped about 40 points.[2] The actual size of the decline may be somewhat greater than this because "scale drift" research indicates that after 1963 "it was somewhat easier to get a high score than before."[3] Though scores rose again through 1985, they remain at that level which is still about 55 points below the 1967 level.[4] Specifically, according to the most recent scores (1989), average national verbal scores dropped one point from the 1988 level to 427 and national math averages remained unchanged at 476.[5] Even after discounting the decline for the effects produced by the changing composition of students taking the test, [6]the decline appears to be a real one. Other nationally administered tests show a similar decrease in the mean score of students taking the tests, so the downturn does not seem to be limited to the particular instruments or testing approaches used to conduct the SAT.[7]

If one shifts to other forms of *national* assessment, such as the First National Assessment of History and Literature, given to approximately 8,000 eleventh grade students covering the fundamental content of American history and literature, the results are similarly disturbing. Ravitch and Finn, writing about the scores on that 1987 test, summarize the outcomes this way:

On the history portion of the assessment, the national

average is 54.5% correct; on the literature portion, the national average 51.8% correct...[8]

The authors go on to say:

If there were such a thing as a national report card for those studying American history and literature, then we would have to say that this nationally representative sample of eleventh grade students earns failing marks in both subjects.[9]

Just a few examples are revealing. Few students could identify the major Old World influences on American history. So, only about 39% of the students could identify the Renaissance, a sparse 29% the Reformation, and about 30% the primary source of English liberties, the Magna Carta.[10] A scant 13% could answer questions about Bunyan's classic story of sin and repentance, *Pilgrim's Progress*.[11] Only about 36% knew that Chaucer wrote *Canterbury Tales*.[12]

Besides standardized tests other developments mirrored a growing discontent with American elementary and secondary education in the 1980's. One such development was the publishing of many reports by study commissions and educational agencies. Probably the best known and most often quoted is *A Nation at Risk*, produced by the National Commission on Excellence and issued in 1983 by the U.S. Department of Education. The eighteen-person commission warned that the nation was at risk due in part to a rising tide of educational mediocrity. It went on to say in direct language what it had found by reviewing existing studies and hearing advisory presentations:

We have, in effect, been committing an act of unthinking, unilateral educational disarmament...Our society and its educational institutions seem to have lost sight of the basic purposes of schooling, and of the high expectations and disciplined effort needed to attain them.[13]

The same tone of alarmed concern pervades another report penned by a prestigious advisory group meeting under the auspices of the National Endowment for the Humanities. The name of the report, *The American Memory*, states in clear language, among other things:

> In our schools today we run the danger of unwittingly
> proscribing our own heritage...Both the process and
> the content of learning are important, but so much
> emphasis has been placed on process that content has
> been seriously neglected...Textbooks are tangible
> evidence of how little we are doing to make our
> children shareholders in their cultural heritage.[14]

Other reports identified areas for educational improvement
in the decade of the eighties. Although exhibiting differences in
reform proposals and tone, none were satisfied with American
education the way it was.[15]

The general public continues to be concerned about educational quality. The most recent annual public opinion poll
conducted by Phi Delta Kappa and the Gallup Poll organization on the subject of American public education shows that
when those polled are asked to grade the public schools in their
own communities, about 8% give the schools an "A", about 35%
a "B" and about 33% award a "C". The remaining 24% say that
the schools deserve a "D" or "F".[16] It should be noted that the
public apparently sees some improvement since 1983 when a
total of only 31% of those answering gave an "A" or "B" to the
schools.[17] Education writer Barbara Lerner argues that these
polls show a public consensus for change that corresponds with
what the research evidence suggests is needed.[18]

Finally, three out of four professors at U.S. colleges and
universities think that students are seriously unprepared for
doing college-level work according to a recent Carnegie Foundation study, the results of which were made public by Foundation President Ernest L. Boyer.[19]

Pennsylvania: Is the Story Different Here?

Has Pennsylvania avoided the national trends that have been
referred to above? No, not according to the evidence that is available. Although average Pennsylvania SAT scores did not fall as
much as the national averages during the years for which statistics are available, nevertheless, neither did the Pennsylvania
averages recover as much as the national figures have.[20] The
averages for 1988[21] and the newly released numbers for 1989[22]
place Pennsylvania students taking the SAT, *17 to 18 points*

below the national average. National scores (1989) are 427 verbal and 476 math. Pennsylvania averages are 423 verbal and 463 math. Coming out below the national average might not be so bad if the national average were on the increase. But, as mentioned above, the current level of national performance on the test remains low compared with twenty-five years ago.

Other assessments have included Eastern states in the sampling. For example, the National Assessment of History and Literature made certain that regions of the country were represented in proportion to their current population estimates, so that the results could be said to be representative generally.[23] In like manner the national polls have fairly represented all regions including Pennsylvania.[24] Moreover, in a recent Pennsylvania poll those polled evidenced strong support for fundamental structural changes in public education as will be more fully explained later.[25] In summary, the national downturns in educational results appear to have had their harmful and widespread impact upon the Keystone, just as in other states.

Educational Reform by the States — The Standards Approach

In the face of continuing complaints about educational quality the states have responded with a variety of educational reforms. Following the issuance of *A Nation at Risk*, in the period from 1984-1986, more than 700 state statutes dealing in some way with teaching and education were enacted![26] Pennsylvania is no exception. During the 1980s a number of reforms have been proposed and implemented by either the Pennsylvania Department of Education or the state legislature. Before looking at specific reforms, their strengths and weaknesses, it should be pointed out that educational reforms promoted by the Commonwealth illustrate what commentators call the "standards approach" to educational improvement.[27] The "standards approach" is the use of standards or requirements established by the Department of Education or the legislature which the local districts must meet. The hallmark of this approach, which is by far the most commonly followed in public education today, is centralization. A central legislating body delivers mandates and regulations to school districts throughout the state. The "standards approach" does not alter fundamentally the way in which the educational system is organized. In addition, the "standards approach" views the district, not the school, as the unit through which change and improvement are to be accomplished.

Four Pennsylvania Reforms

Four major public school reforms were accomplished in Pennsylvania during the 1980s. They were (1) the increase in high school graduation requirements, (2) the addition of continuing professional development requirements, (3) the mandating of standardized certification testing for new teachers, and (4) the requirement of TELLS tests which tested and then remediated students who had reading or mathematics deficiencies in various selected elementary grades.[28] Let's take each reform in turn and review its strengths and weaknesses.

Graduation Requirements

When the Pennsylvania Department of Education adopted new regulations in the fall of 1985 which boosted high school graduation requirements in mathematics and science and which increased total graduation credits from 13 over 3 years to 21 over 4 years,[29] it was responding in part to one of the recurring recommendations of various reports and commissions, namely, that high school graduation requirements be strengthened so that students receive more substantive academic content from their high school courses of study.[30] Nobody can disagree with the intent of such regulations. However, the likelihood that these additional requirements, *per se*, are producing real results is doubtful.

On the plus side, commentators studying six state reforms, including Pennsylvania, describe such increases in student standards as producing some additional exposure of students to academic courses such as math and science.[31] However, the gains may be illusory. The fact is that most local districts studied by these authors had *already* been requiring that much academic work of their students.[32] Further, even when districts themselves were requiring only the previous minimum, college-bound students have already elected to take more academic courses than the new requirements.[33] Under the assumptions above, one would not expect the scores of college-bound (academic track) students to increase because what was required by the Pennsylvania Department of Education was already being done by local boards or individual students anyway. But, how about general or vocational track students? Would they not be forced to take more academic courses? Yes, but the gains would be produced only if the courses they take are established rigorous academic courses. For example, if the general track student takes the traditional high school chemistry course as a result of the new requirements, he will clearly be exposed to greater content. However, if the local schools respond to the added requirements by creating special science or math courses that are, for lack of a better term, "watered down" versions of their academic counterparts, then the gain intended is less likely to be realized. Again, the study referred to above, including Pennsylvania, explains that this latter approach and others exist by which some local districts avoid the intended impact of the newly required regulations while technically meeting them.[34]

Furthermore, such beefed up graduation requirements do not remedy the complaints about sparse content in existing courses or deficient textbooks used in those courses, and, it is only fair to add, they are not designed to do so. In other words, if poor quality science and math courses with weak textbooks are being offered to students, then requiring *all* students to take the courses will not improve the students' preparation or their scores on standardized tests.

Some states, seeing this, have attempted to go several steps further using the "standards approach" by mandating specific course content and by directly controlling textbook adoption.[35] Pennsylvania has not followed that course. It has eschewed detailed standards regulation of courses and texts and has instead relied upon local districts, teachers, and regional accrediting agencies to monitor and make decisions about course content and textbooks.

In summary, the "graduation requirements" reforms are not likely to produce much measurable change in educational outcomes. Standing alone, such "standards" changes do not alter content covered or texts used in courses. Neither do they necessarily increase actual academic content received by Pennsylvania students either because the students were already performing above the requirements or because the extra courses taken are emasculated versions of normal academic courses.

Teacher Continuing Education Requirements/Teacher Education

Another "standards approach" reform of the 1980s in Pennsylvania established the requirement that school districts adopt a professional development plan which requires professional employees to take additional graduate work, to attend professional conferences or to attend "in-service" programs of continuing education for the teachers arranged by the district.[36] Those teachers who have earned Master's degrees receive a kind of exemption from the continuing education requirements because their continuing certification is not threatened as it is for non-Master's teachers who fail to accumulate the requisite credits. This latter exemption was obtained by teacher organizations which put pressure on the state legislature for the exemption.[37]

Requiring teachers to learn more about teaching and about the subject they are teaching are laudable goals worthy of any reform effort. Some would go so far as to say that without improving and encouraging teachers, little else that one does can hope to produce any significant results. However, once again one must ask if the means chosen are likely to produce the goals which are sought.

One must review the recommendations which various reports and commissions have made about *teacher education in general*, including continuing professional development (CPD) requirements. They can be summarized this way.

Undergraduate teacher preparation and continuing education suffer from being too heavily weighted with methods courses, curriculum planning techniques and workshops on current teaching novelties, and are too light or even devoid of contact with the subject matter of the specific intellectual disciplines that teachers are teaching. One noted educator calls the curricula of teacher training institutions, the tendency of schools and training institutions to think of teachers primarily as "facilitators" rather than as practitioners of the discipline of the mind and the reinforcement of the above tendencies by certification standards of the various states, "primary obstacles" to a literate teaching professoriate.[38] We will have something to say below about undergraduate teaching preparation. For now, it is the continuing educational development to which we turn.

Unfortunately, nothing in the continuing educational development requirements of the Commonwealth produces much hope that Pennsylvania teachers will gain both content and form, both substance and method from the professional development programs. There is every reason to believe that the bulk of the professional development that will be offered by the districts and in the education graduate courses will be predominantly "methods" and "processes", not subject matter. If the Commonwealth is determined to improve teaching by a single standards type requirement, it ought to insist that only substantive courses or substantive in-service programs will count toward continuing professional development requirements. In other words, the social studies teacher ought to be enrolled in or receive in-service instruction in "Europe in the Late Medieval Period", not "Contemporary Methods of Teaching Social Studies II." The requirement of improving subject-matter knowledge could be met by a teacher in a number of ways. Teachers could take traditional graduate courses in the subject areas. Teachers could take upper-level undergraduate courses in the subject area. Many teachers say that as undergraduates they were unable to take 300 and 400 level courses in their field because of the press of education requirements, other requirements, and teaching practicums. In order to meet the requirement teachers could attend in-service *subject matter* presentations provided by nearby college or university faculty or by some of their own experienced high school teachers. For instance, the high school biology teachers in a certain geographic area should be able to attend a one-day update program on "Recent Developments in Micro-Biology", offered by Professor X of ABC University. But what about elementary teachers? Can they also benefit from such an emphasis upon subject matter study? They, more than all other teachers, are called upon by students to have a broad knowledge of the world in which we live. Instruction in history, literature, economics and astronomy, to name a few, will produce surprising dividends for the elementary teacher's students.

Such an emphasis on substance will have three effects besides expanding the knowledge of teachers about the subjects they teach: (1) It will help to swing the pendulum in their prior education back toward a proper balance between content and method. (2) It will reinvigorate the interest of the teachers in their subjects; (3) It will help to counter the understandable, yet corrosive, skepticism with which teachers themselves[39] and the general public view continuing education activities.

Undergraduate teacher preparation suffers from the same thing that ails continuing teacher education: there are too many form, process and methods requirements. The Commonwealth through its certification process can begin by reducing its requiments as to form, process and methods, thereby freeing students to take other non-education courses in their field of study. Let us hasten to add that we are aware of institutions that stress student mastery of content as a major part of education courses.

Teacher Testing and Certification

Pennsylvania uses a uniform teacher exam[40] to test those who seek Pennsylvania certification for the first time. The exam tests basic knowledge, teaching skills and subject matter knowledge. One does wonder why the subject matter portion of the test is not simply the requirement that education graduates take one of the many existing, excellent achievement tests in that subject area. But, that aside, once again the test requirement is an example of standards regulation. It has these beneficial effects. It screens out the obviously ill-prepared graduates from being certified, assuming they do no further work to improve their performance on the test, as well as serving as a check on higher educational institutions that train such graduates. It gives them an incentive to make certain their grads are at least minimally prepared. Pennsylvania, in short, is justified in not wanting to stamp with its imprimatur any substandard performers.

The problem in the certification area is not this one additional requirement but the whole structure of certification and its underlying assumption that state occupational licensure is the only effective means to make certain that those who practice the teaching profession are qualified to do so. At least this much can be said: In those areas of the curriculum where there are shortages of certified candidates, Pennsylvania should make every effort to simplify entry into the classroom for those who hold degrees in the fields of study where the short supplies exist. In addition, districts ought to be free to make imaginative use of part-time but well-educated members of their school communities, who nevertheless have not taken teacher certification courses. What better way to improve instruction than by the creation of additional smaller sections or completely new offerings in the areas where students perform poorly on national tests, all taught by uncertified staff. Instead of taking a punitive attitude toward districts which made use of technically uncertifiable teachers, Harrisburg should praise such resourceful districts. It is time that the severely limiting maxim that only the certified or certifiable can teach be discarded in favor of the proposition — education of quality whatever the source.

The TELLS Test

Pennsylvania's initiative to test students at various points in elementary and junior high and then deal with the problems displayed by some students is a sound educational reform in two important ways. It stresses basics, i.e., reading and math, and it is administered early enough in the child's schooling so that the district, the parents, and the student are able to devise a plan to improve his performance. TELLS initially stood for Test of Essential Literacy and Learning Skills but its acronym is now shortened to TELS. It is given in the third, fifth, and eighth grades.

The Choice Proposals

Approving or disapproving various kinds of centralized regulations, all illustrating the "standards approach" to educational reform will undoubtedly continue to have its place in future policy debates about Pennsylvania's schools. However, at best the "standards approach" will produce incremental and peripheral change in some cases, not the kind of fundamental changes that are necessary if citizens are once again to be satisfied with the education of their children.

A promising new approach to educational reform has been advocated and is in the early stages of being implemented in several states. It has been referred to by various names: schools of choice, the choice approach, the opportunities approach, or educational competition.

Think about it this way: The corner grocery store manager is kept on his toes because of educational alternatives available to his customers. If he is not sensitive to their demands for good wholesome food at a reasonable price, he stands to lose their patronage.

In like manner, shouldn't the principal of a public community high school be kept on his toes because of educational alternatives available to his "patrons" — the parents with school-age children? If he isn't sensitive to parents' legitimate demands for basic rigorous education and an orderly school, shouldn't he stand to lose students and thereby funding? The answer is an obvious yes. Educators, like Massachusetts educator Dr. Charles Glenn, agree with the idea of putting choice to work in education. He says that options like those mentioned above allow "parents to vote with their children's feet."[41] But, how can that be accomplished? What do educational choice or educational competition systems look like in practice?

First, there are examples of limited choice, called magnet schools [42]such as those found in Pittsburgh, Pennsylvania, Cambridge, Massachusetts and in many other cities. There the school system is modified so that parents are given an opportunity to select a school in the system which meets their child's interests and needs, and send him there even though the school may be located across town. These schools are called "magnet" schools because their programming *draws* students like a magnet from different residential neighborhoods to a single school.

On the other end of the spectrum are full-choice options found in states like Minnesota,[43] the acknowledged pioneer in the adoption of educational competition and choice. In such a state, parents, no matter where they reside, can opt to transfer their students to any school district in the state. There are limitations even here, but this open enrollment option is the most ambitious choice scheme in the nation. What is the theory behind the choice options and what are the advantages and drawbacks?

Choice Theory

The theoretical justification for increasing choice in schooling has come from combining economic and educational theory. Researchers John E. Chubb and Terry E. Moe built upon previously existing research which had determined that certain effective schools possessed common characteristics — clear goals, strong leadership and a collegial relationship between administration and teachers.[44] Furthermore, Chubb and Moe found that schools with a maximum of local autonomy, i.e., schools which were freest from oppressive regulation, political infighting and centralized controls developed these characteristics which led to their being effective.[45]

These effective schools were largely suburban public schools and private schools.[46] It seems from their research that the independence of these schools was protected by interested parents who either were consumers or came close to viewing themselves as customers of educational services. In other words, effectively organized schools were produced by circumstances that most closely resembled a market or quasi-market model. Therefore, concluded Chubb and Moe, why not introduce greater amounts of choice and competitiveness into our current elementary and secondary school systems and by so doing stimulate even greater numbers of effectively organized schools, that is, schools which will do a superior job of teaching our children.[47]

The Public and Choice

Their proposals and those of other choice advocates have been greeted enthusiastically by the general public according to the pollsters. The most recent Gallup (mid-1989) poll registered a startling two to one margin in favor of parents being able to choose which school their children attended regardless of where they lived.[48] The idea is especially popular among *non-whites* and young adults. Non-whites favored an increase in school choice at the rate of three to one. Sixty seven percent of non-whites favored choice while non-whites opposing choice made up only 22% of those polled.[49] This probably represents substantial discontent with poorly administered city schools. A poll conducted by The Commonwealth Foundation reflects similar sentiments. When Pennsylvanians were asked if they favored a system where parents had the choice as to which public school they could send their children, 61.5% favored the proposal. In Philadelphia the support for the proposal was a whopping 78.4% and in Pittsburgh a substantial 68.5%.[50]

The National Governors' Association also supports expanding parental choice of schools. One of the Association's task forces recommends that states "adopt legislation that permits parents to enroll their children in the public schools of their choice."[51] The National Education Association, however, took official convention action opposing choice programs that would "give students the freedom to move between school districts", although the vote was a close one.[52] The American Federation of Teachers is more favorable to educational choice.[53]

The Advantages of Schools of Choice

Public support aside, what commends the adoption of choice and competition in Pennsylvania education? A system of expanded choice, one in which parents could enroll their child in a school that they had selected either within the district or without, would encourage a fundamental revolution of organization in Pennsylvania's public schools. Why?

First, the unit of improvement and change would now be the *individual schools*, not the districts.[54] Under a choice system, parents choose to send their children to particular schools, not to school districts. Upon the introduction of choice reforms, it would be individual schools which would no longer have "captive" enrollments virtually guaranteed to them by the residing of the students in the school district. That fact and that fact alone drives the system of choice in the direction of individual schools and their staffs having more *direct* incentives to give careful attention to the quality of educational services. If the school serves parents and students well, it will prosper. On the other hand, if the school staff becomes complacent and other "competing" schools attract some of their existing students away, *the school* is the unit that will suffer loss of funds. Such a choice system then will place the individual school and its staff in a more prominent place in the educational scheme of things. Centralized control, either from Harrisburg or from the local district superintendent's office will be open to more frequent challenge, particularly when what is being proposed by either central authority is thought by the individual school to go counter to the legitimate demands of the school's parents.

Secondly, the impact of choice systems upon teachers appears to be positive. Indications from places like East Harlem, where an intra-district system of choice is being used, are that teachers are encouraged by the system to reach new heights of ingenuity, creativity and dedication to make their school succeed in the new competitive atmosphere.[55] Furthermore, principals who are leading schools which are no longer guaranteed students, must take seriously the wisdom, ideas and needs of his or her classroom teachers. After all, it is their contentment and performance that will ultimately determine the future of the school.[56]

Thirdly, students who have chosen a school, even if they chose to remain in their own neighborhood school, will have enhanced motivation[57] for making the most of the choice. Parents also will be likely to be more interested and supportive of a choice which they considered rather than one that was decided for them by the location of their residence.

Fourth, the introduction of competition does not detail the educational changes that schools ought to undertake in order to improve, but leaves specific directions (other than certain minimum requirements) to the imagination of the school and its staff. One thing is certain, though, if and when schools have to compete for students, the procedures, plans and policies that are central to student learning will be retained, but those that are peripheral, make-work, or irrelevant will be unceremoniously jettisoned.

Objections and Concerns

What are some of the specific objections to choice/competition being introduced? Are there not schools that will fail to attract any students or so few that they will have to close? That result is possible in some of the worst cases. Imagine a case where, upon educational choice reform being instituted, School A, which had heretofore possessed 400 students, after choice has only 50 students returning. Obviously something is quite wrong with the education being offered there. The remaining 50 students ought to be given the alternative of attending any of the surviving schools. The result, when one considers it, is no harsher than allowing the lives and minds of our young to go unchallenged, wasting away in unresponsive school environments.

What has happened in this rather unlikely case is that 400

students are now attending schools which in the judgement of most parents are superior to School A. That cannot be viewed as a bad result. What about the teachers who were employed in School A? If they are generally effective they may very well be picked up by School X or Y. These schools are the beneficiaries of the choice system, but now, with 25 or 30 more students, are in need of extra staff. However, actual experience with Minnesota suggests that the number of students transferring between schools or districts will be very small.[58] However, *possibility of transfer*, the availability of the option, is what will keep schools responsive to parental concerns.

Another fear among opponents of choice and competition in education is that schools will find it hard to anticipate how many students they will have for the next school year.[59] Students moving from district to district will have a disruptive effect on personnel planning and a destabilizing effect on budgeting. These are reasonable concerns. Minnesota has alleviated the problem of last-hour transfers by setting and sticking to a deadline for such transfers. Also, schools that are simply out of classroom space can refuse a transfer request. By the same token, it does not appear from the budgetary standpoint that student numbers will significantly fluctuate in most districts.

Another objection is that choice means parental choice and there are parents whose ability to choose between alternative schools is limited. Moreover, there are other parents who simply take no interest in their child's education.[60] Won't these students be left in their own neighborhood schools like so much residue, while other aggressive, educated parents see to it that their children get into better schools across town?

One answer to this problem of the unqualified or uninterested parent consumer is provided by Cambridge, Massachusetts. The Cambridge district pays for an information campaign in the period just before the parents are supposed to exercise their choices in the spring.[61] However, just as in the marketplace all consumers benefit from competition, so in Pennsylvania competition would have the effect of raising the quality of educational services, even for the ill-informed or indifferent. How would it work?

Suppose School B lost 10 of its students out of 400 the first year. Suppose further that Bob, who lives in the School B district, is a student whose parents are not knowledgeable about school choice. Let's eliminate the very real likelihood that Bob's parents seek information from others such as their friends, relatives or neighbors to make the school decision. In our hypothetical situation they do nothing, and therefore Bob will continue to go to School B in his own neighborhood. However, School B is not immune from the effects of competition. It has lost ten students and its staff is now mobilized to make certain that no more of its base is eroded. Let's further assume that the staff manages to stabilize or improve the offerings of School B. Bob will benefit from the forces of choice and competition. Said another way, Bob benefits from the conscientious, even fastidious parent consumers who transferred out of School B. They did not intend to help Bob, but they did so unwittingly. Their exodus provided the incentive for School B to improve itself, thereby benefiting Bob and others. There is no reason to believe that this projected set of events would not repeat itself many times under a choice system.

Along similar lines, isn't it likely that some schools would furnish an easy, breezy and trendy curriculum? It is possible, although choice systems usually do not advocate the dismantling of the minimal state requirements i.e. four years of English, three of history, etc. So those minima would be in effect for any and all schools. Of course, as with any service, parents would have to monitor quality. If the instruction provided was insubstantial, then a change of schools would be in order. As things stand now, poor instruction must largely be endured where it is found.

It is said that Pennsylvania has had virtually no experience with the choice system and we shouldn't experiment with our children. Let's take the last complaint first. How can fear of experimentation suddenly become an obstacle when the story of modern educational theory is an account of one new experiment after another. But going back to the question of experience, magnet schools have been successfully used in Pennsylvania school districts. Also private schools — parochial, independent, Christian, homeschools and others — are currently providing wider educational choice to parents. In fact, parent groups representing Christian Day Schools and home schoolers were able in the last three years to get legislation passed which further protects private educational alternatives to public schooling.[62] In other words, right now parents who are disatisfied with their own public community school can avail themselves of these other options (Christian schools, homeschools). Therefore, we *have had* some experience with choice in education in Pennsylvania.

In this regard, the legislature at the same time that it is encouraging choice among public schools, should strengthen private schools. One way this could be done is by granting a tax credit of up to $250 to families who pay tuition or make expenditures for private educational materials. This would have the effect of reducing the inequity which results to families who purchase non-public educational services and yet must pay school taxes. By offering a credit, the Commonwealth would further its general policy of expanding the educational choices open to parents by creating an educational services marketplace with as many options as possible. The educational policies of Pennsylvania in the 1990's should be characterized by emphasis on substance and choice.

Summary of Recommendations

I. In an effort to promote an expanded educational services marketplace, Pennsylvania should:

A. Institute a system of statewide choice under which parents are permitted to transfer their children to any public school in the Commonwealth, regardless of where they reside, as long as they give reasonable notice to both the schools involved.

B. Offer a tax credit of $250 for expenditures by private school and homeschool parents for tuition, books and other educational expenses.

C. Encourage the view that the individual schools in the Commonwealth should be free to respond to educational demand with the least interference from the state or the district, consonant with certain minimal curriculum requirements.

II. In order to bring modern education's emphasis on methods and processes back into a proper balance with content, Pennsylvania should:

A. Study its teacher certification requirements and reduce mandated methods and process courses.

B. Encourage the further integration of liberal arts courses into the undergraduate education major's program of study.

C. Declare a moratorium on in-service and graduate pro-

grams which concentrate primarily on methods and processes and, instead, allow teachers to take graduate,
undergraduate and in-service courses that expand the
knowledge of teachers about the subject they teach.

III. In an effort to increase the pool of persons who would
bring benefit to our children by their knowledge as
classroom teachers and to encourage diversity in the use
of texts and books, Pennsylvania should:

A. Relax certification rules to allow persons to teach who
hold substantive degrees in the appropriate fields of study,
but who are virtually uncertifiable because they have not
taken education courses.

B. Continue to refrain from centralized textbook adoption.

CHAPTER FOUR

EQUITY, EXCELLENCE AND CHOICE:
THE PITTSBURGH PARADIGM

By Richard C. Wallace, Jr., Patricia A. Crawford, and Mary Ellen Kirby

EDITOR'S SUMMARY

Pittsburgh has developed one of the nation's most successful magnet school programs. Magnet schools specialize in the individual talents and needs of students. Specialities range from vocational and technical experience to training in the fine arts.

The magnet programs are highly attractive to both students and parents. Instituted on a district-wide basis in 1979, Pittsburgh's magnet programs were started to help promote student integration. Other districts interested in providing choice may benefit from studying the Pittsburgh experience.

Magnets have brought growth in public confidence and educational excellence to Pittsburgh schools. Thousands of students have been drawn back to the public schools from private institutions, which has contributed substantially to the dramatic turnaround in public confidence the District experienced in the 1980's. The magnets also offer the educational opportunities needed to prepare students more effectively for higher education and the work force of the 1990's.

Precautions were taken to ensure that magnet schools would be committed to equity. As the public began to recognize that magnet schools placed a special emphasis on "better" and not merely different, parents of non-magnet school children began to question the magnet school's commitment to equity. The District has been careful not to create a dual system, in which several elite schools operate at the expense of the rest of the system. To face this challenge, the District attempted to avoid attracting too many students from any one attendance area or "skimming" higher achieving students away from standard schools.

Through continued improvement and expansion, Pittsburgh magnet schools have achieved a racially balanced student body and have main-

tained academic integrity. The magnet schools' success can be measured in part by their growth and popularity among students and parents, as well as by their impact on integration.

Magnet program students now comprise 22% of the District's student body of 39,459 students. The number of students enrolled in the magnet schools has tripled in nine years from fewer than 3,000 in 1979-1980 to more than 8,600 in 1988-1989. All of the programs have been able to achieve a racial balance of at least a 60-40 ratio.

Most of the funding for magnet schools has come from Pittsburgh's General Fund. These costs included additional transportation, personnel, equipment and other start-up costs such as curriculum writing and student recruitment. Some costs can be expected to increase in proportion to the growth of the magnet, while others are a onetime expense.

Richard C. Wallace, Jr. is Superintendent of Schools for the Pittsburgh Public School District.

Patricia A. Crawford is Director of Public Information for the Pittsburgh Public Schools.

Mary Ellen Kirby is Coordinator of Parent/Community Involvement for the Pittsburgh Public Schools.

"Choice" — the right of parents to choose a school or program for their children — has been one of this decade's hottest educational issues. Legislators, parents and educators alike are closely watching the handful of states which have already adopted or are about to enact legislation granting parents some measure of choice in selecting their children's schools.

The pros and cons of such legislation are being debated widely across the nation in public forums and through the print and broadcast media. Choice will force a healthy competition among schools, some say, and will involve parents more actively in the educational process. Others point to obvious equity problems when the choice legislation does not provide the necessary resources, such as transportation, for all students to take advantage of the program.

These issues become particularly troublesome when inter-district choice is proposed because established policies and practices may differ vastly from school system to school system. On the other hand, intra-district choice through magnet programs is already available to students in many large American cities. These magnet programs, which provide a workable "choice" paradigm, have a long history of success in the United States, both in terms of enhancing racial balance and in improving quality education. Pittsburgh's magnet programs, which were instituted on a district wide basis in 1979 to help promote student integration, provide an excellent case study. Though there have been growing pains and annual changes, these magnets have demonstrated significant success.

It became clear early in Pittsburgh that parents were much more willing to accept a move to a school beyond their neighborhood boundaries if there was an educationally exciting program at the end of the bus ride. Thus, magnet programs, with their special focus, were highly attractive to both parents and students. Magnets alone, however, were not expected to achieve the level of integration demanded of the district. Additional measures including school closings and student reassignments were to be enacted.

Over the years, Pittsburgh has faced several challenges and attempted to forestall potential pitfalls, as well as resolve problems as they developed.

One of the first and greatest challenges was communicating to *all* parents and students in the district that choices were available to them through magnet programs and schools. While the central administration assumed responsibility for disseminating general information about programs and registration/acceptance procedures, the responsibility for recruitment was assigned to the staff and parents in each specific program. Technical assistance and marketing strategies were shared impartially among all who needed such support.

Sufficient resources and time to become established were critical to the success of fledgling programs. Courage to cancel unsuccessful programs was also essential.

As the public began to perceive some schools which had a special emphasis as "better" (in part due to the energetic marketing pitches by enthusiastic parent recruiters), and not merely different, questions of equity were raised by groups of parents in non-magnet schools. The district has been careful not to create a dual system, that is several elite successful schools operated at the expense of the rest of the system.

Another challenge was not to attract too many students from any one attendance area, or, worse, "skim" too many higher achieving students away from the standard schools. Precautions were also necessary to prevent inequities from developing in staffing, facilities and resources, thus creating a morale problem within the District.

Because Pittsburgh has wrestled with these issues as the magnets evolved over 10 years, other districts interested in providing choice, whether or not integration is a factor, may benefit from studying the Pittsburgh experience.

Program Description

Racially balanced magnet programs have served as a tool to promote student integration in the Pittsburgh Public Schools since September 1979. The initial programs, 17 specialized courses of study spanning kindergarten through grade 12, were developed on the recommendations of staff and a community advisory committee which had been formed by the Board of Education to study successful programs in other cities.

Pittsburgh's magnets initially were open to all students in the District regardless of academic achievement or ability. In subsequent years, however, standards have been adopted for the creative and performing arts schools and for selected high schools which are more academically rigorous. By contrast, other districts have established magnets as gifted programs with very high admission standards. Pittsburgh did not have to establish magnets in this way, because it operates a separate gifted program which serves eligible students in all schools, magnet and mainstream.

From the beginning the Board of Education has demonstrated its commitment to having magnet programs serve a racially balanced student body, maintain academic integrity, and meet valid educational needs. Thus, magnet programs have changed gradually over the past 10 years. Some programs have been expanded and replicated. Others have been relocated, and nearly all have undergone revision or refinement of curriculum and objectives.

Of the 16 magnet programs currently in place at 61 of the district's 75 elementary, middle, and high schools, 14 are whole school magnets; that is, located in schools that serve students only in that magnet program. All others are school-within-a-school magnets located in a building that also serves a standard elementary, middle or high school population assigned to that school.

Programs at the elementary level are: International Studies with a foreign language curriculum, Montessori, Traditional Academy, Open Education and Full-Day Kindergarten. Middle School programs are International Studies, Traditional Academy, Classical Academy, Geographic and Life Sciences, Polytechnic Academy and Creative and Performing Arts. Offered at the high school level are: Computer Science, Creative and Performing Arts, High Technology, International Studies, Law and Public Service, Junior ROTC, Vocational-Technical, Traditional Academy, Math and Science, Teaching Academy, and Public Safety Academy.

Impact of Magnets — Equity, Excellence and Choice

Desegregation Tool: Pittsburgh's initial magnet programs, launched in 1979, were designed for the purpose of desegregation. They were incorporated into a comprehensive systemwide desegregation plan in 1980. This plan, with amendments, satisfied the requirements for desegregation established by the Pennsylvania Human Relations Commission. In addition to furthering integration, these programs also had potential for improving the quality of education and increasing the level of parental choice in the educational process.

Since 1982, the Board has amended the original desegregation plan, closing and opening additional schools and enhancing and expanding magnet programs. The number of integrated schools and the percentage of students served in an integrated setting continue to increase each year.

Program Growth: The success of Pittsburgh's magnet programs can be measured in part by their growth and popularity among students and parents, as well as by their impact on integration. The number of students enrolled in magnet programs has almost tripled in nine years from fewer than 3,000 in 1979-80 (7% of the enrollment of 45,000 students) to more than 8,600 in 1988-89, 22% of the District's student body of 39,459 students. All of the programs are racially balanced with at least a 60-40 ratio. Most of the programs are able to achieve a racial balance that is closer to the goal of 50% black students and 50% students of other races, which mirrors the overall racial balance of the District.

Growth in Public Confidence: In Pittsburgh, the magnet programs are in large part responsible for drawing thousands of students back to the public schools from the private sector, and they have contributed substantially to the dramatic turnaround in public confidence the District experienced in the 80's.

Educational Excellence: Magnet programs enhance educational opportunities for certain students and offer educational opportunities needed to prepare students more effectively for higher education and/or the work force of the 1990's and beyond.

Healthy Competition: Magnet schools which succeed in creating a healthy inter-school competition often have a positive impact on the entire district as well. In many instances in Pittsburgh, standard schools without magnets have worked hard to attract their constituent students through new programming and parent involvement, ensuring that parents have viable choices to make for their youngsters, choices that include the standard school of assignment as well as magnets.

Potential Pitfalls

Although magnets offer many advantages to a school district, there are some side effects which can cause problems unless corrective action is taken. Equitable access, funding, and impact on other schools and feeder patterns are three areas which require close attention.

Equitable Opportunity to Participate: The registration or sign-up procedure for magnets must assure that all interested applicants have an equal opportunity to participate, even though all applicants cannot be assured of acceptance into their first choice of program. "First-come, first-served" was the original sign-up procedure for magnet schools in Pittsburgh. This method served the district well in the early years. As lining up became a ritual, however, the popularity of Pittsburgh's magnet schools and programs attracted nationwide publicity. Zealous parents camped out on the sidewalks and schoolyards of their favorite schools, days in advance of the registration time, braving inclement weather and foregoing civilized amenities to guarantee their place in line. Signing up had become a test of endurance, not a measure of interest, and a change was called for. "Line sitting" raised questions of equity particularly for single parents and others unable to spend time in line.

In 1987 a two-week general registration period replaced the first-come first-served sign-up, with a lottery held wherever applications exceeded the number of available openings in one or both racial categories.

Community reaction at first was mixed. While the change pleased those parents who were unable to line up, it angered those who felt a loss of control in the change to a lottery system. They were no longer guaranteed a place for their child in the school of choice by virtue of their place in line.

The change to a lottery, however, was accompanied by "sibling preference," assuring parents that families would not be fragmented by participation in magnet options. In addition a telephone bank, funded by the Allegheny Conference on Community Development and staffed by more than two dozen volunteers, helped parents understand and adjust to the new procedures. As a result, the district has made a very smooth transition to the lottery system, with no lapse of confidence or good will in the community it serves.

Funding: In Pittsburgh, the General Fund has financed the lion's share of additional costs for magnets, including additional transportation, personnel, equipment and other start-up costs such as curriculum writing and student recruitment. Some costs can be expected to increase in proportion to the growth of the magnet. Others are a one time expense.

Pittsburgh applied for and received a $4 million federal Magnet Assistance Grant in 1985, renewed in 1986, six years after magnets were in operation. These funds were used, in accordance with the law, to offset local expenditures and to purchase new equipment. Very little was allocated for expansion. Subsequent proposals in 1987 and 1989 were not approved for federal funding and full funding of magnets once again reverted to the district. Although federal dollars provide additional resources for magnets, the district has not been dependent on "soft money" to sustain or expand its magnet schools and programs.

Impact on Other Schools: The impact of an attractive magnet program/school on a school or schools within an assigned attendance area can be very unsettling, in the long run as well as the short. The so-called "skimming" effect — whether real or perceived — can demoralize the staff, students and parents of the school students are choosing to leave. This phenomenon has a devastating impact on certain middle and elementary schools. To help them fight back and remain competitive, the Board has placed special programs and resources at these schools which continue to serve their assigned student population.

One example is the Fulton Academy for Geographic and Life Sciences which now provides an exciting new curriculum for students who reside in the school's attendance area. In the first year alone, enrollment increased by 50 students.

A magnet program within a standard school also has the potential to divide and discriminate, as well as resegregate, creating a "have and have-not" atmosphere between magnet and non-magnet classes. A symbiotic relationship must be maintained between the add-on magnet and the host school. Strong staff cooperation and a healthy balance between integrated whole-school activities and magnet special events can help achieve and sustain the desired symbiosis.

Conclusion

Magnet schools have succeeded in Pittsburgh because they are an integral part of a strong public school system, serving a wide diversity of urban students with different needs, talents, and expectations. No effort has been spared to ensure that the neighborhood school of assignment is a viable choice. For most applicants to magnet programs in Pittsburgh, the school of assignment is an acceptable second choice if the magnet application cannot be approved.

In the 1989-90 school year, three new magnet programs are opening. One is the middle school Academy for Geographic and Life Sciences. The two at the secondary level, the Teaching Academy and Public Safety Academy, are a direct response to future area employment needs. These programs will prepare students for professions where job opportunities are expected to be plentiful.

In Pittsburgh, however, future expansion of new magnets will be limited. The District will increase choice for students by providing schools of emphasis in standard elementary and middle schools, and schools-within-a-school at the high school level. For any new magnets, the district will seriously consider several modifications; for example, looking at "restricted zone" magnets (magnets open only to students residing in a limited geographic area.) Restricted zone magnets would help maintain integrated schools in a specific region and would minimize transportation costs.

The way school districts attempt to provide choice for students and parents can have great impact on school reform as we close out this century. States and districts should carefully consider all the issues and must be willing to monitor the impact of choice programs on the total population, looking to see that equity and excellence are not compromised. Equity of opportunity for all students and excellence in programming must be maintained as top priority if true reform is to be achieved.

CHAPTER FIVE

HIGHER EDUCATION:
ARE WE GETTING OUR MONEY'S WORTH?
By Robert V. Iosue

EDITOR'S SUMMARY

Pennsylvania's higher education institutions have lost their direction when it comes to cost. Costs have risen beyond reason and the challenge is to set a new standard of expectations. The expectations should be increased productivity, improved quality, reduced costs, and more affordable access for all students.

Annual tuition increases have been more than double the yearly increase of all goods and services. From 1980-86, tuition increased 10.6% annually, while the Consumer Price Index averaged 4.8% during the same period. However, quality has not increased proportionally during the 1980's and educational value lags far behind cost.

Faculty teaching loads have decreased in the past decade. Teaching loads have declined from an average of 10.2 hours per semester in 1980 to 8.4 hours by 1985. Reduced loads have not strengthened colleges and universities since evidence shows that released time contributes to nothing but less teaching.

Administrative costs have risen even more rapidly than instructional expenditures. Administrative positions have increased to include vice-presidents of all types, and each new position has its associates and assistants. A $60,000 vice-president actually costs the institution well over $100,000.

Costs have been rising, due in part to higher education interest group pressure on legislators. Major universities hire expensive legal talent in order to lobby the Legislature for increased funding. However, increased financial support usually leads to increased costs since there are no meaningful incentives to limit tuition increases.

Public monies should be redirected into more functional modes. These include teaching, scholarship, and adequate facilities. Above all, a sense of vitality and mission must return to educational institutions, beginning with a lean, forthright administration and staff.

A bitter irony is being perpetuated at colleges. As the cost escalates at private colleges, they price out of the market many of the economically disadvantaged and increasingly large numbers of middle to upper-class families. This allows public institutions to become more selective and SAT's go up at these public colleges. The increasing selectivity at public universities forces a large segment of our minority population to abandon hope of ever getting to college. Thus, public educational institutions fail to fulfill their obligation to those who cannot afford the high tuition at a private college.

Robert V. Iosue is President of York College and a U.S. Department of Education appointee to the Congressional Advisory Committee on Student Financial Aid.

Pennsylvania's rich and diverse collection of higher educational institutions has, in general, lost its direction when it comes to value received for money spent. Costs have risen beyond reason, providing less value than it should — or did.

The challenge is to restore integrity to our higher educational system by setting a standard of expectations that may bring about a much needed change throughout the country. Policy discussions include productivity, institutional administration, and priorities on campus design.

The expectations should be more productivity, increased quality, reduced costs, and, most important, easier and more affordable access for *all* who can benefit from a higher education.

Our Hallowed Halls

> The way college costs are skyrocketing at most colleges is tragic. Our middle class family is considering not sending our three kids to college, even though they test in the 99th percentile on school achievement tests and my husband and I both graduated from college. We would feel more inclined to sacrifice our retirement savings for their education if there was less waste of our money.

One can pick and choose the problems that confront higher education; some picayune, some more serious; its vastness affects all aspects of society, causing it to be an easy target for anyone's imagination. Without doubt, the most serious problem higher education faces today is pricing out our future. The letter above states it clearly and poignantly.

Pennsylvania has a wonderfully diverse system of higher education consisting of 115 private institutions (colleges, universities, seminaries) and 32 public institutions (universities, community colleges). In addition, there are 29 branch campuses serving mainly as two year community colleges, and 102 specialized institutions, many of which grant the associate degree. All in all, it is a rich mix that far exceeds all states in the United States with the exception of one or two.

In the Keystone state, approximately 70% of all students attend a public institution with the remaining 30% in private institutions. Nationally, the figures are approximately 80% in public, 20% in private. The difference between Pennsylvania and the national average can be explained by the exceedingly large number of private colleges that were developed here long before the development of the present public system.

Salaries for faculty in Pennsylvania are near the national average: $38,700 vs. $39,400 nationally, for the academic year 1988-89. Fringe benefits as a percent of salary were approximately 25% in Pennsylvania as compared to 22.9% nationally. The combination of salary and fringe benefits compares well with national averages; the problem is not that college staffs are overpaid. Most have doctorates in their field of expertise and are well trained and capable of providing students with a fine classroom education. The problem is that most faculty members no longer wish to teach an adequate number of classes or students. Teaching on too many of our college campuses is playing a secondary role to other more self-serving pursuits.

If quality in higher education is defined as value received for money spent, then we are in dire need of change. The cost of higher education has risen dramatically over the last decade, so much so that the media has grabbed onto it with the tenacity of a pit bull. The media is doing no more than reflecting the frustration and outrage of the general population, reflecting a disillusionment with how we tend our shops, how we mislead the public, and how we do a disservice to our students.

The Rising Cost of Higher Education

In June of 1988, a Special Advisory was issued by the National Task Force on Higher Education and the Public Interest. Quoting directly:

> Of the five public interest questions, the price and cost of higher education is of greatest concern to the public and educators alike.
>
> The price/cost question also has become closely tied to an urgent national problem. When the principal economic challenge for the nation is whether American goods and services can be made and marketed as cheaply and as well as those of other nations, it should not be surprising that concerns about productivity have spread to higher education.

How colleges and universities respond to the price/ cost issue will influence long-term regulatory responses by federal and state governments. The imposition of governmental controls on the health care industry is particularly instructive, and a similar fate may await higher education.

The public doesn't necessarily want more information on the reason behind tuition increases. Parents and students, especially, want reassurances that college will be affordable. Not being able to attend college is an unacceptable alternative.

During the period 1980-86, there had been an average annual increase in tuition of 10.6%. This yearly increase is more than double the yearly increase of all goods and services, which was 4.8%. And it continues roughly at that rate going into the 1989-90 school year.

Our derelict behavior can be more forcefully demonstrated by pointing out that higher education's increases during the period 1980-86 exceeded the increases of medical care by 25%. During this period when medical care had risen dramatically and we subjected it to blistering attacks, higher education had outperformed them. During the same period, housing rose an average of 6.1%; food, 2.9%; new cars, 3.8%; and energy was fairly flat. It would be difficult to find a commodity or a service that rose faster than higher education costs.

A ten year comparison of tuition measured against the Consumer Price Index indicates how wildly out of line we are.

Academic Year	Public	Private	C.P.I. (Yearly)
1980-81	4%	10%	11.6
1981-82	16%	13%	8.7
1982-83	20%	13%	4.3
1983-84	12%	11%	3.7
1984-85	8%	9%	4.3
1985-86	9%	8%	3.6
1986-87	6%	8%	1.9
1987-88	5%	8%	3.6
1988-89	5%	9%	4.1
1989-90	7%	9%	Estimate: 4.5

For private institutions, the method for determining tuition increases is a heady combination of what the market will bear and what is wanted at the school. For publics, it is a noisy mix of politics ("We will have to triple the costs to the students and their parents if the legislature and the governor don't fall into line.") and what is wanted at the school.

Privates also consider the competition, and in a two-step maneuver that runs counter to the free enterprise system *and* possibly the legal system, raise the price to outbid the competition, but only after alleged informal price-rigging sessions.

Our credibility is suffering and rightfully so. For the year 1987-88, the C.P.I. was a meager 3.6%, while the increase for private colleges was 8%. There was a justifiable outcry, so we responded by promising that increases for the next year would slow down to 4 or perhaps as high as 5%. The 1988-89 year arrived and with it came a 9% increase, and with the increases came another round of flimsy excuses.

The problem of runaway costs goes further back than most people realize, including those who claim the dramatic tuition increases are recent and serve to make up lost time. Between the period 1970 and 1986, the Consumer Price Index rose 182%, while college tuition soared by 232%. The high cost of college is not a recent phenomenon; it has just become more noticeable, more outlandish, and those defending it, more arrogant, and at times, just plain silly in their defense.

First it was the high cost of energy, in 1972-73 and again in 1978-79. But energy costs subsided, yet college costs continued to soar. Then it was the high cost of computers, yet the 1960's saw the real brunt of high computer costs without irresponsible increases in tuition. Besides, as every administrator knows, the costs of equipment, especially in physics and other sciences, have always been high, especially during the Sputnik years.

The blame shifted to cost of maintenance of campuses, not realizing or remembering that on December 29, 1975, we collectively and openly acknowledged in a national journal that our goal was to raise record sums of money to curb tuition increases. We stated that our physical plant was up to snuff, no new buildings needed. No sooner had we made this pledge, and consequently fattened our endowments, than the unending exorbitant tuition increases started.

Is it not ironic that the institutions with the largest endowments (private and public) are also the most costly? Shouldn't questions be raised when one of our state universities in the fall of 1988 gathered all its resources so it could raise $200 million allowing it to endow $1,000,000 chairs, resulting in less teaching, less availability, and strangely enough, more costs. It is very much like putting our state's resources into a precious gem or an antique auto; wheel it out once in awhile, put it on display, then tuck it away. Its price is high, its value low. In academia, as in the art world, we judge the worth of our product by how unavailable it is.

The government, state and national, is a perennial favorite to lay the blame on. "If only they gave us more, we would not have to charge so much" goes the oft heard lament.

The very latest excuse indicates our willingness to abdicate any semblance of leadership or direction. With a shrug of the shoulders, we say the high cost is for all the upscale extras that "they" want. "They," are the students. In order to satisfy "them," we need to go the extra mile and that, of course, is the most costly one.

Another excuse that just now surfaced, and defies logic, is that the high cost is due to an emerging part-time population. If any group is cost efficient, it is the part-time student; they always have been and continue to be so.

Peter Drucker described our failure best of all. "Unless challenged, every organization tends to become slack, easygoing, diffuse." Our colleges and universities exemplify this indictment. Cost containment is seen as a sign of weakness. Being upscale is in vogue; why bother with a functional gym when an oversized athletic facility would look much better? We can then market the campus more on its designer appeal than on its educational potential. Since the money is not ours, throwing it around is not a primary concern. We can peddle quality and everyone is brainwashed into believing that quality comes at a phenomenally high cost. But it need not!

Decreasing Faculty Productivity on College Campuses

Dr. Myron Tribus, Director at the Center for Advanced Engineering Study at M.I.T. (and a protege of Dr. W. Edward Deming, the person most responsible for setting Japan on the road to recovery and success), wrote:

When I speak of quality, I do not mean adding bells

and whistles. I do not mean buses made by Rolls Royce. I simply mean doing the job the way it is supposed to be done.

For those who all too often use the unimaginative excuse, "quality is the reason for the higher costs in education," then required reading for them should be Dr. Tribus who states, "Increasing the quality of what is done leads to less waste, less cost, more satisfaction on the part of everyone, higher productivity and a better product."

Dr. Tribus, and his mentor Dr. Deming, were talking about quality and productivity as it applies to running a hospital, making cars, or administrating a college.

Let us examine the problem whose major observable symptom is runaway costs that cut across both public and private institutions, even though the uninformed assume that because a college is public, it is low cost. Public colleges have a financial one-upsmanship over privates because about 65% of their cost is hidden in tax subsidies thereby allowing them the luxury of low tuition. However, this low tuition comes at a high cost. In Pennsylvania, the average salary and fringe benefit package available at public institutions exceeds that of most privates. Any information on the subject has shown that, on average, the real costs of public and private institutions are approximately equal. And why not — they are equally derelict, on average, when it comes to administering campuses.

Most people out of university life do not realize the scant teaching load far too many of our faculty enjoy. We have always known about the long summer break, and we learned about the fall break, the four week semester break, and the spring break along with other smaller ones as we saw our children come home from college as often as they were in session. We also have seen the 17 week semester of 20 years ago reduced to 15 weeks, and in some cases, 14 weeks. The Governor of Missouri has concluded that today's students receive a semester and a half less education than previously.

Surveys show the average professor works from 50 to 60 hours per week, but unfortunately the surveys are self-serving.

Dr. Chester Finn, an astute observer of the higher education scene, has this to say about faculty workloads:

A great many faculty do very little work, at least on

behalf of the institutions that pay their salaries. Although practically all of them appear to think they do an enormous amount — certainly they assert that they do — the basis for these self-estimates is a set of norms that practically nobody outside the academy would credit.

About 25 years ago, the standard teaching load at many colleges and universities was 15 credits (hours) per semester. This compares with a 25 to 30 hour workload for high school teachers. The primary reason the load was one-half lighter for the professor was not because it is a more difficult assignment. Not only do public school teachers work a longer school year, teach more classes, work in a more difficult environment, especially if they are in the inner cities, but they do all this for about $9,000 less than your typical college professor. Since both the professor and the high school teacher have preparation of classes and correcting of tests and curriculum development, these are not the reasons.

The principal reason the college professor is allowed to teach one-half the load of the typical public school teacher is scholarship required of the professor that is generally not required of the high school teacher. A secondary reason, one that has grown in favor simply because there is virtually no accountability attached to it, is committee work, or faculty governance.

Professor Myron Lieberman of Ohio University writes:

> From the rhetoric of higher education, one would think that academicians are grievously overworked. Actually, a significant proportion of faculty time is devoted to collective decision-making, often on the trivial issues. Even when issues are resolved by individual decisions, there must frequently be a prior collective decision to delegate the decision to the individual. Despite the fact that they teach only three to nine hours a week, most professors do not conduct any meaningful research. It is, therefore, essential for most to find another justification for their lack of productivity; faculty self-governance meets this need very nicely, since its demands can be interpreted expensively and implemented with minimal effort and no accountability.

The teaching load of 15 credits per semester was reduced to 12 credits for most colleges, and there it should have stopped. Unfortunately, far too many let it go to 9 and even 6 credits.

The very detailed work of Thomas P. Snyder and Eva A. Galambox reported a decline in teaching load from an average of 10.2 hours per semester in 1980 to 8.4 hours just five years later. That is a 17.6% decline in productivity between 1980 and 1985. This helps explain why tuition skyrocketed.

A university might report a teaching load of 12 or 9, but this official version may differ dramatically from what actually goes on.

Reductions (or released time) are routinely given from the official workload so that a professor who should be teaching 12 credits will teach only 9, or if the official load is 9, some will teach only 6 or even 3. In one survey at a relatively large institution, we were all surprised, including the faculty, at just how much teaching reduction had accrued over the years. A course less for this, another for that, the end result was that about one-third of the official load was not being taught. We even uncovered one bizarre case of a professor who, for a variety of reasons received 15 credits of reductions against a 12 credit load, so he was paid a 3 credit overload. Yet this college would claim it has a 12 credit teaching load.

The more common inside story is told by a professor who just retired. He wrote that he had taught in major universities and small colleges, private and public. When he started he taught 15 credits per semester and published 8 books. During his last years his teaching load was reduced to 6 credits per semester, while his publishing ceased. He went on to write that his last university (a large state university), if asked, would report a 9 credit teaching load.

> But, that is by a rather dishonest system of counting 3 hour courses as 4.5 if there are more than 30 students and double if there are graduate students. Serving on committees earns points as does every dissertation. But many professors want to get out of directing such things as well as teaching.

Some colleges award 4 credits to the student but only provide them with 3 hours of teaching. The student pays the 4 credit rate and the professor can log in 4 hours of teaching so his workload appears more fulsome.

Research is most often given as the reason why reductions in workload are wanted. And, what is given to one faculty member, must be given to all. There are 450,000 faculty members nationwide, about 20,000 of them in Pennsylvania. To assume they are all engaged in seminal research and deserving of a 9 credit load is in one's self interest.

Some publications are very important, many are not, and even those in the field do not take them too seriously. Many of the published articles do not represent advancement of knowledge broadly defined. Many do not pose new philosophic theories or advance the work of others. Rather, they are a compilation of data emanating from hypothesis of such limited scope and value as to be ultimately confined to the dust bin of intellectual irrelevancy.

The duplicity used in reporting the teaching load is also used in measuring research. Presidents of colleges and universities are not naive. They wheel out the one or two professors who are doing frontier research, whether laser or robotics or history, and then leave everyone with the impression that all faculty are similarly engaged.

Professor Peter Drucker, in a 1979 article titled, *"The Professor as Featherbedder,"* said it most colorfully.

> By the time faculty members reach their early or mid-forties, they typically have been in academic life for 20 years — and typically have not worked in any other environment. Most faculty members, by that time, have done all the research and have written all the books they will ever write. Beyond that age, only a very small number of first-rate people remain productive. To be sure, these scholars and teachers who continue to produce are the people of whom everybody thinks when talking of historians, anthropologists or metallurgists, but their number is very small indeed. The rest have, in effect, retired into boredom. This middle-aged faculty member is far from burned out. But he is bored. And the common remedies — to get a divorce and take up with a nineteen year old undergraduate, to take to the bottle, to take to the psychoanalyst's couch — do not cure the disease.

Those who defend reduced teaching assume it will strengthen the program and the college, *but* are unable to offer even a hint of

confirmation that such an assumption is true. By having reduced loads (anything lower than 12 credits per semester), goes
the argument, we can show the world of our commitment to
quality. However, evidence shows that released time contributes to nothing but less teaching and less value for the
costs incurred.

Dr. Robert Boice, Director of the Center for Faculty Development at California State University, has conducted research on
the subject of released teaching time and has concluded:

(1) faculty given released time usually persist in old
    habits;
(2) verified assessments of normal workloads contradict
    faculty claims of being too busy for additional schol-
    arship;
(3) new faculty showed no obvious benefits of a typical
    released time program;
(4) faculty in released time programs verbalized real
    doubts how to use extra time for meaningful schol-
    arship.

In our own state of Pennsylvania, we have many cases of
quality taking a beating at the hands of insufficient teaching.
Some public and private institutions erroneously define an
excellent higher education in terms of how little they must be in
the classroom. Some do it by giving a paid sabbatical every four
years. Some do it by giving four academic credits for only three
hours in the classroom. Our state university feels that nine
credits for all its faculty is appropriate even though a vast number of them teach in two year facilities where the labs and the libraries and other resources are not (nor should be) available to
accomplish the traditional kind of research normally accomplished by less than 10% of the full faculty population.

Reduced teaching loads are attractive, but they may also be
counterproductive and ineffective. By offering reduced teaching, the college or university is making a loud statement about
campus values in terms of research. But, and this is an important but, *no* lasting changes are made by the faculty who
receive the reduced teaching loads.

These are the sentiments of people like Professors Boice,
Eble, and McKeachie, who go on to state that,

Not only were the accomplishments often small, and

often what might have been expected in the ordinary course of a faculty member's carrying out of responsibilities, grants seem to go first to those already teaching at a high level ... Relevant evidence suggests that productive faculty surpass other colleagues in finding ways to make time for research and writing. The factor that predicts productivity seems to be individual patterns (such as habit of regular writing) that begin early in careers.

What is needed is a statewide mandate that calls for 12 credits of teaching at all of our four year and graduate colleges and universities, and 15 credits at all of our two year colleges and branches.

For those capable of accomplishing seminal research, and having a continuing track record of so doing, reductions may be absolutely necessary, but they should be limited to a relative few, and when important research slows or stops, the 12 credits of teaching should once again be in effect.

A 12 credit teaching load, a standard sabbatical program, sufficient breaks in the academic year, and the four month summer break, provide ample time to continue with one's scholarship. There is confirming evidence to support this practice just as there is evidence to show that less in-class teaching does not guarantee or even seriously indicate progress in research that would justify being unavailable for teaching of students.

Restoring the time honored kinship of teaching and scholarship is a sorely needed policy that should be adhered to on a statewide basis.

The Growth of Administrative Staffs

Stop faculty bashing and show us just what the hell you have contributed and how you justify your big salary. Administrators are nearly all fakes and nonperformers.

It was an unsigned letter from an irate professor who was expressing how he and countless others feel about the bloat at the top. His expression lacks civility, but it indicates quite clearly the common view of too many administrators receiving large salaries. The salaries are not too large, but the growing numbers of administrators do tend to clog up the system.

There has been a decided growth in the size of the bureaucracies of many of our institutions; many of our public institutions have raised it to an art form, but many of our privates are just as gluttonous. We recently received an invitation to a three day conference where presidents' assistants were planning a growing network for people of that ilk. Among the steering committee were: Assistant to the President, Special Assistant to the President and Executive Assistant to the President. The purpose of the three day affair was, among other things, for reasons of "personal convenience, the meeting of colleagues, comparing notes, finding solace, and simply enjoying time together."

As colleges build bureaucracies, the inevitable yearly conference helps to perpetuate the various levels of bureaucracy by bonding the newly created positions in permanent self-proclaimed importance. Vice-President of Enrollment Management is a perfect example. Unheard of just a few years ago, it is today a necessity on most college campuses, and more than yearly conferences are already a staple of this bureaucratic genre.

Referring once again to the work of Snyder and Galambox, we read in their conclusions: ". . . the cost of administering higher education has risen more rapidly than 'Educational and General' expenditures and more rapidly than 'Instructional' expenditures." They go on to say that, "Staffing data indicates a more rapid growth of nonteaching professionals than of faculty."

In one state the professionals with general administrative titles grew more than twice as fast as faculty. In one institution, the number of administrators actually equaled the number of faculty.

Athletic teams at the Division II and III level are overstaffed with coaches, assistant coaches, equipment managers, trainers and former jocks whose exact role is often not known and never fully justified. Their teams go south for practice, demand outlandishly large facilities, use lots of equipment, and pretend the large outlays of money are important to the quality of the academic programs.

They are, in a sense, very much like the majority of professors who claim that because one or two of their number do seminal research and teach less, they all deserve the reduced teaching.

Our Division II and III brethren eye with envy the Division I prerogatives and constantly put pressure for more of everything, forgetting that the Division I program is probably a moneymaker, at least in some of its sports.

U.S. Department of Education studies confirm the view that disproportionate growth has occurred in the administrative side of things. Administrative positions have increased to include vice-presidents of all types, and each new position needs its associates and assistants, along with offices, secretaries, travel funds and other accouterments worthy of the title. A $60,000 vice-president actually costs the institution well over $100,000.

Justifying new positions, or even existing ones, is a difficult job, yet the new positions keep coming until there is a budget problem, either at the college or within the state, and then the painful job of letting people go takes place — most often without any diminution of quality.

Consider how unhelpful a large bureaucracy was at one of our big state universities where a student wrote:

> Is there really excess fat in State's bureaucracy that could be cut to help prevent tuition increases? I'm sure there is, because I received a three dollar refund ($3.06 to be exact) that required the involvement of at least five people, a two part form, and it took over two weeks to process.
>
> The refund procedure began on February 24 when the two part form was typed by the person officially requesting the refund. Three days later my three dollar refund was 'recommended' for approval by a budget administrator. Final approval required the signatures of two untitled bureaucrats — one on the 3rd of March and another on March 4. Then the two part form was sent to the controller where a check was finally issued on March 9.
>
> This is just one example of the bureaucratic monster our tuition money feeds. It makes one wonder what kind of bureaucratic red tape is involved in spending a larger amount of money. This is certainly the kind of bureaucratic fat that can be cut to help reduce tuition increases.

Marketing and Hyprocrisy

Consider the case of a top-notch business school that failed, in 1987, to make the top 20 survey in *U.S. News and World Report*. The next year was devoted to a study of the problem, with the end result being a new director of marketing. The 1988 *U.S. News and World Report* came out with the school of business placed in the top five. Brightness and a spirit of well-being replaced the anger and finger pointing. Applications skyrocketed as did the tuition. What is ironic, few other changes occurred. Aside from the smoke and mirrors, nothing of substance was altered.

We stake our reputation on such inappropriate accrediting mechanisms such as a *U.S. News and World Report* survey, the best 10 list, the best 100 list, all far removed from education. But that is because our goal is more to market the place than to teach the students. We overbuild our buildings, most especially our athletic facilities where everything is twice as big as needed, and marble and copper adorn everything.

One of our public institutions was taken to task for spending $5,000 on a one shot, two-color ad in an expensive magazine touting its low tuition even as it knew about its high cost.

Another plastered billboards at a phenomenally high cost, beseeching the public to accept its purported high quality even as it wasted the public's tax dollars on such foolish high jinx.

The university president then went on the radio to announce, well in advance so students could be prepared, that there would be a 5% tuition increase. Benevolence turned to sanctimoniousness when he said, "Of course, this 5% increase is predicated on us getting a 14% increase from the state legislature."

We all know the rules of the game, and they include politics, but hypocrisy of this magnitude is not worthy of any university president.

The Business of a University

A Capitol Hill staffer learned quickly during hearings and concluded with the following observations:

> We saw the kind of expensive legal talent that some of
> the major universities had hired to lobby us; it sud-

denly dawned on us that we weren't just dealing with higher education in the nation's service. Rather, we were dealing with universities that looked and acted like the very large and very wealthy business corporations that they are. Suddenly, there was a consensus on the part of Hill staffers that these university representatives were well-heeled business people who were out after even more money. 'Greed' seemed to us to be an appropriate term. We immediately resisted.

Legislators at the state level especially, because of their proximity, and the national level are very susceptible to the entreaties of some from higher education who advance their cause as noble and in the national interest. Legislators should learn well the dictum put forward by the respected educational economist Howard Bowen who wrote in 1980 that:

...each institution raises all the money it can.
...each institution spends all it raises.
...the end result is toward ever-increasing expenditures.

If educators were sincere, they would point out that education's problems, society's problems, fall most heavily on our public school system starting with Head Start, and kindergarten, and working its way upward to a disgraceful dropout rate from high school. Surprising as it may seem, the problems faced by the inner cities are matched by those of the rural Pennsylvania countryside. While the problems are not the same, the dropout rate, the unwanted pregnancies, and the poverty cause the education system some of its biggest problems.

If we are genuinely concerned about our state's future, we should focus on the real problems, not on the areas that have become quite adept in self-service.

The Minorities and Disadvantaged

Consider the bitter irony colleges perpetuate. As the cost escalates at private colleges, they price out of the market many of the economically disadvantaged *and* an increasingly large number of middle and upper-middle class families. The middle and upper-middle class correctly concluded that public institutions can get their child to his or her destination as well as a costly private college, causing the ranks of those wanting to attend public institutions to swell. This allows the publics to become more selective, which they have, and to even draw from some upper class families. SAT's go up at these public institutions accompanied by new goals and visions of becoming "great" research or high profile universities. In either case, their primary mission of fulfilling a special obligation to those who could not afford the high tuition at a private college has dramatically changed.

The unwitting conspiracy between high tuition at privates and increasingly high selectivity at publics has forced a large segment of our minority population to abandon hope of ever getting to college, a hope that fades well before the eleventh grade in high school.

Some statistics are in order. Following World War II, access to private colleges increased dramatically both for whites and blacks, with the period between 1960 and 1981 showing an increase in non-white students from 6.4% to 14.6%, a 128% increase.

The dramatic increase in tuition for private colleges started about 1980 resulting in a 33% rise in three years. Black enrollments started to drop and have continued to drop even today, especially among black males.

There are other important reasons why the black student population in college has decreased rather than increased, the unattended problems in elementary and secondary schools chief among them, but certainly the high cost of education has done nothing to encourage attendance. To compound the problem, the financial aid we claim is being used for the economically deprived is mainly for the benefit of middle class kids.

Many college presidents claim that the solution to both the high costs and the dwindling minority enrollment is more state and federal aid. Federal aid now exceeds $20 billion a year to all institutions while Pennsylvania contributes more than $1.3 billion to its institutions.

In seeking to absolve ourselves of the blame for increased costs and decreased value, we point the finger at our state capitol or toward Washington. We gobble up favorable responses, often for nonessential things, and come back knocking for more. Yet the costs continue to soar.

Cost Analysis

The question legislators must ask themselves is, "Does increased financial support cause costs to go up?"

We all seem to hold the view that government support of health care has caused everything connected with the medical field to increase, from prescriptions to operations to office visits, all of us except those in health professions, that is. We all hold the view that the billions of dollars spent on defense contracts and other implements of defense cause the price to go up, except those in the industry. Why should it be different for higher education? In 1961, the federal government spent about $400 million for student aid. Including loans, it's now over $20 billion, not counting state aid. Who, except educators, believes the increased support and the increased costs are not connected. There is just too much evidence to the contrary. After all, the formula for determining a student's need includes the cost of the school the student wishes to attend, so why not raise the ante. If social security worked the way student aid does, our government would give a larger monthly payment to those with richer tastes.

Not only does it provide an incentive for institutions to raise costs, or at the very least it does not provide an incentive to hold down costs, it also helps them to more fully use the questionable practice of discounting. This is where a school raises the costs so the student can obtain more aid, then lowers it by giving in-house scholarships, some of it pure paper.

The latest fad, unfortunately, one that discourages a value-oriented, cost containment program, is the tuition prepayment plan. Some colleges tried it, prematurely, as have some states. Not only is it fraught with uncertainties and unknown tax consequences, it may well encourage another long round of tuition increases. A well intended yet irrational piece of legislation floating around Harrisburg will, if enacted, be an invitation to raid the treasury. It is a prepayment plan designed to get parents or grandparents to pay into a fund from which the child can draw when college time comes. If the amount of money contributed by the family is not sufficient to cover the cost, "...the state would cover the difference for public institutions by supplementing their annual state appropriations. A reserve fund would be set up to cover any difference for private colleges and universities."

The incentives to raise tuition are overt in this proposed policy.

Conclusions

1. First and foremost is to return a sense of vitality and mission to our institutions beginning with a lean, forthright administration and staff in place of a bloated bureaucracy.

2. Restore respectability to the teaching of students. Establish a 12 credit *hour* teaching standard, with few exceptions for seminal research.

3. Reestablish educational mission over costly marketing endeavors which, at some schools, cost more than $2000 to "land" a student.

4. Direct public monies into more functional modes; i.e., teaching, scholarship, adequate facilities; discourage the present direction of insufficient teaching, inadequate scholarship and grand edifices.

5. Recapture athletics. If Division I is the category, then it should carry itself financially. All others (Division II, III) should cease the excess spending and discard the excess baggage.

6. Lastly, seriously consider a redirection of our public educational funding, reducing that which finds its way into higher education and increasing that which is needed in those programs and schools that will help Pennsylvania reduce its high school dropout rate. The workplace as well as higher education will benefit from a sharp decrease in the number of dropouts we have, each one of whom is potentially a noncontributer to society. Worse, they tend to become a drain. A zero dropout rate by the year 2000 is a most worthy goal and will set a standard for the nation. It may be impossible to reach, but no more important goal can come out of Harrisburg.

CHAPTER SIX

THE ROLE OF BUSINESS IN IMPROVING EDUCATION
By Edward Donley and George J. Evans, Jr.

EDITOR'S SUMMARY

American industry is moving from labor intensive operations to knowledge intensive operations. Future business success will increasingly depend upon a well-educated population which possesses the skills to adapt to technological advances. This need for a better-educated workforce will require changes in our education system.

Changes in public education are needed since current worker skills are deficient. A study commissioned by the Governor's Office of Policy Development found that 86% of Pennsylvania companies surveyed had productivity losses caused by deficient worker abilities. These deficiencies were primarily in reading, writing, and math skills.

Businesses have recently become involved in improving the education system. Partnership projects that bring together schools and local businesses have succeeded throughout Pennsylvania. Examples include the Committee to Support Philadelphia Schools and the Lehigh Valley Business-Education Partnership. These partnerships allow for education and business leaders to explore the educational needs of the region and to formulate action programs which will assess these needs.

In Western Pennsylvania, the Allegheny Conference Fund has channeled private money into public education initiatives. This fund was created as a flexible link between schools and Pittsburgh's business, government, civic, and foundation leaders. A number of programs are supported by the fund including grants to school principals, management training of middle management school personnel, and school-neighborhood consortiums.

Another form of business-education involvement is the corporate academy. This concept provides an alternative educational experience for young people who are at risk of dropping out of school. The academy involves the school system, the social service organizations, business, and volunteers in an organized effort to support the at-risk young person.

There are several guidelines for business-education partnerships that should be followed. Model partnerships have clearly defined, measurable goals for both business and education. Underlying every successful compact is the premise that genuine economic opportunity can encourage young people to stay in school and learn the necessary skills.

Business stands to be a major benefactor of successful educational improvements. However, for changes to ultimately succeed, cooperation must be developed between educators, school boards, and the general public. The business community can assist in this effort by contributing to an environment of trust and commitment to a long term relationship.

Edward Donley is Chairman of the Executive Committee of the Board of Air Products and Chemicals, Inc. and is a member of the Senior Council and Executive Committee of the U.S. Chamber of Commerce.

George J. Evans, Jr. currently serves the Iacocca Institute at Lehigh University as the IBM Executive in Residence.

A movement to involve the American business community in an evermore substantial way with education reform is gaining momentum throughout the United States. Many business organizations including the Business Roundtable, the National Alliance for Business and the U.S. Chamber of Commerce are working cooperatively in this important field. The widely recognized influence of quality education upon the competitiveness of American industry is a vital driving force in this growing activity.

The U.S. Chamber of Commerce is particularly well-positioned as a national business organization to tap into a nationwide network of business groups committed to enhance education quality. The U.S. Chamber has 2,800 local and state chamber members and 180,000 corporate members strategically placed in cities, suburbs and rural areas nationwide. This creates a solid infrastructure now in place to contribute to the nation's efforts to improve our schools.

To empower local chambers and business leaders to be the catalyst for education reform, the U.S. Chamber has established the Center for Workforce Preparation, a separate, nonprofit corporation which stresses action — not more research of the problems. Through local chambers, it will equip business leaders with the tools they need to shape meaningful education policy at the local level.

A broad array of materials will be dispersed to local chambers and business leaders through the Center. The Center will:

- Develop a campaign to link business, education and community leaders together and show them what works in education reform, what does not, and why.

- Empower local chambers and business leaders to be key players in the education reform movement.

- Identify the most successful and results-driven education partnership activities and show business leaders how to get these initiatives underway.

- Disseminate information on national reform issues such as school restructuring, core competencies, accountability, alternate teacher certification, and national goals to key local chambers and business leadership.

- Initiate a campaign to help students understand the necessity of a quality education for work and career participation.

The U.S. Chamber's Center for Workforce Preparation promises to put local chambers and business leaders on track with educators in achieving education reform. In doing such, it will institutionalize throughout the nation the business role in education as a tool for long-term economic growth and prosperity.

This paper describes some of the experiences which business organizations have had working with educators in Pennsylvania and in other parts of the country. Fortunately our state has a good history of business support for education and this will help us as we face the complex task of orienting our education system to the needs of the 21st century.

Changes in the Business Environment

The business environment of the 1980's has been one of major structural changes during a period of unprecedented economic prosperity. Daily we read about the effects of the new "global economy" in which we now live. Approximately 79% of all products manufactured in the United States now have competition from overseas sources, and it is no longer possible to be a truly successful businessman if competition from our overseas trading partners is ignored.

This heightened competition from countries which operate from an environment which is different from the United States has forced a reexamination of all facets of business operations. In most cases this results in the recognition that a number of fundamental changes will be required to meet the new challenges. It is becoming increasingly clear that success will depend upon a well-educated population which possesses the skills to adapt to the changes which must be made if we are to continue as a strong economic leader.

Reasons For Business Involvement

A successful business provides a product or service which

offers the buyer the right combination of quality, function, service and price when compared to its competitors. While overseas wage rates have been increasing, they have not reached the level of the U.S. Therefore, it is virtually impossible for a U.S. company to compete on the basis of lower wage rates. Consequently, most labor intensive jobs have gone overseas either as subsidiaries of U.S. corporations or as suppliers. With the shrinking value of the dollar from its 1985 peak and the general increases in wage rates overseas, this trend has diminished. The effects, however, are not reversible unless we are willing to accept a much lower standard of living in the U.S.

Automation and the use of technology have been the tools necessary to reduce the labor content of most business operations. They have also made it possible to provide improved quality products and services as a result of the reduction of sources of human error. By effectively using the new technologies, a business can also reduce the time necessary to design and produce the product. This makes it possible to get to the market ahead of competitors and capture the lead for introduction of the product or service.

Moving from labor intensive operations to knowledge intensive operations requires a higher level of skills for all parts of the organization. Management must be willing and able to adapt to new ways of organizing and operating the business. Workers must possess the basic skills to learn how to operate in an environment which uses new technology. It is no longer possible to look at the mechanism of a machine and see how to fix it. The operator must understand how it works and be able to deduce what to do based upon the symptoms which are observed. These higher order skills are becoming the norm for U.S. businesses rather than the exception, and we depend upon the education system to produce a population which possesses these skills.

Increasingly, business leaders are speaking out on the need for change in the way we educate our young people. David T. Kearns, Chairman and CEO of the Xerox Corporation, has noted:

> Public Education in this country is in crisis. America's public schools graduate 700,000 functionally illiterate students every year, and 700,000 more drop out. Four out of five young adults in a recent survey couldn't summarize the main point of a newspaper article, or

read a bus schedule, or figure their change from a restaurant bill.

At a time when our preeminent role in the world economy is in jeopardy, there are few social problems more telling in their urgency. Public education has put this country at a terrible competitive disadvantage.

Colby H. Chandler, Chairman and CEO of Kodak, writes:

The education gap between the United States and its major competitors is even more alarming. We are failing as a nation to provide this country with a properly educated workforce. This shortfall ranges from entry-level jobs to the next generation of scientists and engineers to ensure continued leadership for the United States in the fields of science and technology. Twelfth grade students from the U.S. consistently score below their counterparts from Japan, Singapore, Hong Kong and a host of other countries in international math and science tests.

Investment in education must become a national priority, fully involving parents, teachers, communities, states, the federal government and the private sector. Investing in education does not necessarily mean more money needs to be spent. What it does mean is an unrelenting commitment to excellence which has been lacking.

The Governor's Office of Policy Development working through the Pennsylvania Occupational Information Coordinating Committee, commissioned a study to assess how Pennsylvania employers perceive that education deficiencies affect their ability to do business. Participants were asked a number of questions concerning their perceptions of entry level workers' abilities. Three responses were possible: Pleased With Entry Level Workers; Slight Problem: Business Somewhat Affected; Extreme Problem: Business Seriously Affected. The percentage of responses in the last two problem categories were:

Workers Abilities	Percentage With Problem
Reading Ability	32%
Writing Ability	45%
Math Ability	51%
Ability to Communicate	49%

Effects on Business	Percentage With Problem
Inefficiency & Productivity Loss	86%
Higher Accident Rate	32%
Greater Wastage	76%
Confused or Lost Orders	75%
Poor Relations with Customers	69%
Introduction of New Technology	66%

Since this survey recorded perceptions rather than absolute measurements, the responses must be interpreted accordingly. No doubt they are also influenced by the relatively low unemployment rate in Pennsylvania as well. Given the rather high percentage of responses which indicate that skills are deficient and that business is negatively affected, however, it must be concluded that a significant level of impact exists. Any improvement in the quality of the education system which improves the skills of the graduates should therefore result in improved business operations.

Structural Problems Associated With Involvement

Interacting with the education system is not an easy task due to the structure of the system. Education is also highly influenced by events which take place outside the school itself. Therefore educators should not always bear total responsibility for the problems in the system. The issue is not so much how we got here, but how do we move on to a system which is more responsive to the needs of the future.

Public education in the United States is the responsibility of local school boards operating under rules and regulations set forth by state government. A district may be very large such as the city of Pittsburgh with 39,672 students or one with fewer than 1,000 students such as the Weatherly Area School District with 740 students. Socioeconomic factors of the community play an important role in education due to the use of local property taxes to finance a significant proportion of the costs. In Pennsylvania local sources provided 49.9%, state sources 45.6%, and federal sources 4.5% of funds in the 1985-86 school year. Nationally, the figures were 44.4% local, 48.9% state, and 6.6% federal. Depending upon the local emphasis on education there can be great diversity from district to district and each locality frequently has its own set of problems.

Models For Business Involvement in Education

Business has been involved with education for many years and in many ways. In the Lehigh Valley, many companies have adopt-a-school programs in operation. The Allentown-Lehigh County Chamber of Commerce and the Lehigh County school districts have a "School Works!" program which functions to create partnership projects between schools and area businesses. The Lehigh Valley Partnership, an organization of business leaders and industrial development organization leaders, through several committees has been actively working with Vocational Technical Schools and in assessing the needs for business to become more involved.

At Lehigh University, the Iacocca Institute was established to address the problems of U.S. industrial competitiveness. The advisory board, which is made up of industry leaders and chaired by Lee Iacocca, identified education as one of the major issues which needed to be addressed by U.S. industry in its efforts to become more competitive.

Working together, the Lehigh Valley Partnership and the Iacocca Institute developed the concept of a Lehigh Valley Business-Education Partnership (LVBEP) which was put forward and supported by both the education and business communities. The purpose of the LVBEP is to bring together the district superintendents, the college and university presidents, and the CEO's of the area businesses in a forum which will allow them to explore the educational needs of the Lehigh Valley and to formulate action programs which will address these needs. Membership in the partnership is limited to the top executive of each organization. The work of the partnership will be done through various task forces which will be responsible for developing the background concerning the issues and making recommendations to the full membership. Participation on the task forces will include members of the partnership plus community experts who have experience concerning the issue.

In the city of Philadelphia, the Committee to Support Philadelphia Public Schools (CSPPS) has been in operation since 1983. It was formed under the leadership of Mr. Ralph S. Saul who was CEO of CIGNA Corporation at that time. CSPPS is an umbrella group whose mission is to stimulate, coordinate and focus private sector resources on priority problems of education, with emphasis on the Philadelphia public schools.

Its activities are coordinated by a number of task forces and subsidiary organizations, each led by a member of the committee. These include:

- **Paths/Prism:** an organization which draws on resources of colleges, cultural organizations and corporations to provide intellectually rigorous professional and curriculum development for teachers.

- **Education for Employment/Cities in Schools:** a broad and growing initiative whose goals are to reduce the dropout rate and increase the employment rate of high school students.

- **Financial Resources:** a task force which reviews school district financial matters with the goals of identifying areas for management savings and/or needs for added revenue.

- **Management Assistance:** a variety of involvements of corporations in improving school district management, with a major emphasis on human resource management.

- **Celebration of Excellence:** an annual spring dinner honoring outstanding contributors to public education and a fall event providing cash awards to outstanding teachers.

CSPPS stresses long-term, major, systemwide improvements. It uses corporate dollars to leverage support from other sources; corporate leadership to get a range of institutions working together and following through; and corporate staff, as well as those of other organizations, as a source of expertise. CSPPS and its subsidiary activities have built a budget in excess of $5.5 million on a base of $280,000 in corporate investments. Foundation, government and school district dollars comprise the balance, with approximately $200,000 in additional corporate support to related programs. The funds CSPPS raises are used as seed money or "venture capital", with the school district picking up the cost of successful programs. Mr. Richard H. deLone of deLone, Kahn & Associates, a management consulting firm, is retained by CSPPS to direct its activities. PATHS/PRISM and Education for Employment are nonprofit subsidiaries with their own staffs.

One of the original Pennsylvania programs was the Allegheny Conference Fund which was started in 1978. The Fund is a program of the Allegheny Conference on Community Development and was created as a flexible vehicle for building links between the schools and Pittsburgh's business, government, civic, and foundation leaders; for increasing community confidence in an urban school system; and for channeling a limited pool of private dollars into a range of efforts to support the schools.

The fund supports a number of programs:

1. **Small Grants for Teachers.**

2. **Principal Grants** — This program offers grants in the range of $1,500 to principals to develop programs not possible within the school budget, which will make systemic changes and improvements in the schools. A focused component within this program offers grants averaging $500 to project teams with innovative approaches to increasing parental involvement in their children's education.

3. **Partnerships-in-Education** — This program pairs 39 businesses and associations with Pittsburgh public middle and high schools and offers system-wide assistance of 29 associate partners.

4. **Educator-in-Residence** — Several times a year, prominent persons in the education or business community are brought to the city to speak to a variety of different audi-

ences, such as business leaders, foundation leaders, community representatives, and school personnel.

5. **Counselors Career Update** — This is a series of four workshops to update high school and college counselors' knowledge about career trends and economic development in Allegheny County. It includes speakers, workshops, and shadow day experiences.

6. **Schenley Teachers Center** — A development officer was supported by local funders in order to develop and implement a fundraising plan for this teacher training center. The Fund continues to provide technical assistance.

7. **Management Training** — This program provides the opportunity for middle management school personnel to participate in existing company training programs in eight companies. In addition, two companies will offer specialized training as needed.

8. **Mon Valley Project** — Technical assistance has been provided to the McKeesport School District regarding the development of an education fund to carry out four projects: 1) mini-grants for teachers; 2) increased and improved public information; 3) community development; 4) a Mon Valley Counseling Center that will provide assistance to counselors in all the Mon Valley districts. This fund expanded into the Mon Valley Education Consortium.

9. **Principals Academy** — A support network for 30 selected principals from a three-county area. Using business resources, the Academy offers opportunities for professional development and the discussion of educational issues within a peer group setting.

10. **School-Neighborhood Consortium** — The Fund established the Consortium to ease transitions created by school and community changes that result from neighborhood demographic shifts, school closings and the reorganization of feeder patterns. The Consortium's director works with community leaders to select communities and develop action plans.

11. **Urban Math Collaborative** — Pittsburgh's Urban Math

Collaborative is one of 11 nationwide collaboratives established to encourage the professional development of secondary mathematics teachers and connect them to resources
to enhance mathematics education.

12. **Ad Hoc School Finance Committee** — A group of local school
district and government leaders meet to discuss school
finance in southwestern Pennsylvania and to develop
strategies for building support in the public and private sectors for adequate public finance of public education.

13. **Parent Involvement** — The Fund has hosted two half-day
workshops focusing on increasing parent involvement in
the Pittsburgh Public Schools in conjunction with the offering of focused grants.

14. **Special Projects** —
     a) Private Industry Council (PIC)
     b) Discretionary Fund
     c) Public Information
     d) Woodland Hills Comprehensive Inservice and
        Community Outreach Program
     e) Employers and Child Care

Another form of business-education involvement is the Corporate Academy. This concept was pioneered by Cities In
Schools, Inc. in conjunction with the Burger King Corporation.
The CIS/Burger King corporate academy is an alternative educational experience for young people who have been identified
as being at risk of dropping out. It provides students and their
families with specialized educational instruction, assistance
with personal and social service needs, enrichment activities,
and employment training and placement opportunities.

A corporate academy involves the school system, the social
service organizations, Burger King franchisees and volunteers
in an organized effort to support the at-risk young person. Cities
in Schools has developed a manual and training program to provide instruction in creating a corporate academy. Their experience to date with the program has been outstanding and
anyone interested in learning more about it should contact
Cities in Schools.

Choices of an organization for any particular area is necessarily dictated by the needs of the area, the level of commitment by the community, and the skills and leadership available. In most cases the organizations have changed over time and as they have matured, the needs have been better understood and the level of trust between educators and businessmen has developed. In no case has a quick fix solution been found.

Guidelines For Business-Education Partnerships

The National Alliance for Business began a project which provided guidance and support to twelve communities attempting to build partnerships among schools, employers, local elected officials, and youth at risk of not making a successful transition into the workforce. The model for the project was the Boston Compact which featured a written agreement representing a five-year commitment by business and education leaders to work together to improve public education. The key to this agreement was several clearly-defined, measurable goals for both business and education. A fundamental premise of the Compact was that genuine economic opportunity could encourage young people to stay in school and learn the necessary skills.

After six years of experience the Boston business community did not feel that the results met their expectations. While the minority youth unemployment rate in Boston was lower than in other urban areas, the high school dropout rate remained virtually unchanged and progress toward other academic goals was poor. In fall 1988, the Boston business community initially refused to reauthorize the agreement and sign Compact II. Business leaders did not want to abandon the schools but did feel that renewed emphasis on fundamental school change and accountability was necessary. Compact II was signed in spring 1988 and adds new goals to the original efforts to improve test scores and lower dropout rates. The new goals include: increasing parental involvement in school children's education, creating a post graduate support network that Boston high school students can tap into for up to four years after graduation, and putting in place a school based management program to decentralize the system and make each school accountable for its own success or failure.

The National Alliance for Business prepared a report of its

experience with the twelve demonstration cities entitled *The Compact Project: School-Business Partnerships for Improving Education*. It profiles the twelve projects and also describes the lessons learned and makes a number of recommendations.

Lessons from the Compact Project

- Business still does not adequately understand the magnitude and seriousness of the problems of our public schools.

- Many business leaders in a community must be brought together to coalesce support for education issues.

- An institutional structure is needed at the local level to orchestrate ongoing business commitment and build the likelihood of continuity of business involvement.

- Partnerships require a long-term commitment. Most partnerships are formed out of a sense of crisis, but reform is complex and efforts may lose momentum.

- Reform requires a high level of interest from at least three groups: educators, business leaders and government officials.

- Business needs to become involved in the governing structures of the schools.

- It is imperative to develop agreed-upon measurable goals that clarify intent, focus, commitment, and permit periodic assessment.

- Large infusions of funds are not necessary to maintain partnerships, but information and assistance are essential.

- Business people have only limited knowledge of education reform issues.

Recommendations

• A carefully structured and organized school-to-work transition program or "Jobs Collaborative" can be an effective first step in bringing together the necessary individuals and organizations required to establish a Compact. The business community can provide meaningful employment opportunities and the schools can agree to better prepare young people for tomorrow's jobs. The intermediary organization can organize and develop the jobs and work with business and education to ensure that they are each meeting the needs of other partners and of the young people in the program. NAB details the benefits of the process for developing effective Job Collaboratives in the publication, *Who Will Do the Work? A Business Guide for Preparing Tomorrow's Workforce*.

• If partnerships are to achieve their maximum potential, it is important to coalesce committed, high-level leadership from many organizations and sectors. While one leader's energy and organizational skills are helpful, a broader coalition is imperative if significant changes are to be made. Business people must work with educators, community-based organization staff, and local elected officials to help find lasting solutions to their community's problems.

• It is imperative that all partners make a commitment to be involved for the long term. There are no quick fixes in improving public education — problems that took such a long time to develop will take a longer time to solve. This long term commitment is especially important because changes continue to occur even as solutions are being developed and implemented.

• It is essential that all partnership members understand and articulate a shared vision of what the changes should be. There is no place for separate agendas. Indeed, openness to a redefinition of roles is imperative.

• Business-education partnerships are most effective when all who are involved develop, agree upon, and regularly measure long and short term goals and objectives. Student, staff, administrative and system progress — not just test scores, the number of jobs filled, and other objective data — should be measured.

• It is important to establish an organization to manage day-to-day efforts and to measure progress against predetermined objectives. The Private Industry Council or the local Chamber of Commerce can serve as the organization, or a new organization can be formed for this purpose.

Blueprint For the Future

Since 1983 when *A Nation at Risk* generated widespread attention to the problems of education in this country, there have been many reports on the topic. The Business-Higher Education Forum examined 20 major reports and recorded 285 distinct recommendations. Only 9 appeared in 5 or more reports and 70% appeared in only one. The Forum observed at the time, "It is little wonder that progress in raising student achievement has been much too slow: As different pilots seize the helm of educational reform, the ship goes round in circles."

Observers have noted that the reform movement went through a "first wave" from 1983-86 which was mostly dictated by the states and focused on stiffening standards on teachers and students. Beginning in 1986, a "second wave" of reform emerged with its focus more on improving teaching and learning at the school site. These "second wave" issues are often referred to by the term "restructuring" and call for significant changes in the way education is managed and operated.

President Bush in his education summit with the governors identified a set of topics for their discussion which serve to categorize the issues into six general areas. These can serve as a starting point for examining the issues in local areas of interest:

The Learning Environment

  • Providing appropriate preschool and early-childhood experiences to prepare children for primary school.

- Identifying at-risk youths and reducing the number of dropouts.

- Creating safe, violence-free schools.

- Establishing and maintaining drug-free schools.

- Assessing student performance and establishing appropriate goals.

- Engaging teachers, students, parents, and the community in partnerships.

Teaching: Revitalizing a Profession

- Identifying, recognizing, and rewarding excellence in teaching.

- Enriching the teaching profession by providing more flexible routes to certification.

- Attracting enough qualified teachers for elementary and secondary schools.

- Meeting the nation's needs in science and mathematics instruction.

- Increasing the number of minorities entering teaching.

Governance: Who is in Charge?

- Defining the appropriate role of the federal government in education.

- Defining the appropriate role of state and local governments in education.

- Reforming federal and state education guidelines.

- Ensuring that schools are publicly accountable for their

performance, that there is adequate opportunity for innovation, and that exceptional performance is recognized and rewarded.

- Ensuring parent and citizen involvement in local governance.

Choice and Restructuring

- Evaluating the experience with choice across the nation.

- Assessing transportation and equity issues involved in choice.

- Considering ways of expanding choice and strengthening accountability.

- Evaluating the experience with magnet schools across the nation.

- Instituting performance-based restructuring initiatives.

- Evaluating the experience with site-based management and program restructuring.

A Competitive Workforce and Life-Long Learning

- Ensuring that adult Americans are sufficiently literate to perform effectively as parents, workers and citizens.

- Determining what institutions, public and private, bear responsibility for various aspects of worker training.

- Enhancing public-private partnerships in education.

- Communicating the needs of consumers of products of the nation's education system.

- Creating incentive programs to produce more high-school graduates.

- Enhancing the quality of training and vocational education.

Postsecondary Education: Strengthening Access and Excellence

- Enhancing opportunities for disadvantaged youths and their access to higher education.

- Strengthening science, mathematics, and engineering teaching in American universities.

- Strengthening university entrance requirements and reducing the need for remedial courses.

- Recruiting and retaining more minority students and faculty in higher-education institutions.

These issues will not be easy to address. Business stands to be a major benefactor of successful improvement of the outcomes of the educational system and should be willing to help lead the way. More importantly, the nation stands to benefit even more significantly if the population becomes better educated and able to function in a free and democratic society.

Business alone can not be successful in this effort. It will take strong political leadership to develop the consensus among the general public, educators, school boards and businesses. Partnerships made up of these constituencies, operating in an environment of mutual trust and understanding, with a commitment to a long term relationship, will be necessary to achieve success. The business community can be a catalyst to make this happen at the local level where change must take place.

SECTION THREE:
Human Resources

CHAPTER SEVEN

INVESTING IN THE FUTURE: STRATEGIES FOR HUMAN SERVICES IN PENNSYLVANIA
By Harold D. Miller

EDITOR'S SUMMARY

Pennsylvania controls its own destiny in the area of social services. States must take the lead in human services innovation as the federal government becomes less able to address social needs. Federal funding has been decreased and the largest source of funding for child welfare services, services for the elderly, mental health services, and other community social services is the state budget.

The Commonwealth spends much of its human services budget on the elderly. This is due to the fact that Pennsylvania has the second highest percentage of elderly of any state in the nation. In addition, the number of persons age 85 or older is projected to increase by 46% in the next ten years.

The most critical areas of needs for senior citizens are long-term care and assistance to the low-income elderly. Because of the high cost of nursing home care, most persons placed in nursing homes must ultimately rely on Medicaid to pay their bills. As a result, this is one of the fastest growing items in the state budget.

The most obvious area where investments made today will have long-term benefits is in programs for children. The children born over the next ten years will represent the entry-level workforce by the year 2020, and their ability to develop into skilled and productive workers will determine the competitiveness of Pennsylvania's economy. However, problems of poverty, abuse and development along with increasing problems of teenage pregnancy represent barriers to success.

There must be a priority for parenting and education support. The existing social systems — the family, the schools, and the community — should be strengthened to respond to the needs of children facing problems. Programs must be emphasized that will provide support early in a child's life rather than waiting until they have more serious problems.

There has been a dramatic growth in programs and services for the disabled. A multifaceted strategy that addresses both the causes of handicaps and the needs of handicapped individuals must be pursued with private sector involvement. It is in employers' best interests to hire handicapped individuals as labor shortages are expected to occur, particularly in entry-level positions.

Human service problems will only increase in the future. We must not be so short-sighted and focused on immediate problems that we fail to face up to the problems that are just around the corner. Political leaders must recognize that long-term priorities must be established for human services needs into the next century.

Harold D. Miller is Associate Dean of the School of Urban and Public Affairs at Carnegie Mellon University and formerly served as Director of the Pennsylvania Governor's Office of Policy Development from 1980 to 1986.

The historical dominance of the federal government in American social welfare policy and the traditional focus of the news media on federal programs have created the impression for many citizens that human services are primarily funded and controlled through the federal government. The federal government continues to play a major role in funding for income maintenance, health care programs, and institutional programs for the poor. However, its role in community social services is relatively small. In Pennsylvania, the largest source of funding for child welfare services, services for the elderly, mental health services, mental retardation services, drug and alcohol treatment services, and other community social services is the state budget. Moreover, as a result of deficit pressures, the federal government has become less able to address new needs, and the states have taken over the lead role in innovation and expansion of human services in recent years. Therefore, Pennsylvania controls its own destiny in the area of social services, and it cannot depend on federal legislation or funding to respond to human services problems.

It is critical that the state plan carefully for this responsibility because of the dramatic changes that will be occurring in its population over the next decade and beyond. Demographic shifts, changes in lifestyles, advances in technology, and other trends will result in fundamental changes both in the needs of the Commonwealth's citizens and in the resources available to address those needs. It will not be financially or managerially feasible to address all needs in the fashion that many advocates might like, and Pennsylvania's leaders will have to make difficult decisions about where to focus their time and resources. It is important that they do so strategically.

This chapter will examine four major areas of human services — services to the elderly, services to children, services to the handicapped, and services for the homeless. In each of these areas, the decisions made now will have significant long term effects, and an understanding of future trends can help guide the decisions made today. In addition, a series of general principles will be identified that can help to make the entire human services system more efficient and effective in improving the lives of Pennsylvania's neediest citizens.

The Elderly in Pennsylvania

The elderly in Pennsylvania are a very large and diverse population. There are an estimated 1.8 million persons age 65 or older in Pennsylvania in 1990, representing 15.2% of the total population. This is the second highest percentage of any state in the nation. Over half (58%) of the elderly are between the ages of 65 and 75, one-third (32%) are between the ages of 75 and 85, and 10% are 85 years of age or older. Many individuals continue to work into their 80's and beyond, while others have impairments of varying types and degrees that prevent them from working or socializing and that may even require their institutionalization.

Pennsylvania has one of the most extensive systems of benefits and services for the elderly of any state in the nation. Pennsylvania spends over $1 billion in state funds annually for programs that benefit senior citizens. These include social services for the elderly through Area Agencies on Aging; low-cost pharmaceuticals for the elderly through the PACE program, nursing home care through the Medical Assistance Program, cash assistance through Property Tax and Rent Rebates and Inflation Dividends, and a variety of other programs throughout state government.

There are two key trends which policies on aging in Pennsylvania must consider over the next decade — changes in the number and characteristics of the elderly; and reductions in the availability of family and community support for the elderly.

Short-Term Stability, Long-Term Growth: Although the number of senior citizens in Pennsylvania increased significantly (by an estimated 20%) in the past decade, it is projected to remain almost unchanged through the year 2000. This stability, however, will be short-lived. The elderly population will grow dramatically after the turn of the century as the post-World War II "baby boom" finally reaches the retirement ages. The baby boom group will begin reaching age 65 in the year 2010 and every baby-boomer will be a senior citizen by the year 2030. National projections indicate that the number of elderly will more than double in the next 40 years, and the percentage of the nation's population which is elderly will increase from 12.6% in 1990 to 21.8% in 2030. The increase in Pennsylvania will probably not be as great, as a result of the extensive migration of young people out of the Commonwealth which has occurred in recent years, but a 30-50% increase in the number of elderly by the year 2030 seems likely.

Growth in the "Old Old": Despite the fact that the total number of elderly will remain stable over the next decade, dramatic increases are expected in the "old old" — those who are 85 years and older — as a result of advances in nutrition and health care that have lengthened expected life spans. The number of persons age 85 and older in Pennsylvania increased by an estimated 34% in the last decade, and is projected to increase by an additional 46% by the end of the century — a doubling in just twenty years. These individuals are the most severely impaired, and are the least likely to be able to care for themselves. Their needs may range from occasional assistance with chores or housecleaning, to daily assistance with meal preparation and other essential activities, to extensive personal and health care. Those over age 85 are 10-15 times as likely to need nursing home care as those between the ages of 65 and 75.

Reduction in Caregivers: Families have traditionally been a principal source of care for the elderly who have impairments. Yet several trends are reducing the availability of family members to perform this function. First, children are more likely to live long distances from their parents, making it difficult or impossible to care for them. Second, women, who have traditionally been the primary caregivers for dependent parents, are more likely to be in the workforce and unable to care for those parents. Third, the reduction in birth rates, combined with the increasing longevity of the elderly, make it more likely that an elderly individual will have no children living or that their children will be elderly themselves. And finally, an increasing number of elderly will be living alone, making them dependent on formal services when they need help.

A Time for Planning, Restructuring and Restraint: These trends make the 1990's a critical period for planning, restructuring and restraining services to the elderly. The elderly have become a powerful political force, and there are always strong pressures to increase the number and types of services available to all senior citizens. There is already significant pressure to increase funding for services provided through senior citizen centers to respond to inflation and increased participation rates. In ad-

dition, the incomes of senior citizens are likely to increase during the 1990's due to cost-of-living adjustments in social
security, better pensions, and other factors. As a result, there will
be fewer individuals below any particular level of income, and
state programs which use fixed income thresholds to determine
eligibility, notably the PACE program and the Property Tax and
Rent Rebate Program, can expect to see reductions in the eligible population. As seniors lose their eligibility for programs
due to increases in income, there is likely to be strong pressure to
raise the income eligibility thresholds.

These expansions of services and eligibility may be affordable
in the 1990's, given the stability in the total number of elderly
during this period. Yet every expansion made in the 1990's could
well become an unaffordable burden in the next century, when
the number of eligibles increases dramatically. It is unlikely
that the Lottery Fund will experience the growth necessary to
keep up with the increase in demand for services, and it will be
difficult to use tax revenues to make up the shortfall, since the
size of the working age population will be stable or even decrease. In 1990, there are 2 persons in the age 25-44 age group for
every person age 65 or older (which is already below the national
ratio of 2.6), but that ratio will drop to 1.5 within twenty years.
Despite the understandable political pressure to provide short-
term benefits, strong leadership is needed to keep the Commonwealth's vision focused on the future. It is much easier to resist
creating new programs now than to face eliminating them in
the future.

The 1990's should represent a time to target increases in state
funding to the highest priority programs, and to find ways to cut
back or find alternative sources of funding for other programs of
lower priority. This will assure that the most critical needs are
met, and that Pennsylvania is positioned to be able to continue
to meet those needs in the future.

Priority for Long-Term Care: The highest priority for attention
in the near future must be in the area of long-term care services.
As a result of the declining availability of family members as
caregivers for the elderly, there has been increasing pressure on
nursing home care. Although there is a widespread and longstanding misperception by the elderly and others that Medicare
pays for long-term care in nursing homes, the fact is that
Medicare will only pay for short-term skilled care in nursing

homes. Most elderly individuals must pay directly for their nursing home care or, after exhausting their assets, rely on the state's Medical Assistance (Medicaid) program. Because of the high cost of nursing home care, most persons placed in nursing homes ultimately must rely on Medicaid to pay their bills. As a result, this is one of the largest and fastest-growing cost centers in the state budget.

There are two complementary ways to address this problem. First, some of the elderly who go to nursing homes could stay in their own homes and communities if they could receive personal care and other supportive services, which are typically called "community long-term care services" or "in-home services." These services can be significantly less expensive to provide, and more attractive for the client, than nursing home care. Pennsylvania has dramatically increased funding and programs for these services in the past decade. For example, the Long-Term Care Assessment and Management Program (LAMP) has been able to help approximately 10% of those elderly individuals who would go to nursing homes to stay in their own homes or communities. However, the LAMP program is not yet operating statewide, and there are long waiting lists for individuals who need other in-home services.

The second approach to long-term care services is to encourage the development and use of long-term care savings plans or insurance policies, so that individuals will save money during their working years to pay for the long-term care they need when they are older. Although there are a growing number of long-term care insurance policies available, most have been marketed to individuals who are already elderly, and the policies have been limited both in terms of the benefits provided and the eligibility criteria. It will probably not be possible for such policies to provide truly meaningful coverage at an affordable cost unless employers begin offering them to employees as a group benefit.

Priority for Low-Income Elderly: While there is considerable pressure to make services available to all elderly regardless of income, it is clear that low-income elderly are the most disadvantaged when insufficient services are available, since they cannot afford to purchase private services. This is particularly true in the area of long-term care, where even community-based services can be unaffordable for low-income elderly. Many

higher-income elderly who need human services can contribute
to their cost. This type of cost-sharing is a well-established principle in some public systems, such as mental health services and
drug and alcohol treatment, but there have been prohibitions
against charging for services in aging programs. Such charges
can both provide revenue to expand services and deter unnecessary utilization, thereby reducing the gap between need
and availability. Obviously, care must be taken to insure that
individuals who genuinely need assistance are not prevented
from receiving essential services because they cannot afford
them; sliding fee scales and other procedures can provide
appropriate protections.

The need to focus on low-income elderly is not just an admonition for government, however, but for the private sector as
well. While no statistics are available, it is likely that corporations invest large sums of money each year to provide
"senior citizen discounts" to a wide range of elderly, regardless
of their income level. Obviously, many higher income elderly
would likely buy the products or services without the discounts.
If businesses were to take even a small proportion of the funds
these "discounts" represent and give them to agencies which
provide social services for low-income elderly, it could significantly reduce the funding problems which are now being
experienced. The existence of the PACE card, which is only
available to senior citizens with incomes below $12,000
($15,000 for couples), makes it possible for both publicly-
funded programs and private businesses to easily differentiate
between higher and lower income elderly.

Pennsylvania's Children

The most obvious area where investments made today will
have long-term benefits is in programs for children. Many
studies and program evaluations have shown that relatively
small investments in programs which address the problems of
children, particularly young children, can reduce or avoid more
serious problems later in their lives. For example, programs to
provide early prenatal care for pregnant women can significantly improve infant birthweights and thereby reduce the
likelihood of handicaps and developmental delays. Programs
like Head Start, which provide comprehensive educational and

family support services to preschool children, reduce the need for special education and decrease the likelihood of delinquency and unemployment later in their lives.

Such improvements are becoming increasingly important to Pennsylvania's future. As a result of the continued aging of the baby-boom cohort and continued low-birth rates, the size of the labor force in each age group will continue to decline. For example, in 1990 there are an estimated 3.7 million Pennsylvanians aged 25-44, but the size of this age group is expected to decline by nearly 1 million, or 25%, in the next 20 years. Even more striking is the fact that the number of individuals aged 20-24 — the traditional source of entry-level workers — will decrease by 25% in the next decade. The children born over the next ten years represent the entry-level workforce of the year 2020, and will represent about 20% of the total workforce for the first half of the next century. Their ability to develop into skilled and productive workers will determine how effectively Pennsylvania can compete in the world economy, and the health and social problems they experience will represent the burdens of the state's human services system in the future.

Yet if the trends of the past 10 years in poverty, abuse, and family structure continue, many of these children will not be born or raised in ways that are conducive to successful development.

Problems of Poverty, Abuse, and Development: Although the average child is better off economically than in the past, due to rising incomes and decreasing family size, many children still grow up in poverty. In 1985, 14% of all children in Pennsylvania, and 20% of children under age 5, lived below the poverty level. This is a higher proportion than any other age group, including the elderly. The rate of poverty is even higher among minority groups: over 42% of black children and over 64% of Hispanic children were living in poverty in 1985.

Other measures of the well-being of children also indicate problems:

- Substantiated child abuse cases in Pennsylvania increased by 70% between 1978 and 1988, and sexual injuries account for almost half of all injuries suffered by abused children.

- In 1987, 5.7% of white babies and 13.4% of non-white

babies were born with low birthweights; such children have the highest risk of developmental delays.

- One-fourth of the births in Pennsylvania in 1987 were to single mothers, compared to only 15% a decade earlier. Because of the problems they face from working and raising a child, and the problems they experience getting child support from absent fathers, single mothers are particularly likely to have low incomes; national estimates indicate that nearly one-third of the women heading single-parent families had incomes below the poverty level in 1985.

Increasing Problems of Teenage Parenthood: A special problem of children and parenting is teenage parenthood, or what is often described as "children having children." Not only does having a child disrupt the lives of these parents at a key time in their own development — many will not finish high school due to the responsibilities of parenthood — but their immaturity and lack of parenting skills make it less likely that the child will grow and develop normally. Although there has been considerable attention to the problem of teenage parenthood in recent years, teenage birth rates have not increased. In fact, the rate of teenage birth rates have declined significantly in the past two decades, from 53.2 births per 1000 women ages 15-19 in 1970 to 38.8 in 1987, a 27% reduction. However, an increasing proportion of teenage pregnancies and births occur out of wedlock or in low-income families. In 1987, 74% of teen mothers in Pennsylvania were unmarried, compared to 45% in 1977 and only 26% in other age groups. National statistics indicate that teenagers in poor families are 2.5 times more likely to become teen parents than teenagers in higher-income families. This results in serious economic problems for the mother and her child, which compounds the problems caused by poor parenting skills. Further, many teenage mothers do not seek or obtain appropriate prenatal care or refrain from using drugs and alcohol during their pregnancy, which increases the likelihood that their children will be handicapped. In 1987, only 52% of teen mothers in Pennsylvania obtained prenatal care in the first trimester, compared to 80% of mothers in other age groups; 9.8% of teen mothers' babies were low birthweight, compared to 6.6% of the babies born to older women.

Priority for Parenting and Education Support: It is likely that without help, many of the children facing significant economic and family problems will develop other problems when they mature. We must find ways to strengthen the ability of existing social systems — the family, the schools, and the community — to respond to the needs of children facing problems, and we must emphasize programs that will provide *parenting and education support* early on in a child's life rather than waiting until they have more serious problems.

It is important to distinguish between *parenting* support that will benefit the child and support that will benefit the parents. For example, day care is an important mechanism for enabling parents, particularly single parents, to work, and this can improve the economic status of the family. However, if properly structured and targeted, it can also provide important parenting support for parents whose inability to care for their children is unrelated to employment. Child care services can serve as respite for a mother who is ill; as a model for a teenage mother whose parenting skills are limited; and as an intervention for a child who is abused or developmentally delayed. Moreover, if educational programming is combined with more traditional day care services, the children's development can also be improved. Evaluations have demonstrated the ability of programs such as Head Start to make dramatic improvements in the lives of disadvantaged children and their families.

Since child abuse, poor parenting skills, and other problems exist in rich families as well as poor ones, there is a need to insure that quality child care and early childhood education are available to families at all income levels. However, because of the problems that low-income families have in paying for and gaining access to these programs, public funding must be used primarily to insure that disadvantaged children have access to quality programs. Businesses must increasingly take responsibility for providing child care and other parental support programs to their employees, which will in turn allow public funds to be targeted to help the most disadvantaged children.

More Comprehensive and Coordinated Services: Children and their families are not likely to have a single or simple problem that can be addressed by a single, specialized program. A child with a learning disability may have a mother who is alcoholic or mentally ill, a father who is abusive or absent, and a home that is cold and dirty. Yet the services such a family needs are provided not only through several different programs, but several different levels of government, with no system for coordination. Depending on the child's age and residence, he or she may get services through a county funded early intervention program, an Intermediate Unit preschool or special education program, a federally-funded Head Start program, a school district special education program, or no services at all; the mother might get services through a county or private mental health or drug and alcohol treatment program; the father might get attention from the county child welfare agency, the municipal law enforcement agency, or the county court system. Is it any wonder that their needs are not resolved?

The answer is both simple and complex. Children and their families need *comprehensive* services that are tailored to their *needs*, rather than independent, uncoordinated programs that implicitly expect that the family can diagnose its problems, determine its needs, and negotiate the maze of programs to obtain services. Rather than forcing families to find the human services they need, the human services must be brought *to* them through systems they are likely to be familiar with or using, such as hospitals, day care centers, and schools. Case managers should be available on a full-time or part-time basis at these sites and have the ability to initiate a wide range of services from many different programs. Pennsylvania's Human Services Development Fund could provide a mechanism for accomplishing this, since its funding can be used to pay for services from any state human services program.

It is particularly important to pursue coordination between the social service system and the schools. Too often policy has cycled between two extremes: either expecting schools to be multipurpose institutions that can provide both education and social services to children, and finding that they do neither well; or focusing solely on educational achievement and casting off those students who cannot function within the schools without extensive support. Juvenile delinquents are a classic case of this: a youth who commits a crime and is institutionalized will receive intensive social services during the institutionalization, but may then be returned to school and expected to function without any continuing support services. Similarly, teenage mothers are often forced to drop out of school because of the lack of day care services and other supports. A child who has problems outside of school needs help both with those problems and with his education; his teacher(s) and his social worker(s) must work hand in hand to insure that he gets both in an effective way, and that the whole family's needs are addressed.

Greater Community Involvement: Not all of the answers rest with government programs, by any means, and it is unlikely that there will be sufficient tax revenues at any level to address all of the problems that exist. All citizens must take more responsibility for addressing the problems of their community's children and parents. Senior citizens can make an invaluable contribution to future generations by providing their time and attention to help care for children and to train and support young parents; they should recognize that they have an unprecedented opportunity to leave a lasting legacy through their attention to the development of today's children. Business and community leaders can serve as role models and "Big Brothers/Sisters" for youth whose only exposure to "success" is the neighborhood drug dealer. The investment they make in today's children will determine the quality of the society in which they will retire.

Handicapped Persons in Pennsylvania

Services for handicapped individuals have changed dramatically over the past two decades. The passage of landmark federal and state legislation in the 1970's (e.g., the Rehabilitation Act of 1973, the Developmental Disabilities Assistance and Bill of Rights Act of 1975, and the Education for All Handicapped Children Act of 1975) have resulted in many opportunities and services for handicapped individuals that were previously not available. Prior to these laws, individuals with severe handicaps were typically institutionalized, and many individuals with mild or moderate handicaps were denied access to schools, employment, and transportation. Today, however, an extensive range of services and accommodations are available to assist handicapped individuals to integrate effectively into society. Special education programs in schools, handicapped access provisions in buildings and streets, paratransit services, vocational training, attendant care, and community and independent living arrangements now exist, and many severely disabled individuals can receive the training and support they need to live and work in the community.

Despite the dramatic growth in programs and services for the disabled, the amount and types of services are falling short of the needs of the handicapped population. Substantial waiting lists currently exist for many types of services, and funding increases have not always kept pace with inflation, much less with increases in the eligible population. Moreover, it appears that the problems may increase in the future, due to two important trends.

Changing Needs of Handicapped Persons: First, the needs of the handicapped population are changing, in many cases as a result of the programs put in place over the past two decades. For example, it has only been 15 years since passage of the Education for All Handicapped Children Act, and only recently have substantial numbers of the children who received expanded and improved special education services graduated from public education. These young adults have abilities and needs which are different from those of older handicapped adults, and they will represent a larger and larger share of the handicapped adult population in the future. Community programs for handicapped adults have not always been prepared to continue the kinds of support and training that these individuals received while they were in school, and without continued support, their skills and abilities will deteriorate. Many community programs were established to provide services appropriate for individuals who were previously institutionalized, not for those who have benefited from public education programs.

Moreover, many of these adult handicapped individuals now live with their parents. As their parents become elderly or die, these individuals will need to move to residential programs if they are to remain in the community. This will dramatically increase demands on a system where significant waiting lists already exist. This pressure will likely become more severe over the next decade, as more and more parents of the handicapped subset of the baby-boom cohort reach retirement age.

Changing Causes of Handicapping Conditions: At the same time, the causes of handicapping conditions have been changing and will likely continue to change. There have been notable efforts to prevent handicaps, such as educational programs to reduce alcohol use during pregnancy and prevent fetal alcohol syndrome, improved prenatal care and nutrition, and programs to eliminate lead paint. But there are other forces which are working in the opposite direction. Many medical advances, such as neonatal intensive care units, trauma care, and transplant surgery, have been lauded for saving lives that would previously have been lost. However, many of those who now survive have disabilities, often severe ones, and the funds available for rehabilitation have not matched those provided for the lifesaving interventions. For example, victims of severe head trauma have achieved growing visibility in recent years. Many have characteristics and needs similar to those of the mentally retarded, yet Pennsylvania law specifically limits eligibility for mental retardation services to individuals whose condition occurred prior to age 21. The increase in longevity for the elderly has resulted in more persons with disabilities, and we can only speculate about the kinds of disabilities that drug-addicted infants will have if and when they grow up. There is evidence that individuals with chronic illnesses and childhood handicaps may become more impaired as they grow older; for example, individuals who had polio as children have experienced unexpected weakening of their limbs as they reach middle age, leading to more serious disabilities than they had previously experienced. There are no data available which allow the impacts of these trends to be analyzed, but aggregate statistics indicate that the proportion of the population with disabilities has increased markedly during the past two decades, and the increases may well continue.

These trends call for a multifaceted strategy that addresses both the causes of handicaps and the needs of handicapped individuals. Significant increases in funding will be needed to meet the increasing need for services and costs of programs, and this should be a high priority in the state budget over the next decade. In addition, policies should be pursued which would help to reduce the pressure on public funds.

Expansion and Adaptation of Service Programs: Programs serving the handicapped must receive sufficient funding to provide essential services in a quality fashion to individuals who have no other alternatives. At the same time, these programs must be flexible enough to respond to the changing needs of handicapped persons. Programs that are now serving young, handicapped adults must be prepared to respond to their needs as they grow older; programs that have been geared to providing minimum services for low-functioning individuals must be prepared to provide services for higher-functioning persons; sheltered workshops must be prepared to provide more supported work programs in conjunction with private sector employers.

New Forms of Prevention and Early Intervention: It is clear that many types of handicapping conditions can be prevented, and those prevention efforts that can be demonstrated to be cost-effective should be vigorously pursued. For example, efforts to provide early prenatal care and reduce alcohol use among pregnant mothers have been demonstrated to reduce mental retardation. These programs should be expanded, and similarly effective programs must be found to address drug addiction among mothers. Expanded accident prevention programs may be able to help reduce the number of crippling injuries from highway and workplace accidents. Similarly, well-designed early intervention programs have been shown to dramatically reduce the lifetime costs of support for handicapped individuals, and these programs should be expanded and new ones developed.

Private Sector Involvement: Employers can and must play a stronger role in efforts to assist handicapped individuals. As the baby-boom cohort grows older and as birth rates continue to decline, employers are likely to experience labor shortages, particularly in entry-level positions. Persons with handicaps will represent an increasing opportunity for employers to avoid these shortages if the employers establish training programs and provide accommodations to help handicapped individuals fill entry-level jobs. In addition, many experienced workers now leave their jobs due to work-related and non-work related accidents; it will increasingly be in the interest of employers to provide rehabilitative services and workplace accommodations to enable experienced workers to continue working despite disabilities.

Homelessness in Pennsylvania

Housing is not traditionally considered a "human service,"

nor are housing programs traditionally administered, planned, or even strongly influenced by human services agencies. Yet a growing problem for many low-income individuals, and one of the most serious impediments to the success of the human services programs that try to help them, is a lack of affordable housing.

Changing Characteristics of the Homeless: Many still imagine that the homeless consist solely of "skid row bums" and "bag ladies," and that homelessness is caused by drug addiction, alcoholism, or mental illness. The evidence of recent years indicates that substance abuse and mental illness are important contributors to homelessness for many individuals, but for a growing number of homeless individuals and families, their only problem is that they simply cannot find housing that they can afford. It is difficult to sort out the extent to which the problem is due to their wages or welfare checks being too small or due to the cost of housing being too high. It is likely that it is a combination of both. Perhaps the most troubling trend in recent years has been the increase in the number of women and children, and even families with two parents, who are homeless. It has been estimated that one out of every eight homeless individuals in Pennsylvania is a child under age five. There are many reasons for the homelessness of families. Many women and their children leave their homes to escape abuse; others find it impossible to obtain housing that they can afford or that will accept children. National estimates indicate that single parents between the ages of 25 and 34 pay an average of 58% of their incomes for rent, and single parents under age 25 pay 81% of their income for rent.

Services Beyond Shelter: The most common response to homelessness is the provision of emergency shelter facilities. Such facilities provide only a temporary solution, however, since they are explicitly short-term, and many represent an undesirable environment for families with children. There is a need for more facilities that can accommodate families with children, and a need for better coordination and planning between the homelessness programs and domestic violence programs in the Commonwealth, both of which provide funding for shelters for women and children. However, shelter is a treatment for the symptoms, not the causes of homelessness. Greater emphasis is needed on services that will help to address the problems and conditions that lead to homelessness. An integral part of these programs must be the provision of low-income housing, since programs to provide job training and social services will not effectively help those with multiple problems if they do not have a decent place to live. Pennsylvania has taken a leadership role in the development of "bridge housing," — programs which provide both housing and a range of services, such as mental health or drug and alcohol treatment, job training, and other services, designed to enable a formerly homeless individual to achieve self-sufficiency. More of these programs are needed, particularly to address the problems of the chronically mentally ill, and systematic efforts to evaluate their effectiveness must be instituted.

Greater Investment in Truly Low-Income Housing: The weakest link of all, however, is the development of permanent housing for low income individuals and families. Many homeless individuals and families have a small income through work or through welfare; their primary problem is a lack of affordable housing. Traditional housing development programs for "low and moderate income" families have focused more on moderate-income homes than on housing which is affordable for those with very low incomes. This is largely because the structure of the programs — low-interest loans, interest subsidies, and modest write-downs funded through government bonds — do not provide sufficient incentives or subsidies to make truly low-income housing profitable for private developers. It is likely that in most cases, direct government grants for a significant portion of construction or renovation costs will be needed to develop housing units affordable for individuals who are on welfare or work at low-wage jobs. Pennsylvania undertook a limited effort to develop "Single Room Occupancy" (SRO) housing in the mid-1980's, and this program should be reinstituted and expanded, with a strong planning and technical assistance component. Greater support is needed for nonprofit organizations seeking to develop innovative and low-cost approaches to the construction and renovation of housing.

This is a relatively new role for Pennsylvania and other states. Housing development has traditionally been a federal responsibility, but the federal government has substantially reduced its commitment to housing programs in the past decade, and is not likely to return to previous levels. Moreover, existing housing programs at the local, state, and federal levels have such strong vested interests that it will be difficult, if not impossible, to redirect them to truly low-income housing. Pennsylvania should provide new funding for initiatives that will increase the supply of low-income housing for the next century.

Cross-Cutting Issues

The trends and ideas described in the previous sections cover only some of the many issues facing the human services system in Pennsylvania through the year 2000 and beyond, and it is impossible to cover all of the others here. However, there are several general principles which can provide guidance in establishing human services policies in the coming decades.

Entitlements: In the face of limited public funds and many competing needs for services, it is natural for advocates to push for legislation that establishes "entitlements" to a particular service for a particular group. Entitlements are viewed as guarantees of access to services for the population in need, and as protections against the effects of changing priorities in the future. Entitlements, however, may not always be uniformly positive for those they are intended to benefit. Creation of an entitlement presumes that we know what kinds of services are needed and who should receive them. In many cases, though, our knowledge of what works and what does not work in human services is very limited — a program or service may work for some people and not others, but we cannot predict who will be in which group. Despite these uncertainties, entitlement legislation establishes rigidly defined eligibility and service criteria. This can result in provision of a mandated service to some who do not need it, and prevent delivery of a non-mandated service to those who do. Examples of such problems abound: mandated early intervention services for children rarely permit the provision of preventive services to "at risk" children, and even definitions of "at risk" provide no flexibility to include unique cases; health insurance programs which mandate coverage for institutional care may preclude the flexibility to use less expensive and more desirable home-based or outpatient care; programs that mandate free transportation for those who would otherwise have no access to services often spend large sums on transporting those for whom access is not a problem.

Thus, flexibility may be as important as guarantees in enabling a needy individual or family to obtain the most effective and appropriate services. Flexibility is also important in insuring that limited funds can be spent as efficiently and effectively as possible. From a broader perspective, entitlements reduce the state's flexibility in establishing priorities and changing those priorities in response to changing needs. As is evident from previous sections, the needs in human services have changed dramatically over the past two decades, and are likely to change equally dramatically in the coming ones. The state needs the ability to reallocate resources to where the needs are most pressing, and where research indicates the returns on investment are greatest. Great caution should be used in establishing entitlements that constrain this flexibility.

Prevention: Time and time again, it has been shown that an effectively designed and targeted prevention program can save far more money in the long run than it costs. For example, postnatal screening programs have virtually eliminated the problems of phenylketonuria (PKU); education efforts designed to reduce alcohol use among pregnant women have prevented many cases of mental retardation due to fetal alcohol syndrome. Unfortunately, prevention programs all too often are the least attractive politically, since their costs are immediate, while their benefits are long-term. Higher priority is needed for prevention and early intervention programs, particularly those oriented towards children, such as improved prenatal care, Head Start, and other programs where effectiveness has been clearly demonstrated.

Caution must be used, however, to insure that prevention programs are, in fact, cost-effective before they are implemented on a wide scale. Three conditions are important in assessing prevention programs. First, it must be possible to predict with reasonable accuracy which individuals will have the problem to be prevented. Second, there must be strong evidence that the intervention that is planned will, in fact, prevent the problem. And third, the costs of the prevention program must be less than the costs of treating the problem directly. For example, it is frequently observed that a nursing home placement for an elderly individual could have been delayed or avoided had certain community services been instituted earlier, while the senior was still in the community. Creation of a true prevention program, however, requires that we be able to predict which senior citizens would ultimately be institutionalized in the absence of the program, and be able to provide the right mix of services that would prevent institutionalization. Many attempts to establish such programs often have simply resulted in a general expansion of services for all elderly individuals, with limited impact on nursing home placements.

Salaries: Often forgotten in the debates on policies, programs, requirements, and funding are the service providers and their staffs. Each social service program has an extensive network of private providers, generally nonprofit agencies, that deliver services to the programs' clientele. These agencies are generally staffed by dedicated, caring individuals who provide services with limited budgets to large caseloads of individuals.

One of the most severe problems these agencies face is attracting qualified staff at the salaries they can pay. Human services workers typically make very low salaries; for example, the average salary of a personal care worker is between $10,000 and $11,000, and the average salary of a case manager is between $15,000 and $17,000. This is not just an issue of providing decent compensation for individuals who provide critical services, or of attracting individuals with experience and education, although both are important goals. Increasingly, agencies are finding it difficult to recruit anyone at the salaries paid; new vacancies are created as soon as they are filled due to high turnover. It is estimated that the average human service agency has to hire 41 new workers each year for every 100 staff positions. As a result, agencies are often unable to provide the services they are funded for, further worsening the shortage of services. Their costs increase due to the need to constantly recruit and train new staff, and their service quality suffers due to a lack of experienced staff.

These problems will only increase in the future as the tightening of the labor market makes it even more difficult to get qualified individuals to work at low salaries. The aging of the baby boom cohort has already reduced the number of young people in the workforce, and they have traditionally been important sources of human service agency staff. As a result, state funding decisions in the future will need to address not only the need for new services, but also the need to boost salaries of workers and to provide other incentives to insure that positions can be filled.

Coordination and Flexibility: While the vast majority of funding for social services is provided by the state, the responsibility for delivery rests with county governments, which in turn either provide the services directly or subcontract them to private providers. Unfortunately, due to inconsistent requirements across the various human services programs, there is a crazy-quilt structure imparted to the human services system. Some programs require county governments to "match" (i.e., provide local funds to supplement state funds) the state allocation, but some do not; some require a 10% match, while others require a 25% match; some programs are always administered by county governments, while other programs fund private, nonprofit organizations directly in certain counties. Some programs have complex formulas for the distribution of funds that attempt (generally unsuccessfully) to provide "incentives" for certain kinds of performance; some funding allocations are so heavily rooted in historical funding patterns as to preserve serious inequities in funding.

Human needs rarely fit neatly into the program categories that have evolved over the years. Although many efforts have been made in the past decade to improve planning and coordination of services across program lines, the system in Pennsylvania remains highly categorized and inflexible. More dramatic changes are needed if it is to respond effectively to the complex problems of children, families, the homeless, the handicapped, senior citizens, and others — particularly given the rapid changes which are expected in the coming decades. More authority and flexibility must be granted to county governments that demonstrate the ability to plan and deliver services effectively. With appropriate enabling legislation, waivers of regulations could be made to permit innovations in services and programs, and true human services block grants could be provided that would give counties the ability to identify their needs and set funding priorities appropriately.

Investing in the Future

An important theme of this chapter is that there are many

human services needs today, but we must not be so short-sighted and focused on immediate problems that we fail to prepare for the problems that are just around the corner. Investing in the future requires strong leadership and self-sacrifice. Political leaders must educate the public about long term needs, and resist the temptation for short-term political credit by creating programs that are not priorities for the future. Voters and interest groups must support leaders who take a long-term view, and not base their support solely on immediate gains.

In addition, we must all recognize that public funding is limited, and that effective human services are expensive. This inevitably means that priorities will have to be established, and not all desires will be met. Each special interest group needs to recognize and accept this, and participate in good faith in the overall priority-setting process and support its outcomes. The elderly must recognize that an expansion of Head Start may be more important than an expansion of the local senior center, and handicapped individuals and their families may need to concede that prevention and early intervention programs may take precedence over recreational services.

And finally, we must all contribute to the financial health of the human services system. This is not just another admonition to dig deep and give to your favorite charitable organization. There are more direct contributions that can be made that are also in the giver's self-interest. Individuals can save for their long-term care needs so that they are well-cared for if and when they need it, without placing demands on the public funding system. Businesses can provide workplace accommodations for the handicapped and child care benefits for employees; these can help them attract and retain a productive workforce, while at the same time reducing the pressure on publicly funded rehabilitation and day care services. After all, human services are not just for "them;" they benefit all of us.

CHAPTER EIGHT

RETHINKING THE WELFARE STATE: A CRITICAL LOOK AT THE UNDERCLASS
By William A. Donohue

EDITOR'S SUMMARY

The nuclear family has always been a key part of the fabric of American society. However, there has been an unprecedented increase in one-parent families — they now constitute one in five families in the United States. In addition, the U.S. has the highest divorce rate and teenage pregnancy rate in the world, making family disintegration a problem of major proportions.

Juvenile crime and violence reflect the breakdown in the family structure. For example, between 1960 and 1980, the juvenile delinquency rate rose by 130%, while the number of juvenile arrests more than doubled. Violence in the schools, once rare and episodic, now centers on such things as drug abuse, pregnancy, suicide, rape, robbery and assault.

Members of the underclass are afflicted with the most severe social problems. Many of these problems have been present in the underclass throughout history, but never has there been the rampant social and moral destitution that we see today. It is this — the near total collapse of the family among the underclass — that separates our age from any other.

Problems that stem from dysfunctional families are manifold. Children who are raised in one-parent families are more likely to live in poverty than children who live with both parents. They do less well in school and are more likely to exhibit discipline problems. They also are more likely to have psychological problems and show a greater tendency to use drugs.

Problems of the urban poor cannot be blamed on the loss of low to medium skill jobs. Pennsylvania's economy is close to full employment, with "help wanted" signs in abundance in Philadelphia and Pittsburgh. The heart of the problem of the urban poor can be attributed instead to the decline of human resources.

Beginning in the 1960's, there was a radical change in the ethos of the dominant culture. American society largely abandoned the value of self-denial and in its place introduced a hedonistic strain of self-actualization. This "new freedom" did much to damage the American family as a whole since it promoted rights at the expense of responsibilities.

Welfare reform must be a priority in the 1990's if the debilitating effects of the underclass are to be mitigated. For one thing, law makers and policy analysts need to become much more sensitive to the impact that government programs have on weakening the authority of families, schools and churches. Greater autonomy should be provided to these value-forming institutions.

William A. Donohue is Chairman of the Department of Sociology at La Roche College and an Adjunct Scholar at The Heritage Foundation.

There was a time, not too long ago, when the absence of one parent from a family was known as "a broken family." But because there has been an unprecedented increase in such families — they now constitute one in five families in the United States — and because we think it compassionate to speak more neutrally about this condition, the term "one-parent family" is now the preferred neologism, having entered the lexicon of sociologists and the popular culture alike. No matter, the United States has the highest divorce rate in the world, and the highest teenage pregnancy rate in the industrial world, making it all but academic what we decide to call the reality of problem families. After looking at these figures, Cornell University psychologist Urie Bronfenbrenner exclaimed that the problems "are part of the unraveling of the social fabric."[1]

The decline in the nuclear family, which began in a major way in the 1960's, was accompanied by a marked decline in civility as well, as the rates of crime and delinquency make clear. For example, between 1960 and 1980 the juvenile delinquency rate rose by 130%, while the number of juvenile arrests more than doubled. The death rate among adolescents due to violent causes tripled during the same period; murders of ten to nineteen year-olds rose 200%. There was a decline in the overall level of crime in the 1980's, though this was hardly the result of a new found respect for civility: almost the entire decrease was due to a decline in the teenage population, that segment of society most prone to engage in antisocial behavior. And the downturn may prove to be short lived, as the crime rate for 1987 and 1988 inched upwards again.

Violence in the schools, once rare and episodic, is now commonplace, especially in the inner cities. According to a California study, in the 1940's the most common school discipline complaints centered on such things as talking, chewing gum, running in the hallways, getting out of place in line and not putting paper in the wastebaskets. In the 1980's, the most common complaints centered on such things as drug abuse, pregnancy, suicide, rape, robbery and assault.[2] It should be noted as well that the decline in academic performance — by now well-reported — paralleled the decline in manners and morals; both problems surfaced in a dramatic way in the 1960's.[3]

The Challenge Ahead

The social problems of illegitimacy, divorce, one-parent families, crime, delinquency, drug abuse and the like are widespread, cutting across racial, ethnic, class, religious and regional lines. But if there is one segment of the population which constitutes the lion's share of the problem, it is the underclass.

To be poor is not necessarily to be a member of the underclass. In fact, most poor are not of the rank of the underclass. To be poor is to have significantly less income than the median income, or to have relatively inadequate resources. But to be underclass means to be poor in *values*, as well as in material wealth. The underclass are, quite simply, the most recalcitrant segment of the urban poor, proven to be the least amenable to reform, whether it be in the nature of an expanding economy or new government program. Almost nothing seems to affect them. Largely illiterate, they have no work skills, no life skills of any sort.

Before the term underclass was first used in the 1970's, social scientist Edward Banfield captured the phenomenon when he explained the difference between a low-income person and a low-class person.[4] Both of these persons may reside in the same housing project, but the difference is this: the low-income person has middle-class values, that is, he is future-oriented and possesses the work ethic; by contrast, the low-class person has low-class values, that is, he is present-oriented, possesses no work ethic and is likely to be on welfare for a long period of time. The former will become upwardly mobile (surely his children will), while the latter will remain right where he is. In short, the term *underclass* is a good one, for it accurately conveys the reality of those who are literally outside the class system, so thoroughly beyond reproach are they.

Another way to look at it is like this: there have always been dysfunctional families, among the rich as well as the poor, but only recently have poverty stricken children been expected to assume the role of parent. Drugs, more specifically crack — a cocaine derivative — have literally disabled thousands of underclass families. In an insightful piece on the effects of crack, *New York Times* reporter Gina Kolata concluded the following:

> Children are taking over as heads of families, largely because of their incomes from selling crack.
> Young pregnant mothers are endangering their lives

to get the drug, and in many cases, people describe mothers or brothers procuring sex for the young women in their families to raise money to buy it.

Teen-age girls are abandoning their families and forming what social scientists say are new and violent gangs to sell or buy crack.

And in some neighborhoods female users outnumber male users for the first time. For years, it had been the women, more often than not, who held poor families together. Yet almost worse than the breakdown of the family are the isolation and sad acceptance expressed by so many people in the affected communities — as if crack has become a final plague they cannot overcome.[5]

This report is not just another commentary on the poor. Nothing like it could be found by any social scientist researching the poor of 30, 50 or 100 years ago. Yes, there have always been the indigent, and yes, people lived in crowded, unsanitary conditions in the past, and yes, there have always been neglectful fathers, but never has there been the near total collapse of the family and rampant moral destitution that we see today. It is this — the near total collapse of the family among the underclass — that separates our age from any other.

Pennsylvania

Pennsylvania is a good state to study because in many respects it is prototypical of U.S. characteristics. A large state, with significant urban, suburban and rural populations, Pennsylvania also has a racial breakdown close to that of the national average.[6] Furthermore, the figures on percent of births with low weight babies, percent of births to teenage mothers, percent of births to unwed mothers and percent of families living below the poverty line (all related characteristics), are nearly identical to the national average in every category.[7] As to be expected, the state's two largest urban areas, Philadelphia and Pittsburgh, make up a disproportionate share of these problem statistics. But even here, the figure of one-third of all black families who live below the poverty line in Philadelphia and Pittsburgh is identical to that of the national average for black families.[8]

Pennsylvania's two largest cities have witnessed a large decline in manufacturing jobs, a situation which contributes to, but is not sufficient to explain, the growing problem of the urban poor. Between 1959 and 1985, Philadelphia lost 187,000 jobs requiring less than a high school education. Similarly, in Pittsburgh, in 1975 manufacturing jobs accounted for 28% of all area jobs; today the figure is less than 15%, due largely to the almost total disappearance of the steel industry.[9]

Tempting as it might be to blame the loss of low and medium skill jobs for the status of the urban poor, it doesn't quite add up: Pennsylvania as a whole, and Philadelphia and Pittsburgh in particular, are today at full-employment, with "help wanted" signs in abundance in both cities. It is not the decline of jobs that better explains the situation, it is the decline of human resources that is the heart of the problem.

The key to economic vitality in any country, and at any time in history, has always been human resources, not natural resources. To be specific, economic growth and upward social mobility are predicated on a system of economic incentives and a bountiful supply of self-disciplined individuals who are capable of realizing their potential. The former predicate is largely a reality, though that is not to say that further privatization would not make for a healthier market economy. It is the latter condition that is the problem, as the number of self-disciplined individuals capable of realizing their potential is regrettably small.

To get a better appreciation of what is meant by the "human resources problem" consider the situation of young black males in Allegheny County, one segment of the urban underclass: a) more than half of the teenage males live in households with one or both of their parents absent; b) in a third of the families, neither parent works; c) more than 40% live or have lived in poverty; d) nearly 30% of young black males drop out of school; e) 45% have used drugs or alcohol; and f) black males make up 9% of the county population aged 13-17 but account for 57% of the juvenile court convictions.[10] These youngsters are not likely to realize their potential, nor are they likely to break out of the poverty trap. Indeed they, and their offspring, are likely candidates for welfare dependency.

It is actually much worse than this. Realizing one's potential is conditioned, at bottom, on normal physical and mental development; normal moral development is crucial, but pales in significance to normal physical and mental development.

Unfortunately, the condition facing many black infants is such that they will not develop normally in any way. Pittsburgh has the highest infant mortality rate among blacks of any city in the United States, and the figures for Pennsylvania as a whole exceed the national average.[11] Even more discouraging is the fact that infant mortality rates are an index of the poor health of those children who do survive, thus compounding the human resources problem.

Just as disturbing is the fact that although blacks make up 13.2% of the student population in Pennsylvania, they constitute 21.7% of the students enrolled in classes for the educable mentally retarded and 27.6% of the classes for the socially and emotionally disturbed.[12] Many of these youngsters were not provided with the kind of physical care that is necessary for normal mental development, being victims of child abuse or neglect. And that is because, in most cases, they were born to unwed teenagers, who themselves were physically neglected.

The problem is bad and bound to get worse. Why? Because crack and AIDS are increasingly taking their toll on children before they are born. Keep in mind that Philadelphia has the highest rate of drug abuse in the nation (82%), and then consider the following.

In the first scientific study of pregnant mothers who use cocaine, it was found that babies born to women who used cocaine during their first trimester of pregnancy may suffer neurological damage, making it more likely that they will suffer future learning disabilities as well. According to one of the scientists who undertook the study, Ira Chasnoff of Northwestern University Medical School, "Cocaine-exposed infants are either very irritable or they become so overwhelmed that they shut down and go into a deep sleep." Chasnoff adds that this condition makes it difficult for mothers to sustain normal interaction with their babies, thereby impairing an important part of the learning process. In another study, it was found that women who used cocaine and/or marijuana during pregnancy ran an increased risk of having underweight babies, a condition linked to greater risk of medical problems and death.[13]

Unborn children who have been infected with the AIDS virus, or HIV (and this includes a disproportionate number of black babies) suffer from brain damage. "The vast majority of children born with congenital HIV infection exhibit retarded

neurological development," says William D. Lyman, a neuro-
pathologist at Albert Einstein College of Medicine in New York
City. Dr. Lyman notes that such children speak late, walk late,
have facial deformities and most important, perform among the
lowest 2% for their age in tests of cognitive skills.[14]

It should be clear that Philadelphia and Pittsburgh face enormous social problems, the roots of which go way beyond conventional descriptions of poverty. We are faced with a growing
abnormal society, housed within a normal dominant culture
that seems unprepared to face the challenge ahead. Before
policy recommendations can be made, an effort to understand
the causes of the problem must first be made.

Understanding the Origins of the Problem

The underclass have received a great deal of attention in
recent years, as more and more social scientists have come to
recognize the enormousness of the problem. While there is consensus as to the effects of underclass status, there is division
among experts as to its origins. Edward Banfield blames "short
time horizons" as the central problem.[15] Douglas Glasgow
credits the existence of a "survival culture."[16] For Nicholas
Lemann, it is the residual effect of entrenched patterns of
Southern culture that handicaps Northern blacks.[17] Princeton
scholar John DeIulio fingers crime as the most serious cause of
underclass status.[18] George Mason historian Roger Wilkins
cites "the legacy of slavery" as the most convincing explana-
tion.[19] The welfare system is the culprit for Charles Murray.[20]
And University of Chicago sociologist William Julius Wilson
speaks to the effects of deindustrialization as the most important factor contributing to the existence of the underclass.[21]

Perhaps the most revealing portrait of the underclass comes
from the work of Ken Auletta.[22] Unlike other students of the
underclass, Auletta is more concerned about letting the underclass speak for themselves, and is less preoccupied with understanding the origins of the problem. Though he eschews any
dogmatism and does not hold to any one school of thought, it is
clear from his work that Auletta recognizes the primacy of
behavioral characteristics in the formation of underclass status.
"Whatever the cause — whether it is the fault of the people
themselves or of society, whether poverty is a cause or an ef-

fect," argues Auletta, "Most students of poverty believe that the underclass suffers from *behavioral* as well as income deficiencies."[23]

Auletta is quite right: we have come a long way from the days when entrenched patterns of poverty was seen only as a lack of income.[24] As Nicholas Lemann recently put it, "Of the millions of black Americans who have risen from poverty to the middle class since the mid-sixties, virtually all have done so by embracing bourgeois values and leaving the ghetto."[25] Indeed it is no exaggeration to say that the prime reason why *any* ethnic group has been able to become upwardly mobile is due, first and foremost, to bourgeois values. For middle class status to be attained, middle class values must first be possessed. No amount of redistribution can ever change that fact.

What are middle class values? Self-discipline, individual responsibility, punctuality, future orientation — in essence, the values that constitute the Protestant work ethic. Their absence is called lower class values, associated as they are with improvidence, irresponsibility, impulse and present-time orientation. It should be clear that for the underclass to change, a radical change in values must be achieved. But for that to change, the sources of lower class values must first be addressed.

The traditional sources of values have not changed as much as some pundits allege. True, there is the role of the media and the ubiquity of peer group pressure to contend with, but the bedrock of individual values continues to center on the family, schools and churches. It is these institutions that define the nature of society, the culture and the individuals that inhere in it. Above all it is the family that matters most. As Confucius noted thousands of years ago, the quality of family relations determined the quality of the society. It was just that straightforward.

It is the weakening of the nuclear family, then, and not race, which is the key to understanding the pathologies of the underclass. When the family weakens, so too do the prospects for upward mobility, as the very existence of the underclass amply demonstrates. And when a weakened family conjoins with the loss of authority in the schools and churches, the recipe for social disorganization is complete.

If it were race that accounts for the existence of the underclass, then there should be noticeable behavioral differences between whites and blacks at the bottom of the socioeconomic structure. But such is not the case. As Ken Auletta found out, the same social characteristics that are evident among the black underclass in the inner city are present among the white underclass of Appalachia:

> The similarities between the rural and urban underclass are striking. There is the same general lack of exposure to the world of work, the excessive violence in the home, the absence of role models, the same dependency on and rage at the degrading welfare system, the same lack of confidence.[26]

Another way to show that it is class, and not race, that accounts for the underclass, is to consider illegitimacy rates among the white and black poor. There has been much discussion about the record high 60% illegitimacy rate among blacks, and the fact that in some inner city neighborhoods the figure exceeds 80%. But there has been relatively little interest in explaining the rising illegitimacy rate among whites. More important, there has been little in the way of analysis regarding the social dynamics of illegitimacy rates, independent of the influence of race. The work that Charles Murray has done (after his major work, *Losing Ground*, appeared) is the exception to the rule.

Murray's investigation into the dynamics of white illegitimacy rates proved revealing. He was able to establish that a) there is a white underclass and b) the illegitimacy problem is concentrated among that segment of the white population. More to the point, Murray was able to conclude that "the same factors that explain white illegitimacy explain black illegitimacy," making it plain that it is class, not race, that is the operative variable. Murray implored researchers:

> Take a hard look at the proposition that there is a white underclass that looks very much like the black underclass. It by no means includes everyone in poverty or everyone on welfare. But a large part of the white welfare caseload on any given day, in many towns the majority, consists of long-term recipients.[27]

The problems that stem from dysfunctional families are manifold, regardless of race. We know that children who are raised in one parent families are more likely to live in poverty than children who live with both parents. They do less well in school, are more likely to exhibit discipline problems and are more likely to become drop outs. They are more likely to have psychological problems, more likely to use drugs[28] and are more likely to run afoul of the law.

In terms of teenage pregnancies, it is known that the rate doubled in the 1970's, and reached a level of more than 3,000 a day in 1988. There are now more than one million teenage pregnancies each year, resulting in a half million abortions; the majority of those children who aren't aborted are born illegitimately. Illegitimacy rates among teens jumped by more than 200% in the period between 1960 and 1980. In 1985 almost 60% of the 478,000 teenagers who gave birth were unmarried, a sharp increase from 1970 when the figure was less than a third. Among black teen mothers today, it is known that 90% give birth out-of-wedlock. Three in four teenage mothers say their mothers were unwed and, in two years, most teenage mothers become pregnant again, making arguments about lack of sex education positively incoherent.

The association between single parent families and poverty is strong. In a detailed study of income inequality, Heritage Foundation policy analysts Robert Rector and Kate Walsh O'Beirne found that marital status, and not race, explained the gap in income earnings between whites and blacks. They found, for example, that black married couples with children had post-tax incomes only 12% lower than the incomes of similar white families (half of the black population resides in the South where wages are depressed, thus accounting for a large part of the remaining gap). Rector and O'Beirne concluded that the overall difference between white and black income earnings "arises mainly from the disintegration of the black family structure."[29] In terms of poverty, O'Beirne found that only 10.8% of married black families were below the poverty threshold, as compared to 50% of female headed families, thus making clear the association between marital status and poverty.[30]

The Role of the New Freedom

Beginning in the 1960's, there was a major increase in one-parent families among whites and blacks. To understand what happened, due respect must be given to the cultural climate of the 1960's; the role of government was actually of secondary significance. To take one example, it is known that as recently as 1950, only 17% of black families were headed by one parent, a far cry from the 60% figure of today. Something more profound than government programs must have been at work.

What happened in the 1960's was a radical change in the ethos of the dominant culture. American society largely abandoned the value of self-denial and in its place introduced a hedonistic strain of self-actualization. Most important, a new concept of freedom took hold, one which sported a belief in liberty without limits, a kind of go-for-broke, skys-the-limit interpretation of freedom. Central to this redefinition of freedom was the uncoupling of rights from responsibilities and the promulgation of a doctrine of moral neutrality. Once freedom was seen as the absence of constraint, it was only a matter of time before individual responsibilities — and burdens of any kind — would be targeted for assault.[31]

This "new freedom" did much to damage the American family as a whole and wrecked havoc with the black family, in particular. Strong families are based on commitment and sacrifice, and that means that all members must subordinate their interests to the interests of others. This is not easy to achieve when the reigning cultural definition of freedom equates liberty with license. By attacking bourgeois values, the new freedom model of liberty undid an important cultural support of strong families. Unwittingly, the government chimed in, hurting blacks more than others.

What happened in the 1960's was that the same government that awarded blacks their long-overdue rights, simultaneously socialized responsibilities for them as well, thus uncoupling the traditional relationship between rights and responsibilities. Within the space of just a few years, a large segment of the black population went from a position of many responsibilities and few rights to many rights and few responsibilities, as the welfare rights movement clearly demonstrated. This is exactly the logic of the new freedom, promoting as it does an inflation of rights and diminution of responsibilities.

It is not welfare, per se, that is the cause of so many social problems, it is the reasons why welfare is sought that matters most. Consider this: twice in the twentieth century there has been a welfare explosion, once in the 1930's, and once in the 1960's.

Only in the 1960's did the pathological conditions normally associated with public assistance evidence themselves. The difference is that those who sought relief in the 1930's did so for economic reasons, while those who joined the dole in the 1960's did so for political reasons. There was no "welfare rights movement" in the 1930's, even though 25% of the workforce was unemployed. But there was one in the 1960's, even though the unemployment rate was only 3.5% (the figure for blacks was 4%).

When relief is interpreted as an entitlement, two status changes occur in the recipient: a) he acquires newly awarded rights, allowing him to make claims on the earnings of others, and b) he loses financial responsibility for himself, transferring that burden to the taxpayers. The net effect of this redistribution of rights and responsibilities is to nurture in the recipient an impoverished set of values: he learns to take, but not to give, expecting more from the community than he is willing to contribute. Not only are prospects for self-reliance dampened, the damage done to the social bond is incalculable.

What the ethic of entitlement has done is to foster a sense of non-responsibility. Journalist William Raspberry has caught its essence:

> There is no more crippling an attitude than to think yourself primarily as a victim. Victimism is a disease that blights our best-intended social programs...because it attacks the ability and the inclination of people to look after themselves...[32]

Lawrence Mead, another astute student of the poor, agrees: "At the core of the culture of poverty is the conviction that one is not responsible for one's fate, what psychologists call inefficacy."[33] It is this disabling attitude that must change if the condition of the underclass is to be demonstrably improved.

Proposals For Reform

Howard Smith is not an ordinary teacher. Unlike most teachers, he spent his youth and young adulthood as a member of the underclass, experiencing poverty, drugs, sex and prison. His students today are not ordinary either: they are members of the underclass, and it is his job to try and help them overcome their condition. What does Smith attribute the problem of the underclass to?

> We have a generation of people coming up now with no family structures. The traditional institutions that taught them what was good and bad, church, schools, the family unit itself —there's an entire generation out there that has not had the benefits of family, church, school.[34]

Cure and diagnosis may not be identical, but there is much in Smith's diagnosis that lends itself to public policy prescription. For one thing, lawmakers and policy analysts need to become much more sensitive to the effects that government programs have on weakening the authority of families, schools and churches. To that end, the first recommendation would be for a state-appointed commission to review all existing social policy with an eye toward providing greater autonomy for families, schools and churches; recommendations for changes in policy should be made to the Pennsylvania Legislature. The state can never be an adequate substitute for these value-forming institutions and it is dangerous to even try. Social authority must always be seen as preferable to state authority.

If the debilitating existence of the underclass is to be resolved, then welfare reform must be a priority. Because this is such an important issue, two different proposals will be made. The first recommendation would be to limit welfare benefits to one year for all able-bodied adults. Unemployment compensation should remain available for those workers who, through no fault of their own, have been victims of economic exigency. This proposal would not stop the counties from providing additional relief, if so decided. But it would discourage the present practice of having children as a way to maintain welfare benefits.

The second proposal would be to do away with the present system of welfare altogether (save for Medicaid) and adopt an incomes policy. Cash grants should be awarded to welfare recipients instead of the present practice of non-cash transfer payments. This proposal would do away with food stamps, free lunch programs, housing subsidies and the like, and would not require any additional funding (it may very well save money). What it would do is shift the money now spent on administrative overhead directly into the hands of the poor. When the poor are required to budget their money the way others do, character traits such as self-discipline will surface. That is why voucher programs should not be used as a substitute: they don't allow the poor to make adult decisions on how best to spend their money.

There are some other things that should be done, regardless of which of the two proposals is considered. Health care for indigent children should remain a government responsibility, as it would be cruel to deprive innocent children of such care; unlike the cost of food, medical care may be prohibitively expensive for the poor.

Central to both proposals must be the principle of family responsibility. Specifically, parents should be required to assume full responsibility for the welfare of their children. What this means in effect is that fathers should be held legally responsible for their children. If he does not support his child, legal action should be taken against him. If the parents are not minors, then the parents of both the father and mother should be held legally responsible for the welfare of their grandchild, as well as for the support of their own children. If no one can be deemed responsible for the welfare of the baby, then the child should be put up for adoption.

The idea that there is a shortage of day care in general, and that mothers on Aid to Families with Dependent Children are faced with a particularly bad shortage, is not born out by the facts.[35] If the state is to have any role in this area, it should be guided by two overriding concerns: a) do nothing to treat unfairly those mothers who choose to provide home care and b) respect the day care choices that working mothers presently opt for, namely placing their children with family members, neighborhood sitters or church day care providers. There is no justification whatsoever to create a new, huge day care government bureaucracy to attend to this "crisis." That is why the preferred method of dealing with this issue should be to extend tax credits to all mothers, independent of whether they work outside the home; the poor should receive direct cash assistance.

More can be done to help the working poor. State and local taxes should be eliminated entirely for any household that earns less than half the median state household income; these taxes should be gradually phased in thereafter. This proposal is similar to the earned income tax credit idea in that it would give the working poor incentives to continue working, thus reversing the perverse incentives of the present welfare system.

In the area of housing, tenant ownership is a must. When the poor are allowed the prerogative of ownership, they gain control over their lives and thus have a stake in seeing to it that their housing units are well maintained. The Kenilworth-Parkside project in Washington, D.C. provides an existing model of what can be done.[36] It should be the goal of Pennsylvania to make the Kenilworth-Parkside example the norm.

Education is one area where a voucher system would help enormously. In a poll commissioned by The Commonwealth Foundation, 83% of black Pennsylvanians already support "choice" in education.[37] The only thing lacking is the will of the state legislature. Insofar as the Catholic schools have had a superior record in teaching inner-city children,[38] any attempt to eliminate parochial schools from the voucher system should be resisted.

No progress against the abnormal condition of the underclass can proceed until the drug problem comes under control. Eight in ten Americans now support tougher laws against users,[39] and lawmakers in Harrisburg would be wise to appease the public's outcry. By concentrating law enforcement on users, as well as pushers, progress in the war on drugs can be made.

The problem of teenage violence needs a new approach. In the 1960's, black psychologist Dr. Kenneth Clark proposed a "Cadet Corps" program of handling youthful offenders. He envisioned a quasimilitary program that could be organized "to use the natural appeal of uniforms, rank, insignia, and other concrete symbols of status to involve young people in more serious programs such as developing reading skills, a sense of reliability, and a sense of responsibility for the welfare and performance of others."[40] The idea has merit. Something like it, perhaps military boarding schools, should be tried as a way of stemming this problem.

Finally, it should be kept in mind that the root cause of the underclass problem is cultural, not political in nature. To change the norms and values of the underclass, a cultural assault must be waged on the pernicious effects of the "new freedom." This means that parents, together with elites at every level — neighborhood, police, government, business, education, media, religious, medical — all must do their job of holding individuals accountable for their behavior and insist on standards of right and wrong. In short, parents and elites must come to understand that true freedom is conditioned on the exercise of social constraints, not the abandonment of them. And no segment of society needs to have that pressed on them more than the urban underclass.

CHAPTER NINE

HEALTH CARE: ACCESS, COMPETITION AND CHOICE
By Peter J. Ferrara

EDITOR'S SUMMARY

The U.S. health care system provides the highest quality care in the world. Americans take for granted the advanced health care that is more readily available here than in most other developed countries. However, there are several problems present in the U.S. system such as inadequate coverage for the uninsured, spiraling costs of health care, and care for the elderly.

Most Americans receive health insurance coverage through their employment. The ones that do not have coverage comprise between 10 and 15% of the population and are mostly in families where the head of the household works regularly. Providing for the health care needs of these individuals is a problem that state governments can solve through imaginative policies.

The U.S. spends about 25% more on health care than most other advanced countries. This is the result of rapidly rising health care costs, particularly in recent years. One of the primary reasons for skyrocketing health care costs is the malpractice liability crisis.

State governments can take certain steps to limit malpractice liability. For example, health care legislation could specify that doctors and hospitals be allowed to offer lower prices in return for waivers of liability. States can take further steps to remove imposed barriers to health care competition and allow consumers to determine standards of liability.

National health insurance is not a solution to health care concerns. Government administered health care would eliminate competition and leave no market incentives to limit high costs or avoid unnecessary care. Such a program would also likely add roughly $300 billion per year in net new government spending.

Medicare for the elderly is one of the fastest growing items in the federal budget. The program currently costs about $90 billion per year and at its current pace, Medicare may soon exceed Social Security in size. Despite Medicare's rising budget, many elderly costs are uncovered, such as nursing home care.

Nursing home care is a state government issue. Such care is provided primarily through Medicaid, which is financed in equal amounts by the federal government and state governments. However, changes need to be made in Medicaid to ensure that needy elderly persons can afford nursing home care.

Home health care is less expensive to provide than nursing home care. States should provide home care for those who don't have the money to pay for their care. For senior citizens with significant resources, state governments should promote the development of private long-term care insurance and other private options.

Peter J. Ferrara serves as Director of the Cato Institute Center for Entitlement Alternatives and Associate Professor of Law at the George Mason University School of Law.

In considering the problems of America's health care system, we should not forget that this system provides the highest quality care in the world. Americans receive the most advanced care available, more so even than most other developed countries. Americans take for granted the sanitary conditions and procedures that are routine here yet are still considered beyond reach in most other countries. Moreover, the U.S. health care system is the engine that produces the innovations, medical breakthroughs, and pathbreaking new treatments that are then followed elsewhere. While designing reforms to address the problems of the system, we must be careful not to undermine the high quality it offers, which Americans demand.

One problem with the U.S. health care system is that a number of Americans lack any health insurance, public or private, and therefore may find themselves without the resources to obtain needed care. Another problem is that the U.S. system is quite expensive, with costs continuing to rise rapidly. A third set of issues relates to the financing of health care for the elderly, particularly the viability of Medicare and the means of financing expenses not covered by that program, particularly nursing home costs. Each of these issues will be discussed below.

The Uninsured

The great majority of working age Americans receive health insurance coverage for themselves and their families through their employment. Indeed, for these Americans the problem may be that they have too much insurance, as discussed in the next section. The elderly are covered by Medicare and private supplemental insurance. Medicaid provides coverage to many but not all of the poor. Despite these different sources of coverage, somewhere between 10% and 15% of the American population lacks significant health insurance. This is a problem that state governments can tackle successfully through imaginative policies.

Most of the uninsured are in families where the head of household works regularly, so extending employment related coverage would solve most of the problem. One approach often suggested is to require all employers to provide health insurance for their workers.[1] But the problem with this approach is that the employers who do not provide health coverage now are primarily small or start-up businesses that cannot afford the extra costs. Imposing this heavy cost burden, amounting to several thousand dollars per year for each worker, would force these businesses to cut back on employment or possibly to shut down altogether. Indeed, this added cost burden would likely cause many firms to fail to start up in the first place. The end result would be a significant loss of jobs and employment opportunity.

For years, small businesses have been generating most of the net new jobs in the American economy, particularly for the less skilled. Placing heavy new burdens on this sector would particularly damage job creation in the most critical areas. It would also limit the opportunity of small entrepreneurs to start up and expand their businesses. Consequently, this approach would likely do more harm than good. The most important employee benefit is a job. Mandating new benefits at the expense of jobs and opportunity is not social progress.

An alternative approach would greatly expand health coverage without adverse employment effects. Employers would simply be required to report to a state or local agency whether their employees had health insurance. For those employees who were not adequately insured, the agency would package attractive groups of employees and shop for the best coverage from private insurers.

For example, suppose 40 small employers in Fisherman's Wharf in Philadelphia had 650 uninsured employees. A local agency could market the uninsured employees of those employers as "The Fisherman's Wharf Health Insurance Group." Or the employees at two or three small tool and die shops in Pittsburgh could be marketed by an agency as another group.

The agency could even solicit competitive bids from potential insurers. For large enough groups, the employees could choose from a smorgasbord of possible insurance coverage, just as under the federal employees health benefits system.

The agency should primarily seek insurance with relatively high front end deductible[2] and coinsurance fees[3], leaving the employee responsible for the first several hundred dollars of expenses each year. This would keep the cost of the coverage low, but provide the protection people need for essential, highly expensive, medical care for critical illnesses. The front end deductibles and coinsurance fees would also provide badly needed incentives to economize on more routine medical expenses, helping to counter rapidly rising health costs. Purchasing the insurance on a group basis would also help to keep costs low.

With these low costs, and the agency bearing the costs of searching for the most suitable coverage, many more employers may be willing to finance, or at least contribute to, health insurance for their employees. Otherwise, the employees would each have the choice of whether to accept the insurance negotiated by the agency, and would pay for the coverage themselves if they chose to participate. Employee premium payments should be tax deductible, just as those paid by employers are.

While workers would not be legally mandated to purchase the insurance, one of the functions of the state or local agencies responsible for the program would be to educate employees about the need for health coverage and repeatedly urge them to obtain it. Local churches and community groups, and even national public interest organizations, could assist in organizing workers into attractive groups and encouraging them to obtain coverage.

Under this proposed initiative, the state or local agencies could design the insurance groups to allow workers between jobs to maintain coverage more easily, since the insurance would not be tied to any one employer. The worker could simply continue paying the premiums until a new job was found. A chief cause of lack of coverage — temporary unemployment — would be more successfully countered as a result.

State governments could adopt this initiative on their own, without federal action. The initiative would require only minimal state outlays for the agencies that would market the worker groups and find the best coverage. Federal action would be needed to make employee premium payments tax deductible, but the initiative could go ahead without this element. Some federal revenues would be lost due to such a deduction, but no federal outlays would be required. Moreover, this revenue loss would result from expanding to a minority of excluded workers the tax deduction for employer paid premiums that effectively benefits the great majority of workers overall now. Expanding this benefit for all would only seem fair.

This proposal focuses directly on what is professed as the key concern — expanding health coverage to the uninsured. The key fallacy in other approaches to this goal has been the attempt to also shift the cost of the insurance from employees to others —

employers, taxpayers, or somebody. The problem with this cost shifting effort is that there is no available candidate to whom the costs can be shifted. Such cost shifting would always be both economically counterproductive, destroying jobs and economic growth, and unfair, as some working people, whether employers through mandates or employees through taxes, should not be required to pay the bills of other working people who are poor. Those who are working and are not poor must take the responsibility to provide for their own basic needs.

If this practical alternative were pursued with as much energy as currently is devoted to obtaining impractical legislative mandates, the problem of the uninsured could be sharply reduced. For those uninsured who do not work regularly and are poor, but are not currently covered by Medicaid, government assistance to obtain insurance could be provided in the context of overall welfare reform designed to most effectively address the problems of the poor.

Health Care Costs

The U.S. spends about 11% of GNP on health care, which is about 25% more than most other advanced countries. Moreover, health care costs have been rising more rapidly than inflation for years, and have soared in particular over the past two years. These rapidly rising costs are becoming a heavy burden on businesses paying for health insurance and on health care consumers generally.

The causes of these rapidly rising costs are complex. One of the most important factors is overinsurance. The employer-provided insurance for workers often includes only minor deductibles up front and little or no coinsurance fees for additional expenses. This broad coverage sharply reduces incentives for patients and doctors to keep costs down, as the patient does not bear the added fees and the doctor does not need to worry about collecting them. A second factor is runaway malpractice liability.[4] Courts today no longer hold doctors liable solely for bad, unprofessional judgement or negligence, but simply for bad results. Consequently, many doctors must pay tens of thousands per year and more in malpractice insurance premiums, which raises the fees they charge consumers. The liability threat also raises costs by causing doctors to practice defensive medicine — prescribing treatments and tests that are not medically necessary but may help the doctor to defend against a malpractice claim should one arise.

Another factor raising costs is cutting edge, high technology, medical equipment and treatments that are quite costly. The U.S. develops and provides access to these new breakthrough medical services more quickly and more broadly than other countries. A final factor is that the market for medical care seems to lack true competition, particularly on price. Doctors and hospitals don't seem to compete to provide services at lower cost. This may be due in part to broad insurance coverage leaving consumers unconcerned about costs. But something else seems to be at work. Perhaps the lack of competition is cultural — both doctors and consumers may feel uncomfortable with price competition in medical care. More study is needed to determine whether government policies and regulations have effectively structured the market for health care to preclude serious price competition, which may be the most important cause of the problem.

State governments can't eliminate high health costs on their own, since the problem is national. But they can take certain steps to help. The most important would be to eliminate the malpractice codes that specify that doctors and hospitals are to be held liable only when the party suing can prove that the doctor failed to act in accordance with accepted professional standards of conduct and care. The code should specifically grant doctors reasonable leeway to exercise their judgement, and specify that they should not be held liable simply because some doctors might have provided different care.

An even better approach would be to specify by law that doctors and hospitals would be allowed to offer consumers lower prices in return for waivers of liability, or for agreements to pursue any malpractice claim in an alternative arbitration system with specified liability standards. The law must specify as well that the courts must enforce such agreements when the consumer has been allowed a true choice. Through this approach, consumers in the marketplace would be able to determine the standard of liability that should prevail. States can take further steps to help by looking for ways to increase competition in health care, and removing any government imposed barriers to such competition.

The federal government would have to address the problem of

overinsurance. This problem occurs because employers are allowed an open-ended tax deduction for the health insurance premiums and the employee bears no tax for receiving the insurance. Consequently, the employer can compensate workers tax-free with the health insurance, but workers must pay stiff income and payroll taxes if the employer paid workers the equivalent value of the health insurance in cash. This tax treatment encourages employers to compensate their employees with as much health insurance as possible, leading to little or no deductible and coinsurance fees.

This problem could be corrected with the idea of Health Banks. Under this proposal, workers with employer provided insurance would be able to direct their employers to pay the tax deductible amounts the employers now pay for costly first dollar health coverage into investment accounts called Health Banks. Employers now can pay $300 per month and more for each employee for their health insurance. A portion of this amount, perhaps $75 per month, could be used to purchase catastrophic health coverage with high front end deductibles of perhaps $1,000 to $1,500 per year, as well as significant coinsurance fees. The remainder of the funds would be invested with the returns tax free, and could be used to pay for the deductible and coinsurance expenses. Workers could withdraw the funds without restriction after retirement, or use them to pay for nursing home care or to leave to their children or other heirs. Workers without employer provided coverage could make tax deductible contributions to Health Banks themselves.

The higher deductible and coinsurance fees would provide workers with strong incentives to avoid excessively costly or unnecessary care and to shop for lower cost care. With consumers showing greater concern for costs, doctors and hospitals would also likely devote greater effort to providing care at less cost. At the same time, with the Health Bank reserves workers would have the funds to cover the higher deductible and coinsurance fees when necessary. Through this system, workers would have more control over their health care finances, with the opportunity to conserve funds for their own future use rather than have it all used up for excessive insurance coverage. The opportunity for uninsured workers to make tax deductible contributions to the Health Banks might lead more of them to purchase coverage through this option.

As for high cost new medical technologies and treatments,

Americans seem to want to spend part of their substantial wealth on the best medical care available, which includes the latest breakthrough medical advances despite the cost. If that is the preference of the American people, government policy should not seek to stop it. This is a legitimate reason for rising total medical costs.

National health insurance would not be a helpful solution to these problems, but rather would make matters worse. Instead of adding to competition in health, such a national program would be a bureaucratic government monopoly, eliminating what competition there is. Moreover, such comprehensive monopoly insurance would leave no market incentives to avoid high costs or unnecessary care. These factors would worsen the medical cost spiral. The only effective counter to such rapidly rising costs under this system would be to strictly ration medical care, which has been the traditional response of governments that have adopted such programs. Such rationing, however, would sharply reduce the high quality of medical care in the current system that Americans demand and that should be preserved. Government cost controls would also probably eliminate the incentives to develop new medical breakthroughs and path-breaking new treatments that are the hallmark of the U.S. system.

The government monopoly bureaucracy running the program would have no incentives to serve consumers well, likely leading to even lower quality care. National health insurance would probably provide for health care consumers the same quality of service that is provided by the government monopoly post office or the public schools.

Moreover, such a program would likely add roughly $300 billion per year in net new government spending. Raising this huge amount in taxes would have a disastrous effect on the economy, with a huge cost in lost economic growth, employment opportunities, and misallocation of resources due to tax distortions. Indeed, no tax sources to raise such sums are remotely available, which means that national health insurance is not a viable approach in any event.

Health Care and the Elderly

Health care for the elderly is dominated by Medicare, which

has its own grave problems. The program currently costs about $90 billion per year, and is one of the fastest growing items in the Federal budget. At its current pace, the program may eventually grow larger than Social Security. By the time today's young workers retire, paying all the program's promised benefits would likely require an increase of 2 to 4 times in the Medicare payroll tax.[5] Yet, the payroll tax is already too high, destroying jobs and employment opportunities.[6]

To counter rapidly rising costs, the Federal government has adopted restrictive reimbursement regulations for hospitals and most recently doctors, specifying amounts health care providers may receive under Medicare for their services and prohibiting them from charging patients any more. These regulations effectively operate like price controls, and will ultimately cause a decline in the quality and availability of care under Medicare.[7] Already we have seen media reports and Congressional hearings echoing claims that hospitals are discharging patients too early and too sick in response to the regulations.[8]

Most remarkably of all, despite Medicare's high costs, the elderly pay as much or more of their incomes for medical care today as they did before the program was adopted.[9] The cost burden includes the rising Medicare premiums imposed on the elderly, which amount to close to $800 this year for an elderly couple. Medicare also leaves many costs uncovered, including prescription drugs, dental care, various doctor and hospital bills, hearing aids, eyeglasses, walking aids, nursing home care, and most home health care. The government recently attempted to expand Medicare to cover some of these items through the catastrophic health care legislation adopted in 1988. But the massive tax increases imposed on the elderly to finance the benefits caused a wave of opposition among the elderly themselves that forced Congress to repeal the legislation. This episode shows that we have reached the limits of the public sector's ability to finance these expenses, as no further tax sources are available to finance added expenditures, including the steep projected increases in unfunded costs of the current Medicare program.

Nursing home care and home health care are state government issues because government assistance for such care is provided primarily through Medicaid, which is financed half each by the federal and the state governments, and through other state programs. In fact, these programs already spend about

$25 billion per year for nursing home and home health care.

Through these programs, federal and state governments should ensure that if an elderly person does not have the money to pay for necessary nursing home care, the government will pay for it. These programs currently seem to perform that function. In the past, real hardship would often occur in the case of married couples, where one spouse had to go into a nursing home and the other spouse remained in the community. Until recently, Medicaid would not provide assistance until virtually all of the couple's savings and almost all of its income (except for a modest sum of about $350 per month) had been used to pay for the nursing home bills. In this case, the noninstitutionalized spouse suffered the financial hardship, being left with inadequate income and no back up savings. However, under new provisions now phasing in, the noninstitutionalized spouse would be able eventually to keep income equal to 150% of the poverty line for a couple, which would total roughly $14,000 today. In addition, the spouse would be able to retain a minimum of $12,000 in savings plus, at state option, 50% of savings above $12,000 up to a maximum of $60,000 in retained assets. These provisions sufficiently avoid this problem.

Home Health Care

Another difficulty in some states involves home health care. In about half the states, the government will provide home health care to an elderly person who would otherwise have to go into a nursing home on Medicaid at greater expense. All states should adopt this policy, as it allows the elderly person to stay in the community while actually reducing costs to the government.

Only the government has provided for those that don't have the money to pay for their care, then the remaining issue is for those that do have the money to pay for it, at least for a while. The concern here is how to avoid the problem of nursing home costs wiping out the life savings of retirees.

This concern is not a matter of access to needed care, which is assured, but rather how to protect the significant assets that a high proportion of the elderly do have. Consequently, this is not really a health policy issue at all, but an estate planning issue, which is more appropriately addressed through the private sector. The government should not be using taxpayer funds to preserve substantial private estates. Those in this situation can and should use part of their accumulated savings to purchase private nursing home insurance to protect the rest. Over 70 companies now offer such insurance.[10] The elderly with substantial accumulated resources surely can afford to purchase that insurance with a portion of those resources.

The elderly with more modest savings of $15,000 or so may feel that purchasing insurance to protect this smaller amount is not worthwhile. For a couple in this situation, the savings would be protected under the new provisions discussed above. This problem would apply only to single elderly persons, who account for 88% of nursing home residents. In this case, it is not too much to ask of those who do have some money they can contribute to their own care to do so before the taxpayers are asked to pay for their care. This is especially true since we are talking about a single elderly person with no spouse dependent on such savings, receiving his or her necessities through the nursing home care.

Some suggest that the government should go beyond the role of providing for those in need, and instead pay for the nursing home and home health care costs of everyone through a new entitlement program. But such a program would be enormously costly for the taxpayers. Total nursing home expenditures in the U.S. are roughly $50 billion per year, and more than $10 billion each year is spent for home health care.[11]

But this is only the beginning. Only 29% of those who need long term care are in nursing homes.[12] The remaining 71% are in the community receiving care from their families and others.[13] If the government started to pick up the bills for everyone, many of those now remaining in the community would likely enter nursing homes, sharply increasing program costs with unnecessary utilization.

Moreover, the problem for home health care is far worse. This care primarily involves assistance in the activities of daily living - cooking, cleaning, bathing, dressing, eating, going to the bathroom, moving around, shopping, and similar activities. Currently, 74% of the elderly who need such care receive it without charge from family and friends.[14] Another 21% receive the care partly from family and friends and partly from paid professionals.[15] Only 5% receive such care entirely from paid professionals.[16] If the government offered paid professional care to everyone, this care would massively displace the voluntary care now provided by family and friends. This is especially so since the volunteers find providing the care quite burdensome, and unlike nursing homes, the elderly and their families find the home health care services so attractive. People don't want to go into nursing homes, but home health care is the equivalent of receiving the services of free maids and cooks. All of the elderly who can qualify for this service will want it, and their family members will want them to have it. Indeed, the energy of family members that formerly went into providing the care will go into lobbying the bureaucracy to get the paid professional care from the government.

In addition, because the home health care services are so attractive, many of the elderly who do not receive such assistance now will try to qualify for the government provided professional care. The history of the Social Security Disability program shows that the government is unable to prevent many ineligibles from receiving assistance even when the qualification criteria are far more stringent.

Taking the abuse even further, many family members who formerly provided free care will instead arrange to receive free services themselves when the government is paying the bill. When the home health aide is shopping for the groceries of the elderly recipient, the aide will often end up shopping for the whole family. When the home health aide is doing the laundry for the elderly person, the aide will often end up doing the laundry for the whole family. This is so natural when the elderly recipient lives with his or her elderly spouse. But it will also happen often when the elderly recipient lives with his or her adult children and their children. It happens today with Medicaid financed home health care. Because home health care is provided in the privacy of the home, controlling these abuses will be impossible. All this abuse and unnecessary utilization in regard to home health care would again sharply increase the costs of the program.

An entitlement program would also eliminate incentives for consumers to shop for the lowest cost care and for providers to attempt to keep costs down, just as in the case of overinsurance for ordinary health care costs as discussed above. This would further increase the costs of the program. The massive increase in demand for nursing home and home health care services resulting from an entitlement program would also increase the fees charged for such services, as has been the experience with other government programs from health, to education, to defense.

Adding up all these factors, the costs of a universal entitlement program for nursing home and home health care would likely be $60 to $80 billion in net additional government spending. Adopting such a huge new entitlement in the face of larger budget deficits, the huge long-term Medicare financing gap, and the impending retirement of the baby boom generation would be foolhardy. Indeed, no revenue sources are available to finance such additional spending, so such an entitlement program is highly unrealistic.

Instead, federal and state governments should promote the development of private long-term care insurance and other private options to assist those who do have significant resources. One attractive option is life insurance policies which phase out the death benefit after retirement and phase in nursing home coverage instead. Many state governments have been slow to approve such policies for sale in their states, without good reason. States should approve this and other helpful insurance innovations quickly.

At the federal level, the proposal for Health Care Savings Accounts (HCSAs) would address the broader Medicare problem as well as nursing home and home health care.[17] Under proposed bipartisan legislation spearheaded by Rep. French Slaughter (R., VA.), each worker and his employer could contribute to a HCSA up to certain limits, in return for a 60% income tax credit. To the extent this option was exercised during working years, the worker would bear a higher deductible under Medicare in retirement, perhaps as high as several thousand dollars per year. But the funds in the HCSA, with tax-free investment returns over the years, would be available to purchase insurance to cover these expenses or to pay them directly.

By design, retirees would likely have extra funds in their HCSAs to purchase nursing home and home health care insurance. Workers who exercised the option substantially over their career would also receive extended catastrophic benefits under Medicare that were withdrawn when the catastrophic health care legislation was repealed as discussed above. On net, the increased deductibles for workers exercising the HCSAs would substantially reduce Medicare expenditures over the long run, possibly eliminating the program's long term financing gap without tax increases or benefit cuts. The bill also provides that those who spend less than a specified proportion of their HCSAs each year on health care could withdraw the difference without restrictions. This would give retirees strong incentives to shop for lower cost care and avoid unnecessary expenses, helping to counter rapidly rising health costs.

This innovative legislation would, therefore, comprehensively address a broad range of problems, and should be widely supported.

Conclusion

While the U.S. health care system does provide the highest quality care in the world, it does have major problems concerning the uninsured, high costs, and health care for the elderly. In each case, however, more heavy government involvement would add to rather than solve the system's problems. These problems can each be far more effectively addressed through reform that would expand the role of the private sector and competitive free markets in meeting health care needs.

SECTION FOUR:
Labor/Business Issues

CHAPTER TEN

COPING WITH A CHANGING LABOR MARKET
By Kevin C. Sontheimer

EDITOR'S SUMMARY

Pennsylvania's labor market is undergoing significant changes. It is difficult to predict future economic trends, but they are likely to fall somewhere between total employment and possible recession. A mix of economic policies should be set to deal with both brisk expansion and periods of slow growth.

A labor shortage in Pennsylvania may be a blessing in disguise. These shortages are caused by increases in labor demand relative to supply and shifts in the composition of labor supply relative to demand. The shifts in labor demand reflects improved market conditions and increases in profits.

The greatest source of decline in Pennsylvania's labor pool is the outflow of workers in the 15-34 year age group. There is also a mismatch between the skills of the labor supply and qualifications demanded due to continuing technological changes. The outmigration of young skilled workers will slow if work opportunities in Pennsylvania improve relative to other regions.

State economic policies should let the market cope with most potential labor shortages. A demand-induced labor shortage is not a cause for concern since the population as a whole and state tax revenues share in the gain. The market mechanism produces higher wages, which bring forth greater willingness to work from the existing labor supply.

However, the market mechanism by itself cannot adequately cope with the problem of training the undereducated worker. Firms do not have adequate incentives to provide workers with general education and other skills not specifically related to the company. Therefore, state policy has a role to play in filling shortages of skilled workers through education and retraining of dislocated workers.

Little is known about the performance of current educational and training programs. The Commonwealth may have overestimated its ability to shift experienced workers from declining to expanding industries. Sound changes will be realized only after an evaluation of current labor policies is undertaken.

Policies should seek to move uneducated, unskilled and dislocated workers from dependency to self-support. A labor shortage could provide employment to most individuals, but effective means must be found to educate young workers and retrain older workers. With proper planning, potential employment problems can be turned into significant opportunities in a period of future labor shortages.

Kevin C. Sontheimer is Chairman of the Department of Economics and Director of the Economic Policy Institute at the University of Pittsburgh.

Recent discussions of labor markets are marked by a state of confusion about what the future holds, and what ought to be done about it. The confused commentary pertains to both the national scene and Pennsylvania, but the discussion here will focus on Pennsylvania only.

Some commentators foresee a period of labor shortages looming in Pennsylvania's future. Others foresee a second scenario — a future decade of neither overall shortage nor surplus, but a period of mismatch between occupational skill requirements and labor force composition. Yet others foresee a third scenario, a continuation of Pennsylvania's surplus of workers relative to positions. Notably in the latter category is The Pennsylvania Economic Development Partnership. The Partnership in 1988 set forth a development goal of creating 50,000 net new jobs per year, many of which are perceived to be necessary just to absorb growing numbers of workers.[1] Given the alternative forecasts, it is natural for policy makers and legislators to ask which is correct.

But predicting the future is an error prone activity. No one, and no econometric model, does an adequate job of forecasting the future. The 1982 recession was as hard on econometric forecasters as it was on members of many other occupations. The post-1982 decline in business by the large econometric consulting firms was due to the realization, however delayed, by corporations and other clients that the track record of econometric forecasts is quite poor. The decline in the number of "corporate economist" positions since 1982 also is a result of the same realization. No econometric model and no economic forecaster has any significant degree of success in predicting turning points in the economy, yet the successful prediction of turning points is precisely what is needed. The upshot of the situation is that policy makers and legislators will have to continue to work in the same environment in which they have worked historically, i.e., a decision environment in which the future twists and turns of the economy are uncertain, a vision of multiple images moving in a murky fog.

In this essay, no foolish forecast of the future is offered. Between now and the year 2000 all three of the above scenarios could and might well occur. The great American job machine could churn on for another 2 or 3 years and tighten Pennsylvania labor markets even further, perhaps even generate a period of shortage. But recession, defined as a sustained period of labor surpluses across a wide range of industries, occupations, and areas cannot be ruled out of our future either. Intermingled with the cyclical scenario is the virtually certain continuation of the restructuring of the American and Pennsylvania economies and the induced shifting of skills demanded versus skills available. The future is likely to be like the past in that it probably will not be pure prosperity or unremitting recession, but some of both along with something in between. That is the only reasonable long-term forecast.

If there is no sure answer to the question of which forecast is correct, what should policy makers do? What does the situation mean for policy makers? It means that the mix of policies to be established, or to be kept in place, should not be based on an expectation of either boom or bust, one scenario or another. Rather the mix of policies should be set to deal with not only recession and brisk expansion, but periods of slow growth or near stagnation as well. It also means that policies should have "on-off" switches so that they are effective when needed but benign and nonburdensome when not needed. It further means that policies should not have the effect of stimulating or amplifying cyclical swings in the economy.

What does the mixed vision of the future mean for labor policies in particular? Before answering that question, it is appropriate to address a few other points and questions first.

Is A Labor Shortage A Good Thing?

It is generally agreed that unemployment is bad, at least the secular and cyclical varieties are bad, and frictional unemployment is a necessary evil. Therefore a policy posture by government, including state government, that can minimize unemployment and its side effects is appropriate to consider. But what about shortages of labor? If a surplus of labor (unemployment) is undesirable, does that mean a shortage of labor is good? And if not, is a shortage of labor necessarily bad? Finally, is there a role for state policy to combat labor shortages?

In trying to address the issue of whether labor shortages are good or not, and whether there is a role for state government in combating shortages, it should be first noted that the economy responds to decreases in the demand for labor (unemployment) differently than it does to increases in the demand for labor (shortage of labor). Similarly, it responds to increases in the supply of labor (unemployment) differently than it does to decreases in the supply of labor (shortage of labor). The main difference is that for both cultural and contractual reasons, reductions in wages and benefits are not the first means adopted to counteract unemployment, whereas society places no obstacles to promptly increasing wages and benefits to eliminate labor shortages. That is, the price mechanism can readily be employed in response to labor shortages, but not labor surpluses. The empirical evidence is overwhelming that our society prefers to respond to either decreases in the demand for labor or increases in the supply of labor via unemployment and safety nets rather than wage adjustments, however unwise the preference might be.

Why is the price mechanism an acceptable means of coping with labor shortages when society resists its use as a means of dealing with labor surpluses? This question is unrelated to the question of whether or not a shortage of labor is good, and so both questions can be answered together. Also, since the demographic situation of Pennsylvania makes the likelihood of reductions in total labor supply to be low, and modest increases in total labor supply to be likely, if labor shortages occur they will be caused by increases in labor demand relative to supply, and shifts in the composition of labor demand relative to supply.[2] So the two questions will be answered within the appropriate demographic context for the coming decade.

Demand Induced Shortage

If labor shortages occur because of an increase in real labor demand relative to labor supply, it can be said to be a good thing. From the perspective of employees, the adjustment of wages and benefits upward to gain additional employees while retaining old ones is good. The increase in real purchasing power provided by higher real wages and benefits promotes greater economic well-being for both old and new employees and their dependents. From the perspective of employers, the shift in the real labor demand reflects unrealized increases in profits. The increase in profits can be realized even as wages and benefits are increased. The latter fact is reflected in the history of the willingness of firms to grant wage and benefit increases during upswings in business activity. So the conclusion is clear: demand shifts that create labor shortages are good for both shareholders and employees.

Are there other considerations that might tilt the argument the other way? Two commonly mentioned issues that might affect the argument are the effects of rising wages on the long run growth of Pennsylvania industry, and the competitiveness issue. The first issue is that if growth in the demand for labor results in rising wages, the wage increases will limit the rate and ultimate amount of industrial growth. In other words, greater growth would occur if wage levels were not allowed to rise. The second is that if wage levels rise in response to growing demand for labor, then the future competitiveness of Pennsylvania will be adversely affected by the higher wage base, i.e., the competitiveness of Pennsylvania based industry will be greater if wages are not allowed to rise in response to rising demand. The two concerns are not independent, and the problem with both arises in considering how wage levels might be kept from increasing in response to an increased demand for labor. One way would be to legislate wage controls. However, state wage controls are not only politically nonviable, but economically counterproductive. State wage controls, even if they were feasible, would only restrain any labor supply response to the increased demand, i.e., wage controls would only perpetuate a shortage of labor and prevent employees and shareholders from realizing potential gains. The employees would be deprived of the higher real wages, and shareholders would be deprived of the higher profits. The competitiveness that would derive from artificially capping wages and benefits would be illusory. Firms would see low wages but would not be able to attract workers to fill positions. What good is a low wage if workers will not work for it? The second way of holding down the wage increases would be to stimulate an increase in the labor supply that was proportionate to the increase in labor demand. However, the state does not have instruments available that can induce such a change in the labor supply. Indeed, it is precisely because there is no magic way of increasing the labor supply that the market mechanism produces higher wages as a means to bring forth greater willingness to work from the existing labor supply.

The appropriate conclusion to draw then is that the state policy toward a potential period of labor shortage, due to an increased demand for labor in Pennsylvania, should be a policy of letting the market cope with the problem. Wages and benefits for Pennsylvania workers will rise and the profits of Pennsylvania enterprises will rise also. Such increases will benefit the state population as a whole and state tax revenues will similarly share in the gain. Another benefit that might accrue to Pennsylvania could be a reduction in the outflow of people seeking work elsewhere (though this effect would depend on the comparative labor and wage situations in other parts of the country too). To the extent that the retention of state residents can be associated with maintaining family and community cohesiveness, the rising wages could contribute to greater social stability — a not inconsequential benefit.

The lesson is not that the impending prospect of demand induced labor shortage (such as Chester County is experiencing) is a cause for concern, but rather it is the kind of problem that is worth hoping for. The Swiss and West Germans know the lesson very well. Let us hope for a labor shortage, and let us allow private individuals and enterprises to eliminate the shortage through better work efforts, wages, salaries, benefits, and employer-employee relationships.

Market Mismatches and Shortages

But what about the scenario that foresees labor shortages due to a mismatch between the skills and qualifications of the labor supply and the composition of skills and qualifications demanded? The scenario has three causes: a) continuing changes in the economic structure of Pennsylvania; b) deficient training and education of part of the workforce (the so-called underclass); c) a continuing increase in the average age of the Pennsylvania labor force, which is exaggerated by a disproportionate outflow of workers in the 15-34 year age group.

Besides the multiple sources of the scenario, the scenario has other complexities which are:

1) Because the disproportionate outflow of workers in the 15-34 age group exaggerates the natural demographic aging of the workforce in Pennsylvania, the dislocations associated with industrial restructuring falls disproportionately on older workers.

2) The outflow of workers in the 15-34 age group appears to

contain a less than proportionate share of the under-educated and unskilled young people, so that the resident proportion of undereducated and unskilled workers is enlarged.

3) There is a potential labor surplus in the 60-74 age group that is obscured by high marginal tax rates that fall on social security recipients.

Thus the mismatch scenario incorporates two mismatches, each of which reinforces the other's effects in creating a shortage of suitably skilled workers. The first is the mismatch between the skill composition of labor demanded and the skill composition of labor supplied. The second is the age distribution mismatch with a labor shortage in the 15-34 age group and a potential surplus of workers in the 60-74 age group. The reinforcing effect occurs because too high a proportion of the 15-34 age group lack marketable skills and capabilities, and a significant proportion of the 60-74 age group have marketable skills and capabilities but lack adequate incentives to stay in the labor force.

What policies are appropriate for dealing with this scenario? The first point to consider in assessing the policy approach to the problem is to note that one of the sources of the problem is, from another perspective, an asset to Pennsylvania. The fact that Pennsylvania exports young workers means that it has the capability within its population base to enlarge the younger portion of its skilled resident labor force. The outmigration of young skilled persons will slow and stop when work opportunities, wages, and the quality of life in Pennsylvania improves relative to other regions (such as the Southwest and California). So, to the extent that the vision of a labor shortage in the younger age groups is realized, it can be rectified in part by relying on the linkage between higher wages and higher profits in situations of excess demand for labor, even if the excess demand is part of a mismatch scenario. The conclusions that a labor shortage is the kind of problem that Pennsylvanians should want, and the market should be relied upon to resolve the problem, are apparent again with regard to young, skilled, and capable workers.

A less satisfying assessment obtains when causes a) and b) listed above are considered. The question is what to do about the unskilled and untrained, and the workers who have the skills that are specific to firms and industries that no longer need them, but not skills suitable for firms and industries who need additional workers. In these cases firms do not have adequate incentives to provide workers with general education and other skills that other firms might want to capture. The more general and less firm-specific the skill or capability, the less incentive an employer has to help workers acquire it. Thus the market process will stop short when it comes to the problem of filling shortages of skilled and educated workers by educating the uneducated, training the unskilled, and retraining or reeducating the capable but industrially dislocated worker. So in these cases there is a need and a role for state policy.

There is another area in which there is a role for state policy, and that is to help lower the costs of information in labor markets. There are large costs of gathering information about job vacancies and job candidates. They are reflected in the fees charged by commercial job placement enterprises. The high costs of gaining information in the job and candidate search process results in an uneven performance by the market mechanism in the labor/employment sector. For high value positions, commercial firms can offer cost effective services to help find matches between vacancies and qualified individuals.[3] On the lower side of the value spectrum, the costs of information are such that extensive advertising and search efforts by employers or commercial agents is often not perceived to be cost effective. Similarly, candidates for lower value positions do not see extensive search to be cost effective. The result is that for occupations and professions for which there is a national market, the flow of information is relatively effective. But further down in the value-of-position spectrum, labor markets become increasingly segmented regionally and locally. The segmentation reflects the declining ratio of value-of-position to search costs. The segmentation is not necessarily efficient, however, since the segmented information flows can result in vacancies in one region or locality being unfilled while qualified candidates are unemployed in other regions or localities.

Part of the problem of inefficient information flows and search arises because of the discrepancy between the private and total costs of unemployment. Firms with unfilled vacancies factor into their decisions the revenues lost due to the vacancies, but see only a tiny fraction of the other costs of unemployment (via taxes). Similarly, unemployed persons receiving unemployment compensation or welfare and other public support see only the difference between employed income and unemployed income as the opportunity cost of remaining unemployed. However, society at large bears the full cost of unemployment. So from the point of view of state government, there is a clear rationale for supporting better information flows if it will result in moving persons from the lists of state support programs to the lists of the employed and taxpaying public.

Reconsidering the questions of whether labor shortages are good, and is there a role for state policy to combat labor shortages within the mismatch scenario, it is concluded:

1) Pennsylvania could make a positive response to the demand induced shortage of workers. Further, the response would be beneficial to employees, employers, and to the state as a whole, and no state government intervention is required or appropriate.

2) The market mechanism by itself will not cope adequately with the problem of repairing the deficiencies of the undereducated, the unskilled, and the dislocated worker. Nor do private market actions provide for adequate information flows between regionally and locally segmented labor markets.

The second conclusion tells us that there are roles for state government to play in conjunction with and supportive of market processes.

State Policies

The Commonwealth of Pennsylvania already is engaged in policies that seek to educate and train the uneducated and unskilled portion of the labor force. Similarly, Pennsylvania is involved already in policies designed to retrain and reeducate the industrially dislocated worker. The state also tries to effect better information flows about job vacancies, job requirements, and job candidates locally and regionally. So the state has a policy program that will help to relieve future labor shortages due to mismatches between the composition of skill and capabilities demanded by employers and the composition of skill and capabilities suppliable by Pennsylvania workers, and to

remove local and regional labor shortages by making information available in labor surplus areas. The question therefore
becomes "What additional, or what different, policies should
state government pursue?"

Asking what state government should do to help unskilled,
uneducated, and dislocated workers might seem to presume
that the effects and performance of current policies are known.
That presumption, whether implied by the question or not, is
false. There is in fact relatively little known about the effects of
present educational and training programs for young, older, or
dislocated workers. The situation that The Rand Corporation
uncovered in the Pittsburgh region is all too true across the
state.

> Making improvements in the region's work-related
> education and training system will be difficult. Little is
> systematically known about the performance of ele-
> ments of the system.[4]

The same is true of efforts to match the unemployed to vacant
positions. Little is systematically known about what happens to
dislocated and other unemployed workers and why, even
though a great deal of information could be made available to
policy makers.[5] The information void might well have led the
state to overemphasize the need to induce workers to shift from
one industry to another as a means of coping with industrial
decline.[6] Or, to put it another way, the information void might
have resulted in an overestimation of both the need and the
ability to shift experienced workers from declining to expanding
industries as a means of coping with industrial restructuring.

So what ought to be concluded about the mismatch scenario
with regard to state government policy for the uneducated,
untrained, and dislocated portions of the labor force? First, no
hasty actions are appropriate. A rich mixture of private and
government supported education and training programs is in
place. Second, a systematic assessment of the effectiveness of
the existing programs is needed. Policy makers need to know
what is working well and what is working poorly, and why.
Sound and cost effective policy changes and new directions will
be realized only after a foundation of information and policy
evaluation is made available to policy makers in the legislative
and executive branches of government.

State government officials also need to learn more about what happens to dislocated workers and why. What are the typical reaches of local and regional labor markets for various skill and occupational categories? What proportion of workers laid off in declining industries can be expected to be recalled, and what proportion will need to make inter-industry moves? How mobile are dislocated workers? Relatively little is known about such fundamental matters, even though data exist in state files to provide the answers and means to better policy formation. Preliminary evidence exists to suggest that both the need and the ability to shift workers between industries might be more limited than generally believed.

It cannot be overemphasized that labor shortages that would be part of a mismatch scenario also would be part of a potential cure to a real problem, how to help remove the uneducated, unskilled, and dislocated workers from a circumstance of dependency to a position of dignified self-support. A labor shortage would provide the potential employment, what would remain would be to find effective means to educate and train young workers and retrain older workers. It is the problem of education, training and retraining that needs to be made the focus of state government efforts.

Finally, future labor shortages could be alleviated in part by making better use of workers who are now are in the ranks of the capable but retired category. However, the impediments to drawing such potential workers back into the labor force are largely due to federal tax and social security policies. Thus the ability to tap the reservoir of older and capable workers is largely out of the reach of state policy.

Conclusion

If the labor shortages would become a more common and sustained circumstance in the Pennsylvania economy, the state would be confronted with a welcome problem. The more serious and burdensome problems of unemployment, welfare dependency, and associated behavioral and social ailments could be reduced; the stability of family and other relationships could be enhanced; and overall labor incomes, corporate incomes, and the state tax base could be improved. It would be a welcome change for Pennsylvania from the experience of the last quarter century or so.

The key to taking advantage of a future period of significant labor shortages is to have an effective mechanism for education, training, and retraining in hand. It also will be helpful to know what are the characteristics of dislocated workers, why and how they react to new opportunities, what the skill and education requirements of new and replacement vacancies are, and what the geographic extent of local and regional labor markets are across the spectrum of skills and occupations.

Pennsylvania already has a rich mix of private and public providers of work-related education and training. Not the least among these are the relatively new system of community colleges, the Area Vocational Technical Schools, and a large number of proprietary schools and adult education programs. What is needed is a comprehensive assessment of the effectiveness of each of these and other components of work-related education and training system. While the system seems to work relatively well, there clearly have been significant numbers of unemployed persons who have not been served, or served well. Before any major initiative or expansions should be undertaken, the present system should be assessed and evaluated. It does not pay to fix what is not broken, nor does it pay to alter or repair without knowing what the failures are.

CHAPTER ELEVEN

LABOR LAW: A MANDATE FOR CHANGE
By Nevin J. Mindlin and Joseph Horton

EDITOR'S SUMMARY

Pennsylvania labor law is antiquated. It reflects the discredited notion that all aspects of the economy are proper subjects for government regulation. As the 21st century approaches, the Commonwealth's labor laws must be updated if the state is to maintain its general economic vitality and competitive position in global and regional markets.

Labor laws have hindered economic growth in the Commonwealth. Unwarranted intrusions into the market, such as the minimum wage and prevailing wage laws have served to maintain a preferential position for labor unions, while weakening Pennsylvania's competitive position.

Economic research shows that a minimum wage set above the market scale means the loss of jobs. The higher the minimum wage is above the market wage for unskilled labor, the fewer unskilled positions are created. The minimum wage is also inflationary, since there is no corresponding increase in productivity with a raised minimum wage.

The prevailing wage rate is excessively costly to government. The price of service contracts between private contractors and government is raised substantially due to this wage setting. Prevailing wages serve to maintain the competitiveness of unionized contractors while harming the interests of merit employers.

Mandated benefits are another attempt at politicizing the employment contract. Adding mandated benefits to a wage has the same effect on less skilled workers as the minimum wage law. If the cost of such mandates to the employer is greater than the value a worker can produce, then a job opportunity is lost.

Unemployment compensation is a case of a labor law that has exceeded its legitimate boundaries. The problem with unemployment compensation is that it is not structured as an insurance program since there is no correlation between benefits and taxes. Pennsylvania's benefit costs are the highest among the major industrialized states.

Industrial homework restrictions work to the benefit of labor unions. Homework provides advantages for many different types of workers. In some cases, it may mean the difference between self-support on the one hand and welfare and poverty on the other.

The Pennsylvania Public Employee Relations Act should be amended. The existing Agency Shop statute should also be repealed so that employees can decide for themselves whether or not to join a union. All meetings related to collective bargaining should be open and subject to the Sunshine Act.

Nevin J. Mindlin is Minority Staff Director of the Pennsylvania House of Representatives Labor Relations Committee.

Joseph Horton is Dean of the School of Management at the University of Scranton.

How Pennsylvania addresses labor law in the coming years is of critical importance to the economic well-being of the Commonwealth and its citizens. Because labor and employment are fundamental aspects of human life, the Commonwealth's general economic vitality and its competitive position in global and regional markets are directly and profoundly affected by the labor policy we adopt.

The Politics and Economics of Work

For over fifty years, governmental power has been directed at politicizing the private economic sector in order to achieve desired social goals. No distinction has been made between what might be considered public or private matters. All aspects of the economy, including the fundamental economic relationship of employment, have been considered the legitimate subject of government intervention.

It is time to rethink the role of government in regulating the relationship between employees and employers. Modern economic analysis shows that markets of all types work better than we once thought. Government simply cannot guide or direct the "unseen hand" of the economy. Very often, government actions are harmful, particularly to the people that they were intended to help. For the economy and the individuals within it to prosper, government must foster private economic relationships which are substantially free of government interference.

Most of the employment relationship is essentially a private matter. The agreements that are arranged between employees and employers as to the wages, hours, terms and conditions of employment establish an economic, contractual relationship between these individuals. These private contracts are not the concern of government. On the other hand, there is a part of the employment relationship which is societal in nature. Indeed, certain parts of the employment relationship have been part of our legal and moral code since the Bible.

Pennsylvania's labor law, in far too many instances, reflects the discredited idea that all aspects of the economy are proper subjects for government regulation. Our law is antiquated; it substitutes the inefficiency of politics and bureaucratic regulation for the flexibility and progress encouraged by market relationships. Our labor law has simply not kept up with our improved knowledge of how the economy works. We must, therefore, differentiate between that which should rightfully be left to the efficiency of the market, and that which is a societal concern that should be regulated by government. The time has come for Pennsylvania to revise its labor law in recognition of how a free enterprise economy functions.

Distinctions, to be sure, are not always clear; and, differentiation is not always easy. From the present political perspective, these distinctions, or the lack or blurring thereof, present no public policy problem. From a pro-market perspective, the blurring or elimination of distinctions between private and public domains in the area of labor law is precisely the public policy problem that demands attention and must be addressed in the 21st century.

Labor Unions and the Political Process

Before attention can be directed to the consideration of various individual public policy issues, the subject of labor unions must be addressed. Labor unions play a significant role in our society. The political agenda, particularly with regard to labor law, but also with regard to broader economic issues, has been, by and large, controlled by labor unions during the last fifty or more years. It is, therefore, imperative that the integrated role of labor unions in our society and in our political culture be understood, if the reversal of the politicization of Pennsylvania's economy is to be achieved.

Labor unions grew and became a dominant political and social force only after the New Deal legislation of the 1930's.[1] New Deal legislation not only transformed American society by establishing the politicization of our economy as the predominant political culture, it also established labor unions as basic liberal, political organizations.

Labor unions are inherently collectivist in their organization. Their purpose is to control or influence the use of the wealth and income that flows from the ownership of private capital for their own purposes and, ostensibly, for general social purposes. Labor unions were empowered by the New Deal with quasi-governmental privileges, exclusive representation and union security, and they were granted immunities, from taxes, from antitrust, and from damage suits and prosecution that would otherwise result from the labor unrest that sometimes stems from statutorily protected activities. From a functional standpoint, labor unions have become, through these privileges and immunities, a sort of lowest level of government, firmly establishing the process of politicization within private enterprise. This functional integration of government and labor unions is further reinforced through government unionization, and through statutorily mandated representation by labor unions on governmental boards and commissions.

In addition to empowering labor unions directly, labor laws also serve to reinforce union strength and privilege indirectly by providing labor unions with a preferred economic position. These types of labor laws, although customarily cloaked in declarations of public policy that indicated that their intended purpose is the general welfare of society, are, in reality, designed to maintain or expand union control over a targeted segment of the market, or to uphold the unions' premium wage scales. In fact, these laws more often than not have adverse and detrimental effects on other (nonunion) participants in the economy.

We must recognize that the interests of individual workers is often not the same as those of the managers of labor unions. The prosperity of working people depends upon the general prosperity of the economy of Pennsylvania, not upon rules which grant special privileges or which prohibit the changes needed to utilize more modern and more productive methods in order to meet our competition.

Despite these governmental efforts at maintaining and expanding the preferred status and power of labor unions, union strength in the private sector is clearly in decline.[2] This decline would strongly appear to be based upon the flaws within the structure of unions themselves in relation to a competitive market economy, and upon the inherent flaws within labor policy, which works to stultify, rather than to promote a vital and expanding private sector economy.[3] The general decline of labor union strength and the failure of the policies of the past to promote our general economic welfare, which is now beginning to be understood by the general populace, affords policy makers an excellent opportunity to begin putting forward a coherent program of labor policy for Pennsylvania's future.

Harmful Government Intrusion into the Labor Market

How do Pennsylvania's labor laws hinder economic growth

and the welfare of Pennsylvania workers? First, there is government action which is clearly an unwarranted intrusion into the market. The minimum wage law and the prevailing wage law are particularly interesting examples of this type of legislation. Both intruded into private contractual relationships, and both serve to maintain a preferential position for labor unions. This preferential position is at the expense of other workers including would-be union members.

Minimum Wage: The minimum wage imposes a specified wage into the employment contract between an employer and an employee that is very different than the value of the work to be performed or the capability of the employee to perform the assigned work. The major argument offered in support of the minimum wage, and of increasing it, is that the minimum wage establishes the lowest wage that should be socially acceptable, and thus, raises the working poor out of poverty. These arguments, however, do not hold up to scrutiny.

Studies by the Minimum Wage Study Commission, the United States Congressional Budget Office, and others have repeatedly shown that only 10 to 20% of minimum wage workers live in poverty-level households, while a substantial share of those who earn the minimum wage live in households with incomes that are double the poverty level. Moreover, economic research and market experience have both demonstrated that a minimum wage set above the market scale is harmful to the economy, and more importantly, to the very people that it is intended to help.

Increasing the minimum wage above the market scale inevitably results in the loss of employment opportunities that would otherwise be available, and the outright loss of jobs. People with few productive skills often cannot produce output worth as much as the minimum wage requires that they be paid. Employers cannot, therefore, afford to hire these people. The higher the minimum wage is above the market rate for unskilled labor, the more unskilled people there are who cannot find jobs at all. A law which was intended to raise the wages of the working poor prevents them from earning any wage at all. The minimum wage is also inflationary, since there is no corresponding increase in productivity when the minimum wage is increased by government fiat.

Who are these people who are hurt by the minimum wage?

They are disproportionately young minority group members who have been short changed by public education. The minimum wage law keeps many of them from getting the job experience and the on-the-job skills needed to move up to higher paying jobs. It keeps them from competing at all with more productive workers who are more likely to be union members. Since those who are denied the opportunity to gain work skills become permanent additions to the welfare rolls, they are supported by taxpayers, including union members. In the long run even union members may lose as a result of this short-sighted policy. A state minimum wage higher than the federal minimum wage would be even more destructive as it would export jobs from the Commonwealth to other states.

Nobel laureate Milton Friedman and other noted economists forcefully argue that the primary beneficiaries of a minimum wage set at a level above the market scale are labor unions. This occurs for two reasons: 1) increasing the minimum wage makes union scale wages more competitive and 2) employers often substitute capital equipment (frequently manufactured in unionized plants) for the employees who are laid off or who are not hired due to an increase in the minimum wage.

Prevailing Wage: The prevailing wage purports to protect workers in a local labor market from unfair competition due both to the willingness of outside labor to work at wages lower than the local market, and to cut-throat contract bidding practices that only serve to harm construction workers. The fundamental justification for prevailing wage laws is that the price of labor should not be an element in the competition for government construction projects. It is argued that by establishing a prevailing wage, government assures that workers receive "a fair day's pay for a fair day's work," and that government obtains the highest quality of work by highly skilled workers. In the case of the prevailing wage, public policy intrudes not only into the employment contract between construction contractors and their employees by setting wages, but also into the contract for service between government and the construction contractor by substantially setting the contract price due to this wage setting. Again, these arguments do not hold up to scrutiny.

Research by the United States General Accounting Office indicates that, because the administration of a prevailing wage is so impractical, the intent is seldom carried out. When the intent is met, the study showed that the established prevailing wages were actually below local market wage rates. Additionally, the General Accounting Office found that the prevailing wage is excessively costly to government, and that it is inflationary. The report concluded that the prevailing wage's intent is best met "when wages become a competitive bidding factor in construction contracting."[4]

Invariably, the prevailing wage rates set by government are the prevailing union-scale wage rates of a labor market that is defined in a manner most advantageous to labor unions. This setting of the union-scale wages as the prevailing wage serves to maintain the competitiveness of unionized contractors, to maintain the employment levels of union workers, and to lower the resistance of nonunion contractors to unionization because of their interest in bidding for large, lucrative government contracts.

Mandated Benefits: More recently, there have been various efforts at mandating benefits that are often provided by employers as compensation in lieu of other forms of remuneration through statutory enactment. These benefits include, among others, medical coverage, and leave programs for parenting, and for personal and family emergencies with some form of compensation. It should be expected that additional benefits will be proposed in the future, given any success with those proposals already on the political agenda. Despite efforts at characterizing these benefit proposals as labor standards, they are clearly a means of imposing through law benefits that are not attainable through contract negotiations or collective bargaining. Mandated benefits are, therefore, yet additional attempts at politicizing the employment contract. Any demand for compensation, including benefits, through statutory enactment clearly falls within the area of government intrusion, and therefore, should be resisted and opposed.

The cost to an employer of employing a person includes the cost of benefits, not just the wage paid. Adding mandated benefits to the wage has the same effect on less skilled workers as prevailing wage or minimum wage laws. The added cost to the employer of mandated benefits is greater than the value some workers can produce. If, as a result, the employer cannot afford to hire or to continue to employ these workers, they lose the opportunity to work in these jobs. Jobs of the already skilled, often union members, are protected from this competition. If mandated benefits are greater in Pennsylvania than in other states, this, too, exports jobs to these states.

There is, however, an element to these demands for mandated benefits that has some level of legitimacy. That exception has to do with the ability of an individual to attend to necessary family matters or emergencies without fear of losing his or her job. It is this consideration that places family and maternity leave proposals at the point of possible conflict between the social contract and the employment contract, which has the potential of being a difficult conflict to resolve. So far, there is no evidence of any social irresponsibility by Pennsylvania's employers where family matters are concerned. The public policy caveat for any legislation on the subject of job security as it relates to family issues is that there must be a demonstrated need and justification.

Excessive Government Actions

There are several existing labor laws in which government exceeds its proper role. These include unemployment compensation, industrial homework, and public employee labor relations laws. There are a few other statutes that could be added to the list, such as workers' compensation, but these laws currently seem to function at a reasonable equilibrium level. Future developments with regard to workers' compensation and other laws must be monitored, but these laws do not warrant comment at this time.

Unemployment Compensation: Unemployment compensation is a classic case of a labor law with a proper social purpose that has exceeded its legitimate boundaries. The program's purpose is to insure individual workers against the loss of wages which is the result of becoming unemployed through no fault of their own. The program was originally designed and was intended to be structured as a public insurance program. It is, in fact, called "unemployment insurance" in federal law.

The problem with unemployment compensation is that it is not really structured as an insurance program. Its fundamental flaw is that there is no correlation and connection between benefits and their associated cost, and taxes. Taxes are, in effect, premiums, and premiums under concepts of insurance must be reasonably related to the cost of the liability. Another major problem is that there is no separation between the administration of the program and the political process. As a result, the program is highly politicized. Since there is no connection between benefit costs and taxes, and since the statute is highly susceptible to amendment to meet political demands, benefits are increased and expanded at every opportunity regardless of whether there exists a justifiable relationship between the benefits provided and the attachment by the employee to the workforce. This politicization is evidenced by the program's excessive cost. An analysis of Pennsylvania's benefit costs in comparison to the other major, industrialized states indicates that Pennsylvania ranks as the state with, by far, the highest benefit costs among its competitors.[5] This makes it more expensive to do business in Pennsylvania and costs the state jobs.

Industrial Homework: The legislative purpose for industrial homework is not wholly without merit. The absence of government regulation does invite abuse of legitimate labor standards, and does place individuals who may be vulnerable at an unfair disadvantage in protecting their legal rights. The problem really is one of overkill, which purposely works to the benefit of labor unions and their organizing efforts. Limitations on industrial homework are so restrictive, they effectively disallow industrial homework except in the most severe cases. This level of restriction forces almost all work into factory and other formal work settings which are locations most accessible to union organizers.

Homework provides advantages for many workers who find it difficult to commute to work in a factory or other setting. The beneficiaries of homework include the disabled, single parents of small children, mothers or fathers of small children whose spouse works outside of the home, people who must be at home to care for an elderly parent, and many other such cases. Excessive restrictions on homework deprive these people of an opportunity to earn an income or force them to find impersonal care, often at high cost, for children or parents. Relaxing regulation of homework to the minimum necessary will help some of those who are worst off in our society. In some cases it may mean the difference between self-support and self-respect on the one hand, and welfare and poverty on the other.

Public Sector Unionization: Pennsylvania labor law is, by and large, limited to the treatment of public employee unions, since federal laws cover any significant aspect of private sector labor relations and collective bargaining. The highest rate of unionization is now found in the government sector. Because public employee unions are increasing in strength in relation to private sector unions, these unions are the rising power center of organized labor and are becoming an ever increasing factor in the political equation. Government unionization is, in some respects, the most insidious and the most problematic, precisely because it merges union and government power so effectively.

All of this said, there is and will likely always be a role for labor unions in employer-employee relations. The problem with collective bargaining laws is excess, not that they exist at all. The essential concept of employees banding together for concerted activity is somewhat akin to the public right to assemble peaceably, and is often borne out of a need for mutual protection against employer disregard or abuse. If certain societal concerns within the employment relationship were adequately addressed in law, labor unions would not be as attractive.

Inadequate Government Actions

There is also the issue of inadequate government involvement in areas of legitimate concern. Given the history of the last fifty years it might be expected that this issue would hardly be a problem from the standpoint of policy-making. That is not the case. The preferential position of labor unions works against placing such policy matters on the political agenda. Employee ownership, for example, which is not, strictly speaking, a labor law issue, has generally not been supported by labor unions. The concept has only recently gained a level of acceptance by labor unions when understood as a means, through friendly or even hostile takeover of a business, of maintaining employment levels in the face of a real or threatened plant closing, or of furthering other social goals not otherwise attainable. Labor unions will generally advance politicization either directly or indirectly by government, but they themselves do not want the responsibility of ownership. The controversial issue of just cause dismissal has, likewise, generally not been supported by labor unions because it presents a direct threat to union organizing. Job security is a powerful organizing argument.

A Pro-Market, Pro-Growth Labor Agenda

What will the labor policies of the Commonwealth be in the 21st century? The proposals that follow are an outline of what those policies should be from a pro-growth perspective. This outline, although offered as a coherent labor policy, presupposes changes in other areas of Pennsylvania law.

Recommendations

1. The minimum wage and the prevailing wage laws should both be repealed. Neither of these laws are justified, and there is little evidence that either ever were. Both only serve the special interests of organized labor unions.

The repeal of the minimum wage, however, does not eliminate the need to address the financial problem of the working poor. As an alternative to the minimum wage, a minimum income supplement should be enacted. The concept of a minimum income supplement is based on the principles of the current federal earned income tax credit. To be eligible for the supplement, an individual should be responsible for the support of a dependent child, or children. The actual amount of the supplement should depend on the number of children in the family and the total annual income of the claimant. The targeted supplement for a family with two children should be equal to, at least, the calculated poverty level for the year. Although the supplement would not affect tax liability, the income tax system should be used as a means of verifying income, and efficiently distributing the compensation either during the year or at year-end.

In stark contrast to the outdated concept of a minimum wage, the minimum income supplement would result in no loss of jobs or job opportunities. It would actually help to stabilize employment. It would have no effect on productivity, and would not be inflationary. It is an effective, targeted public policy that would compensate those citizens who earn low wages and who live in families below certain recognized poverty levels. By so doing, it would serve to increase the attractiveness of work and reduce the attractiveness of welfare.

2. The unemployment insurance program was originally designed and was intended to be structured in a manner that applied the basic principles of workers' compensation insurance to the problem of insuring against the loss of wages by workers who became involuntarily unemployed. The instability and financial excesses of Pennsylvania's unemployment compensation program are a direct result of the failure to structure and maintain our program as an insurance program, using sound insurance principles.

If federal law can be changed to allow it, then the program should be privatized, and operated by the private insurance market. If privatization is impossible, at least the unemployment insurance program should be removed from direct political control and established as an independent state insurance agency which would be responsible for the administration of the entire program, subject to Insurance Department regulation.

Unemployment taxes (i.e., premiums) should be made a direct function of benefit costs, and based upon actuarial calculations and legal principles of insurance rate-making. To the extent permitted by federal law, rates should be classified in a manner similar to the workers' compensation classification system. Adequate reserves should also be established as determined by the responsiveness of the tax program to the changing frequency and severity of claims. Finally, the benefit program should be restructured to eliminate elements of politicization, inequities in the eligibility requirements for claimants, and inequities in the benefits received by claimants. Consideration should be given to what constitutes a fair, sustainable, total cost to employers as a measure of reasonableness.

3. The industrial homework law should be amended to eliminate the provisions that essentially prohibit industrial homework, and to shift the purpose and focus of the law to the regulation of industrial homework. This regulation should be kept to a minimum, with the degree of regulation commensurate with the demonstrated need for it. Federal law has recently been refocused administratively toward this end, with no ill effects.

4. The Pennsylvania Public Employee Relations Act should

be amended to provide for (a) proportional representation by
labor unions, as well as the right of individuals to bargain on
their own behalf, (b) the right of individuals to belong to any
union, or no union at all, (c) contracts for specified services between a labor union and individual nonunion employees, with
the agency fee based on the services actually rendered, (d) non-
collusion, antitrust prohibitions between unions, and (e) secret
ballot strike votes by union members. As an alternative to proportional representation (other of the above items remain the
same), the act should restrict exclusive representation by (1)
requiring regularly recurring elections for representation certification every four years, (2) limiting the length of collective
bargaining agreements to four years, (3) changing the above
noted fee for service contract concept to apply to any employee
who is not a member of the representative union, and (4) requiring that all meetings relating to collective bargaining issues between the public employer and the union be open and subject to
the Sunshine Act. The existing agency shop statute must, of
course, be repealed.

Taken together, these proposed changes will allow for legitimate concerted activities among employees, through labor
unions, if desired. They will also remove the governmental
powers and immunities from labor unions, and restrict their
activities to employment contract concerns.

5. A right to work statute should be enacted, and efforts should
be made to have federal law amended to apply the principles of
the above recommendation (item #4) to private sector labor
unions.

6. The Pennsylvania constitution should be amended to prohibit strikes and lockouts involving all essential public employees, not just police and firemen and, thereby, secure the
right of uninterrupted government service for Commonwealth
citizens.

7. Because work is a fundamental condition of mankind and a
fundamental element in the social contract, the principles of
reciprocity and just cause dismissal should become applicable
for employees who continue employment with an employer
after a probationary period of some number of years. During the
initial probationary period, the doctrine of at-will employment

should remain in force. If an employee is dismissed for reasons other than just cause after the probationary period, dismissal should be with adequate notice or compensation to allow the employee to seek another position. Reciprocally, employees should be required to provide adequate notice of a termination of employment in order to allow an employer sufficient time to hire and train a replacement. Such an arrangement, which is based on biblical principles, would allow for labor market flexibility with stability, and would provide for justified job security. It would also reinforce the basic principle of the right to work by removing a major reason for the need for union representation.

There are three additional proposals of a somewhat different nature that should also be given consideration.

8. Under situations of bankruptcy, the wages of workers are placed in a position in line with creditors to a business. The payment of wages should be set apart and paid first. Employees are not creditors or speculators in a business; their wages are their very livelihood.

9. Efforts should be ongoing to maintain and improve a system of continuing education and job training. The Pennsylvania constitution's mandate for "a thorough and efficient system of public education" is not limited to primary and secondary education. Education is a continuum. The Commonwealth's future economic success and prosperity will depend upon the abilities and the creativity of its citizens more than any other factor. Technology and materials are transferable; our education and skills are rooted solely within the Commonwealth.

10. The labor laws of Pennsylvania should be rationalized and codified, and a unified administrative judicial system for labor law should be established, which should include a corps of administrative law judges, and a restructured and expanded Pennsylvania Labor Relations Board to serve as an appellate administrative law court.

CHAPTER TWELVE

TRANSPORTING PENNSYLVANIA INTO THE 21ST CENTURY

By Kant Rao and James I. Scheiner

EDITOR'S SUMMARY

Transportation is central to Pennsylvania's economy and quality of life. Highways and other modes of transportation are heavily used in the Commonwealth since the state is located astride the Northeast and Midwest regions, with over 40 percent of the nation's marketplace located within a 300 mile radius. Pennsylvania must continue to upgrade its transportation facilities if it hopes to be competitive into the 21st century.

Looking to the future, the Commonwealth's transportation system will be called upon to accomplish two broad missions. 1) To provide safe, dependable, convenient and affordable passenger transportation for Pennsylvania's residents and 2) To provide responsive and competitive goods movement to support Pennsylvania's economy.

New mechanisms must be found to adequately finance the state's capital program. These include public-private partnerships, privatization, and greater use of toll roads. These approaches are needed since it has been estimated that meeting the state's highway capital needs will require a minimum of $100 million in additional state funds annually.

To maximize the amount of money actually spent on road and bridge improvements, it is necessary to slow down the drain on state revenues. In order to accomplish this, PennDOT personnel costs must be held in check to no more than inflation. Also, the program to transfer low-volume roads to local jurisdictions needs to be expanded.

Highway transportation needs require special attention. For example, heavy hauling is of major economic importance, so PennDOT should identify, map, and schedule heavy haul routes which can accommodate oversize shipments. Pennsylvania should also actively participate in national and multistate experiments to apply "smart" technology to the Commonwealth's highways.

Public transportation has a vital role to play in Pennsylvania's future. However, billions of dollars of capital investment are needed to restore and modernize aging physical facilities. In order to bring appropriate equipment and efficient work rules into play, the privatization of mass transportation systems should be considered.

Aviation, rail freight, ports and waterways, and pipelines are other areas of transportation concern. These sectors do not currently receive as much funding and attention as highway issues but will continue to grow in importance into the next century. Recognizing the diversity of transportation modes, PennDOT should establish priorities based on projected ridership, financial commitments from benefiting businesses, and efficiency of service.

Kant Rao is Associate Professor of Business Administration at The Pennsylvania State University and was Associate Deputy Secretary of the Pennsylvania Department of Transportation from 1979-1980.

James I. Scheiner is President and Chief Operating Officer of Stoner Associates, Inc. and served in Governor Richard Thornburgh's Cabinet as Secretary of the Pennsylvania Department of Revenue from 1983-1987.

Transportation is central to Pennsylvania's economy and quality of life. As the "Keystone State," Pennsylvania is strategically located astride the Northeast and Midwest regions. Over 40% of the nation's marketplace is located within a 300 mile radius of Pennsylvania. The provision of safe, efficient and well-managed transportation facilities reduces the cost of conducting social and business activities and provides a competitive advantage to Pennsylvania firms in securing raw materials, providing a quality work environment and reaching markets. The Commonwealth has a rich transportation heritage, including the nation's first toll road (Lancaster Pike) and the nation's first modern limited-access highway (Pennsylvania Turnpike).

Looking to the 21st Century, the Commonwealth's transportation system will be called upon to accomplish two broad missions:

- To provide safe, dependable, convenient and affordable passenger transportation for Pennsylvania residents and visitors;

- To provide safe, responsive and competitive goods movement to support Pennsylvania's economy.

Under these broad missions, there are a large number of transportation issues facing Pennsylvania. In 1989 alone, the Transportation Committee of the Pennsylvania Chamber of Business and Industry has dealt with at least two dozen different transportation issues. In order to provide a brief overview of salient transportation issues facing Pennsylvania in the decades ahead, this chapter is organized around the following transportation modes: highway, public transportation, air, rail freight, waterway/port and pipeline.

Highway Transportation

During the past ten years, Pennsylvania has made dramatic strides in restoring a considerable part of the Interstate System, resurfacing roads and repairing or replacing hundreds of critical bridges. These improvements were made possible by productivity improvements (such as merit hiring practices, value engineering), selected increases in user fees (gas tax and truck fees) to generate more revenues, and leveraging of federal funds.

These accomplishments occurred without any substantial use of general obligation debt, thus avoiding any further increase in the already sizeable debt retirement legacy from the 1970's.

But just as a homeowner must regularly repair his or her home, and just as these repair bills increase as the home becomes older, our 43,000 miles of roads and 27,000 bridges require greater maintenance and repair each year. As Exhibit 1 shows, funds for highway and bridge improvement activities through construction and reconstruction will precipitously decline.[1] According to a 1986 report, repairing our highways and bridges at the cost effective engineering cycles would require about $100 million more expenditures in 1990 than is currently available[2]. The failure to invest this amount, to invest properly, results in longer cycles — i.e., fewer roads and bridges are repaired each year. The results may not be immediately obvious, but they accumulate leading eventually to serious "infrastructure deterioration."

The story is the same nationally. As *The Wall Street Journal* noted,

> Everyone with a car knows that the interstate highway system has a pothole problem. In fact, it's a whole lot worse than that. This vast public works project — by some reckonings the biggest such project in history — is literally falling to pieces . . . This is no mere nuisance; some economists consider it a threat to the nation's productivity as the U.S. relies ever more heavily on highways to move its goods. David Aschauer of the Federal Reserve Bank of Chicago goes so far as to argue that highway deterioration is 'a root cause of the decline of American Competitiveness.'[3]

Inadequate funds for maintenance and upkeep causes a vicious cycle of deferred maintenance, and fixing only when there is failure. Since costs of repair are much greater at failure than preventive maintenance, the budget does not go as far, causing more deferred maintenance. The only cure is to establish a "maintenance first" policy as the Pennsylvania Department of Transportation (PennDOT) has done and get on a preventive cycle of repair. An inadequate maintenance budget also intensifies parochial concerns for allocation of resources. Funds for maintenance should be allocated among counties based on the condition of roads and bridges. PennDOT now has objective systems to collect these road conditions data. Their use in the allocation of funds is the best means of ensuring that the funds will be fairly distributed.

Pennsylvania's current highway capital program has correctly focused on the priority areas of interstate restoration and critical bridge replacement. However, Pennsylvania also has a large number of missing links and much needed bypasses such as on Route 23 in Lancaster County, and Routes 22 and 30 east-west across Pennsylvania. The hilly terrain of the state also has created several hazardous locations especially for truck traffic. Improving these locations and completing missing links and bypasses is enormously expensive and beyond the scope of the current capital program. In addition, the state faces several other pressing issues such as: suburban congestion around our metropolitan areas; needs of fast growing areas such as in the Route 29 and 202 corridors outside Philadelphia; rural Pennsylvania needs both for general mobility and for specific industries such as agriculture, lumber and coal; as well as the deployment of transportation as a tool for economic revitalization in the Mon Valley and in other parts of the state.

Since transportation funds are derived from multiple jurisdictions and multiple tax and debt sources, leverage is an important fiscal factor. Pennsylvania's capital program was leveraged with bond funds in the 1970's and with federal funds in the early 1980's. Looking ahead, the use of bonds must necessarily be limited (due to the already large debt burden), although toll-revenue-supported bonds can play a role as discussed below. On the federal side, current budget deficit problems have capped federal aid for transportation. Unless federal grants for capital programs are substantially increased, it has been estimated that meeting the state's highway capital needs will require a minimum of $100 million in additional state funds annually.[4]

Even with more state funds derived from user fees such as the gas tax, new mechanisms must be found to adequately finance the state's capital program, mechanisms such as: private-public partnerships, privatization, and greater use of toll roads. First phase projects called for in the 1985 toll road legislation improving and extending the Turnpike System are currently progressing towards construction; however, additional toll road projects and expanded use of public-private partnerships may require changes in state and federal laws and these should be pursued through our state and Congressional representatives.

To maximize the amount of money actually spent on road and bridge improvements, it is also necessary to slow down the drain on state revenues. For instance:

- Aggressive risk management and fair tort laws are needed to reduce the millions of annual tort liability payments.

- Personnel costs must be held in check to no more than inflation, offsetting cost increases by productivity savings and personnel reductions.

- Drawdown of highway funds for State Police should be limited to increases of no more than the rate of inflation.

- The program to transfer low-volume roads to local jurisdictions needs to be expanded with additional earmarked funds to increase the service and the efficient maintenance which is possible at the local level.

In Pennsylvania, local jurisdictions (counties, townships, cities, boroughs) are responsible for approximately 66,000 miles of roads and 26,000 bridges. Increases in funds to state programs should be accompanied by increases in payments to local governments for road and bridge maintenance and inspection.

The recommendations suggested above will necessitate raising the state gasoline tax by several cents per gallon over the next few years. This does not mean, however, that the gas tax should be the sole source of new revenue. Automobiles probably should pay about half of this amount. Revenues should be borne fairly by both motorists and commercial vehicles through a combination of fuel levies, licensing fees, and other taxes. The only systematic method for achieving this fairness objective is to base revenue increases on the results of cost allocation studies. Such studies are performed periodically by the federal government and by many states, including recently Pennsylvania. As further experience improves the accuracy of Pennsylvania's studies, they can provide a firm basis for evaluating the fair apportionment between autos and trucks of alternative levels of user fees, and the appropriate mix of specific tax sources.

Since raising taxes, even when they involve user fees earmarked for specific programs, are never quite palatable, the use of long term bonds becomes a tempting alternative for policy makers. Judicious use of bonds can be appropriate, but should be guided by two principles: 1) Issuance of new bonds should be coupled to a new dedicated revenue source for payment of interest and retirement of the principal; 2) Annual debt service (principal and interest payments) should not consume more than one-sixth of annual highway revenues. These benchmarks can prevent the reoccurrence of the fiscal problems of the 1970's.

As Exhibit 1 shows, there are a number of other highway transportation issues requiring attention. Some of these are briefly addressed in paragraphs below:

Uniformity in Commercial Vehicle Transactions: Pennsylvania needs to work aggressively with other states, the National Governors' Association, and the U.S. Department of Transportation to streamline and standardize the processing of commercial vehicle transactions, such as for fleet registration, fuel tax reporting, and permits. PennDOT needs to develop modern information systems in this area to make such standardization possible, as is currently underway in the commercial driver area.

Facilitate Appropriate Heavy Hauling: Heavy trucks can damage roads not designed for such traffic, especially during spring thaw months when the roadbed is in a weakened condition. Heavy hauling can take place with reduced damage when extra axles are added. Recognizing the economic importance of heavy hauling, PennDOT should identify, map, and schedule heavy haul routes which can accommodate oversize and overweight shipments appropriate to the design of the roads involved.

Track Hazardous Cargo: Given the increased truck movements on our state highways, and the potential for hazardous accidents, PennDOT should work with carrier and shipper representatives to systematically monitor hazardous shipments, advise on appropriate routes, and develop contingency plans in the event of mishaps.

Motor Carrier Safety: Research has shown that the most cost-effective way to improve truck safety is voluntary establishment by carriers and shippers of truck safety training programs involving vehicle inspection, preventive maintenance and driver awareness. A modest amount of on-the-road safety inspections is necessary to remove non-complying vehicles off the road, but good results are most likely when the state actively works with the carrier firms to improve self-inspection and training. These actions should be coordinated with appropriate signing on high accident locations, alternate routing, and safety construction improvements.

Use of "Smart" Technology: Pennsylvania should actively participate in national and multistate experiments to apply "smart" technology to roads and vehicles. For example, California is conducting projects to reduce traffic congestion by providing instantaneous feedback to drivers of traffic conditions ahead, while Texas and Michigan are studying automated systems for vehicle guidance and control.

Public Transportation

Public transportation has two vital roles to play. For people without automobile access, public transportation provides mobility. Groups more dependent on public transportation include the young, the elderly, the poor and the physically impaired. In large urban centers, mass transit also provides congestion relief. Commuters can choose to leave their cars at home; those who drive encounter less delays than they would without mass transit.

For these principal reasons, public transportation is subsidized by tax dollars across America. No mass transit system is self-supporting. Typically, half to two-thirds of transit operating expenses are paid with tax dollars, and the entire capital improvement program is funded with federal, state and local grants.

Public transportation in Pennsylvania can be broken down into the following segments:

- Philadelphia Metropolitan Area, with the Southeastern Pennsylvania Transportation Authority (SEPTA) as the primary carrier;

- Pittsburgh Metropolitan Area, with Port Authority Transit (PAT) as the primary carrier;
- Other Urban Areas, with public authorities in a dozen communities (for example, Red Rose Transit Authority in Lancaster and the Luzerne County Transportation Authority in Wilkes-Barre) as primary carriers;
- Small City/Rural Areas, with county governments typically providing and/or coordinating shared-ride services;
- Intercity rail passenger service with Amtrak as the primary carrier and bus service through intercity bus companies.

While issues facing public transportation differ for each segment, one crosscutting issue for the entire Commonwealth is who should pay for the service. What percentage of costs should be paid directly by the riders, and how should local, state and federal governments split the rest of the tab? The federal government has been reducing its funding of mass transportation in response to deficit-cutting pressures. In Pennsylvania, farebox revenue has been relied on for about 50% of operating cost versus a national average that has fallen to about 40%. Annual state appropriations for operating assistance (out of the General Fund) and for senior citizens' rides (out of the Lottery Fund) have grown beyond the rate of inflation as public transportation costs have risen and as federal support has shrunk. Unlike most other states, in which specific taxes are earmarked for local transit support, local funding in Pennsylvania is provided out of general funds via the annual budget process. Pennsylvania's transit agencies have long argued for "predictable funding," a dedicated regional tax piggybacked on either the broad-based sales or personal income taxes.

The sustenance of public transportation into the 21st century depends upon achieving mutual understanding between transit agencies and: 1) their customers; and 2) their supporting governments. Transit agencies must pledge to their customers a high level of service quality — service that is safe, dependable, convenient, and comfortable. In turn, customers must use that service. It makes no sense to run a transit bus for the benefit of a handful of riders. The "use it or lose it" message must be clear.

In return for stable funding, transit agencies must make a pledge of efficiency to their supporting governments. Transit is a labor-intensive industry, with salaries and fringe benefits of bus/rail operators, mechanics and other employees making up 75% or more of total operating expenses. Restraint in growth of salary/fringe costs and increased labor productivity are key to maintaining government support. In Pennsylvania, transit agencies typically enjoy salary scales significantly above those of municipal governments. Transit managers typically earn more than their municipal counterparts (currently, the highest paid public official in Pennsylvania heads a transit agency), and bus drivers typically earn more than police, fire or sanitation workers. Over time, these differentials should become less, not more, pronounced. Transit productivity suffers from the peak nature of the demand for service. Phasing in part-time operators who work either the working or afternoon peak periods, and phasing out full-time work assignments where an operator drives the morning and afternoon peaks while getting paid for much of the time in between, would substantially increase productivity. Competitive procurement of contract services such as for vanpooling or suburban community minibus/van routes could add ridership with less cost and greater flexibility than providing the same service through conventional means.

In the Philadelphia Metropolitan Area, a critical 21st Century issue is the fate of the commuter rail system. Billions of dollars of capital investment are needed to restore and modernize aging physical facilities. There will not be enough public money to do the entire job. Priorities must be established based on current ridership, financial commitments from benefiting businesses and capability to promote higher-density land uses. The politically easy solution of spending a little money on every line must be resisted. Instead major investments should be concentrated on priority lines, to replicate the quality of service achieved by the Delaware River Port Authority's Lindenwold Hi-Speed Line.

In intercity rail service, the 21st Century holds the potential for the use of new technology, some currently in service in Japan and Europe (high speed, steel wheels on steel rails transportation) and some still in experimental stages (magnetic levitation) for medium distance transportation (air has no rival over long distances — i.e., over 500 miles). Studies have shown that the potential of this technology is high for both mobility and service.

Preliminary results also show that, given the current state of engineering, the service may be prohibitively expensive.[5] Until the technology learning curve brings the cost down or conventional alternatives (air, auto, etc.) become more costly due to such factors as rising energy prices or congestion, we must continue to work with and improve upon existing rail service. In the heavily populated Philadelphia-Harrisburg corridor, rail service has deteriorated as a result of Amtrak operating constraints. Privatization of this service, to bring appropriate equipment and efficient work rules into play, would enable the line to add trips and stabilize fares.

Aviation

In the past decade, Pennsylvania has substantially increased state aid for aviation programs, from about $1 million in 1980 to about $6.5 million in 1988. Funded by user fees on jet fuel and aviation gasoline, these revenues finance the state share of federally assisted airport improvement projects, runway and taxiway rehabilitation, runway marking, and reimbursements to public-use airports for real estate taxes paid to local governments on the non-revenue generating portions of the airports. These efforts are designed to slow down or eliminate the decline in the number of airports in the state and to modernize them. This is important because of the shift in the economy from manufacturing to service which places an emphasis on fast, reliable means of transportation, and which has led to increasing use by firms of small shipment air freight carriers.

PennDOT has also improved the financial performance of the state-owned Harrisburg International Airport, so that it can be self-sustaining. However, efforts to interest local governments in taking over the airport have not been successful. The state, through its economic development budget, is financially participating in the building of the new terminal at Pittsburgh which, when completed, should assist further economic development in the area.

At commercial airports, airline deregulation initially increased service, but now threatens to reduce competition as airline mergers take effect. Both state and federal governments can preserve a dominant position at any one hub. When one airline gets more than 50% of gate assignments at a commercial airport, this should be a warning signal that competition could be restricted.

Rail Freight Transportation

During the past two decades, Pennsylvania has seen a vast reduction in its rail network, from over 10,000 miles in 1970 to about 6,000 miles in 1989. The bankruptcies of Penn Central and other northeastern railroads, the subsequent creation of Conrail, the sale of Conrail by the federal government and its successful return to the private sector, all have had a profound change on shippers and goods movement in Pennsylvania.

Despite these changes, the 1987 Comprehensive Rail Study estimated that hundreds of miles of additional rail lines are at risk of being abandoned in the future.[6] The lines most likely to be abandoned are those with low or declining traffic, where parallel or alternative routings exist, and where significant investment may be necessary for continuation of service. Some of these abandonments may be the direct result of anticipated reductions in bulk traffic, such as coal and steel, as the economies of the state reflects the national trend towards a service economy and may have little consequences. Other lines, however, may cause some firms or industries to relocate or cease production, thereby leading to local unemployment and possibly, adverse effects on the highway system due to additional truck traffic.

The Commonwealth has responded to the events of the past with the establishment of several programs to acquire and preserve rail lines deemed essential, to rehabilitate lines to preserve or restore service, and to encourage local communities and shortline operators to actively become involved in maintenance of service. The Comprehensive Rail Study recommends continuation of these programs as well as suggesting several new options. Many of these options can be carried out at no or modest cost, such as suggestions for more active state involvement in assisting shortlines form insurance pools (to deal with liability premiums), joint procurement arrangements (for purchasing track maintenance materials and equipment), and identifying new businesses which can be located on these at-risk lines to generate additional traffic. Existing economic development programs of the state can be expanded and utilized to support investment in rail infrastructures to assist in attracting new businesses.

The Commonwealth faces a number of other rail issues, some of which are noted in Exhibit 1, but the most critical of these involves clearances. Rail lines in Pennsylvania do not have adequate vertical clearances to permit the use, for example, of double stacked trains or tri-level automobile carriers. However, elimination of the clearance issue alone may be insufficient, as other factors, such as the nature of the traffic, and the routes and ports involved in the case of intermodal movements, may also be significant. The state can play a coordination role by working with major rail and intermodal carriers, shippers, and port authorities to determine the set of joint actions needed to facilitate these goods movements. Existing economic development programs can be utilized to undertake public-private partnerships where a state investment can serve as a catalyst and where the benefits are clearly apparent. The state should also continue the policy of eliminating clearance problems on state highway and bridge projects which affect rail/highway clearances.

Ports and Waterways

In a world economy, ports and waterways play an important transportation role. Pennsylvania has three water outlets for world trade: ports of the Delaware River, Pittsburgh area riverfronts, and the Port of Erie.

The ports of the Delaware River consist of facilities along both sides of the river, stretching from Trenton, New Jersey in the north through Philadelphia to Wilmington, Delaware in the south. Nineteen separate organizations, public and private, are involved in port activities. The Delaware River Port Authority (DRPA), created by Pennsylvania and New Jersey state governments, has the title, but not the authority, to coordinate investments in and management of the ports. In Philadelphia, both DRPA and the Port of Philadelphia Corporation have some jurisdiction, but neither has the central authority available to port administrations in Baltimore, New York, or Norfolk.

The ports of the Delaware River have been losing market share to ports in Hampton Roads, Baltimore and metropolitan New York/New Jersey. All of these competing ports have spent far more on landside investments, such as intermodal loading and containerized cargo handling, than has the Philadelphia region. Many of these ports provide various incentives to attract business such as container volume discounts for terminal operators, consolidation of freight for smaller organizations, and ease of billing and documentation. Currently, the Philadelphia Port does much more import than export business. Over 90% of the Pennsylvania exports shipped from the Atlantic ports depart via Baltimore and New York — less than 10% leaves from Philadelphia.[7]

In Western Pennsylvania, the Allegheny and Monongahela Rivers are northeastern branches of our vast inland waterway system, with the Ohio River running generally southwest from Pittsburgh to the Mississippi River trunk. Erie has a Great Lakes port, which can be used for both laker traffic and ocean transport via the St. Lawrence Seaway. In both of these situations, the economic competitiveness of Pennsylvania's facilities is dependent on national investments and national (or international) policies on user charges (the St. Lawrence Seaway is a joint U.S.-Canada agency). Two key facilities in Pennsylvania, Lock and Dam 7 and 8 on the Monongahela River have received Congressional authorization for reconstruction. The competitiveness of the ports is often enhanced by investments made in downstream facilities, such as the Gallipolis Lock on the Ohio River in Ohio, or in the case of the Great Lakes in ice breaking operations to extend the navigation season and improvements at the Welland Canal (connecting Lake Erie to Lake Ontario and the Seaway).

Public monies spent on Pennsylvania ports and waterways should be guided by two principles. First, investments should be export-driven, not driven by the chasing of imports of final goods. (Imports of raw materials and components are also important to the international competitiveness of Pennsylvania firms.) They should be based on a sound export strategy, to include commitments from prospective exporters. Second, investments should be contingent on evidence of professional management in the various port agencies. Qualifications of staff, budget controls, track record or project completions, and success in attracting new business are among the criteria by which port agencies can be evaluated.

Pipelines

Pipelines are the invisible transportation mode. Natural gas pipelines provide more than 600 billion cubic feet of products for Pennsylvania consumption each year — about 25% of this gas comes from wells within our state. Pipelines also transport about 1.5 billion cubic feet across Pennsylvania annually.[8] Pennsylvania is also served by a number of petroleum pipelines, operated by Sun, Buckeye and about another dozen other companies. Pennsylvania's extensive pipeline network is the result of both the state's long history as an oil and gas producer and its location between the principal U.S. oil and gas producing areas and the industrial northeast.

Construction of pipelines has fallen prey to the "NIMBY" syndrome — Not In My Backyard. While this is an understandable individual reaction, governance by NIMBY is bad public policy. Incidents of environmental damage done by pipeline companies, such as dumping of water polluting chemicals, have raised legitimate community concerns. Prior to construction, pipeline companies are obligated to satisfy these concerns.

Pipelines are an important component to Pennsylvania's quality of life. No mode of transportation is safer, less expensive, or less intrusive than pipelines. Putting all petroleum and the oil-equivalent of natural gas onto highways would be a public safety and economic catastrophe.

Public policy should support pipelines by giving their owners an adequate rate of return, and by giving owners a definite timetable for projects subject to meeting clear environmental and safety standards. The Commonwealth should give special priority and assistance to pipeline projects which will more economically transport gas from Pennsylvania wells to markets. As the 10th largest producer of natural gas, Pennsylvania should improve access to this domestically produced, environmentally superior energy source.

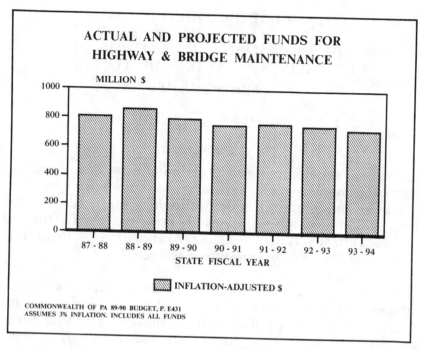

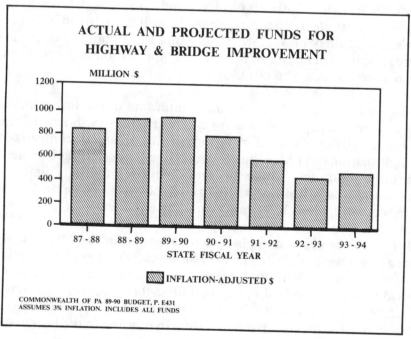

EXHIBIT 1

CHAPTER THIRTEEN

THE INFORMATION REVOLUTION IN PENNSYLVANIA'S ECONOMIC FUTURE
By Kevin F. Harley

EDITOR'S SUMMARY

The most powerful force changing our world today is the continuing information revolution. This revolution has spawned a new era of computer and communications technology. Like electricity, the information revolution is a source of power which, if harnessed and used effectively, will transform a range of fields, including: politics, technology, business, and science.

If Pennsylvania is to become a national and world leader in this new information economy, then our policy makers must prepare for the future. Pennsylvania policy makers must realize that while technological breakthroughs and advances are likely to occur and have positive impacts our lives and economy, they are by no means guaranteed. In the absence of a well thought out information technology policy, the Commonwealth could become increasingly dependent on other states and nations for products, labor, services, and technological direction.

Smaller is better. This is a fundamental fact of the information revolution, and is born out of quantum physics. Some of the characteristics of the information revolution are: decentralized organizations replace large centralized bureaucracies; geographic boundary lines become inconsequential; distance evaporates as a limiting social and business barrier; and most importantly, ideas have powerful consequences.

Just as the combustion engine produced power for the 20th Century industrial revolution, the computer is producing the power for the information revolution. Although computer technology has made great strides in a relatively short span of time, today's computers have barely begun to reach their full potential and are roughly the equivalent of the telegraph machine in relation to the latter version of the telephone.

A fiber optic network is the cornerstone to the future development and modernization of information technology. The fiber optic network will serve as the communication highway for the information age in which our economy will flow. Many state policy leaders recognize its economic importance. Iowa Governor Terry Branstad in his most recent State of the State Address, called for the development of a state-wide fiber optic network to strengthen Iowa's economic position in the 21st century.

Pennsylvania policy makers must aggressively set in motion policies which will make Pennsylvania the keystone of the information age. Such polices would include using state and local governments as a catalyst for the widespread implementation of a fiber optic network and creating a regulatory climate that will keep pace with evolving technology and marketplaces.

Kevin F. Harley serves as Legislative Liaison and Research Associate for The Commonwealth Foundation.

The most powerful force changing our world today is the continuing information revolution. This revolution has been spawned by a new era of computer and communications technology. Just as our great-grandparents had no idea what impact electricity would have on their lives, today many feel that we have just begun to witness the potential impact that the information revolution will have on our lives. Like electricity, the information revolution is a source of power which, if harnessed and used effectively, will transform a range of fields, including politics, technology, business, and science. The information revolution will undoubtedly alter the way in which individuals live their lives.

If Pennsylvania is to become a national and world leader in this new information economy, then our policy makers must prepare for the future. It has been wisely stated that the most reliable way to anticipate the future is to understand the present. Pennsylvania policy makers must realize that while technological breakthroughs and advances are likely to occur and have positive impacts on our lives and economy, they are by no means guaranteed.

This chapter will briefly examine the effects the information revolution has had on our society. Additional focus will be given to the direction in which information technology is headed, and how Pennsylvania policy makers must prepare for the challenges and opportunities that will be presented.

In the absence of a well thought out information technology policy that reflects a clear understanding of the future, Pennsylvania could become increasingly dependent on other states and nations for products, labor, services, and technological direction.

To have a clear perception of the future direction of the information revolution, policy makers need to have a general understanding of the interaction of its three key components:

(1) The transition from the macrocosm to the microcosm.
(2) The future development of computers.
(3) The fiber optic wiring of our communities.

From the Macrocosm to the Microcosm

Smaller is better. As strange as this may sound, it is nonetheless a fundamental fact of the information revolution, and is borne out of quantum physics. It has produced what George Gilder calls the "microcosm," the overthrow of matter in a quantum world.[1] Some of the characteristics of the microcosm are: knowledge produces power; information wealth replaces material or physical wealth; decentralized organizations replace large centralized bureaucracies; geographic boundary lines become inconsequential; distance evaporates as a limiting social and business barrier; and perhaps most importantly, ideas have powerful consequences.

The microcosm of the information revolution is in direct contrast to the macrocosm of the industrial revolution, which emphasized that bigger is better, and that the value of a product is in its material substance. The effects of the microcosm can be seen in the world of science and technology, as well as in business and politics.

Science and Technology: The microcosm is perhaps best exemplified in the microchip. Most Americans take the microchip for granted, not knowing that it is in products ranging from the automobile to microwaves and thermostats. The microchip essentially functions as a computer, which calculates millions of bits of information at a billionth of a second on an area the size of a fly's wing. In contrast to a traditional product or invention, the material cost of the microchip is less than 1% of the total cost of the product because it is made from the most common substances on earth — sand, metal and air. The microchip derives its value from its intellectual content, based on design and software, not from its material substance.[2]

The principles of the microcosm can also be seen in what is perhaps the greatest scientific breakthrough discovery since electricity, the superconductor. As this technology progresses, the practical applications of the superconductor will have a tremendous impact on our lives. Some of the applications will be: battery operated cars with super lightweight and powerful motors; fast supercomputers the size of a home computer; bullet trains that travel hundreds of miles per hour; and limitless and cheap long-term energy sources which will not threaten the environment, but will dramatically reduce dependence on fossil fuels.[3]

Business: Signs of the microcosm can be seen in business through the movement toward decentralization. In the 1980's, corporations on the cutting edge of their respective fields introduced the small team concept and quality control circles. John Naisbitt writes in his book *Re-inventing the Corporation* that we are entering a dynamic period when a more competitive, productive work force is leading us back to the values of "trust, freedom, and respect for the individual."[4]

Additionally, we have seen small business replace large corporations as the primary source of new wealth and jobs. It is no accident that small businesses are producing the lion's share of jobs and wealth. For example, 97.7% of all businesses in Pennsylvania have less than 100 employees.[5]

Politics: The impact of the microcosm can also be felt in American political circles where greater emphasis is being placed on local and state governments. Today, state legislatures are playing an ever increasing policy making role in national affairs. As John Naisbitt states in his book *Megatrends*, "state and local governments are the most important governments in America — they have rediscovered the ability to act innovatively and to achieve results."[6]

The contrast between the macrocosm and microcosm on a global scale can be seen in the success of the democratically elected Pacific Island countries over the last twenty years, in comparison to the large communist countries of Eastern Europe.

Most of the Pacific Island countries do not possess enormous natural resources. They are not large land masses, nor do they have great armies, yet economically they have become one of the most powerful forces in the world. On the other hand, the communist countries of Eastern Europe possess some of the largest land masses in the world, strongest armies, as well as some of the earth's richest natural resources, yet their economies have consistently been in shambles.

Indeed, we have recently witnessed many of these Eastern European powers succumb to the liberating effects of the microcosm. In the microcosm, power is obtained through information, ideas, and knowledge — not by dictators, walls and armies.

By gaining an insight into the microcosm, one can better understand the changes that the information revolution is having on the world. The main vehicle for this change has been the invention and development of the computer. Just as the combustion engine produced power for the 20th century industrial revolution, the computer is producing the power of the information revolution.

The Computer

A brief history of the computer reveals how rapidly it has developed in a relatively short span of time. In the early days of computer technology, computers were mammoth machines comprised of a maze of wires and vacuum tubes, which had few practical applications. As the computer progressed, only government agencies, large corporations, and universities could afford these oversized computers that required specialized programmers.

During the 1970's most computers still relied on punch cards, were very expensive and were not a practical expenditure for small and medium sized businesses. However, during the 1980's as computer technology progressed, personal desk top computers (PC's) became much more powerful and practical than their large and bulky predecessors. Also, during the 1980's venture capitalists discovered the Silicon Valley, and upstart computer firms cropped up overnight. The computer became as important to American business as the telephone and copy machine.

In addition to computers, the Silicon Valley produced a new breed of inventor/entrepreneur. Men such as Steve Jobs, formerly of Apple and presently with Next Computer Company, and Bill Gates of Microsoft, became known in computer circles as the Thomas Edison and Alexander Graham Bell of our generation.

The Computer of the Future: As computer firms continue to pour millions of dollars into researching new technologies, the next stage of development for computers will likely produce "smart" computer software that utilizes artificial intelligence and which functions on the model of the human brain.

Currently, computers only process information that has been entered, but do not have the ability to act independently or have the capability to "think" logically. If most of today's computers were compared to a human, they would be deaf, dumb, and blind.

Although computer technology has made great strides, compared to what has been projected, computers are indeed still in their infant stages. Today's computers have barely begun to reach their full potential and are roughly the equivalent of the telegraph machine in relation to the modern version of the telephone. Nevertheless, today's computer is four million times as powerful per dollar of cost, as its 1962 predecessor.[7] In addition, between 1961 and 1989, the speed of a computer operation increased 230,000 fold.[8]

It is difficult to fathom the technological changes that are likely to take place as we approach the 21st century. Yet one needs only to take an inventory of their office or home to see how far we have advanced in just the last two decades. Twenty years ago, color television sets were just beginning to be mass produced, the VCR and camcorders had not been invented, and nobody had heard of personal home computers. And the wide spread use of cellular phones, compact discs and fax machines were nothing more than an inventor's dream.

The next stage of technological development will likely take all of these wonderful and time saving inventions and combine them into one remarkable machine that will serve as a super-computer; videophone; compact disc player, (that will store video as well as written data); and a printer/fax machine (that will be able to transmit data with near perfect clarity). The uses of such a machine in the home and office will be boundless. Some of the varied uses will be:

Telecommuting and Teleworking: By working at home on a personal computer, an individual will be able to access information and materials as well as teleconferencing face-to-face with colleagues.

Personal Libraries: Consumers will have a limitless capacity for the storage of print, music, video, and still pictures. Additionally, it will provide a remote library service to remote electronic access to virtually any material published.

Retailing: Consumers will purchase a full range of consumer goods via their TV screen. Customers will be able to try on clothes on their TV screen by a computer simulated image that is proportionally correct to the consumer. Products would be delivered to their residence and payment made by direct debit.

Information and Entertainment: The sale of up to the minute news, instant stock information, pay-per-view movies, special sports programs, pay-per-listen radio, and video games will all be accessible to the consumer.

Educational Process: Remote classrooms will make it possible to see and hear a class via a home screen. Class assignments, exams, and submission of student homework will be done through the computer screen or keyboard. Students will also be able to access information through electronic libraries and be able to have face-to-face counseling by videophone.

Documents: The home computer screen will act as a means of distributing documents such as: coupons, tickets, newspapers, etc., and allow for two-way capability letting consumers send out letters, forms, and photos.

Financial Services and Banking: Stocks and other financial transactions will be made via computer screens. Consumers will be able to bank at home and have direct electronic deposits and checkbook balancing through their computer.

Security and Surveillance: Telemetric (remote) monitoring alarms will automatically notify police if an intruder breaks into a house or an apartment.

Travel: The bookings of flights, hotels, and tours will be made over a screen similar to those already used by travel agents. The computer will also be used as an electronic travel brochure for information and promotion.

Medical Consultation and Monitoring: Telemetric devices will enable a doctor at another location to monitor an individual's heart rate as well as other vital signs. This data would also be able to go directly to a medical computer for automatic analysis. Sophisticated computer imaging such as (MRI, CAT, X-ray) will be transmitted over phone lines or from emergency vehicles via cellular telephones. Face-to-face counseling from a doctor in a remote location will be possible by videophones.[9]

Following the lead of the telephone, television, and VCR, the computer will eventually become more affordable and "user friendly". By the turn of the century, the computer will become an accepted consumer staple, used by the young and old alike, in nearly every American household.

The Fiber Optic Wiring of Our Communities

While the future "Information Age" promises to be exciting with products that will make our lives easier and more productive, many of the services that can be available to consumers and business hinge on the installation of a fiber optic network.

The fiber optic network is the cornerstone to the future development and modernization of information technology. The fiber optic network, or more accurately called a "broadband" network, is a complicated system of powerful computer switches, complex computer software and optical fiber cable. It is known as broadband because of its ability to carry a broad range of telephone, video, radio and computer signals all at the same time. The most important aspect of broadband is the optical fiber wiring, which would replace traditional copper wiring. Seventy pounds of fiber optic cable can transmit as many messages as one ton of copper wire, and those seventy pounds of fiber optic cable require less than 5% of the energy needed to produce one ton of copper wire.[10]

A Communication Highway: The fiber optic network will serve as the communications highway for the information age in which our economy will flow. Throughout our history we have seen important advances made in the field of transportation to promote economic growth and expand individual opportunity. In the early 1800's the Erie Canal was built, which was followed by the transcontinental railroad. In this century, we saw the construction of the Pennsylvania Turnpike, the first of its kind in the nation, and the establishment of the interstate highway system. Additionally, nearly every major city in America has made capital expenditures for airports.

Competition with Other States and Nations: Already nations such as Japan, Spain, France, and even Singapore are building telecommunication networks at a much faster rate than the United States. The United States, had a projected telecommunications growth rate for 1988-89 of .06%, in comparison to West

Germany's expenditures, which grew at 4.9%, and Singapore, which had a projected rate for 1989 of 25%.[11] In these countries the political and business leaders recognize the economic advantages of upgrading their existing telecommunication networks. For example, Japan is in the process of spending $150 billion to modernize its fiber optic network.[12]

The race for the expansion and modernization of the telecommunications infrastructure is not limited to other nations. Many state policy leaders also recognize its economic importance. Iowa Governor Terry Branstad, in his most recent State of the State Address, called for the development of a state-wide fiber optic network to strengthen Iowa's economic position in the 21st century.

A fiber optic network wired directly to the home is being established by various phone companies to a limited degree in some U.S. communities, including the town of Perryopolis, Pennsylvania. However, at the current rate of installation, it will take approximately 30 years for the United States to be wired with a fiber optic network. This will put our state and nation at a distinct economic disadvantage relative to our foreign counterparts.

Obstacles to the Fiber Optic Network: Looking back on the great transportation projects in American history, it is difficult to imagine what the economic development of our nation and state would have been like without them. However, each of these projects faced roadblocks in one form or another. Obstacles came in various forms: limited resources, short-sighted politicians, businesses that thought they would be adversely affected, citizens who were opposed to change, and from individuals who thought that the money could be better spent on other programs or projects. Not surprisingly, the installation of a fiber optic network also faces many of the same challenges.

Cost: The cost of installing a fiber optic network is monumental. It has been estimated that it would cost $100 billion to install a fiber optic network in just half of the U.S. households.[13] This high cost is a major reason for the slow progress.

Regulations: Besides the high cost of installation, another obstacle to the fiber optic network is the current regulatory climate of the telecommunications industry. Most notably are the regulations on the Bell operating companies, which were born out of Judge Harold Green's famous consent decree that resulted in the breakup of American Telephone and Telegraph. The consent decree prohibits the Bell operating companies (Baby Bells) from three areas of activity: information services, long distance, and manufacturing.

The Bell companies would like the regulations to be relaxed, which would allow them to offer new customer services, thereby giving an incentive to install and finance much of the fiber optic network. Under the current regulations, there is not enough of an economic incentive for the Baby Bells to make such a move. Their current situation could be compared to a computer company which is only allowed to produce computer hardware (the actual machine), but would be prohibited from developing or manufacturing software, which is the real source of wealth and power.

Regulatory policy both throughout the United States and in Pennsylvania is not keeping up with technological changes. Regulations that may have been effective when our goal was to reach every home in Pennsylvania with basic telephone service, are today undermining incentives to modernize our infrastructure and improve our economic competitiveness. Regulators should not view themselves in a reactive role, but rather should perceive their jobs as developers of technology, which in turn will have long term benefits to the economy and consumers.

The installation of a fiber optic network also faces opposition from vested business interests who feel they would be adversely affected by the network or through the relaxation of regulations. One such group is the American Newspaper Publishers Association which is afraid that revenue currently obtained from classified advertisements would sharply decline because the consumer would be able to obtain information services through a fiber optic network. Other groups include the National Cable Television Association and the National Association of Broadcasters who are opposed to the Baby Bell's entry into the information service field because of competition.

Conclusion

This year Pennsylvania is celebrating the golden anniversary of the Pennsylvania Turnpike, our nation's first superhighway.

Just as we led the country with a modern highway system in the 20th century, we also have the opportunity to be the first state to construct a telecommunication network that will serve as the highway system of the 21st century.

In order for Pennsylvania to develop such a communication highway, local and state policy makers must consider the following policy recommendations:

— Use state and local governments as a catalyst for the widespread implementation of a fiber optic network by installing the network in government buildings.

— Create a regulatory climate that will keep pace with evolving technology and marketplaces.

— Explore innovative financing measures and favorable tax laws which will stimulate investment to build a fiber optic network.

Today, Pennsylvania policy makers must realize the permanent socioeconomic changes that were a result of the transition from the industrial age to the information age. They must have an unblurred vision of what a positive impact computer and telecommunication technologies will have on our economy and quality of life. Pennsylvania policy makers must aggressively set in motion policies which will enable Pennsylvania to be the keystone of the information age. If they fail, the future may leave us behind.

CHAPTER FOURTEEN

PRODUCING GROWTH: INFRASTRUCTURE IMPROVEMENT, ENTERPRISE ZONES AND SOUND ECONOMIC DEVELOPMENT POLICY

By Jordan P. Krauss

EDITOR'S SUMMARY

Pennsylvania has suffered economic dislocation on a grand scale, losing 400,000 manufacturing jobs between 1974 and 1983. However, during this time the state underwent a metamorphosis whose visible signs were not seen until 1985, when the state began to keep pace with the national economy in new job creation and in reduced unemployment.

The state government has some important responsibilities to promote continued economic growth in the future. The state must remain strong and competitive by insuring that government is well managed; that infrastructure is modern and well-maintained; that environmental quality is uncompromised; and that the education system produces a well-qualified workforce. Also direct state investment in economic development should avoid chasing private dollars in an effort to turn bureaucrats into dealmakers.

High quality infrastructure most immediately bears on a state's competitive advantage. Deferring infrastructure investments any longer will result in fewer business investments and threats to the safety of citizens. Without these investments, Pennsylvania cannot hope to remain an attractive place to live and work.

The state remains the one governmental body with the management capacity and the ability to find the resources needed to make these investments. It will take dollars to pay for improvements. Among the funding possibilities that state policymakers are using are private sector-public sector infrastructure funding partnerships, privatizing certain municipal services, user fees, and transportation taxes. A special 21st Century Fund could be established to oversee these infrastructure improvements.

The state-administered enterprise zone program begun in 1982 represents a basic state allocation of only $7 million a year, but to date has stimulated hundreds of millions of dollars in new private sector investment. Enterprise zones are a partnership venture between the public and private sectors that is administered by the state. In the first four years of operation, over $225 million in private investments were made, and 5,400 new jobs and 377 new businesses were created.

The U.S. Commerce Department in 1989 noted that Pennsylvania's enterprise zone program is more successful than those in other states. To ensure this success, state funds budgeted for "legislative initiatives" should instead be used to support and expand the enterprise zone program which could result in more than a billion dollars in new private investment, thousands of new jobs, and hundreds of new businesses in the state's most distressed areas. A renewed emphasis on enterprise zones would have a significant impact on Pennsylvania's economic performance in the coming decades.

Jordan P. Krauss is a policy consultant and former Executive Deputy Director of the Pennsylvania Governor's Cabinet Committee on Economic Development.

In their recent study entitled *The Book of America: Inside the 50 States Today*, Neil Pierce and Jerry Hogstrom began their section on Pennsylvania with the subtitle "State of Magnificent Decline." To many observers in the 1980s the only argument with the authors' title would have been a question on their choice of the word magnificent. "Precipitous" is the word the citizens of Pennsylvania might themselves have chosen.

Between 1974 and 1983, Pennsylvania lost 400,000 manufacturing jobs. Perhaps even more staggering is the fact that the loss of manufacturing jobs in Pennsylvania accounted for roughly 20% of all manufacturing jobs lost nationally during that period. This is economic dislocation on a grand scale. Again this job loss was further compounded by its concentration in two industries, primary metals, and textiles and apparel.

Perhaps the most dramatic and visual change was the shrinkage and restructuring of the domestic steel industry. This major dislocation in our national economy had a tremendous and painful effect on much of western Pennsylvania, especially the historic mill towns of the Monongahela Valley. This same kind of economic loss occurred in Northeast Pennsylvania as a substantial number of textile operations closed down, moved to the South, or went offshore.

Looking at Pennsylvania then, especially in the early part of this decade, an observer might have been tempted to write the state off as an aging dinosaur — a graying population; continued population loss of young people; an industrial capacity no longer in demand; and an infrastructure wholly inadequate for new economic development.

The truth, however, was that Pennsylvania was undergoing a metamorphosis in the early part of the decade whose visible manifestation would not be readily apparent until 1985 — when Pennsylvania began to keep pace with the national economy in new job creation and in reduced levels of unemployment.

The purpose of this very cursory survey is to identify two important responsibilities of state government to promote continued economic growth in the coming decades.

First, the state's most important obligation is to remain strong and competitive by insuring that state government is well managed; that its infrastructure is modern and well-maintained; that environmental quality is uncompromised; and that the system of education produces a well-qualified workforce.

Second, that direct state investment in economic development should avoid chasing private dollars in a copycat effort to turn bureaucrats into dealmakers.

In particular, this chapter focuses on the need to introduce, finance, and manage a *21st Century Fund* to promote the rehabilitation and development of our infrastructure as a critical ingredient in the state's global obligation to promote competitive advantage. It also briefly examines the state funded enterprise zone program as an example where discrete state investment has won national recognition in achieving results and as a program where renewed investment is needed.

The Politics of Economic Development

Beginning in the 1980s, government at all levels both here and throughout the country was concentrating on supporting and securing new private, job-generating investments. Governments were also busy taking credit for every new investment made, no matter how tenuous or chimerical the public sector support given. I recall one particular state Department of Commerce memo in the mid-1980s which sought to show the ability of state investment to leverage private investment by pointing to a leverage ratio of one public dollar for every 15 dollars of new private investment made within a particular program. No doubt it never occurred to the author of the memo that at that rate, public funds had long since passed from the category of leverage to one of gravy.

This is not to say that government, particularly state government, does not play an important, even crucial role in the economic well-being of its citizens; but rather that its direct investment in economic development generally has more to say about political goals than economic development.

There are numerous reasons for the public sector's limited role in guiding economic development, not the least of which is the nominal amount of funding support for investment in economic activity. As recently as 1986, the Pennsylvania Business Roundtable estimated that less than 1% of Pennsylvania's $9 billion annual general fund budget was allocated for direct support of economic development projects. Beyond that, there is some question whether government is institutionally equipped or sophisticated enough to guide an overall economic policy. The forces and demands of the marketplace — its sense of urgency, risk taking, and entrepreneurship seldom find a receptive audience in the world of the public sector, with its endless reporting forms; risk aversion, and near glacial bureaucratic response to every new initiative.

Further, the market economy — global and diffuse, with its enormous capital and technological resources routinely outstrips the capacity of even its most knowledgeable experts to direct its performance or behavior. Government, at any level, is even less likely to have the capacity to understand the marketplace. Still, nearly all politicians find it difficult to resist seeking the warm glow of achievement which comes from announcing the creation of new jobs and building a better tomorrow.

For example, in the early 1980s, then Governor Dick Thornburgh vowed that his administration would not be a smokestack chaser — a reference to earlier attempts among the various states to lure new large-scale industrial facilities within their borders. Given that the primary metals industry was suffering billions of dollars in losses and that the automotive industry was reeling from loss of market share to imports, the likelihood of any smokestacks available to chase was remote at best. Yet when General Motors announced its decision to build a new modern facility to construct the "Saturn", even Governor Thornburgh was compelled to join the pilgrimage of governors to Detroit to compete in the Saturn sweepstakes.

An additional charm is the tremendous discretionary nature of so much of the public money targeted to economic development. In Pennsylvania, the General Assembly has entered into the economic development act, not satisfied with merely allowing governors to spend all the money and get all the glory. (Of this recent phenomenon there will be more later.) For this reason, states and cities have created a plethora of programs designed to spur new development. A recent catalogue of state programs, listed 26 state-backed programs aimed at securing new private investment with public sector financing.

States have also entered into the "numbers game" by identifying the number of jobs created that would not otherwise have occurred absent public investment. For example, the Commonwealth recently published its program performance on job creation, citing nearly 50,000 jobs created with public sector support in the combined calendar years of 1987 and 1988. Yet the state Department of Labor and Industry identified total employment in the non-agricultural sector increasing by only 132,000 positions during that period. Subtracting the number of jobs created in government and retail trades, an area not supported by public finance, reduces the number to 100,000. Again, while the Department of Labor and Industry identifies 13,000 new manufacturing positions created in the 1987-88 period, the program performance publication identifies 10,561 manufacturing jobs created during that same period through government financial assistance.

This kind of data collection is either cause for rejoicing or alarm depending upon one's point of view. If the Commonwealth is responsible for generating half the new jobs created in the state, and well over two-thirds of all the manufacturing jobs, it is a testament to the targeting of very modest resources relative to the investment of the private sector. If these jobs would not have occurred, absent public sector support, which is one of the criteria for providing public investment, then clearly these state programs are the principal engine running our economy, and any reduction in funding could have the most dire consequences.

An alternative conclusion, however, could be drawn that statistics such as those provided by the various state press operations may not be the most accurate or valid means to measure the effectiveness of public sector support in spurring economic development, even while conceding their efficaciousness in mobilizing political support for public investment in the work of economic development.

Still, the purpose here is not to disparage the role of government, especially state government, in supporting new economic development. Strong evidence exists in both the current and previous state administration to support the argument that public sector support can be a critical element in bringing specific projects to fruition, where resources are carefully targeted. This discrete and targeted role of government as a partner is lost; however, in the headlong rush to generate numbers and other unreliable statistics to prove the taxpayer is getting a "bang for his buck." This frenzy for job creation as the yardstick to measure the value of government investments further obscures the areas where government can be most helpful in improving the economic vitality of Pennsylvania.

The Need For Infrastructure Improvement

Tolstoy begins his famous epic *Anna Karenina* with the remark that, "All happy families resemble one another, every unhappy family is unhappy in its own fashion." The same analogy could be drawn between successful and unsuccessful states. The unsuccessful ones are each struggling in their own unique fashion. The successful ones all have something in common. Generally, this includes a well-managed and predictable state government; a system of fair, affordable, and equitable taxation; strong transportation systems; modern infrastructure with capacity for expansion; a superior quality of life; and a strong system of public education.

At the beginning of this decade, Pennsylvania would have been hard pressed to point to any of these six core areas as assets to our competitive position, as against other states, either regionally or subregionally. State budgets were not produced on time; tax dollars flowed into a government which had a national reputation for corruption; the transportation system was in decay and the funding system bankrupt; the infrastructure system was in ill repair and at capacity; and public education had been in a downward spiral from which it is only beginning to recover. Thus, when the worldwide recession began in the late 1970s, Pennsylvania was almost entirely unprepared to respond to the challenge, further contributing to our precipitous economic decline.

During the past ten years, however, in both the Thornburgh and Casey administrations, tremendous strides have been made to address these six critical areas of state capacity. It is one of the ironies of public life that while the public relations teams of Governors Thornburgh and Casey have devoted enormous attention to ribbon cutting and economic development photo opportunities, neither is likely to be remembered for his economic development nor is this the area where their greatest contributions to Pennsylvania's competitiveness has occurred. More likely, Thornburgh will be remembered as a great manager, the man who restored respect, honesty, integrity, and predictability to state government at a crucial hour in the life of the Commonwealth. And while it is still too early to tell, Mr. Casey with his commitment to the environment, education, and local tax reform appears to be the most committed reform governor since the illustrious Gifford Pinchot. Yet it is through these contributions that these two men have created the climate and set the agenda for a stronger economy, without which any recovery would have been impossible.

Meeting Core Responsibilities

It is through the provision of the core responsibilities of government that states remain attractive places to do business for the overwhelming number of firms which have never sought any assistance from state government except to ask that the state's basic operations and infrastructure support rather than diminish their competitiveness. Among these various core responsibilities of state government, is the basic provision of high quality infrastructure, i.e. roads, bridges, water systems, waste management, air and water ports, development and redevelopment of industrial and manufacturing sites, which most immediately bears on the competitive advantage which a state enjoys. It is these items which are incorporated in the discussion that follows.

As evidence mounts that at least a brief recession will occur in the early years of this decade, a mechanism to maintain appropriate levels of state investment in the six critical areas of state responsibility identified earlier, will become a major political concern. Such recent program initiatives as PennVest, designed to assist local governments in financing water system improvements and the state supported waste recycling program, both funded out of revenue surpluses, are only modest downpayments on the work which lies ahead.

While no reliable figure exists, the costs of restoring Pennsylvania's water and sewer systems, managing both residential and industrial waste, rebuilding and maintaining its water and air ports, maintaining its system of highways and bridges, and reclaiming major underutilized and abandoned industrial and manufacturing centers (especially in the southwestern part of the state) will total tens of billions of dollars in the next decade.

For example, in the early 1980s, when Department of Environmental Resources staff made an informal tally of statewide water infrastructure needs, in preparation for initiating a state-sponsored infrastructure bank program, they stopped counting at $2 billion. The costs appeared so enormous, the infrastructure bank idea was shelved.

However, to defer these infrastructure investments any longer will result only in greater costs of doing business and most likely fewer business investments. Delay may also result in very real threats to the health and safety of our citizens. Without these investments, Pennsylvania cannot hope to remain an attractive place to live and work.

The Problem of Funding

Where will the money come from for these investments? Surely not from local governments. The number of local governments in Pennsylvania and the less than cooperative spirit that exists among them has been, on more than one occasion, a barrier to improved state economic vitality. In any case, many are at the limit of available taxation. Neither can we anticipate increased federal aid in the future.

The state remains as the one governmental body with the management capacity and the ability to find the resources needed to make these investments. Under our federal system, the heaviest burden for infrastructure maintenance and replacement falls to state governments, though the federal government continues to play a significant role in funding assistance.

With persistent federal deficits and the scaling back of federal dollars to state infrastructure improvement, the burden of financing these projects will increasingly fall to state governments, where the burden arguably belongs.

Although the purpose of this chapter is not to engage in fiscal policy setting or to critique current state spending priorities, the task of infrastructure improvement will unavoidably require dollars. Naturally, several immediate options the state has are: to insist that it gets its fair share of federal dollars; re-direct funds from elsewhere in the budget and consolidate state programs; and reduce administrative staffing and overhead funding to the maximum extent possible.

Beyond that, however, states are increasingly engaging in innovative funding arrangements that include any number of the following:

(1) Private/public sector infrastructure funding partnerships for road construction and transit services in areas of urban and suburban growth, such as Pennsylvania's transportation partnership program.

(2) Privatizing infrastructure improvement, including the capitalization of projects. Municipalities are increasingly turning to this option in such areas as waste water

treatment facilities, solid waste incineration facilities, road maintenance, and even ports and utilities. Auburn, Alabama for example, became one of the first American cities to privatize a waste water treatment plant which had been held up ten years due to lack of funding. A private firm financed, built and now operates the $36 million facility.

(3) User fees. With state governments strapped for general funds, an increasingly popular method of highway and bridge improvement is simply raising the user fees for highway passengers. In Pennsylvania, proposals are pending in the legislature to expand the use of self-financed toll roads to ease congested urban traffic.

Pennsylvania may find the above options insufficient to meet the infrastructure modernization task. As legislators search for additional revenues, they should be aware of a growing body of research that points to the deleterious effects of high individual and corporate tax structures on state economic development. It makes little sense to invite business development through infrastructure improvement, only to drive it away through burdensome tax policies.

The key is to find revenues from sources that are least destructive of economic growth and development. A little known fact of the Thornburgh administration is that while taxes were raised for specific purposes no less than six times during the Governor's eight-year tenure, those targeted increases were linked to overall tax decreases for businesses and individuals. In other words, sound tax policy, particularly for the improvement of roads, bridges, sewers, and waste water treatment, is to target those taxes to those specific uses which demonstrably improve the overall wealth of the state.

By combining the funds raised in the above methods with a matching investment of $100 million annually from the combined state-supported pension funds, a substantial annual pool could be secured. These funds, both as direct investments and as security to bond issues could insure significant improvements in our infrastructure system.

Given the notorious capacity of infrastructure programs to degenerate into the quagmire of corruption — the municipal building built by the Tamany Hall gang comes to mind — a dedicated fund proves more accountable as well.

The fund, perhaps called the *21st Century Fund*, would be managed as a corporate entity, removed as far as possible from the ward healer level of politics, while allowing for overall political direction. It would be chartered as a corporation and independently managed. The board of directors, however, would contain both public and private members. The Secretary of the Budget could serve as chairperson of the board.

To move toward this objective, the Governor should consider reactivating the State Planning Board, the most prestigious public policy planning group in the nation. The board would be charged with identifying the infrastructure costs confronting the Commonwealth and the return on investment in terms of jobs, new private investment, and reduced liability which would occur as a result of satisfying our infrastructure needs.

Beyond this, the board would establish a mechanism to identify which kinds of investments should occur and in what order of priority. From this, a mechanism for project selection, based on clearly articulated public policy goals, economic opportunities, and provision of public health and safety would be established. This mechanism, and the criteria for specific project selection would be published by the board and used in the determinations of the board of directors of the envisioned *21st Century Fund Corporation*.

While this concept may not immediately take hold, the overwhelming need to make major, multi-billion dollar strategic investments in our Commonwealth's infrastructure base is unavoidable. Delay would be unwise, perhaps even foolhardy.

Direct Partnership — Enterprise Zones

If we are successful in setting the table as envisioned above by continuing to address Pennsylvania global problems, especially our infrastructure needs, then the discrete investments made to support public/private partnerships become much more valuable.

In this paper, we are interested in a particularly focused partnership venture between the public and private sectors, the state-administered enterprise zone initiative.

As discussed earlier, public sector support of economic development is fraught with difficulties. This difficulty is exacerbated when government promotes a "deal making" mentality unrelated to any specific public policy goals. In that kind of environment, the danger is always great that political, as opposed to financial, criteria will be the yardstick against which public funds are awarded.

One recent program example has by and large avoided this problem. The state-administered enterprise zone program initiated in 1982 represents a basic state allocation of only $7 million a year, but to date has stimulated hundreds of millions of dollars in new private sector investment. By 1986, the last available year in which program statistics were provided, over $225 million in private investments had been made in the ten original designated enterprise zones. By that period as well, more than 5,400 new jobs had been reported by the 26 communities participating in the program overall. More than 377 new businesses had been formed.

Pennsylvania's enterprise zone program has a number of unique aspects which separate it from the programs of other states and the envisioned federal program. Four of these elements are particularly important:

First, it is the only administratively established program in the nation. This has allowed the Commonwealth to carefully manage the number of zones designated. In a state of more than 2,500 municipalities, and after nearly a decade of operation, only 30 zones have been established.

Second, this universe of a manageable number of zones has allowed the state to target substantial financial and management resources to such zones, thereby assuring a high level of performance.

Third, an array of state program resources have been set aside as prioritized both statutorily and through regulation for use by the enterprise zones. This includes millions in industrial development, housing, infrastructure, and transportation dollars, as well as various investment tax credits.

Fourth, when it established the program, the Commonwealth set as a standard for participation that communities would not only have to represent measurable levels of distress, but just as importantly, local leaders would be required to commit substantial local and financial resources to the effort.

In a major study authorized by the U.S. Department of Commerce, completed in April 1989, evaluating state enterprise zone programs, these aspects of the Pennsylvania program were identified as reasons for its success to date. The authors of the study concluded that the "... program has achieved more success than many of those in other states."

Earlier in the document, the authors stated that "... other states may want to take a closer look at how this approach (i.e. Pennsylvania's enterprise zone program) could be used in their situations to target the financial, infrastructure and coordination resources of many state agencies into the enterprise zones."

Finally, the authors note that "...the Pennsylvania program is associated with higher zone performance...of investing firms."

Unfortunately, the recognized success of Pennsylvania's enterprise zone program has not translated into any recent significant enhanced commitment by Pennsylvania's state government. It is difficult to avoid the conclusion that the association of the concept in the United States with the Republican Party has made it less than a priority with a state Democratic administration. This concept is somewhat ironic.

First, because the lion's share of the program's resources have always gone to democratically controlled municipalities.

Second, when the democratically controlled legislature attempted to eliminate the program in 1984, it was local government that lobbied the hardest to restore the program.

Moreover, the resources needed to expand the program, more than $12 million, are at hand without taking funds from any other state administrative program.

The reference here to the almost uncontrolled growth of the budget item known as "legislative initiatives," or more precisely WAMS — walking around money — for state legislators. This is the practice of giving legislators' funds for special projects in their districts, free from executive branch management, administrative review and in some cases, program monitoring. The practice first surfaced in the early 1980s as a mechanism by which the legislative whips could win votes for the budget from various legislators without going through the time-consuming process of public debate on the state budget, a document now representing a $22 billion annual expense. The need for this arises from the General Assembly's tendency to take up the budget only days before the June 30th date on which it is constitutionally mandated for adoption.

In the early eighties, this money amounted to a few hundred thousand dollars. In 1988-89, it amounted to anywhere between $12 and $15 million dollars. This amount is equivalent to two-thirds of the entire annual state allocation to support housing and redevelopment in the Commonwealth. This is a process which should be modified; even if the budget process is lengthened because of it.

Moreover, as stated earlier, it could be more effectively used to support and expand the enterprise zone program. For example, with only half of those funds the program could be expanded by as many as 25 to 30 new zones over the next four years. A tremendous pent-up demand for participation in the program exists throughout the Commonwealth. More than a dozen communities are already positioned to participate in the program should expansion occur. Moreover, if the data on the program identified earlier is accepted, this expansion could result in more than a billion dollars in new private investment, thousands of new jobs, and hundreds of new businesses occurring in some of our state's most distressed communities.

Conclusion

Taken together, the development of a multi-billion dollar infrastructure fund and a renewed emphasis on the carefully targeted and the well-managed enterprise zone program could have significant and measurable impact on Pennsylvania's economic performance in the coming decades.

These suggestions are not intended to minimize other important related state activities, but rather to highlight the tangible advantages of getting down to basics and targeting resources against the allure of dealmaking and the politics of chasing private dollars with public funds.

State administrators cannot hope to compete with the private sector in such deal structuring, rather they should return to the two economic development activities they perform best — providing sound tools for economic development: good roads, bridges, ports, industrial sites, water and sewer systems, and in targeting direct state financing to areas of the Commonwealth which have suffered from disinvestment in recent years, but whose citizens are committed to restoring local economic vitality.

CHAPTER FIFTEEN

ENTREPRENEURSHIP AS A SOURCE OF NEW PROSPERITY

By William C. Dunkelberg

EDITOR'S SUMMARY

The 1980s was the "Decade of the Entrepreneur." Small firms, those with under 20 employees, appeared to the major creators of new jobs for the economy. While small businesses flourished, large firms were unable to respond to rapidly changing markets. "Small" and "flexible" became desirable firm characteristics.

While communist governments failed in Eastern Europe in the 1980s, the U.S. experienced an unprecedented economic expansion. A record-high percentage of the employable population was employed and major shocks to the financial system were easily digested by an economy freed from the shackles of government intervention.

Entrepreneurs perform the most vital function for strong economic growth — the research and development for an economy. Individuals are responsible for all new ideas. Successful ideas are rewarded with profits that finance expansion and attract new competitors anxious to "cash in" on a good thing.

Some government policies discourage entrepreneurial activity. Among these are employment taxes and minimum wage laws which discourage hiring and training. These taxes create more paperwork which diverts valuable time from the main tasks of entrepreneurs. This is clearly a tax that diminishes the effectiveness of entrepreneurs and the amount of entrepreneurial activity.

Firms, especially small firms, are not efficient administrators of social programs or tax collectors. They are best at producing goods and services. The more of an entrepreneur's time that is diverted to doing paperwork, managing health care programs, running child care operations, etc., the less successful he or she is at producing low-cost goods and services.

Successful economic development requires the provision of a climate conducive to entrepreneurship. Each new law has the potential of raising the cost of doing business in the state. Each regulation must be carefully examined for its "tax consequence" for entrepreneurship.

Businesses can no longer rely on "federal subsidies" or "federal spending" to support the economy. Instead, the "core" assets (location, natural resources, natural attractions) must be identified and a climate that is conducive to entrepreneurship must be actively built.

Government's biggest challenge is to keep out of the way and not impede the critically important work of the entrepreneur. It will not be the firms that we attract to the state that make Pennsylvania an economic success. Rather, our success will depend on how effectively the government avoids discouraging the entrepreneurs we now have through various forms of taxation, and how effectively we attract and retain the talent we develop.

William C. Dunkelberg is Dean of the School of Business and Management at Temple University.

The term "entrepreneurship" became the buzz-word of the 1980s and legislators and the press became aware of the tremendous importance of small business in U.S. development. So-called "Corporate America" was adversely impacted by the economic environment of the early 1980s which required "down-sizing" and "streamlining" , polite terms for shedding employees. Academic studies began to show what we really knew all along — big firms did not create new jobs. Small firms, those with under 20 employees, appeared to be the major creators of new jobs for the economy. The inability of large firms to respond to rapidly changing market conditions became very apparent. "Small" and "flexible" became desirable firm characteristics. It would seem that the 1980s became the "Decade of the Entrepreneur."

The 1980s were a period of sharp contrasts. The early years included one of the worst recessions in our history, with unprecedented rates of inflation, interest and unemployment. This was followed by the longest peacetime economic expansion in our history, with dramatically lower inflation rates and the highest employment rate in the population ever recorded.

Perhaps the most memorable event of the decade of the 1980s was the unraveling of the communist/socialist experiments in Eastern Europe. "From each according to his ability, to each according to his need" just didn't stir people to high levels of effort. Economic planning, targets and computer models failed to invigorate these large economies, even those that possessed plenty of raw potential. Graft and corruption flourished, and a select few still lived better than the majority of the workers in spite of the official objectives of the system. But everyone lived more poorly than was necessary in light of the resources available to these countries. The ultimate collapse of these political systems was a direct result of the failure of their economic systems to improve the standard of living for their people.

In the free world, the role of government was being diminished through great waves of "deregulation" and changes in the tax laws that reduced marginal tax rates, leaving more of each extra dollar earned in the hands of the individuals doing the work. In this supportive environment, the U.S. experienced an unprecedented expansion, employing a record-high percentage of the employable population. Even the numbers of individuals with more than one job reached new highs. Major shocks to the financial system were surprisingly easily digested by an economy freed from the shackles of government intervention, flexible and resilient enough to change quickly to altering market conditions.

The reasons for the tremendous expansion of the 1980s will be debated for the next decade. And, it seems likely that one of the most important keys to this success is likely to be overlooked as we debate the impact of federal policies, exogenous shocks and large deficits. Very simply, this very important key to our success was entrepreneurship, functioning in a deregulated economic environment.

The Crucial Role of Entrepreneurs

Entrepreneurs perform the most vital of all functions for strong economic growth — the R&D for an economy. Individuals are responsible for all new ideas. Those with the most freedom to exploit these ideas will be the most successful (meaning they create lots of wealth and jobs for others as well as themselves). Thus, each year in the U.S., thousands of entrepreneurs try out thousands of new ideas, new products, new services, new ways to do things, and new ways to organize production or delivery. No board of central planners, even with the largest available computers, could conceive of and test all of the ideas generated by entrepreneurs. Successful ventures are rewarded with profits that finance expansion and attract new competitors anxious to "cash in" on a good thing. This simply assures that more of the firm's product is provided to the economy at a competitive price.

Not all of these ideas are successful, of course. Thus, for 1989, Dunn and Bradstreet will report about 50,000 business failures, one of the lowest figures in years. Beyond those, there were additional thousands of "terminations" of various sorts that never produced an official bankruptcy record. Associated with these statistics are many personal losses and the displacement of hundreds of thousands of workers. From society's perspective, the whole process looks a bit different. First, on balance, there are more successes than failures — the number of firms keeps growing and the number of people employed keeps rising. Second, a "failure" does not represent a "loss" to society. All of the assets, human and real, that were involved in the "failure" are still available for new experiments. These assets are simply "repriced" and used again. This process continues until a "success" results. Thus, the assets are continually re-employed in new business experiments.

Viewed in a somewhat different perspective, it is the freedom to seek out the best paying jobs and uses of our resources that is critical to the success of this system. "Success" means that something is being done by the firm that is valued by the market. When an individual finds the highest paying job available, that individual has also found where his/her talents have the highest value to society.

Encouraging Entrepreneurial Activity

There is a fundamental principle that is often forgotten in the rush to raise revenue to finance government activities: If you tax something, you will get less of it. Now, what is a "tax"? Beyond the obvious monetary schemes (sales, profit, employment and income taxes), a tax is anything that makes it more difficult or more expensive to get something done. Liquor taxes discourage liquor consumption. Speeding tickets discourage reckless driving. Employment taxes and minimum wage laws discourage hiring and training. Income taxes discourage work and provide incentives to devote resources to finding ways to avoid taxes. Indeed, so called "progressive taxes", when effective, provide the largest *disincentives* to our most productive people as indicated by the high salaries their talents command in the marketplace.

Since entrepreneurship is something that we should encourage, perhaps we should examine our governmental policies more carefully to see how they impact on the entrepreneurial process — as a tax or as a subsidy (which encourages entrepreneurial activity). Founders of new companies in Pennsylvania in the mid-1980s worked many hours in their new firms. Three quarters spent more than 50 hours per week, and over half worked over 60 hours per week in their new ventures. Half utilized unpaid family members to help out as well, with a fourth of these firms receiving more than 40 hours per week of unpaid assistance. However, these entrepreneurs can easily spend 8-10 hours each week on "paperwork" (over and above tax-related and accounting activities). Diverting valuable entrepreneurial time from the main tasks of entrepreneurs is clearly a tax that diminishes the effectiveness of entrepreneurs and the amount of entrepreneurial activity.

The median amount of capital employed to start these new firms is about $20,000. A rise of $1 in the minimum wage for a firm with just two unskilled workers working 2,000 hours per year raises labor costs by over $4,000, over 20% of initial capital employed by these firms. This increase will encourage the firm to reduce the number of employees and/or hours worked and weaken the firm's financial capital position.

Consider a simple story that illustrates all the ways new firms might be adversely impacted by government action, as well intended as it might be. You and I decide to open up a pizza parlor. We scrape together $20,000 and enough other financing to get into operation. We employ 20 people the first year (some full-time, some part-time), and manage to make enough each month to take home $15,000 each for the year, just enough to keep us in the pizza business rather than working for someone else. Since there are a large number of pizza places, we can't make much more than this because of the competition. So, each year, we take home about $15,000 each.

Then, we are suddenly required to provide health insurance for our 20 employees (most of whom are young workers covered by family insurance). This costs (for the purposes of our example) $500 per employee per year, or $10,000. At the end of the year, we have only $10,000 each to support our families. We meet to decide what to do. One alternative is to get out of the pizza business and get a job working for someone else. We would, of course, have to fire our 20 employees. Or, we could just be happy with $10,000 each, even though we could earn $15,000 working at other jobs. A third alternative is to raise the price of our pizza. A fourth is to cut the wages of our employees or cheapen our product and service. We opt for raising prices.

It seems that all of our competitors choose to either raise prices or cheapen their product in an attempt to deal with the increase in mandated medical costs. However, it becomes clear that at higher prices, people buy less pizza, and we, as well as our competitors, are forced to fire an employee. At the end of the year, we are able to pretty much restore our $15,000 salaries. But, who paid for the increased cost of medical insurance? Obviously, it was the pizza customers who paid higher prices (or got a cheaper product), and the employees that lost their jobs.

As an alternative, the market may have ultimately reduced the cash wages of employees so that the cash pay plus the new health benefits would equal the old wage bill paid by pizza parlors. In this case, those receiving the benefits would have paid for them directly, but this is a difficult "agreement" to negotiate with our workers, especially since most of them did not want the coverage to begin with. Even worse, those that did probably could have received it cheaper elsewhere. They would be forced to accept lower wages and whatever health care plan we provided if total employee costs were to remain unchanged after the mandated health insurance was put in place.

Now, substitute "profit tax", "minimum wage", "mandatory child care", "paper work" or any other mandated government program or activity for "mandated medical insurance" in the above example, and you get the same results. Firms, especially small firms, are not efficient administrators of social programs or tax collectors. Firms are best at producing goods and services. The more of an entrepreneur's time we divert to doing paperwork, managing health care programs, running child care operations, etc., the less well we do at producing low-cost goods and services. Ninety percent of all employers in the U.S. have 20 or fewer employees and very limited resources. They do not have large pools of capital that they have no use for. They are too small to efficiently deal with the high fixed costs entailed when interfacing with government regulations and programs. Operating in very competitive environments, they must pass on all of the costs of the programs to their customers and/or shrink their operations.

Sensible Public Policy

Especially in these times of tight federal, state and local budgets, the concept of "mandating" firms to organize and finance social programs that governments cannot afford to do directly has become quite popular. The notion that there is some "Robin Hood" process that legitimizes "taxation" in any form remains alive and well in government circles. But the facts of life are quite different. Taxing 100% of the incomes of individuals with six digit receipts would raise only enough revenue to run the government for a matter of days. But, we can seriously damage the incentives faced by individuals who have the creative power not only to improve their own economic situation, but also that of millions of others for whom these entrepreneurs create jobs and wealth. This is the strength of our economic system, the wealthiest in the world, and also the most generous. Few economies are economically so successful that they can finance the relative level of generosity exhibited in our federal, state and local budgets. When the pie gets bigger, everyone benefits.

Successful economic development, then, requires the provision of a climate conducive to entrepreneurship. Relatively few new firms are started with moves from the "home base". Eighty percent of the entrepreneurs starting businesses in the early 1980s did not move, and only 10% moved more than 150 miles to start their new enterprises. When asked to compare the reality of starting a firm to their expectations, half underestimated how difficult government regulations and red tape would be, compared to only about 10% underestimating the problems presented by the competition and 25% underestimating the problems associated with developing sales or managing workers or financing their operations.

Each new law has the potential of raising the cost of doing business in the state — a tax on entrepreneurship. It should be clear now that we cannot rely on "federal subsidies" or "federal spending" to indefinitely support our economy (for example, New England became over-dependent on military spending). Instead, we must identify our "core" assets (our location, our natural resources, our natural attractions) and actively build a climate that is conducive to entrepreneurship. Each law and regulation must be carefully examined for its "tax consequences" for entrepreneurship.

On the positive side, government is in an excellent position to effectively develop our infrastructure to reduce transportation and commuting costs, to impact the general quality of the workforce (education and training), and to provide information and networking capabilities that make it easier for new firms to overcome the hurdles they face (e.g. the Ben Franklin Partnership). It will not be the firms that we attract to the state that make Pennsylvania an economic success. Rather, our success will depend on how effectively we avoid discouraging the entrepreneurial talent we now have through various forms of "taxation", and how effectively we attract and retain the talent we develop. Government's biggest challenge is simply to keep out of the way and not to impede the critically important work of our entrepreneurs.

SECTION FIVE:

Environment/Natural Resources

CHAPTER SIXTEEN

MARKETPLACE ENVIRONMENTALISM
By Andrew S. McElwaine

EDITOR'S SUMMARY

The 1990's will be a decade dominated by environmental concerns. Policy makers at all levels of government must deal with unaddressed cleanup needs and the costs of regulation. Instead of regulating individual behavior and constraining markets, ways must be found to harness the marketplace to not only bring about regulatory compliance, but to reduce costs.

A market-based approach to address environmental concerns is contained in *Project 88*. This report has 33 proposals governing 13 major environmental problems. Its recommendations have been partially incorporated into proposed federal legislation in order to pursue market-based incentives.

Project 88 advances several possible solutions to reduce acid rain. A reduction target for both the nation and individual utilities would be set through an Acid Rain Reduction Credit program. President Bush adopted *Project 88*'s recommendations and both the House and Senate versions of the Clean Air Act contain the tradeable permit program.

Tradeable permits can have a major role in bringing emissions into compliance. Emissions in excess of standards can be offset by reductions beneath the standard at a neighboring facility. Hundreds of millions of dollars can be saved without significant loss of environmental quality in affected areas.

Recycling is another area where tradeable permits would work. A permit system can provide an incentive for private sector recycling of materials which would otherwise become waste. Credits can expand the market for recycled products and grant the manufacturer of virgin inputs far greater flexibility than a traditional regulatory mandate.

States should apply the lessons learned from *Project 88*. Pennsylvania's Energy Office is one of a few state agencies considering the energy strategy recommended by the report. The Commonwealth is analyzing possible utility regulation changes in order to allow conservation to compete with energy production in the rate base.

Marketplace incentives encompass more than recycling and acid rain reduction. *Project 88* also recommends a deposit/refund system for containerized hazardous waste, converting environmental entitlements into marketable commodities, and debt/nature swaps to protect natural areas. These recommendations can help to reduce cleanup costs while maintaining environmental compliance.

Andrew S. McElwaine is Director of Congressional Affairs for the Institute of Scrap Recycling Industries, Inc. and previously served as Legislative Counsel to Senator John Heinz.

As Pennsylvania and the nation enter a decade which many believe will be dominated by environmental concerns, policy makers at all levels must grapple with the complexity of un- addressed environmental needs and the tremendous costs of each additional increment of environmental control. Tra- ditional regulatory procedures would call for specific man- dates, with timetables for industrial or municipal polluters to meet, and sharp penalties for failure to comply. A recent report out of Washington, however, and some new legislation point in a markedly different direction. Instead of regulating individual behavior and constraining private markets, these would-be reformers want to harness the marketplace to not only bring about regulatory compliance, but reduce costs.

Project 88

The report was called *Project 88*, and is available from the offices of Senators Timothy E. Wirth (D-CO) and John Heinz (R-PA) in Washington. Wirth and Heinz convened a staff of over 50 individuals from all sectors of American life — public and private, industry and environment — to prepare the report, which was published in December 1988. It makes 33 recom- mendations governing 13 major environmental problems. In each case the report recommends a market-based incentive approach to advance environmental control at the lowest cost.

Several of its recommendations have been incorporated into proposed federal legislation, but in only limited measures are state governments applying the lessons learned; and there are no good reasons why states cannot already move in the direc- tions proposed. Pennsylvania's Energy Office, for example, is one of a few state agencies considering the least-cost energy strategy recommended by the report. But to address the state's role in *Project 88*, one must first examine the federal precedents and the ways these are now being applied.

Legislative Precedents

The Clean Air Act of 1970 and its 1977 amendments authorize the Environmental Protection Agency to issue tradeable per- mits to bring industrial air emissions into compliance with federal standards. Emissions in excess of the standard may be offset by reductions beneath the standard at a neighboring facility. The emissions source which reduces its output beneath the required level generates a permit equal to the overage, which can in turn be traded or sold to the source that does not meet the requirement. Since 1980, the EPA has conducted nearly 1,000 such exchanges, including several in Pennsylvania, without significant loss of air quality in affected areas. Estimates of the cost savings accomplished have varied, but start in the hundreds of millions of dollars.

The chief criticism of emissions trading over the years has not been based on policy so much as philosophy. Many in the environmental movement have complained that such policies create a right to pollute. The answer to the criticism is to point out that the right already exists and is being given away for free. Under a tradeable permit approach, at least a price can be charged.

Acid Rain

Project 88 builds on EPA's history with tradeable permits, and recommends that they be applied in new fields. For instance, the report's most widely adopted recommendation has been in the area of acid rain. Traditional acid rain legislation has mandated a set level of emissions reduction either from specific locations within the United States or from specific plants. *Project 88* recommended an Acid Rain Reduction Credit program, where a reduction target would be set both for the nation and for individual utilities, but that compliance be made flexible, and cost-efficient, through a tradeable permit program. Utilities which reduce emissions beneath the targeted level would receive tradeable permits equal to their excess reductions. Those which could not, for economic or technical reasons, reach the required level would purchase these credits for a price determined solely by the market.

President Bush adopted *Project 88*'s recommendations on acid rain, and cited the Project in his press statement. The House and Senate versions of the Clean Air Act contain the tradeable permit program. It appears certain that a dramatic expansion of market incentive approaches to air pollution problems will be law in 1990. The key question is, can the same approach be used elsewhere.

Project 88 believes that the answer is a very firm yes. The criticism of tradeable permits in the Clean Air Act legislation has not held up. Some in the environmental community argued that major polluters might choose to purchase credits in lieu of significant reductions, thereby continuing severe regional pollution problems. This argument assumes that emissions reductions can be made elsewhere at little cost. In the acid rain field, this assumption has not held up. The EPA and private sector analysts believe that, under the President's proposal, marketable permits for sulfur dioxide, the primary acid rain precursor, will trade for at least $500 per ton. The President's proposal calls for a ten million ton reduction of sulfur dioxide. Simple math demonstrates how difficult it would be for a utility to make significant reductions in sulfur dioxide solely by purchasing permits; few public utility commissions would allow such a costly option even if private operators chose to follow it.

Market-Incentive Legislation

Tradeable permits and market forces, as recommended by *Project 88*, are turning up in new federal legislation. The pending House of Representatives' bill to reauthorize the Resource Conservation and Recovery Act (RCRA), H.R. 3735, contains legislation offered by Rep. Esteban Torres (D-CA), Sen. John Heinz and Sen. Tim Wirth on oil recycling. For five years environmentalists and industry have fought over whether or not used oil should be listed as a hazardous waste. Under the Torres-Heinz-Wirth proposal, used oil would have to be recycled, and a market-incentive would expand the marketplace for used oil. Over 300 million gallons of used motor oil are discarded each year. Most of it ends up in landfills or dumped down storm drains; it ends up in groundwater and as contaminant in soil. If it is listed as a hazardous waste, however, treaters, handlers, and disposers of the oil come under the heavy hand of RCRA and Superfund, required to install environmental monitoring, maintain financial responsibility, provide closure and post-closure care, and more. Many re-refiners of used oil are relatively small businesses which would be discouraged, if not driven out of business, by hazardous waste regulations. Other recyclers would be similarly affected.

Rather than bring the heavy hand of regulation down on recyclers, the proposed legislation, and the *Project 88* recommendation that preceded it, require that the EPA set a minimum standard for oil recycling. All producers of virgin oil would have to use that minimum amount of recycled oil in their product, or purchase permits from oil recyclers such that they have either permits or recycled oil, or both.

If the legislation required that 35% of use oil be recycled (an increase from today's 33%), a manufacturer of engine oil would have to recycle that amount of his production by himself or contract with an independent recycler to purchase permits. The recycler would receive credits from EPA equal to his overall production of recycled material. The recycler would still be able to market the recycled oil to any buyer. Only the permit would be sold to the manufacturer.

Similar legislation has been introduced governing newsprint recycling and tire recycling. Rather than setting an inflexible mandate, the permit system provides an incentive for private sector recycling of materials which would otherwise become waste, expands the market for recycled products, and grants the manufacturer of virgin inputs far greater flexibility than a traditional regulatory mandate.

Does the relative success of market incentive legislation at the federal level mean that Congress has conceded microeconomic policy to the private sector? Not at all. In fact, the same legislation that includes used oil recycling incentives, H.R. 3735, would require all private sector recyclers, with the possible exception of paper, to obtain hazardous waste recycling permits, purchase liability insurance, install environmental controls, and incur additional costs and constraints on recycling. And, the same clean air proposal that grants marketable permits for acid rain control also sets numerous, Congressionally-imposed deadlines for emissions reductions with no allowance for economic efficiency. The risk in these proposals is not that the private sector will use market incentives to avoid compliance, but that the incentives will not be used because the costs imposed by top-down regulation elsewhere in the bill will leave little room for any marketplace.

Any market, once established, can also be cornered — and not just by speculators. One of the great concerns regarding market-based legislation is the ability of legislators to maneuver the market. For instance, one could target extra permits to specific interest groups on the grounds of "fairness" and grant a market-place advantage to one sector of the economy. Some have proposed doing just this in the acid rain field either to benefit utilities which reduced emissions in the past, or to help utilities which have not reduced emissions at all.

Additionally, there needs to be oversight of the market, just as in stock and commodity markets, to ensure that private interests do not attempt to buy up all existing credits and hold manufacturers hostage. Federal legislation to date has granted the EPA that role.

How can states implement such policies? Several already are. New York State has developed a comprehensive least-cost energy policy based in part on a *Project 88* recommendation. The report urged states to change utility regulations to allow conservation to compete with energy production in the rate base. At present, utilities seldom receive any benefit from conservation programs as most state regulations rewards only energy output. Conservation is often a lower-cost option to new production, and brings additional rewards in reduced sulfur dioxide and carbon dioxide emissions.

But the applications are far broader. Consider how California's mandatory recycling laws might be modified by a market-incentive approach. The California Law requires a 50% recycled paper content in newsprint by 2000, and a 25% reduction in solid waste sources by 1995 (50% by 2000). Those who exceed these targets could generate credits for those who cannot meet them. Maine's mandatory beverage container deposit/return program could reflect the market-based approach taken earlier by California, where private recyclers are encouraged to accept and process discarded containers.

Louisiana is about to embark on a major waste reduction program, including 25% recycling of discarded materials. They could learn from the District of Columbia's failure to find a market for recyclables, and from *Project 88*'s recommendation that markets be stimulated by government action. Without a market, recyclables won't get recycled, and the District is stockpiling waste paper until the time that someone will take it. If manufacturers or distributors of newsprint are given a regulatory incentive to use recycled material, the District and Louisiana could avoid the cost of holding onto recyclables until a market develops.

Conclusion

Project 88 is about more than just recycling or acid rain. The report also recommends a deposit/refund system for containerized hazardous waste, converting natural resource entitlements such as water rights into a marketable commodity to spur better management, debt/nature swaps to protect developing nations' natural resources, and more. It has implications for all levels of government, saving costs and expanding environmental compliance.

CHAPTER SEVENTEEN

MEETING PENNSYLVANIA'S HAZARDOUS WASTE NEEDS
By Carole A. Rubley and Michael D. LaGrega

EDITOR'S SUMMARY

Pennsylvania has modeled its hazardous waste regulations after federal regulations. The Commonwealth's Solid Waste Management Act of 1980 is designed to protect human health and the environment from potential waste hazards. This Act is the state equivalent of the federal Resource Conservation and Recovery Act.

Approximately one million tons of hazardous waste is generated annually in Pennsylvania. At the same time, the Commonwealth is also accepting approximately 245,000 tons from other states for treatment and reclamation. The largest percent of waste is generated by blast furnaces, steel works, and rolling mills.

Serious problems are faced in siting hazardous waste facilities. Changing technologies, tighter regulations, and a better technical understanding of the management of hazardous waste combine to make siting decisions difficult to make. When a decision is made, well-organized citizen groups usually resist the proposed site.

No new permits to operate commercial hazardous waste disposal facilities have been issued by DER since 1980. A hazardous waste disposal crisis is looming since Pennsylvania's last commercial disposal facility was closed in 1987. Due to this dilemma, a Hazardous Waste Facility Siting Task Force was commissioned by Governor Casey to make recommendations on where to site disposal facilities in the state.

Pennsylvania's 1988 Hazardous Sites Cleanup Act also addresses the need for waste disposal. The Act established a state Superfund program to clean up sites where hazardous substances have been released. In addition, the Act calls for the expeditious review of all permit applications for commercial treatment, storage, and disposal facilities.

Hazardous waste disposal facilities can be a great economic burden to the operator. The required liability insurance is extremely difficult for most disposers to obtain. The growing expense of shipping wastes off-site is borne by generators since most current on-site hazardous waste disposal facilities are close to capacity.

Pennsylvania's Waste Facilities Plan advocates the adoption of several specific waste management practices. These recommendations include encouraging source reduction and optimizing the use of treatment technologies. State government and industry should promote these proposals along with educating the public as to the crucial need for siting new hazardous waste disposal facilities.

Carole A. Rubley is a Regulatory Analyst for Environmental Resources Management, Inc. and a member of the Pennsylvania Solid Waste Advisory Committee.

Michael D. LaGrega is Professor of Civil Engineering at Bucknell University and has recently served as Director of Hazardous Waste Planning for the Pennsylvania Department of Environmental Resources.

Pennsylvania was an early leader in recognizing the need to conserve resources and protect the environment. The General Assembly enacted legislation establishing responsibility for damage to forest lands by fire in 1682. The Fish Commission was created in 1866, and the Bureau of Forestry and the Game Commission was created in 1895. A water resource inventory was completed in 1913, and soil conservation and stream protection measures were enacted in 1937.

In the wake of significant citizen awareness during the early 1970s (Earth Day, DDT scare, etc.) the constitution of the Commonwealth of Pennsylvania was amended to define the right of the people to "clean air, pure water, and the preservation of the natural scenic, historic and aesthetic values of the environment" (Article 1, Section 27).

The Commonwealth, as trustee of these resources, created the Pennsylvania Department of Environmental Resources (DER) as an executive agency to implement programs designed to protect the environment, resources, wildlife, and public health. The DER is a unique agency among state environmental authorities because of the scope of its mandate and the responsibilities over all resources.

DER recognized that the existing "Pennsylvania Solid Waste Management Act" did not address the needs of the Commonwealth to control the management of hazardous wastes. In 1978 an Industrial Advisory Committee was formed by the DER to advise the Commonwealth on the matter. This committee included private citizens, industrial representatives, academicians, and engineers. Act 97, the Solid Waste Management Act (July, 1980) required the development of siting criteria, mandated a facilities plan and provided the DER with the legal authority necessary to be in conformance with federal requirements. The Industrial Advisory Committee was recommissioned as the Solid Waste Advisory Committee. Its role is to advise DER on areas relating to hazardous and non-hazardous wastes.

Hazardous Waste Regulations

Most of Pennsylvania's Hazardous Waste Regulations are modeled after the federal regulations. The Resource Conservation and Recovery Act (RCRA) was passed by Congress in 1976.

RCRA was revised in 1980 and then in 1984 to include the Hazardous and Solid Waste Amendments. RCRA regulates hazardous waste, non-hazardous waste, and underground storage tanks. It is a national program designed to protect human health and the environment from current and potential hazards from waste activities by developing standards for facility waste management plans. RCRA is often referred to as a "cradle to grave" law because it regulates everything that happens to a waste material from the time it is generated until the time it is disposed. Pennsylvania has the authorization from the Environmental Protection Agency (EPA) to regulate and enforce most of the requirements under RCRA.

The 1984 Amendments to RCRA closed many of the perceived "loopholes" in the original law. One change brought the Small Quantity Generators into the system. Small Quantity Generators are those facilities that generate more than 220 pounds of hazardous waste per month (approximately one-half of a 55 gallon drum) but less than 2,200 pounds per month, or less than 2.2 pounds of acutely hazardous waste per month. They must now comply with most of the regulations under RCRA including using the manifest system to track the waste and shipping only to permitted hazardous waste facilities. Companies that generate less than 220 pounds of hazardous waste per month are exempt from most RCRA regulations but still are required to meet minimum standards.

The 1984 RCRA Amendments also eliminate the disposal of bulk liquid hazardous waste in landfills as well as banning the land disposal of specific chemicals. EPA has issued treatment standards for other wastes that must diminish the toxicity of the waste or reduce the likelihood of migration. The intent of Congress was to make land disposal of waste a last resort and to move toward managing wastes in accordance with the hierarchy shown in Figure 1.

Congress also mandated that if land disposal sites were to be used then these sites must be "state of the art" facilities. Pennsylvania's regulations required these "state of the art" systems prior to the federal requirements. For example all new land disposal facilities must have:

- Double-liners;
- Leachate collection systems;
- Leak detection systems;

- Groundwater monitoring systems.

What is a Hazardous Waste?

A "hazardous waste" is defined as a waste that may pose a substantial threat or potential hazard to human health or the environment. They may be in a solid, semisolid, liquid, or a containerized gaseous material. Hazardous waste is identified by showing certain characteristics or by being on one of three EPA hazardous waste lists.

The hazardous waste characteristics are as follows:

- Ignitable (e.g. solvents);
- Corrosive (i.e. acids and bases);
- Reactive or explosive (e.g. cyanide);
- EP Toxic — These apply to wastes which when put through the Extraction Procedure (EP) laboratory test are shown to contain one of several specific contaminants (including eight heavy metals and six chemicals used in pesticides). The test is designed to simulate landfill conditions.

The EPA lists (listed waste) include the following categories:

- "K" wastes — Specific industrial waste generated from a specific industrial process; e.g. wastewater treatment sludge from the production of zinc yellow pigments;
- "F" wastes — Nonspecific sources; e.g. spent halogenated solvents;
- "U" and "P" wastes — Acutely hazardous waste and toxic waste; e.g. arsenic acid and benzene listed wastes.

Hazardous Waste Facilities Plans

Act 97 required the Commonwealth to prepare a Hazardous Waste Facilities Plan that would include:

- Criteria for siting hazardous waste facilities;
- An inventory of current waste generation and management;

- A strategy for encouraging source reduction;
- An identification of needed commercial hazardous waste facilities.

Phase I of this plan was published in July of 1986. The Plan serves several basic purposes:

- Provides information about the amounts and types of hazardous wastes generated in Pennsylvania;
- Outlines the types of modern technologies that will be needed to treat and dispose of that waste;
- Establishes basic hazardous waste management policies for the Commonwealth;
- Serves as one of the factors to be used when issuing Certificates of Public Necessity.

The Plan also establishes a preferred waste management strategy, as shown on Figure 1, which encourages the following structure for handling wastes: reduction; recycling; and treatment of wastes where practicable. Land disposal is reserved for wastes that are not affected by the land ban restrictions under RCRA, cannot be managed under the preferred methods, or wastes that have been stabilized before disposal to reduce the potential for leaching of the material.

DER authorized the update of the Phase I Plan to include new waste generation and management data and to include the effect of regulations on the small quantity generators and the wastes treated or disposed of from Superfund cleanup sites. The Phase II Plan is scheduled to be published early in 1990. In this Plan, estimates of waste generation will be made from 1995 through 2010 to evaluate the existing waste treatment and disposal capabilities within Pennsylvania to handle these wastes.

Siting of Hazardous Waste Facilities

The Commonwealth of Pennsylvania, along with most other states, is facing a serious problem in siting new hazardous waste facilities. This dilemma is brought about in part by changing technologies, tighter regulations, and a better technical understanding of the management of hazardous waste. The situa-

tion is exacerbated by public fears, best expressed as the
NIMBY syndrome (not in my backyard). This has caused the
creation of very well organized opposition groups to the few sites
that have been proposed.

In Pennsylvania no new permits to operate commercial
hazardous waste disposal facilities have been issued by DER
since 1980. In addition, with the closing of the last commercial
disposal facility in the state in July of 1987, there are no operating land disposal facilities in Pennsylvania. It is estimated that
Pennsylvania-based industries are exporting approximately
42% of the waste generated to other states for treatment or disposal. The need for hazardous waste disposal firms in the state
has been documented in the Hazardous Waste Facilities Plans.

Hazardous Waste Facility Siting Task Force

Due to the economic and environmental consequences of the
aforementioned situation, Governor Robert P. Casey has made
the siting of commercial hazardous waste disposal facilities a
priority on his environmental agenda. A Hazardous Waste
Facility Siting Task Force was commissioned by Arthur Davis,
Secretary of DER, in April of 1987 to identify the obstacles to the
siting of hazardous waste disposal facilities including the effect
of the Department's environmental policies and regulations
and to make recommendations on how to site one or more
facility in Pennsylvania.

Among other recommendations, the Task Force called for the
formation of a DER Hazardous Waste Facility Permitting Task
Force to address and resolve many of the siting obstacles identified in their report of October 1987. The Siting Task Force also
called for the enactment of legislation to establish a Hazardous
Waste Facility Siting Commission that would establish a siting
process and, if necessary, have the power to implement a mandatory siting process if other alternatives are not successful.

Act 108

Act 108, the Pennsylvania Hazardous Sites Cleanup Act was
signed into law by Governor Casey on October 10, 1988. The
major purpose of this Act is to set up a state Superfund program

to clean up sites where hazardous substances have been released or pose a threat of release. In addition, in response to the urgency of the siting issue, the Act calls for the establishment of a Hazardous Waste Facility Siting Team by DER to review all permit applications for commercial treatment, storage, and disposal facilities. A major purpose of the team is to provide a fast and consistent review of permit applications. This team has been established and is currently reviewing permit applications for hazardous waste disposal facilities.

If no commercial hazardous waste disposal is permitted by July 1, 1992, an independent Hazardous Waste Facility Siting Commission, similar to that recommended in the Task Force report, must be established. The seven members will include three individuals appointed by the Governor, one by the President Pro Tempore of the Senate, one by the Speaker of the House, one by the Minority Leader of the Senate, and one by the Minority Leader of the House. The membership will consist of representation from local government, industry, and public interest groups.

This Commission has the following responsibilities:

- Identification of potentially suitable areas for disposal facilities in Pennsylvania using the siting criteria;
- Review and approving or disapproving the siting sections of pending permit applications;
- Assist local governments in planning for the siting of disposal facilities;
- Submit an application for the Commonwealth to DER establishing a stateowned hazardous waste disposal facility;
- Lease Commonwealth owned real estate for up to 50 years;
- Acquire a site through the power of eminent domain, if necessary.

Siting Criteria

It is well recognized that many geographic areas are not suited for the location of land disposal sites. In developing the criteria for siting hazardous waste facilities, DER undertook one of the

most extensive public participation efforts of any environmental regulation in recent history. The Final Rulemaking
published on September 21, 1985 (Chapter 75, Subchapter F)
marked the culmination of almost five years of effort by DER
and the Department's Solid Waste Advisory Committee.

The siting criteria expressed in the final regulations are
divided into Phase I (absolute prohibitions) and Phase II (regulations which allow for judgement). Phase I excludes hazardous waste facilities from flood hazard areas, wetlands, oil
and gas areas, certain carbonate bedrock areas, national natural
landmarks and historic places, dedicated land in the public
trust, agricultural areas and exceptional value watersheds.
Additionally, facilities may not be located within one-half mile
of water supplies. The Phase I criteria apply to all new or modified hazardous waste treatment and disposal facilities except
those that were sited and substantially constructed prior to the
effective date of the criteria.

Permit applications will be denied without further review if it
is determined that the proposed facility is located in an area
excluded by Phase I criteria.

Where Phase I does not exclude siting, the proposed location
must be evaluated in Phase II. The Phase II criteria require
detailed assessments of nine categories of concern in order to
provide sufficient information for DER to determine whether
the location of a facility is acceptable. These criteria include
proximity of water supplies, geology, soils, mineral bearing
areas, land use, transportation, safety services, proximity of
facilities and structures, economic impact, and environmental
assessment considerations.

Certificate of Public Necessity

Pennsylvania will need to establish facilities to properly
handle hazardous waste for the future. Act 97 includes a unique
provision allowing the state to issue a Certificate of Public
Necessity (CPN) overriding all local laws, including zoning
ordinances, which would preclude or prohibit the establishment of a hazardous waste treatment or disposal facility (Chapter 75, Subchapter G). This provision applies only to hazardous
waste and cannot be used to site municipal waste landfills. The
applicant must meet the following criteria before a CPN can be

applied for:

- Siting criteria are met;
- Meaningful public participation has been obtained;
- Site has been approved for a permit by DER; and
- Site conforms with the Pennsylvania Hazardous Waste Facilities Plan by being shown to be "needed".

The Environmental Quality Board (EQB) has the authority to issue a CPN.

Current Hazardous Waste Generation

Pennsylvania currently generates about 860,000 tons of hazardous waste annually with approximately 364,000 tons exported to other states for treatment and disposal. At the same time Pennsylvania is also accepting waste from other states which are importing approximately 245,000 tons into the state for treatment or reclamation.

Figure 2 graphically depicts the types of off-site hazardous waste generated by industrial sources in Pennsylvania in 1987. The largest percent of waste is generated by blast furnaces, steel works, and rolling mills.

Hazardous waste disposal facilities can be a great economic burden to the operator. Just obtaining the required liability insurance is extremely difficult as well as very expensive for most disposers. Therefore, it is expected that generators will have a tendency to ship more wastes off site. Additionally, current on-site facilities for disposing of hazardous wastes have limited capacity. In many cases the siting criteria will preclude expanding those facilities beyond their current boundaries. This will force those generators to ship wastes off site or to relocate to other facilities that they may own.

Figure 3 shows the percent of hazardous waste by waste type that were shipped off site by generators in Pennsylvania in 1987. Forty five percent was in the form of aqueous liquid waste with approximately 22.5% of this consisting of pickle liquor. Another 34% consists of solids and sludges. The waste in Pennsylvania covers a wide range of activity, but is predominantly inorganic, as compared with hazardous waste across the United States, which tends to be predominantly organic.

Source Reduction and Waste Minimization

The 1976 Federal Resource Conservation and Recovery Act was intended, as its title indicates, to encourage conservation and recovery of materials as opposed to disposal of wastes. In response to more stringent regulations and more costly treatment, industry has employed a number of mechanisms to reduce hazardous waste at the source.

- Process Changes;
- Segregation of Waste Streams;
- New Equipment;
- Improved Operation.

A great deal of the initial reduction was in such simple matters as dewatering of sludges. Some mechanisms that have been used to reduce waste include analysis of the waste to demonstrate that it is not hazardous. An increased emphasis on source and waste reduction is being seen at the state levels and there is some indication that mandatory reduction levels may be written into RCRA when it is reauthorized by Congress.

In Pennsylvania the following programs are being implemented to encourage hazardous waste minimization:

- A Technical Assistance Program (TAP);
- An educational outreach program;
- The Governor's Waste Minimization Award program;
- Participation in the Northeast Industrial Waste Exchange;
- Funding to the Center for Hazardous Materials Research (CHMR) at the University of Pittsburgh;
- Imposition of hazardous waste transportation and management required by Act 108; and
- Grants for recycling equipment.

Capacity Assurance Plans

Under the federal Superfund law every state was required to submit a Capacity Assurance Plan (CAP) to EPA on October 17, 1989 describing the ability of the state to dispose of the hazardous waste generated within the borders for the next 20 years. Pennsylvania's CAP was developed as part of the Northeast States Regional Capacity Assurance Plan in conjunction with the District of Columbia, Connecticut, Delaware, Maine, Maryland, Massachusetts, New Hampshire, New Jersey, Rhode Island, Vermont, Virginia, and West Virginia. The CAP noted disposal deficiencies for sludge treatment and landfill capacity.

The Plan shows that the 13 states as a group have the capacity to treat and dispose of the waste generated within their borders with the following exceptions[1]:

- 76,000 ton incineration shortfall for 1989;

- 11,600 — 16,000 ton sludge treatment shortfall;

- 140,000 — 283,000 ton landfill shortfall in the future.

A committee has been formed to attempt arrangements with other regions to satisfy this shortfall to demonstrate that there is indeed capacity available for treatment and disposal of the waste generated.

Summary

- Pennsylvania has no land disposal facilities currently operating.
- The hazardous waste facilities plan recommends that the Commonwealth should move toward the following preferred waste management practices as shown in Figure 1:
    — Encouraging source reduction
    — Recycling/reuse/recovery
    — Optimizing use of treatment technologies
    — Minimizing land disposal
    — Eliminating land disposal of unstabilized waste
- The Commonwealth currently requires new facilities for incineration, wet air oxidation, advanced thermal destruction, aqueous waste treatment, and land disposal.
- State government, industry and the environmental community are working to educate the public to the potential crisis if new facilities are not sited.
- No acceptable solution is yet at hand.

Figure 1
Waste Management Hierarchy

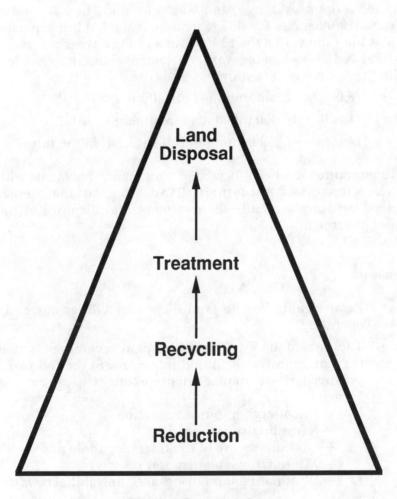

**Land
Disposal**

Treatment

Recycling

Reduction

Waste Generation

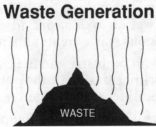

WASTE

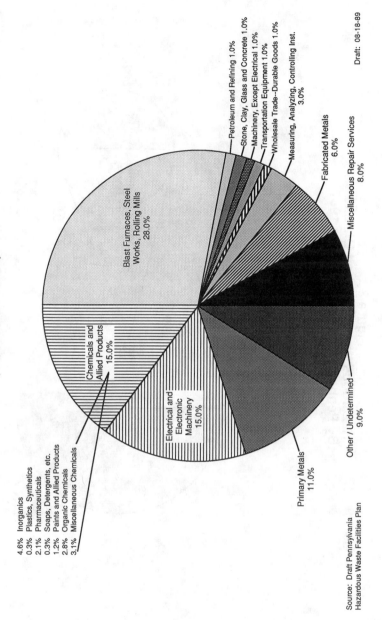

Figure 2
Percentage By Industry of Off-Site Hazardous
Waste Generated in Pennsylvania in 1987
(Before Normalization)

Blast Furnaces, Steel
Works, Rolling Mills
28.0%

Chemicals and
Allied Products
15.0%

Electrical and
Electronic
Machinery
15.0%

Primary Metals
11.0%

Other / Undetermined
9.0%

Miscellaneous Repair Services
8.0%

Fabricated Metals
6.0%

Measuring, Analyzing, Controlling Inst.
3.0%

Wholesale Trade--Durable Goods 1.0%
Transportation Equipment 1.0%
Machinery, Except Electrical 1.0%
Stone, Clay, Glass and Concrete 1.0%
Petroleum and Refining 1.0%

4.6% Inorganics
0.3% Plastics, Synthetics
2.1% Pharmaceuticals
0.3% Soaps, Detergents, etc.
1.2% Paints and Allied Products
2.8% Organic Chemicals
3.1% Miscellaneous Chemicals

Source: Draft Pennsylvania
Hazardous Waste Facilities Plan

Draft: 08-18-89

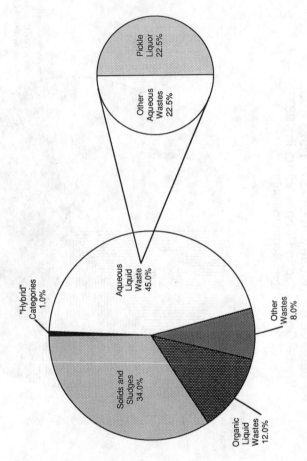

Figure 3
Hazardous Waste Shipped Off-Site
By Pennsylvania Generators in 1987
By Waste Type
(Before Normalization)

Source: Draft Pennsylvania Hazardous Waste Facilities Plan

Draft: 08-18-89

SECTION SIX:

Reforming the Courts, the Legislature, and the Law

CHAPTER EIGHTEEN

PRISONS AND ALTERNATIVES TO INCARCERATION
By Daniel S. Nagin

EDITOR'S SUMMARY

The prison population is exploding in Pennsylvania. With a rated capacity of about 13,000, the state system is now housing nearly 50% more inmates than its designed capacity. The crowding problem in county jails is comparably serious, with 79% of jail inmates incarcerated in overcrowded facilities.

Incarceration is becoming increasingly expensive. Construction costs average about $50,000-$75,000 per cell and the average annual cost of housing an inmate is about $14,000 per year. In Pennsylvania, $254 million has been spent for the renovation and construction of state prisons in the 1980's and the Department of Corrections budget has grown by 40% during this same period.

Alternatives to incarceration must be considered. The high cost of building and operating prisons plus the overcrowding conditions now present in the system are reasons for analyzing other possible sanctions. These "intermediate" sanctions include the use of intensive probation and parole, house arrest, and shock incarceration.

Intensive Supervision Parole/Probation (ISP) programs are less expensive than incarceration. ISP programs include some combination of multiple weekly contacts with the supervising officer, unscheduled drug testing, strict enforcement of probation conditions, and community service. ISP programs attempt to reverse the minimal supervision of parole conditions present in most regular parole programs.

House arrest is an increasingly popular intermediate sanction. House arrest is explicitly intended to be punitive and can be used as a sentencing alternative to a prison or fail. Typically, it is imposed on nonviolent offenders or a probationer/parolee charged with technical or misdemeanor violations.

Shock incarceration is the newest intermediate sanction program. Participants in these programs are subjected to a military bootcamp environment in order to instill a sense of discipline and respect for authority. Admission is generally limited to young offenders who have not been previously incarcerated and have been convicted of a nonviolent crime.

Intermediate sanctions can reduce expenditures for corrections. The cost impact of intermediate sanctions depends on the intensity of surveillance of program participants and types of services made available to participants. It generally costs between $1,500 to $8,500 annually per-participant for intermediate sanctions compared to an annual cost of $9,000 to $20,000 per-inmate for incarceration.

Intermediate sanctions can help to improve the correctional system, but expectations should be modest. There are problems of balancing the costs of imprisonment with just sentencing and public safety needs. Society must ultimately make some tough choices concerning incarceration and intermediate sanctions.

Daniel S. Nagin is Professor of Management at the School of Urban and Public Affairs, Carnegie Mellon University and served as Deputy Secretary of Fiscal Policy and Analysis in the Pennsylvania Department of Revenue from 1981-1986.

Prisons and jails are a growth industry in Pennsylvania. Between 1980 and 1988 the inmate population in state-run correctional facilities increased by 118% from 8,243 to 17,929. In 1980 the number of inmates in county jails stood at about 7,500. By 1987 the population exceeded 13,000. Not surprisingly such unprecedented growth in inmate populations has spawned serious overcrowding. With a rated capacity of about 13,000 the state system is now housing nearly 50% more inmates than its designed capacity. The crowding problem in county jail facilities is comparably serious. The Pennsylvania Council on Crime and Delinquency reports that in 1987 79% of jail inmates were incarcerated in overcrowded facilities.

Incarceration is an expensive business. Construction costs average about $50,000 - $75,000 per cell and the average annual cost of housing an inmate is about $14,000 per year and can be as high as $30,000. The high cost of incarceration is a major factor in the growth of the Commonwealth's corrections budget. Since Fiscal Year 79-80 the Department of Corrections' operating budget has increased on average by 14% per year — twice the rate of growth in General Fund expenditures. Further, $254 million has been spent for the renovation and construction of prisons. Upward spiraling prison populations and corrections budgets are not unique to Pennsylvania. Nationwide prison populations have increased by more than 100% since 1980 and corrections is the fastest growing component of most state budgets.

The high cost of building and operating prisons, the inhumane conditions created by overcrowding, and court orders to improve prison living conditions have combined to create a special urgency to identify alternatives to incarceration. Much of the experimentation with alternatives to incarceration involves the use of "intermediate" sanctions. Among these are intensive probation and parole, house arrest, and shock incarceration.

While in principle criminal statutes afford judges considerable flexibility in sentencing, in reality judges typically have only two choices — incarceration or regular probation. In the sentencing of nonviolent offenders without lengthy criminal histories, neither may be very attractive. On one hand a sentence of regular probation, which in practice involves little supervision, is deemed an inadequate response to a serious, albeit nonviolent, criminal act. On the other hand incarceration seems excessive in terms of the seriousness of the act, the danger the individual poses to the public safety and the threat the typical prison environment poses to the individual. Intermediate sanctions are intended to provide viable sentencing options to the polar extremes of incarceration and regular probation. Compared to incarceration and regular probation intermediate sanctions are intended to hold the middle ground in terms of punitiveness, the degree of safety afforded the public, and their cost.

In this article I will begin by briefly describing several of the most popular examples of intermediate sanctions. I will then focus on the implications of widespread use of intermediate sanctions for issues such as prison overcrowding and costs, public safety, and equitable sentencing. Regrettably, this discussion cannot appeal to the findings of rigorous evaluations because none have been completed. While there have been many purported evaluations, these studies are seriously flawed. Space does not permit an extended discussion of these flaws. For a thorough discussion of the limitations of extant evaluations I refer the interested reader to a monograph by Tonry and Will. Tonry and Will conclude that the often extravagant claims of success in extant evaluations should generally be greeted with more than a little skepticism; I concur.[1]

Examples of Intermediate Sanctions

Throughout the United States, state and local governments are experimenting with a great variety of intermediate sanctions. The most popular are intensive supervision probation/parole, house arrest, and shock incarceration. Such labels can, however, create a deceptive sense of homogeneity. Programs billed under each of these headings come in many shapes and forms. The details of the design have important implications for the program's influence on prison population, cost, public safety and the quality of justice. Thus, the descriptions which follow are intended only to illustrate the prominent features of each of these categories of intermediate sanctions.

Intensive Probation and Parole

Probation and parole officers are commonly assigned several

hundred cases. As a result, the probationer or parolee often receives minimal supervision and enforcement of parole conditions is typically spotty. Intensive Supervision Parole/Probation (ISP) programs are intended to remedy these deficiencies. Most programs include some combination of multiple weekly contacts with the supervising officer, unscheduled drug testing, strict enforcement of parole/probation conditions, and community service. To achieve these goals, case loads of supervising officers are typically in the range of 30 to 50 individuals. As of 1987, ISP programs were underway in at least one county in 40 states.[2]

Beyond the mix of requirements and the intensity of supervision, ISP programs also differ on other important dimensions. One is whether diversion to ISP is controlled by the sentencing judge or corrections officials. In Georgia's ISP program, which is perhaps the oldest, largest, and most publicized in the United States, entrance is controlled by the sentencing judge. Because the program is intended to be an alternative to a prison or jail sentence, I will call this a "front door" design — it is intended to reduce the rate of commitments to jails and prisons. By contrast, New Jersey's ISP is a "back door" program. Admission to the program is administered by the Department of Corrections and the candidate pool is prison inmates.

A second important design feature concerns the definition of the program's target population. The New Jersey and Georgia programs are intended for individuals who are deemed to pose a low threat to public safety. Offenders who have committed violent crimes or who have a history of violence are rarely admitted. The typical participant has been convicted of drunk driving, a drug offense, or a less serious property crime. By contrast, the Massachusetts' ISP program is directed at high risk parolees from the state's prison population. Many of these individuals have been convicted of violent crimes.[3]

House Arrest

House arrest is another increasingly popular intermediate sanction. House arrest should be distinguished from curfew restrictions which are common conditions of probation or parole. Curfew restrictions are typically of limited duration (e.g., being at home between 10:00 P.M. and 6:00 A.M.) and are intended to keep the individual out of "harms way." By contrast, house arrest is explicitly intended to be punitive and requires the individual to remain at his residence at all times except when at work or involved in some specified activity such as drug or alcohol treatment.

House arrest should also be distinguished from electronic monitoring. While house arrest is explicitly intended as a punishment, electronic monitoring is not. Rather it is a technology for insuring that the individual is abiding by the conditions of the house arrest sentence.

Like ISP, house arrest is a very flexible sanction. It can be used as a sentencing alternative to a prison or jail. Florida's program is perhaps the most prominent example of such a "front door" program. Since its inception in 1983, 20,000 individuals have been sentenced to house arrest. Typically, the individual has been convicted of a nonviolent felony or is a probationer/parolee charged with technical or misdemeanor violations. Smaller front door programs are also in place. The target population for these programs are commonly persons convicted of drunk driving or misdemeanors.

House arrests can also be used as a "back door" sanction. In Oklahoma more than 4,000 prison inmates have had the location of their incarceration shifted from a state institution to their home. To be eligible prisoners must have served 15% of their maximum sentence and be within 27 months of discharge. Only persons convicted of nonviolent offenses are eligible.

Shock Incarceration

Shock incarceration (SI) is among the newer of the intermediate sanctions but has already received wide media attention. The National Institute of Justice reports that 11 states have shock incarceration programs.[4] Most of these programs are in southern states, which as a region has the highest rate of incarceration in the country.

Most SI programs operate within the confines of a conventional state prison. Participants are, however, segregated from regular inmates. During their "shock" incarceration — 90 to 180 days — inmates are subjected to a military bootcamp environment, albeit without weapons. The idea is to "jolt" them from their criminal habits and also to instill a sense of discipline and respect for authority. Post-release requirements vary. In some states those who are successful in the shock phase are assigned to regular probation. In others they are assigned to an ISP program. In still others they are released to the community without further condition.

Admission to SI programs are generally limited to young offenders who have not been previously incarcerated and have been convicted of a nonviolent crime. In some states assignment to the program is at the discretion of the sentencing judge. In others it is at the discretion of corrections officials.

Will Intermediate Sanctions Reduce Prison Populations?

At first blush the answer to this question would seem to be an obvious "yes" but, as is often the case, things are more complicated than they first appear. The reason is that despite stated intentions, intermediate sanctions will invariably be imposed on individuals who would not have otherwise been incarcerated.[5]

For shock incarceration the diversion of nonprison bound offenders implies increasing the number of prison admissions. Whether on balance shock incarceration reduces inmate populations depends on a host of factors. Among these are the length of the shock incarceration period, the proportion of participants who would not otherwise have been incarcerated, the proportion of participants who fail and are diverted to the regular prison population, and the amount of time "failures" are incarcerated with the regular prison population.

Ambiguity about the impact of intermediate sanctions on prison populations also extends to programs like ISP and house arrest which do not involve incarceration. Like shock incarceration, some proportions of persons assigned to the program would not have otherwise been incarcerated. Diversion of nonprison bound offenders is particularly likely in "front door" programs where selection is controlled by the sentencing judge. Of this group some proportion will invariably fail to meet program requirements and be incarcerated for either technical violations or for having committed a new crime.[6] Those who are incarcerated for technical violations unambiguously add to the prison population. Ironically, this may also be the case even for those who are incarcerated for a new crime because the close supervision which is the intended purpose of ISP and house arrest may be the basis for their apprehension.[7] Finally, one must keep in mind that failures among those who would have otherwise been incarcerated will further attenuate any positive impact of ISP and house arrest on prison population.

In my judgement it is likely that intermediate sanctions such as ISP and house arrest reduce prison population somewhat but by far less than proponents have argued. For shock incarceration I am less confident of this conclusion.

I emphasize the issue of prison population for several reasons. Prison overcrowding makes this an issue in its own right. If the principle objective of an intermediate sanction program is reducing prison population, it is probably best that it be designed as a "back door" program such as New Jersey's ISP or Oklahoma's house arrest program. Judges may impose a prison sentence in anticipation that the individual will be selected for a "back door" program, but back door programs are undoubtedly a surer way to reduce prison populations than "front door" programs. A second reason I emphasize prison population is that it is a key ingredient in assessing the impact of intermediate sanctions on the cost of running the corrections system. This is the topic of the next section.

Will Intermediate Sanctions Reduce Expenditures for Corrections?

By one estimate Georgia's ISP program has saved the state's taxpayers the expense of constructing and operating two prisons. The Florida Department of Corrections estimates that the state's house arrest program resulted in an annual savings of nearly $75 million.

A major reason for the growing popularity of intermediate sanctions is their promise to check ballooning taxpayer expenditures for corrections. Table 1 reports estimates of the annual cost per person-year of various intermediate sanctions. Compared to the cost of incarceration — $14,000 per person-year plus a $50,000 capital cost per cell — intermediate sanctions appear to be cheap. Moreover, since intermediate sanction programs commonly require the participants to pay a supervision fee, the cost to taxpayers is further reduced. Comparison of annual costs can, however, be deceptive and easily lead to overblown expectations about cost savings.

Table 1
ANNUAL COST OF SENTENCING OPTIONS
(Exclusive of construction costs)

Option	Annual Cost ($)
Routine probation	300 - 2,000
Intensive probation	1,500 - 7,000
House arrest	
Without electronics	1,350 - 7,000
With telephone call-back system	2,500 - 5,000
With passive electronic monitoring	2,500 - 6,500
With active electronic monitoring	4,500 - 8,500
Local jail	8,000 - 12,000
Local detention center	5,000 - 15,000
State prison	9,000 - 20,000

Source: J. Petersilia

Cost savings will depend, in part, on the number of people assigned to the program who would not have been incarcerated. Without the program some individuals would have presumably been sentenced to routine probation (or released unsupervised to the community). As shown in Table 1, routine probation is generally far less expensive than most intermediate sanctions. This will result in an increase in corrections expenditures for this category of program participants. Further, some proportion of this group will fail to meet the program requirements and be diverted to the most expensive sanction option — prison.

Cost savings will also depend on the failure rate of program participants who would have otherwise been prison bound. Whether there are any cost savings for this category of program failures depends on the length of incarceration following failure compared to the time they would have spent in prison had they not been initially diverted. If, for example, there is no reduction in incarceration time, then there is an increase in corrections expenditures for this group. The only group for whom there would seem to be a certain cost savings are those who would have otherwise been sent to prison and who successfully complete the program requirements.

Even for this group, however, there is some ambiguity. The ambiguity stems from a somewhat arcane but important issue of cost accounting. The average annual cost per inmate-year is calculated by dividing the annual cost of operating the prison system by the average daily prison population. The issue is: how well does this average cost calculation capture the incremental savings of avoiding a person-year of imprisonment? Tonry and Will argue that $14,000 per prisoner-year grossly overestimates the true savings. They argue that unless an entire institution, or section thereof can be closed down, or alternatively future construction can be avoided, cost savings will be minimal. For small scale programs involving only the diversion of a tiny fraction of the total inmate population their argument is undoubtedly correct. However, for large scale programs such as those in Florida, Georgia, and Oklahoma their argument is less compelling.

Notwithstanding, Tonry and Will are correct in emphasizing that facile appeals to differences in average cost can result in overblown expectations about cost savings. Average costs are not generally equal to incremental costs. Further, even in circumstances where average cost reasonably approximates incremental costs it is important to keep in mind the full cost savings of diversion pertain only to those individuals who would otherwise have been prison bound and who successfully complete the intermediate sanction program. For the other categories of participants defined above intermediate sanctions either unequivocally increase corrections costs or have an uncertain effect. Consequently, claims of large corrections cost savings should be greeted with skepticism. It is even possible that intermediate sanctions will increase the corrections' bill.

The cost impact of intermediate sanction programs will depend on a multitude of design features including the intensity of surveillance of program participants and the types of rehabilitative services availed to participants. Cost impacts are also likely to be heavily influenced by whether it is a "front door" or "back door" program. All else equal "back door" programs would seem most likely to achieve the largest corrections cost savings.

Do Intermediate Sanctions Jeopardize Public Safety?

This is a complicated question. Its answer turns on issues such as: How well does the program control and monitor the activities of participants? Absent the program, how would program participants been sentenced? Are program participants high risk or low risk offenders? Does the program have a rehabilitative influence? I will address these questions in turn.

Incarceration is the surest way to protect the public safety; while incarcerated an offender is physically constrained from victimizing the general public. Regular probation provides the least public protection. With case loads often in the hundreds, probation officers can typically do little to monitor the activities of their assignees. The degree of public safety provided by intermediate sanctions is somewhere in between incarceration and regular probation and is a function of the type and design of the program.

Shock incarceration provides the same degree of public safety as regular incarceration during the period of confinement. The period of confinement is, however, shorter by design. The enhanced security of ISP and house arrest compared to regular probation is much more difficult to assess and will depend on the design of the program (e.g., intensity of surveillance, whether electronic monitoring is used). Preliminary results of an evaluation of ISP, which is being conducted by the Rand Corporation, suggest that parole revocations are about the same or higher for offenders assigned to ISP compared to comparable offenders assigned to regular probation.[8] A conclusion that ISP is not effective in deterring criminal activity is, however, premature. The higher revocation rate may simply reflect the fact that ISP is doing its job — closely monitoring the activities of assignees.

The threat to public safety will also be affected by other factors. To the extent that an intermediate sanction program is diverting prison bound offenders, there is obviously some diminution of the public's safety. But, as I have emphasized, intermediate sanction programs will invariably cast a wider net and divert individuals who would have been sentenced to regular probation. This is true even for back door programs if some judges anticipate the diversion decisions of corrections officials. Thus, in part the incremental effect of intermediate sanctions will depend on the degree to which it is diverting prison bound vs. probation bound offenders.

A final key factor affecting the threat to public safety will be the types of offenders assigned to the program. Most programs such as Georgia's and New Jersey's ISP, Florida's house arrest program, and Oklahoma's shock incarceration program are targeted at low risk offenders. Persons convicted of violent crimes and offenders with long criminal histories are rarely assigned to these programs. Thus, the selection process itself is designed to minimize public risk.

This focus on the least violent offenders is entirely understandable. Just one bad call can jeopardize an entire program — to wit, Willy Horton. The typical emphasis on the lowest risk offenders may, however, have unforeseen consequences which should be recognized. First, if the program is intended to divert individuals who would otherwise be prison bound, it seems certain that the lower the risk threshold the less likely this objective will be achieved. Second, low thresholds may result in the ironic situation of lower risk offenders being subjected to more intensive and costly supervision than higher risk offenders. An extreme example of this is a situation where drunk driving offenders are sentenced to house arrest with electronic monitoring and offenders with long criminal histories are released from prison to regular probation. At first blush, this may seem like an implausible hypothetical, but it is not; sentencing and parole decisions are highly decentralized.

Do intermediate sanctions rehabilitate? There have been no rigorous evaluations of the rehabilitative effects of the intermediate sanction programs of the 1980's but with one possible exception there is little reason for optimism. A report of the National Academy of Sciences released in 1979 concluded that there is little evidence of rehabilitative programs having had much success in reducing recidivism.

One glimmer of optimism pertains to drug testing. There is good evidence that drug using offenders commit crimes at a higher rate than their nondrug using counterparts and that during periods of nondrug use, offending rates decline. There is also evidence that regular drug testing of offenders known or suspected of being drug abusers reduces recidivism.[9] It thus appears that such testing inhibits drug use. One might question whether this is really rehabilitation. Semantic issues aside, this evidence does suggest that random drug testing should be a prominent component of intermediate sanction programs directed at drug abusers.

Do Intermediate Sanctions Provide Justice?

Intermediate sanctions, as their name is intended to communicate, provide a middle ground between probation and
incarceration. For practical purposes the question whether
intermediate sanctions provide justice is not really quite on
target. The more appropriate question is: Will intermediate
sanctions improve the quality of justice? The answer to this
question turns on many normative issues which I will not
attempt to address here. However, it also turns on an important
nonnormative issue. Namely, what sentence would the individual have received if the intermediate sanction had not been
available? As previously discussed the answer is usually imprisonment or regular probation. This observation has important implications for thinking through the question of the
impact of intermediate sanctions on the quality of justice.
    Intermediate sanctions have earned the rancor of some
groups such as Mothers Against Drunk Driving (MADD).
MADD perceives that intermediate sanctions such as house
arrest are simply "a slap on the wrist" compared to regular
incarceration. As a parent, I share this reaction. Notwithstanding, it is important to keep in mind that the "inn is full." For each
day a drunk driver is incarcerated some other type of criminal
cannot be incarcerated. We do not normally think of prison as a
precious resource, but if the combination of scarcity and high
demand define "precious" then it is. We as a society must make
some tough choices concerning the types of offenders we want to
incarcerate and for how long. Tough rhetoric about "locking
'em all up" may sound good but the reality will be quite different. In the end, like it or not, courts will intervene and force
the release or forever delay the admission of some offenders who
have received prison sentences. In all likelihood the result will
be even less to our liking than that arising from conscious
choice.
    Returning to the example of MADD's displeasure with inter-
mediate sanctions, it may be the case that their concern is based
on a faulty assumption — intermediate sanctions divert prison
bound offenders. An instructive example involves a case study
of a drunk driving crackdown conducted by H. Laurence Ross.

Upon his election, a judge in a central Ohio county began sentencing all persons convicted of drunk driving to jail; no ifs, ands, or buts. Ross found, however, that the likelihood of actually being incarcerated for drunk driving did not increase. The reason is that the jails were full. Thus, for many offenders a sentence to an intermediate sanction program may escalate the severity of the sentence they would have otherwise received — probation.

While the prospect of intermediate sanctions escalating the severity of punishment is of solace to some, for others it is not. Some observers are concerned that intermediate sanctions are a threat to civil liberties because they have the potential for greatly expanding the punitive reach of the State. Every home, for example, has the potential of being converted to a jail. I believe that such net widening concerns can easily be overblown. They also neglect some of the equity benefits which may be achieved. When judges are forced to choose between regular probation and incarceration, the goal of proportionality in sentencing — fitting the punishment to the crime — must inevitably suffer. Whatever their failings in terms of controlling prison populations and cost, intermediate sanctions do provide a middle ground in terms of punitiveness.

Some are also concerned that intermediate sanctions may increase class and racial discrimination in sentencing by reserving incarceration as the sanction of choice for minorities and the poor. This concern is again based on the shaky premise that the "privileged" would otherwise be incarcerated. If this is not the case, and in many circumstances there are ample reasons for believing so, intermediate sanctions could increase the equity of sentencing across classes and races.

Conclusions

Like incarceration, intermediate sanctions are something of a growth industry. This is not a coincidence. In large part the growing interest in intermediate sanctions has been spawned by the growth in prison populations.

In some respects this article might be more aptly titled "A Cautionary Note on Intermediate Sanctions." I have argued that it is far from certain that intermediate sanctions can appreciably reduce prison populations and public expenditures for corrections. Indeed in some circumstances intermediate sanctions may actually increase one or both of these. If the principal goal of an intermediate sanction program is to control prison populations and correction expenditures, then "back door" designs are probably the best bet.

"Back door" programs, however, have certain disadvantages. Compared to "front door" alternatives, they are more likely to involve offenders who pose a greater public danger. Further, for reasons discussed in the prior section, they are less likely to contribute to just sentencing.

There are no easy answers to the problem of balancing the costs of imprisonment and corrections with concerns about public safety and just sentencing. In my judgement, intermediate sanctions can help to improve the balance, but expectations should be modest. There is no easy fix.

CHAPTER NINETEEN

DRUG POLICY IN PENNSYLVANIA
By Charles E. Greenawalt

EDITOR'S SUMMARY

Society must engage all its institutions — families, schools, churches, businesses, civic organizations, and government — to win the war on drugs. There is no panacea for public policy makers as they determine the best way to address the drug problem. An effective strategy should combine the components of education, treatment, and law enforcement in order to achieve victory.

Approximately 60 million Americans spend roughly $150 billion annually on illicit drugs. Drug abuse costs American business each year almost $100 billion. However, in the last five years, thousands of companies have developed their own policies and programs for a drug-free workplace.

In Pennsylvania from 1981-1987, drug arrests increased by 43%. Almost half of all drug arrests in the state took place in Philadelphia within the period, with Pittsburgh accounting for 11%. Treatments for cocaine abuse increased 975% between 1983-1988.

There are five goals any drug policy should meet. 1) Drive all illicit drug dealers out of business; 2) Reduce the state's demand for all illicit drugs; 3) Provide treatment facilities for drug-dependent people; 4) Assist law enforcement personnel to more effectively fight the drug problem; 5) Reduce prison over-crowding.

The best weapon against drugs is parents who properly educate their children about drugs' dangers. Certain proposals under consideration include requiring all teachers to be certified in substance abuse education; enrolling the state's schools in the U.S. Education Department's Drug-Free School Recognition Program; developing a state-financed assembly program; and a special youth education fund on drug awareness.

The Commonwealth should establish special drug courts in Phila-delphia and Pittsburgh that would only handle drug sale cases. The state must also consider adopting a mandatory law to increase deterrence for serious drug offenses, where a defendant convic-ted a third time for felony drug crime is given a mandatory life sentence and is ineligible for parole.

The federal government's emphasis on targeting casual middle class and upper class drug users and dealers should be examined. Research has shown that drug use has declined among the middle class. The federal government's policy of treating all drugs as equally evil encourages dealers to switch from marijuana, which is relatively cheap to the more profitable and dangerous cocaine.

An anti-drug movement is emerging across Pennsylvania and the nation. Help groups for addicts, grassroots organizations, along with neighborhood anti-drug and anti-crime groups, are taking steps to achieve victory in the war against drugs.

Charles E. Greenawalt is Director of Policy for the Pennsylvania Senate Majority Caucus and an Adjunct Professor of Political Science at Millersville University.

J ust as every U.S. President in recent years has declared his own war on drugs, the year 1989 was one during which many state and local governments did the same. Eighteen years ago, President Richard Nixon launched this struggle at the federal level by appointing the nation's first White House Drug Czar, Myles J. Ambrose, and pushed to pursue a "balanced and comprehensive" assault on the "drug menace." In fact, major anti-crime and anti-drug laws were enacted in 1984, 1986, and 1988. While President and Nancy Reagan made a joint TV appearance in 1986 to initiate a more energetic federal government crusade against drugs, President Bush issued his declaration of war against drugs on September 5, 1989, in a televised speech to the American people from the White House. Indeed, perhaps the most prominent issue for state and local government to contend with in Pennsylvania during 1989 was drugs.

With well-orchestrated bursts of publicity, all of the major players in Pennsylvania government have entered the war on drugs. Questions have been posed, such as: How much of a problem was illicit drugs for the nation and the Commonwealth at this time? Furthermore, were the proposals which were advanced by the Governor, the General Assembly, and the Attorney General the most effective responses to deal with this threat?

National Cost of Drug Abuse

New strategies to combat illicit drugs have been sought by public policy analysts because of the magnitude of this problem in our society. According to government studies, approximately 60 million Americans spend roughly $150 billion annually on illicit drugs.[1] Estimates of how much drug abuse costs American business each year range from $33 billion to more than $100 billion.[2] Numerous businessmen now believe that illicit "hard drugs" create more trouble for their operations than the effects of alcoholism. Government figures for the national cost of drug abuse lag by a number of years; however, even in 1983, the cost to the American economy of drug abuse is estimated to be $59.747 billion, up from $46.9 billion in 1980. Costs are incurred by American businesses each year through decreased productivity, absenteeism, accidents, and unrealized profits stemming from impaired judgment and creativity. These costs included the following:

$33.346 billion in reduced productivity;
$10.846 billion for crime careers;
$ 6.565 billion in direct crime costs;
$ 2.425 billion for direct incarceration costs;
$ 2.049 billion in treatment and support costs;
$ 2 billion in treatment services;
$ 945 million in costs to crime victims' treatment.

Drug users are three to four times more likely to be injured on the job, and they are two and a half times more likely to be absent from work. Employers' health costs are normally tripled by the average cost for drug users while these individuals have a 50% greater chance of illness than non-drug users. Studies show that substance abusers are late and absent three times more often than non-abusing employees, use three times the average level of health benefits, are involved in accidents three and a half times more than other employees, and are five times more likely to file a workers' compensation claim.

Approximately 37 million Americans used an illegal drug last year; 23 million, or almost one in every ten Americans, used an illegal drug in the past month. Three out of every four teenagers drink alcohol regularly, and nearly 100,000 ten and eleven year old children report getting drunk at least once a week. One in every eight Americans is a child of an alcoholic.

The cost of this substance abuse is staggering. More than $200 billion is lost in the United States annually to the economic and social drain that substance abuse perpetuates. Crime, unemployment, lost productivity, chronic illness, abusive family relationships, and death are all direct consequences of drug and alcohol abuse by alcoholics and addicts. The relationship between drugs, alcohol, and crime is clear. Nearly three quarters of all persons arrested, for reasons other than drugs, test positive for illegal drugs or alcohol intoxication at the time of their arrest. Juvenile court judges report that 60-90% of their case-loads involve some degree of drug or alcohol abuse.

According to the 1988 White House Conference for a Drug-Free America, the relationship between substance abuse and criminal activity "goes well beyond the commission of crime to support a habit"; substance abuse has "victims beyond conventional crime." These victims include the tens of thousands killed or maimed each year by drunk and drug-using drivers, the babies born addicted or abandoned at birth by addicted and alcoholic mothers, 25% of AIDS victims who acquire the disease through intravenous drug use, and the children — some as young as seven years old — recruited into drug dealing and gang activity.

Even more destructive and irreversible are the consequences of substance abuse that victimize the families. Drug and alcohol abuse are intergenerational phenomena — abusers pass on to their children not only the emotional, social, and financial havoc that drug and alcohol habits create, but also a greater risk of developing addictions themselves. For example, the 29 million Americans who are children of alcoholics — 7 million of whom are minor children currently living with alcoholic parents — are four times more likely to become an alcoholic than their peers from nonalcoholic homes. Even the grandsons of alcoholic grandfathers are three times more likely to become alcoholics, and daughters of alcoholics are more likely to marry alcoholic men.[3]

Children of substance abusers are placed for adoption or foster care more often, have greater incidences of behavioral and educational problems, and are more likely to become runaways. They are also more likely to be born with birth defects and fetal alcohol syndrome; treated for hyperactivity and aggressive conduct disorders; abused physically, emotionally, or sexually; referred to adolescent psychiatric inpatient programs; become pregnant and start parenting as teenagers; adjudicated as juvenile crime offenders; and treated for substance abuse themselves. While 3,600 to 10,000 babies are born each year in the United States with fetal alcohol syndrome, other studies estimate that nearly 175,000 babies annually have been exposed to illegal drugs — frequently cocaine.

Drugs in Pennsylvania

Accurate data on drug usage is hard to obtain and the costs associated with that usage are difficult to determine. Therefore, compiling reliable statistics on drug usage on a statewide basis can be challenging. In the Commonwealth, the Pennsylvania Commission on Crime and Delinquency (PCCD) appears to be the single best source of drug usage data. The PCCD's "Pennsylvania Statewide Drug Law Enforcement and Violent Crime Strategy," reports that "the magnitude of drug abuse in Pennsylvania has increased over the past seven years as reflected in information concerning drug arrests."[4] During the seven year period, between 1981 and 1987, drug arrests in the Commonwealth increased by 43%. This increase is particularly significant since arrests for all other offenses in Pennsylvania dropped by 2% over the same period. Historically, most drug arrests have involved drug possession. PCCD notes, however, that arrests for the sale and/or manufacture of drugs rose a dramatic 92% during the 1981-87 time period.

Philadelphia appears to have the Commonwealth's largest drug problem since 45% of all drug arrests in Pennsylvania took place within the city limits. When the four suburban counties surrounding Philadelphia are included (Bucks, Chester, Delaware, and Montgomery), that figure jumps to 60%. Allegheny County, which includes the city of Pittsburgh, accounted for 11% of all drug arrests. Consequently, the remaining drug arrests occurred in the Commonwealth's other 61 counties.

The most significant rise in drug-related arrests involve cocaine. Between 1981 and 1987, cocaine arrests soared by 357%. Although marijuana-related arrests have historically accounted for the majority of drug arrests, in 1987 arrests for cocaine and related opiates surpassed reported arrests for marijuana. This increase in cocaine abuse is also mirrored in the statistics for the Commonwealth's drug treatment facilities. Treatment for cocaine abuse increased 975% over five years between 1983 and 1988.

Student Use of Drugs

Since 1979, the Primary Prevention Awareness, Attitude, and Usage Scales (PPAAUS) has been used to conduct student surveys of drug usage throughout the Commonwealth. This survey was conducted throughout Pennsylvania in 1989 with 38,000 students in 6th, 7th, 9th, and 12th grades completing the questionnaire. This survey revealed that one-half of high school seniors drink alcohol at least once a month, 24% drink weekly or more, and almost three quarters of the seniors who drink monthly or more often get drunk at least once a month. Beer is the favorite alcoholic beverage of Pennsylvania students. Approximately 14% of the seniors smoke marijuana at least once a month while 8% of the seniors smoke marijuana weekly or more often. This survey also revealed that cocaine use has been in decline among Pennsylvania students during the last three years. Seven percent of Pennsylvania students are willing to use or try cocaine or crack; nonetheless, only 2.5% of seniors report regular cocaine use.

In the hallucinogenic drug group, this survey revealed that only 1.5% of the seniors and 1% of the 9th graders use this type of drug once a month. Eight percent of the seniors and 5.5% of the 9th graders are interested in trying or using LSD or other hallucinogens.

Finally, heroin usage and the desire to experiment with heroin is quite low among Commonwealth students. Only 1.5% of the 12th graders and 2% of the 9th graders are willing to use heroin. Regular use of heroin among Pennsylvania students is .1% in 12th grade and .3% in 9th grade. Heroin has never been used by 99% of Pennsylvania's 9th graders and seniors. In conclusion, the Commonwealth has seen some improvement in the abuse of illicit hard drugs by students.

Drug Policy

There is no panacea for public policy makers as they determine the best ways to address this problem. Although there are a variety of approaches to deal with substance abuse, this is a problem that will be solved on a person-to-person basis. Progress against substance abuse will be made individual by individual, street by street, and community by community. Although public policy makers seek direct solutions to many problems, society must engage all its institutions — the family, the schools, the church, businesses, civic organizations, and government — to win the war on drugs.

Any comprehensive drug policy must be multifaceted and possess components which address education, treatment, and law enforcement. All of these three components are interrelated.

Education: Many examinations of the drug abuse problem discuss the topics of prevention and education separately. Although these items are frequently separated, one of the aims of drug education is prevention. Therefore, this discussion will deal with these items together under the heading of education.

Many states have been responding to the drug challenge

through programs of drug education. These programs normally fit neatly within the mechanisms already in existence for the dissemination of public health information in the education system. Thus, the incremental cost of devoting resources to drug education is primarily the loss of the use of scarce resources (e.g., classroom and teacher time) rather than out-of-pocket outlays by state or local government. Many governors have been using their leadership positions to encourage saying no to drugs and by exhortation and designation of funds for programs, encouraging others to do the same.

On the national level, a Gallup Poll released during August of 1989 revealed that more than four million youngsters between 13 and 17 years of age said that they have been offered illicit drugs in the previous thirty days. The average age which children first try alcohol or marijuana is 12. Further, in a 1987-88 survey of over 200,000 junior and senior high school students by the national Parents' Resource Institute for Drug Education (PRIDE), over 45% said they drank liquor. A third of the drinkers said they "get bombed" when they drink.

Researchers, who have dealt with the issue of substance abuse throughout the country, believe that the best weapon against illicit drugs is parents. They must prepare their children to deal with the scourge of illicit drugs and alcohol just as they prepare them to deal with fire. However, most parents receive their basic training in child rearing from being reared themselves. But their parents never dealt with a drug epidemic, so today's parents find coping with young children who use drugs as an alien experience. Thus, ignorance and denial are typical. Parents cannot teach their children safe passage in a world awash in alcohol and crack cocaine until they learn more about this world for themselves.

Although there is some difference of opinion, most experts believe that lessons of substance abuse should begin no later than third grade. Children who are in third grade are capable of learning how to identify various drugs, their effects, and their dangers. At this time, parents should also review the messages their children are receiving about drugs and alcohol from friends, relatives, day care providers, and baby-sitters.

Parents must explain, truthfully and in detail, that while not everyone who uses drugs or alcohol becomes an addict or dies as a result, many do. Scare tactics and hysteria do not work with children because as they receive accurate information from other sources, they will discount other previous information that they have received from their parents. Dr. Martha Morrison, author of *White Rabbit: A Woman Doctor's Story of Her Addiction and Recovery*, says "research tells us that kids who perceive drugs as potentially harmful are less likely to use them." Parents must also watch their children for the evidence of "gateway drugs" — tobacco, alcohol, and marijuana. Every drug counselor and drug education expert agrees that a drug or alcohol abuser always began this abuse with one of these gateway drugs.

Many experts and teachers believe that educational efforts are not working. In order to succeed, educational efforts in the schools must profoundly influence the students. Programs must be well-planned, well-funded, and appropriately taught. Pennsylvania already has a Student Assistance Program (SAP), which provides school personnel with the knowledge and skills needed to identify students using alcohol or drugs. Students are referred to professional evaluators, if needed, and receive treatment services. At the end of 1989, 386 out of 501 school districts in Pennsylvania participated in this program. The state also has a program called, "Here's Looking At You, 2000." This program consists of a kindergarten through 12th grade curriculum which teaches children about drugs and helps them understand what roles such things as "self concept" and "coping" play in turning students to drugs. There are approximately 320 school districts currently involved in this program.

The Pennsylvania General Assembly is currently considering legislation which would require drug education in all grades, K-12. To complement this measure, the Commonwealth may also wish to adopt legislation that ten other states and the District of Columbia already have adopted which requires certification in substance abuse education for all teachers. If teachers are going to provide substance abuse education to students, they must have the background which is needed to perform this task effectively.

Another educational initiative which the Commonwealth could adopt would be to enroll the Commonwealth in the U.S. Department of Education's Drug-Free School Recognition Program. The program is a competitive evaluation award program to identify and recognize public and private elementary and secondary schools whose comprehensive prevention programs have succeeded in preventing or reducing student substance abuse.

The goals of the program are to focus national attention on drug-free schools in America; to demonstrate by example that drug-free schools can be achieved and maintained by communities which strive for them; and to offer models of success in creating and maintaining drug-free schools that other school systems may emulate. Only two states in the nation have declined to participate in this program as of the end of 1989 — Maine and Pennsylvania.

Yet another state educational initiative to combat substance abuse would be to develop a state-financed assembly program. This program could utilize former addicts, as a condition of parole or a part of their rehabilitation, to speak to high school students in assemblies and in smaller groups about the effects and consequences of drug abuse.

The Commonwealth may wish to establish a special youth education fund on drug awareness. This program would be modeled somewhat after the Neighborhood Assistance Act. Under this program, corporations and individuals would be requested to aid in the fight against drugs by contributing funds into this Youth Education Drug Awareness Fund. Corporations and individuals would be able to deduct their contributions and would also be given a 50% credit on their income tax upon their next filing. This would double the funds available to the educational program through corporate or personal contributions.

Drug Testing

Invariably, the issue of testing always arises during a discussion of drug prevention. During the 1988 National Conference of State Legislatures' annual meeting, one of the speakers remarked that if the public is truly serious about fighting drug abuse, it will have to be willing to relinquish some civil liberties and support drug testing.

Tennessee was the first state in the nation to adopt a statewide drug testing plan. This plan allows school districts to test students who are under reasonable suspicion of drug use. The bill establishes general criteria for student drug testing. These guidelines include the following: a) a school policy must be broken; b) this test must produce evidence that a rule has been broken; c) the test results will not be used in criminal prosecutions; and d) the test must be conducted in the presence of a witness.

Under the Tennessee law, school principals also must notify parents before the test, and districts must decide how to discipline students testing positive for drugs. Negative results will not be placed on the student's permanent record. The adoption of these testing procedures are optional; they are not mandatory.

If some individuals believe that the Tennessee plan seems too radical, a milder but nonetheless effective step would be to require drug testing of those students wanting to engage in extracurricular activities.

Treatment: A crucial component for any drug abuse policy is treatment. In fact, many drug experts believe that it is somewhat futile to pursue drug users when there are insufficient resources to conduct drug treatment and rehabilitation. The Commonwealth has to be as committed to treatment as to any other facet of the drug abuse policy. Treatment consists of not only making the person drug-free, but treatment must also prepare him for reentry into society.

Selecting a treatment program for substance abuse is a difficult process because little data exists to suggest which approaches work best with certain patients. One may choose a variety of inpatient programs, or one may select outpatient therapy for approximately one-third of the cost of inpatient treatment. At any time, some 9,000 programs are helping 650,000 people nationwide to kick their addictions.[5] Substance abuse treatment centers have burgeoned into a $3 billion a year industry.

Nonetheless, most drug treatments fail as often as they succeed. Studies by such groups as The National Institute of Drug Abuse (NIDA) and The Chemical Abuse and Addiction Treatment Outcome Registry (CATOR), a data gathering group in St. Paul, Minnesota, showed that only about half of those who complete a treatment program of any sort are drug or alcohol free a year later. Only 10 to 20% of those who stay clean for a year can be expected to fall off the wagon over the next two to five years. According to research performed by CATOR, inpatient and outpatient programs succeed just over half the time in treating people who will be abstinent two years later.

As the crack epidemic spirals out of control and as the social cost of substance abuse mounts, new interest has been shown in medical approaches to drug addiction. This renewed interest can be seen in a 50% increase in funding for NIDA.

This additional funding has begun to yield benefits with a new array of drugs being developed to combat addiction. These drugs include buprenorphine, flupenthixol, and carbamazepine. Although medical therapy frequently fails to address the underlying psychological and social causes of substance abuse, these new medications provide therapists with tools to assist in weaning addicts from drugs. Buprenorphine appears to be the most promising of these drugs at the present time. It has proven to be useful in treating cocaine abusers who are addicted to heroin. Because methadone has no opiate-blocking effects, buprenorphine possesses clear advantages over methadone as a treatment for heroin addicts who use cocaine, roughly 70 to 80% of heroin addicts do so, as well as cocaine abusers. Flupenthixol and carbamazepine have also proven to be useful in combating cocaine addiction.

In addition to encouraging new medical approaches to treatment, state government should explore other avenues of treatment. For example, research has repeatedly shown that substance abuse treatment is more effective when the family participates in drug counseling. Consequently, the states of New Mexico, North Carolina, and Texas have all adopted legislation that would empower juvenile court judges to require families to participate in drug counseling for addicted juveniles. This concept was introduced in Senate Bill 617 by Senator Robert C. Jubelirer, and this measure has passed the Pennsylvania Senate. It is to be hoped that the Pennsylvania House will pass this bill in the near future.

Another useful tool for the state which has already been placed into bill form is the ability for parents or guardians of minors judged to be dependent on drugs or alcohol to petition the juvenile court to commit them to substance abuse treatment programs. This concept is embodied in Senate Bill 1173, sponsored by Senator Stewart Greenleaf. Conversely, Pennsylvania may also wish to adopt procedures whereby minors who have been judged to be dependent on drugs or alcohol may petition the juvenile court for a waiver to enter substance abuse treatment programs without obtaining parental consent.

Philadelphia has 60,000 regular users of cocaine and 10,000 regular users of heroin. Among all people in Philadelphia arrested for crimes, 80% test positive for drug use and 70% test positive for cocaine. One might reasonably expect a crack baby problem in Philadelphia, and indeed, one of every six babies born in Philadelphia is born to a mother who used cocaine during her pregnancy.[6] At the national level, 1 to 2% of all live births, somewhere between 30,000 to 50,000 babies, are addicted to crack.[7] Because crack appears to destroy maternal instincts and is more difficult to treat than other addictions, different measures may be useful. The insidious nature of crack has been witnessed by Linda Spooner, director of a drug treatment center set up by New York's Jamaica Community Adolescent Program: "I've seen kids on angel dust, acid, speed, heroin, and cocaine; but I've never seen a drug destroy a person as quickly as crack."[8]

While maintaining the goal of keeping families together and in order to better insure the safety of infants, perhaps the Commonwealth should consider legislation which would mandate the testing of all newborns to determine whether they have been exposed to drugs. If an exposure to drugs is present, the state may wish to mandate that the parents complete substance abuse counseling before the child would be considered to be in their full custody. If the parents are unable to rehabilitate themselves, the children should be placed in foster care. Children of this Commonwealth should not be held hostage to the ravages of illicit drugs.   The private sector may also assist in the war on drugs. Thousands of companies since the mid-1980s have developed their own policies and programs for a drug-free workplace. The Executive Director of the Institute for a Drug-Free Workplace, a coalition of corporations that seek to shape public debate over drug legislation, and Special Counsel for Domestic Policy of the U.S. Chamber of Commerce, Mark A. deBernardo, states, "It's nothing short of phenomenal, the extent to which employers have gotten religion on the drug issue in the last five years."[9] Local business people in several cities such as Jacksonville, Florida and Washington, D.C. have formed groups to help small companies establish anti-drug programs. The Commonwealth can assist in this effort by establishing a small "strike force" which would operate under the direction of the Office of Drug and Alcohol Programs.

For those employers who have not established drug policies but wish to do business with the state, the Commonwealth may wish to adopt legislation which would establish that a company must maintain a drug-free workplace in order to obtain a state contract. Under this legislation, contractors would be required to notify the state government if any employee was convicted of a drug offense, and the government could withhold funds. The employer would have the right of a hearing. If he can prove he has made a "good faith" effort by instituting a drug-free policy and if he can show that all his employees are aware of this policy, the government contract would not be lost.

The treatment process is costly and agonizing. A substance abuser has an equal chance to fail or succeed in treatment, but without a treatment component in the war against drugs, many substance abusers would be lost. Society would find it much more difficult to win this war if it ignores its treatment needs.

Law Enforcement

The serious nature of our state's illegal drug problems can be measured by the increase in arrests for the sale and/or manufacturing of controlled substances. PCCD reports that arrests for sale of drugs increased 92% from 1981 to 1987, and that drug convictions increased 32% and incarcerations rose 107% from 1982 to 1986. The noticeable rise in incarcerations can be attributed to a 144% increase in incarcerations for selling or manufacturing drugs. Although no statistics are available, it may be reasonable to assume some of those arrested and convicted of drug activities are repeat offenders. It is time for the Commonwealth to send a clear message concerning its unwillingness to tolerate those who continuously commit drug crimes.

As previously stated, any successful anti-drug policy must incorporate a variety of measures directed toward the users as well as the sellers of illicit drugs. Therefore, states must also evaluate their punitive measures.

One of the first law enforcement tools which the Commonwealth may wish to create at some point would be special drug courts. The National Association of Attorney Generals and the National District Attorneys Association in "A Drug-Free America" recommend that each state consider the need to establish specialized drug courts to process the increasing number of drug-related cases which are backlogging our courts. Judge Eugene Maier of the Philadelphia Common Pleas Court notes that the Philadelphia Common Pleas Court has more than 11,000 active cases, and 70% of these cases involve drugs.[10]

The Commonwealth should establish drug courts in Philadelphia and Pittsburgh that handle only drug sale cases. Several changes in Pennsylvania's rules of criminal procedure will be needed to permit the expeditious handling of these cases. To speed the pace of these trials, the rule permitting preemptory challenges should be eliminated. The attorneys could still challenge the selection of a juror, however, by stating the reason and convincing the court that the juror may not be fair. Further, time limitations should be imposed on opening and closing statements to the jury. These changes may allow a drug-sale jury trial to be completed in one day. After the court backlog has been eliminated in Philadelphia and Pittsburgh, the Commonwealth may wish to review whether to maintain these courts.

Alabama has adopted a law enforcement tool which might prove useful in battling substance abuse among children. This action was the creation of immunity for school personnel. This measure grants immunity from civil liability to all public or private school employees who communicate information to law-enforcement officials or health officials concerning the suspected use, possession, sale, or distribution of any controlled substance by any child. Immunity does not apply to persons who communicate such information maliciously and with the knowledge that it is false.

Shock Incarceration

As one considers innovative approaches to deal with juvenile drug offenders, one cannot overlook the concept of "shock incarceration." Oklahoma, with its Regimented Inmate Discipline Program, was the first state to adopt this program in November 1983 with a similar program in Georgia soon following. Many observers described shock incarceration as military "boot camps." Youthful offenders are subjected to a regimen of strict discipline, hard labor, physical exercise, and educational and counseling programs. This experience substitutes for prison admission or parole. Many variations among the shock incarceration programs exist, and few program evaluations have been conducted because these programs have been so recently established.

By the end of 1988, 15 shock incarceration programs were operating in nine states. Other states such as California, for example, conduct programs which are similar to shock incarceration, but they are not classified as such because they do not place as much emphasis on the military orientation for the program. During 1989, New Hampshire, North Carolina, and Kansas were scheduled to initiate shock incarceration programs. Indeed, North Carolina did initiate shock incarceration in October of 1989 and graduated its first class in January of 1990. New Hampshire and Kansas delayed the implementation of their programs — New Hampshire until 1990 and Kansas until 1992. Other states which are currently utilizing shock incarceration programs include Alabama, Arizona, Florida, Georgia, Louisiana, Michigan, Mississippi, New York, Oklahoma, South Carolina, and Texas.

Shock incarceration has multiple goals — rehabilitation, deterrence, punishment, and reduction of prison crowding and prison cost. It is an alternative sentencing option for the judiciary. Furthermore, most shock incarceration participants must meet a variety of criteria in many of these states. Generally, shock incarceration programs cater to juvenile and youthful male and female offenders who must pass a thorough physical exam, must be physically fit for exercise and hard labor, and must not have had any of the following: severe psychological problems, a history of arson charges or convictions, or a history of assaultive behavior.

Senator Frank Pecora introduced Senate Bill 621 as part of a Senate drug package which would initiate a shock incarceration program in Pennsylvania exclusively for juvenile drug offenders. This legislation would establish separate shock incarceration programs for males and females and would have a duration of six months. Senator Pecora's program would consist of strict discipline, hard labor, physical exercise, educational training to raise one's grade level or acquire a GED, vocational training and substance abuse counseling. This program would not permit any smoking, any visitors during the first thirty days, or any contact with the outside world during the first thirty days of incarceration.

Senator Pecora's bill was adopted by the Senate by a vote of 50-0 and is presently in the House Judiciary Committee. During the latter portion of 1989, Representative Dwight Evans and Representative Lois Hagarty introduced legislation which also proposed variations of the shock incarceration concept.

Tougher Laws

An example of a mandatory law which the Commonwealth

may wish to adopt to increase deterrence for serious drug offenses would be the adoption of the "three time loser" legislation. Under the "three time loser" concept, defendants convicted a third time for felony drug crimes would be given a mandatory life sentence. Under existing law in Pennsylvania, mandatory life sentences apply only to those convicted of homicide, and under Pennsylvania law, lifers are not eligible for parole. Someone serving a life sentence in this Commonwealth any win early release only if his sentence is commuted by the Governor upon a recommendation by the state Board of Pardons.

Another law enforcement tool that would be useful in the fight against illicit drugs would be a ban on the fortification of a building or room to deter entry by law enforcement personnel. A great deal of illicit drug activity takes place "behind closed doors." Many homes, apartments, and other dwellings serve as busy havens for the sale, distribution, and manufacturing of controlled substances. Moreover, a number of these drug-dispensing shelters are heavily fortified to thwart law-enforcement entry. According to an agent with the Attorney General's Bureau of Narcotics Investigation and Drug Control, state drug authorities periodically encounter suspected drug dwellings that are reinforced by various means. In some cases, electronically charged bars are placed across windows and doors to deter "intruders." Obviously, the successful suppression of law-enforcement entry into drug emporiums can prevent the arresting of offenders and the collection of evidence. Also, more sophisticated methods of fortifying or "boobytrapping" dwellings may also endanger the lives of police agents.

Reflecting the increase in cocaine abuse, many law enforcement officials, such as Attorney General Ernest Preate recommend the adoption of precursor legislation. Precursors are substances which are needed to process cocaine. By requiring the wholesalers and retailers of these substances to maintain and provide information about the sale and distribution of these chemicals to law enforcement officers, the investigation of clandestine laboratory operations will be aided significantly. This type of legislation should enable law enforcement officials to more easily identify illicit drug manufacturers.

Albeit this is only a short list of possible law enforcement actions which may be taken, these initiatives would bolden our law enforcement efforts. Numerous states and local governments are currently experimenting with other innovative initiatives to combat substance abuse. Norfolk, Virginia, for example, bars drug offenders who are on parole from frequenting areas of the city which are considered to be drug distribution and drug usage areas.

Future Goals

The goals of any drug policy should be five fold: 1) to drive all illicit drug dealers out of business; 2) to reduce the state's demand for all illicit drugs; 3) to provide sufficient treatment facilities for drug-dependent individuals; 4) to assist law enforcement personnel to more effectively combat substance abuse; and 5) to reduce prison overcrowding.

Our Commonwealth has needs beyond our resources, therefore, our limited state resources must be carefully targeted at problems to obtain maximum effect. To reiterate, one needs to remember that no one policy or set of policies and programs will be able to defeat illicit drugs. An effective strategy must combine the components of education, treatment, and law enforcement throughout all segments of our society in order to achieve victory in this crucial struggle.

Despite the nature of this struggle against illicit drugs, there are glimmers of hope in this struggle. The federal government's emphasis on targeting casual middle class and upper class users as well as dealers should be examined. This examination should occur because the latest studies by the NIDA and the University of Michigan's Institute for Social Research show that drug use has declined among the middle class. Meanwhile, crack cocaine addiction has soared among minorities, the poor, and the unemployed. President Bush's summary of his drug policy indicates that casual drug use has fallen 37% since 1985. The number of such users dropped from 23 million to 14.5 million. The number of individuals who tried an illegal drug even once during the year dropped almost 25%. Marijuana use led the decline, with usage by adolescents and young adults at the lowest level since 1972. The number of cocaine users within the most recent thirty days dropped by half from 1985-88; the number who use cocaine at least once during the year fell from 12 million to 8 million. Hence, the demand among teenagers and young adults for illicit drugs is dwindling despite their increased availability.

Among chronic users of cocaine, however, consumption is mounting. In 1985, 246,000 Americans took cocaine daily. In 1988, the total rose to 292,000. The NIDA study revealed increased use of cocaine by blacks and Hispanics, and drug use among the unemployed between 20 and 40 years of age was double the rate of those individuals with a job.

The seriousness of the cocaine crises is underscored by figures from hospital emergency rooms. In Washington, D.C., the number of cocaine-related emergencies in 1988 was ten times the total for 1984, soaring from 522 to 5,211, according to the NIDA. Hospitals in major cities reported 549 admissions in 1984 for crack cocaine emergencies but more than 15,000 in 1988.[11]

Judith Miller Jones, Director of the National Health Policy Forum at George Washington University, states, "Crack has hit the social fabric of the ghetto like a nuclear bomb, replacing heroin as the drug of choice in many cities." Crack is decimating the lives of low income children and families in inner cities, although it is becoming more of a problem in some middle class neighborhoods and in some pockets of rural America. Many law enforcement measures taken to control this problem have actually created new problems.

By treating all drugs as equally evil, the government regulators have in many instances encouraged dealers to switch from marijuana, which is relatively cheap and bulky, to the more profitable, compact and much more dangerous, cocaine. Furthermore, the government's marijuana enforcement program merely substituted more potent domestic marijuana for less dangerous foreign supplies, according to Mark A.R. Kleiman, a Harvard professor in criminal justice. A paradox of anti-drug enforcement is that the more the government cracks down on illicit drugs, the more worthwhile the business is made for the drug dealers who survive.

Tougher enforcement simply means higher prices, and higher prices produce more street crime among addicts desperate for a fix. Nonetheless, society cannot afford to lose this struggle. All opinion polls resoundingly support the need for renewed war on drugs as the nation's and the Commonwealth's number one problem. Drugs have ingrained themselves in so many aspects of our contemporary culture, such as music, entertainment, and sports, that eliminating illicit drugs will not be easy. The real war on drugs will have to be one on a cultural and behavioral front.

We must indeed win the hearts and minds of the American people, and the struggle has just been commenced.

Conclusion

After this overview of the struggle against illicit drugs in the Commonwealth and the nation, outlines of a anti-drug movement are emerging. First, there is an enormous expansion of 12-step groups such as Alcoholic Anonymous, Cocaine Anonymous, Narcotics Anonymous, and Marijuana Addicts Anonymous. In these 12-step groups, drug users are frequently converted into a powerful anti-drug constituency who encourage others to forego illicit drugs as well as doing so themselves.

Second, in addition to the conversion of many drug users, the self-help groups have mobilized additional constituencies of the families of addicts in such groups as Nar-Anon, Al-Anon, and Adult Children of Alcoholics (ACOA).

Third, early drug education programs in schools have been altering students actions and attitudes. Many school-based programs have had success training students to be peer helpers, peer educators, and peer counselors on drug issues. This is a strategy that research has found to be dramatically more effective than many other types of programs.

Fourth, new therapeutic approaches, such as the use of acupuncture for drug users has proven effective and new rehabilitative therapies related to the 12-step model are emerging. Acupuncture is being utilized in New York City's Lincoln Hospital and early results are encouraging. Dr. Vernon Johnson has developed a new rehabilitative therapy based on the 12-step model which is providing a guide for families and friends of addicts to assist those who do not want help.

Fifth, neighborhood anti-drug and anti-crime groups are forming throughout the Commonwealth and the nation. These residents are banning together to drive drug dealers and users out of their communities and to reclaim the streets by organizing patrols and equipping themselves with radios.

Sixth, major national grassroots organizations like the National Peoples Action and ACORN are developing model anti-drug campaigns to deploy in communities throughout the nation which request this assistance.

Although the six elements of a state and national movement

are emerging, additional federal resources are needed to supplement the increased state finances which have been brought to bear on this problem. As we continue our struggle against illicit drugs, however, all forces in this struggle must remember that they cannot prevail in this battle unless they forge close alliances, cooperate closely with one another, and maintain their patience and vigilance over the long term. In this way, and perhaps with a number of the strategies discussed earlier in this chapter, Pennsylvania will be able to achieve victory in the war on illicit drugs.

CHAPTER TWENTY

IMPROVING PENNSYLVANIA'S CIVIL JUSTICE SYSTEM
By Eugene W. Hickok, Jr.

EDITOR'S SUMMARY

The status of the civil justice system in Pennsylvania has emerged as an important and controversial issue. A number of issues suggest that the Commonwealth's judicial system needs serious reform. Many citizens feel that our judicial system undermines justice rather than promoting it.

Most Pennsylvanians have either lost contact with the judicial system or have lost confidence in it. In 1983, for example, one study found that three-quarters of the Pennsylvanians polled felt uncomfortable with the current method of electing judges. Most citizens lack adequate knowledge to exercise their vote wisely since they know little if anything about the candidates running for judicial office.

A "mixed" system for choosing Pennsylvania judges has been recommended by the Governor's Judicial Reform Commission. Under this system, judges are appointed and, should they seek to continue to serve, campaign for retention. It is an approach to judicial selection that exists in many states.

The entire court system has been plagued by persistent cases of alleged conflict of interest among judges and other equally disturbing problems. All of these problems contribute to a general distrust or wariness about the Commonwealth court system, which undermines public trust and respect for the judiciary.

Pennsylvania has experienced enormous upheaval in the area of tort liability. Major increases in the costs of insurance have occurred and Pennsylvanians have had to shoulder their share of the costs. Tort reform has not helped to alleviate these costs since the focus has been on societal insurance and risk spreading, rather than upon concerns with fault.

The judicial system has seen a dramatic increase in the size of tort damages. For example, from 1975 to 1985, the average medical malpractice jury verdict increased 363%. During this same time, the national average product liability verdict increased 370%. These awards have resulted in an increase in insurance premiums as insurance companies seek to develop adequate resources to pay for litigation costs.

Serious thought should be given to placing caps on the amount of non-economic damages that plaintiffs can be awarded. Compensation for such things as pain and suffering are entirely subjective and unpredictable. Plaintiffs are entitled to reasonable compensation for their pain and suffering, but the key is reasonableness.

Eugene W. Hickok, Jr. is Assistant Professor of Political Science at Dickinson College and Adjunct Professor of Law at Dickinson School of Law.

The status of the civil justice system in Pennsylvania has emerged as an important and highly controversial issue in recent years. The overall quality of the Commonwealth's judicial system has been a topic of ongoing debate for several years now. In addition, issues related to the nationwide transformation in tort liability have captured the attention of Pennsylvanians who care deeply about soaring insurance rates and the ability to secure necessary services.

Pennsylvanians have always taken their judicial system seriously. But more recently, the public's attention has been directed at a number of issues which suggest that the Pennsylvania judicial system needs serious reform. Quite simply, many citizens feel that our judicial system undermines justice and the rule of law rather than promoting it.

Perhaps no single public policy issue more directly affects the daily lives of citizens in the Commonwealth than liability. Although it concerns a complex and, for many, obscure area of law, tort liability law helps to determine our ability to acquire necessary goods and services. In Pennsylvania, a fundamental transformation in the character of tort liability has occurred which needs to be addressed if future generations of Pennsylvanians are to be able to enjoy the quality of life they have come to expect.

The problems affecting the state's civil service justice system illustrate vividly just how difficult the challenges facing Pennsylvania in the future are and how important it is that public officials begin now to deal effectively with these problems. In addition, they are problems which reflect the rich diversity of Pennsylvania's population and socioeconomic status, its changing character within the nation, and the ever growing demands being placed on state governments generally.

In short, the issues outlined here represent contemporary public policy problems which offer rich opportunities for reform and improvement. They are challenges that Pennsylvanians will want to tackle in the coming years and that will require a renewed sense of policy entrepreneurship if they are to be managed effectively.

The Judiciary in Pennsylvania

It is not an overstatement to say that most Pennsylvanians

have either lost contact with the state judicial system, have lost confidence in it, or both. Numerous surveys have produced evidence of this. In 1983, for example, one study found that three quarters of the Pennsylvanians polled felt uncomfortable with the current method of electing judges. Not surprisingly, those same Pennsylvanians said that they planned to vote for a judicial candidate in the next election but could not name a single one of the candidates who were seeking statewide judicial office. In other words, the voters (at least in this case) feel uneasy about the way Pennsylvanians choose judges.

Moreover, most citizens lack adequate knowledge to exercise their choice wisely. Time and again studies have revealed that most voters in the Commonwealth know little if anything about the candidates running for judicial office. They know very little about the responsibilities of judges, the sorts of issues arising under their jurisdiction, and little about the records of judges seeking retention. Yet, citizens feel compelled to choose.

Clearly the legitimacy of the current judicial selection system is suspect, if not the integrity of the Pennsylvania judicial system generally.

In 1988 Governor Casey's Judicial Reform Commission issued its long anticipated report. In addition to substantiating conclusions reached in earlier studies, the Commission brought forth a series of recommendations aimed at ensuring a judicial system that provides for the "prompt, fair, and competent resolution of disputes and the preservation of our fundamental adherence to the rule of law..." Addressing the issue of judicial selection directly, the Commission outlined a proposal for a selection process that would "minimize partisan and special interest influence" and "provide an impartial and competent judiciary."

The Commission recommended what is labeled a "mixed" system for choosing Pennsylvania judges. Appellate court judges would be appointed by the governor from lists of candidates supplied by a Judicial Nomination Commission. Judicial appointment would require confirmation by the State Senate, and at the end of an initial four-year term, judges would be reviewed by that Judicial Nomination Commission to determine whether their term should continue. Under the proposal, judges seeking retention for a ten-year term would then run in "retention elections" in which the voters would either vote for or against retention.

Under a "mixed" system approach to judicial selection, then, judges are appointed and, should they seek to continue to serve, campaign for retention. "Retention elections" are supposed to be non-partisan and do not involve candidates contesting the seat but a sitting judge seeking public support to continue on the bench. It is an approach to judicial selection that exists in many states.

The Judicial Reform Commission seemed generally pleased with the way trial judges are chosen in the Commonwealth and recommended that the current system of electing these judges be retained.

The report by the Judicial Reform Commission elicited enormous media coverage and popular debate. However, the governor has all but ignored the report and the recommendations it contains. The Pennsylvania Bar Association, numerous organizations concerned with legal and judicial issues, and many members of the state legislature have argued that the Commission's ideas deserve serious attention. In other words, while serious students of the Pennsylvania judicial system, and a majority of citizens in the Commonwealth, remain uncomfortable with the current system and recommend important change, the present governor remains reticent to act.

The judicial selection system is not the only problem confronting Pennsylvanians when they consider the quality of the Commonwealth's judiciary. The entire court system has been plagued by persistent occasions of alleged conflict of interest among judges, numerous scandals alleging "kickbacks" for judges, and other equally distasteful and disturbing problems. All of this contributes to a general distrust or wariness about the Commonwealth court system, thus undermining public trust and respect for that branch of the state government in which trust and respect are most critical.

Perhaps the most alarming aspect of the current status of the Pennsylvania judiciary is that very little is being done to improve things. As already mentioned, the Governor has turned a blind eye to the recommendations of his own commission. State legislators, members of the Pennsylvania Bar Association, and even members of the bench have repeatedly called for reform; but there has been little real momentum for change.

There are, no doubt, a number of reasons for the lack of action. Surely the enormous influence wielded by the various law-related interest groups can explain why the state legislature has been less than forceful in a call for reform. In addition, as currently organized, the Pennsylvania judiciary is responsible for dealing with all allegations of misconduct among members of the bench. In other words, it is a self-policing organization. Allegations of misconduct are dealt with "in house." Finally, the judicial system remains, for most citizens, shrouded in mystery due to the complexity of the system. Judicial reform, therefore, while popularly supported, is not considered a high policy priority within the state. Given the nature of the existing judicial system, this is predictable. But given the importance of a principled, prompt, and fair administration of the laws, it is very regrettable.

The current judicial system has evolved over a number of years. The last major change in the court system occurred in 1968 with the creation of the constitutionally mandated Unified Judicial System. As Pennsylvania prepares for the next century, serious attention should be directed to improving the quality of the state judicial system.

Recommendation: The entire Pennsylvania court system should be reformed to provide a more coherent, consistent, and expeditious administration of the laws of the Commonwealth.

Recommendation: The system of judicial selection should be changed. Appellate court judges should not be elected but appointed by the governor and confirmed by the state senate. Serious consideration should be given to the creation of a merit selection system for all judges in the Commonwealth. A system of merit selection that takes into consideration the specific needs of various regions within the Commonwealth, might provide for a judiciary which is both representative of the clientele it serves and highly skilled and responsible.

Recommendation: The present statement of standards of judicial conduct should be revised and those standards must be stated clearly.

Recommendation: The system currently in place for governing the conduct of judges and punishing misconduct needs serious reform. There should be clear and absolute guidelines governing the reporting, investigation and punishment of alleged violations of the prescriptions on judicial conduct.

Recommendation: Any reorganization of the system governing judicial conduct should reflect the need to ensure that those who administer that system are not also those who are to be governed by it.

Recommendation: Serious thought should be given to the creation of additional alternative dispute resolution systems so that the current overcrowding of the judicial system can be ameliorated without any accompanying diminution in the quality of the administration of justice in the Commonwealth.

The Tort Liability Problem in Pennsylvania

Pennsylvania, like every other state in the union, has experienced phenomenal upheaval in the area of tort liability and this has had implications for public policy in a host of related areas. A virtual revolution has occurred in tort law, resulting in major increases in the costs of insurance, the inability to secure some types of insurance, and a consequent loss of many services that most citizens, until relatively recently, took for granted. All of this is the product of a sort of "common law activism" among the states, and Pennsylvanians have had to shoulder their share of the costs such activism incurs.

A tort is best understood as a wrongful act for which a civil action might be brought. Traditionally, tort law was founded upon the idea of fault, or wrongdoing. In other words, individuals who caused harm to others — who could be faulted for the harm — could be held liable for their actions. Fault, or causation, provided the moral and doctrinal justification for and limitations on tort liability. Gradually, however, the concern with fault has been displaced by a growing interest in no-fault liability. Rather than shaping tort law upon concerns with fault, deterrence and compensation, the focus has shifted to concepts of societal insurance and risk spreading.

The desire to fashion tort law so that it might be more economically efficient and so that costs might be spread more evenly throughout society has produced a tort liability system that seems to focus more and more on compensation rather than fault. It is a system that increasingly imposes liability upon persons and companies that have done nothing wrong. What seems to be driving the liability transformation is an almost overwhelming desire to ensure that individuals are adequately compensated for harms that occur.

This undermining of fault or causation has been achieved as newer approaches to tort law have emerged. The increasing use of joint and several liability has helped to shift the cost of compensation to "deep pockets." Today it is not uncommon for defendants with only a limited role in causing an injury to bear the full cost of compensating the plaintiff, even in some cases where the plaintiff may have been largely responsible for his own injury. Apparently what drives the system is not fault or causation but ability to pay. In a related development, "market share" liability allocates liability among manufacturers of a generic product on the basis of their share of the market for that product; discarding almost all concern with assigning responsibility for injuries. More recently, in tort law liability proceedings, the burden of proof has been shifted to the defendants to demonstrate or prove lack of causation in order to avoid liability.

The result of all of this transition in tort law has been a dramatic increase in the size of tort damages and a resulting increase in insurance premiums as insurance companies seek to develop resources adequate enough to cover the costs of these damages. For example, nationwide the average medical malpractice jury verdict increased 363% from 1975 to 1985. During this same time, the national average product liability verdict increased 370%.

A not inconsequential aspect of the problems surrounding the tort system is the excessive transaction costs. The costs of securing counsel and litigation are excessive for defendant and plaintiff alike.

Pennsylvanians are suffering under a tort liability system that can find defendants liable when they should not be, either because they did not cause the injury in question or did not engage in wrongful activity. It is a system in which damages have become excessive and in which the costs of securing adequate legal counsel and pursuing litigation have become excessive. And it is a system that has forced insurance companies to shoulder this compensation burden, thereby driving insurance premiums up dramatically, and, in some cases, eliminating the availability of insurance. All of this has the effect of increased costs to the consumers of Pennsylvania.

It must be recognized that this is a national problem that will require national attention. But tort law remains essentially the province of the state, and Pennsylvania can do much to reform the current situation and improve tort liability law in the coming years.

Recommendation: Pennsylvania should move to reestablish the idea of fault or causation as the foundation for liability. Fault remains the only way to distinguish desirable from undesirable conduct. Without fault as the basis for liability, the tort liability system generates arbitrary and unfair results. For non-product liability issues, negligence should be the applicable standard. For product liability, the doctrine of strict liability should be observed.

Recommendation: Findings of causation should be based on credible evidence. Juries are frequently asked to make difficult decisions about highly technical and confusing issues and are dependent upon the expertise of witnesses when making those decisions. It is imperative that expertise be competent and credible. The information provided to the jury should determine the case, not the demeanor or personality of the expert.

Recommendation: Pennsylvanians should give serious thought to rethinking the concept of joint and several liability. As it currently stands, it is a doctrine that allow plaintiffs to recover substantial awards from "deep pocket" defendants even when those defendants are found to be only minimally at fault. The distinction between joint and several liability and joint causation should be remembered and should underwrite reform in this area.

Recommendation: Serious thought should be given to placing caps on the amount of non-economic damages that plaintiffs can be awarded. Compensation for such things as pain and suffering is inherently open-ended and entirely subjective and unpredictable. Moreover, awards for non-economic damages have increased dramatically in recent years. Certainly plaintiffs are entitled to reasonable compensation for their pain and suffering; but the key is reasonableness. Serious thought should be given to limiting compensation for punitive damages as well.

Recommendation: The system of contingency fees needs to be reconsidered. Currently, attorneys receive a flat percentage of their client's awards. It is in the interest of the attorney, in other words, to seek as generous an award as possible. This only serves to increase the size of liability awards and the costs of transactions. Some reforms in the procedures governing the current system might help to lower the costs of tort liability transactions and eliminate the incentive attorneys have to push for substantial awards.

Recommendation: The Commonwealth should increase the effort to develop alternative ways to resolve tort disputes. While important work has been done in this area in recent years, the Pennsylvania bar and the Pennsylvania bench remain less than enthusiastic to developments in alternative dispute resolution techniques. Moreover, the relationship between the plaintiff and the defendant bar in Pennsylvania is such that it is difficult to get the two groups to even give serious consideration to tort reform.

Pennsylvania is undergoing enormous change. As the final decade of the twentieth century approaches, the Commonwealth must contend with a transformation in its economic growth patterns, the national and international trends in trade, commerce, and technology, and the challenges to governing that are represented by the gap between the demands of the citizens and resources of the state. Recent renewed interest on the part of the federal government in increasing the role of state government in a host of public policy areas suggests that the next decade and beyond will see the states become the focus of increased public attention.

All of this is to suggest that the coming years will see unusual change in Pennsylvania government and politics and, therefore, unusual opportunities for creative and imaginative approaches to dealing with the problems that have plagued the Commonwealth for years. Nowhere is there a greater need for creativity and energy than in the area of judicial administration and civil justice. And there is perhaps no other area of public policy in which reform is so difficult to achieve. The ability of Pennsylvanians to improve policy in this area, therefore, will say volumes about what the citizens of the Commonwealth can expect as they approach the next century.

CHAPTER TWENTY-ONE

MAKING PENNSYLVANIA'S ELECTORAL PROCESS MORE COMPETITIVE

By Charles R. Gerow

EDITOR'S SUMMARY

The power of incumbency in the Pennsylvania General Assembly is overwhelming. In the 1988 general election, only three members of the Commonwealth's 253-seat legislature lost their seats. This trend is disturbing, since without healthy competition in the electoral process, we risk losing accountability and responsiveness to the voters.

Money is the primary reason for declining electoral competition. Money is a critical campaign commodity, with PACs being the most significant money source. Since incumbent legislators hold political power over issues important to the PACs, the overwhelming majority of PAC dollars go to this group.

PACs serve to disenfranchise average citizens by transferring political clout. *The Wall Street Journal* says "America is becoming a special-interest nation where money is displacing votes." PACs fall into this trap by giving to incumbents who lack challengers or financially supporting both candidates in an election.

Strong campaign finance reforms are seriously needed. The aim and effect of legitimate reforms must be to make elections competitive again, to encourage voter participation, strengthen the political parties, and enhance the role of the individual. Any proposed reform must slowly peel away the layers of incumbency insulation built into the current system.

There are several specific reforms that should be enacted. The Pennsylvania Election Code needs to be modified with rules that will require candidates and their committees to raise money in their own name, for their own election, in their own district, in the year they actually stand for election. These changes can help return accountability to the voters in local elections.

The most bold proposal is a constitutional limit on consecutive legislative terms. The precedence for such action is strong since the state constitution limits the terms in office which the Governor, Attorney General, and Auditor General may serve. Legislators should be limited to two consecutive terms in the Senate and four terms in the House in order to guarantee legislative turnover. Limiting terms would go far in bringing new ideas and new blood to the process.

Pennsylvanians want change in the electoral status quo. A recent poll conducted by the Commonwealth Foundation indicated that of 1200 Pennsylvanians polled, 72% believe there should be a limit on legislative terms. The public must be allowed to reassert control over the legislative process through election campaign reforms.

Charles R. Gerow is a practicing attorney and past President of Pennsylvanians For Effective Government.

O ver the past decade, elections in the Keystone State have come and gone without producing any significant changes in the makeup of the Pennsylvania General Assembly. Competitive elections have been replaced by a permanent campaign that keeps incumbents in their seats with the help of taxpayer funded "constituent services," large special interest contributions, and carefully gerrymandered districts. By assuring that incumbents don't lose elections, the electoral process in Pennsylvania has suffered a serious departure from the intentions of the Founding Fathers and produced a legislative body less responsive and accountable to the voters.

Meaningful campaign reforms and serious restrictions on the use of taxpayer money by the state legislature are needed to restore a competitive balance and revive the power of ordinary citizens in Pennsylvania's political process. If the Commonwealth fails to vigorously debate and enact these governmental reforms, we are faced with the prospect of continuing declines in voter turnout and deepening public cynicism toward the institutions of government.

Declining Competition

The results of general elections in recent years clearly show the overwhelming power of incumbency in Pennsylvania. In the 1988 General Election, only three members of Pennsylvania's 253-seat General Assembly lost their seats. In 1984, there were only two partisan changes as a result of the election. In November of 1986, not one legislator was shown the door by the voters. It increasingly appears that the only way to lose a seat in the Pennsylvania House or Senate, short of committing a felony, is to retire, get elected to another office, or die. Even in death, there exists a curious type of perpetuation. An increasingly common trend is for widows or children of deceased or retired Representatives to win the vacated seat.

Virtually every Pennsylvanian believes that competition in the marketplace produces better products and services for the consumer. Healthy competition inevitably leads to excellence. Most would also agree that the truism applies to electoral politics as well. Without healthy competition in the electoral process, we risk losing the essence of representative government — accountability and responsiveness to the voters. When the political process stagnates, the entire system suffers: issues are not sufficiently debated, new ideas are not considered, and voting records are not exposed.

Not only are few incumbents defeated by challengers, scores of seats in the Pennsylvania Legislature, Democrat and Republican, face no challenge at all, and dozens of other legislators face only token opposition. Surrounded by increasingly larger and more expert staffs, armed with taxpayer funded mailing privileges, and enjoying easy access to large PAC contributions and special interest assistance, Pennsylvania lawmakers are not only winning their elections, they're winning by bigger and bigger margins.

Pennsylvania and National Trends

The near automatic reelection of incumbents is not a phenomenon unique to Pennsylvania. Much attention has been focused recently on the problem at the federal level, where most members of Congress enjoy "seats for life," and 98% are returned to office each election. Many states, particularly those with large legislative bodies, have experienced the same problem.

Some of the factors that contribute to Pennsylvania's unusually high incumbency return rate relate to the unique features of the state's legislature: it has more members, meets more session days, and is better paid than virtually any in the nation. Only New Hampshire, with its part-time "citizens" House and Town Meeting system, has more legislators than Pennsylvania's 253.

In Pennsylvania, the legislative sessions have become around-the-calendar events, covering 23 of the 24 months between legislative elections. Besides Pennsylvania, only four states had year round legislative sessions during the last cycle: Massachusetts, Michigan, New Jersey, and Ohio. According to officials of the National Conference of State Legislatures, only New York and California are even considering going to yearlong legislative calendars.

Pennsylvania is also at or near the top of the compensation ladder. Until the beginning of the 1989-90 legislative session, Pennsylvania led the nation in legislative pay. Although we now have been surpassed in that category, when all the additional compensation, benefits, and perquisites are factored in, Pennsylvania may yet lead the country.

Just as the fact of perpetual incumbency is more distinctly seen in Pennsylvania than elsewhere, many would argue that the consequences that spring from such a situation are also greater. One of the major problems stemming from the breakdown of competitive elections is the insulation and bureaucratization of the legislature itself. When the process fails to produce meaningful challenges, officeholders become increasingly remote and isolated from their constituents. Many of the best intentioned lawmakers, once they get to Harrisburg, find a powerful political culture which is eager to win their loyalty. Those who yield to these pressures become less and less tied to and influenced by the people themselves. With the legislative calendar dragging on for most of the year, lawmakers, especially those from geographically distant districts, are forced to spend more time on the shores of the Susquehanna than in their home districts, and more separated from those whose daily lives are impacted by the taxes, laws and regulations adopted in the state capitol.

Many of the state's salons have virtually taken up permanent residence in the Capital City, which means that social acquaintances and neighbors are more likely to be bureaucrats, political insiders or lobbyists than ordinary workers and taxpayers. For legislators trapped in this "Catch 22" situation, they unwittingly, even unwillingly, contribute to a process that is a far cry from what it was ever intended to be.

Original Intent: Robust Democracy

An in-depth reading of the Federalist Papers is not required to understand that our Founding Fathers had something distinctly different in mind for legislative bodies, both state and federal. Real electoral competition in open, free and fair elections is the very heart of the American political system, the centerpiece from which other freedoms spring. Nor can it be denied that the framers of our system intended for the state legislatures to be those closest to the people. As Alexander Hamilton proclaimed, "Here the people govern. Here they act by their immediate representatives." Those wise people of two centuries ago envisioned a system where honest citizens would come from the farm and factory, the home and the office, gather in Harrisburg a few weeks a year to make laws and then return to live with the laws which they had written. Power, especially political power, was seen as temporarily entrusted to the holders of office; something to be held in trust for a short period of time and then handed over to another. The very idea of long terms in political office was a foreign concept.

The deliberative bodies of our tripartite system of government are those which must be closest to the people and consequently responsive to them. The founders would have undoubtedly viewed the absolute disappearance of biannual competitive elections as a death blow to the representative democracy they ingeniously brought forth. Maintaining a republic required an electoral process that was balanced, fair and bolstered by healthy competition, they concluded. They believed that such a system would constantly infuse new blood into the process, and they were correct. During the first Congressional elections after George Washington became President, 40% of incumbents lost their seats. Today, in Pennsylvania, it is remarkable if 4% lose theirs.

An even more worrisome trend which has emerged concomitantly with automatically reelected incumbency is the increasing decline in voter turnout. Of the major free powers in the world today, the U.S. ranks at the bottom of the voter participation scale. In recent Pennsylvania House and Senate elections, more eligible voters have turned their back on the process than have participated. With the outcome seemingly preordained, many just don't bother to vote. Many others believe that their vote, even if cast, just doesn't count — that no matter how they vote, or even if they vote, it won't have any real effect on their everyday lives. There is a clear lack of confidence in the electoral process.

Money: "The Mother's Milk of Politics"

A number of significant factors have converged to produce this departure from the original design of our electoral process. The reasons most commonly advanced have to do with that critical campaign commodity: money. Money is the fuel of the incumbent protection machine. Not only is it used to wage campaigns, but increasingly to scare off all challengers.

Perhaps the most significant source of money readily available to incumbents and not their challengers is the Political Action Committees, or PACs. Most PACs give overwhelmingly to incumbents. A review recently conducted by the *Philadelphia Daily News* of more than 300 PACs showed that PACs paid for 50% of Philadelphia House campaigns in 1988.[1] Another study, published in the *Greensburg Tribune-Review*, showed that nearly 40% of all the money collected by successful candidates in State House elections came from PACs, while the losers got only 15% of their already inferior funding from PACs.[2]

By weighing their contributions so heavily towards incumbent officeholders, PACs promote the accumulation of huge campaign funds which serve not only as a deterrent to any would-be challenger, but to crush any brave soul foolish enough to actually make such a race. The PACs understand and practice the fine art of political survival. Many of them are unwilling to risk the wrath of an incumbent who holds inordinate power over their particular agenda by supporting a "poor-risk" challenger.

So much money has poured through the PAC funnels that most Pennsylvania PACs are in the business of giving large sums to candidates who don't even have an opponent. This, in turn, allows the officeholders to hold the campaign funds in reserve to scare off opposition, or to use them for some future purpose, most likely for higher office. Another increasingly common practice is for incumbent legislators to share their PAC money with other legislative candidates, thereby expanding their personal power base in the legislature.

One thing is sure: there is always enough money left over at the end of the political year to help the incumbent face the future with little fear of opposition. Unlike some of their Congressional counterparts, Pennsylvania legislators are not permitted by the Pennsylvania Election Code to keep excess campaign money for their personal use. Under current Pennsylvania law, funds on hand when a committee is closed must either be transferred to another political committee or returned, pro-rata, to the contributors.

The rapid escalation of campaign costs is not indigenous to Pennsylvania, but is clearly mirrored here, at least in the races for "open" seats (those in which no incumbent is running) or those few marginal districts that remain. The growth of campaign spending has exponentially outpaced the rate of inflation. A serious candidate for an open house seat in Pennsylvania should expect to spend at least $75,000, while a Senate candidate should plan on expenditures of a quarter-million dollars or more. Pennsylvania has already cracked the three quarter-million dollar mark for a single race, and will undoubtedly cross the one-million dollar threshold for spending in a single seat in the 1990 elections.

Few doubt that it costs too much to run for political office these days. Part of the reason for the high costs is the professionalization of politics and the accompanying high costs of pollsters, advertising, consultants, and media consultants, direct mail, computer specialists, and election lawyers. Another reason is job security. With big salaries, expense accounts and benefit packages, politics has become the sole livelihood of most legislators. More than 80% of the members of the Pennsylvania House listed their occupation as legislator, or some variation thereof, on their State Ethics Commission disclosures. By allowing legislative posts to become full time and well compensated, we have compelled members to have, as one of their principle concerns, the protection of their jobs and income. Lawmakers can be expected not only to protect the campaign laws that shield them from external challenge, but also to spend all that it takes to fend off a serious challenge if it comes.

PACS: Their Virtues and Vices

Lest Political Action Committees undeservedly become a whipping boy, it should be quickly recalled that PACs themselves represent a campaign reform. PACs were first introduced to curb the abuses of free-for-all cash giving in the pre-Watergate era. By enacting strict and extensive reporting requirements, the 1970's reformers suggested an increased accountability would be introduced to the system. As Michael Malbin of the American Enterprise Institute correctly points out: "It takes a large set of blinders to miss the fact that the emergence of PACs represents an improvement over what went before."[3] The truth is that PACs are generally involved in very constructive activities including grassroots action, registering and turning out voters, and promoting challengers through candidate recruitment and identification programs. Obviously these types of activities are to be encouraged and promoted.

But even the PACs and their professional managers aren't

happy with the current state of the electoral process and campaign finance laws. Stories abound in Harrisburg about PACs that are fed up with being arm-twisted into making political contributions by purchasing tickets to an endless number of fund-raising social events. PACs are increasingly being asked by incumbents for money earlier, more often, and much more forcefully. One state senator, elected in 1988 to a four-year term, held a $1000 per head fund-raising event before he was even sworn in to his new office. The head of one of Harrisburg's largest PACs was recently quoted in the public press as saying that they "feel compelled" to assist legislators with other than outright PAC contributions.[4]

Some of the staunchest supporters of the PAC system have become increasingly disenchanted. U.S. Representative Guy Vander Jagt, who spent a decade encouraging the growth and development of PACs, recently exploded "The PAC's are... whores!"[5] President Bush has taken a low view of PACs as well. He has said: "PACs weaken the political parties, restrain competition, and deaden the political debate."[6] This comes from a man who has been the recipient of millions of direct and indirect PAC dollars.

The major problem with PACs is that they have become such a dominant factor in politics that they serve to disenfranchise average citizens by transferring political clout to those who control donations. *The Wall Street Journal*'s Brooks Jackson says: "America is becoming a special-interest nation where money is displacing votes." [7] The problem Jackson describes becomes exacerbated when PACs willfully and voluntarily fall into the trap of dependency by refusing to say no to incumbents who lack challengers, by giving to both candidates in an election, and by rewarding hypocrisy found in the pronouncements and votes of office holders.

What is the solution? Many suggest simply outlawing PACs; others suggest severely restricting the contributions they are able to make, or placing a limit on campaign contributions and expenditures. There are several reasons why such reforms would likely fail. First is the simple fact that the electoral process is, and will remain, a demand-side business. Eliminating PACs might not be a bad idea in the abstract. But it probably would not produce fundamental change. The money would still flow, although probably through less accountable channels, such as independent expenditures. Big labor union expenditures would still continue indirectly through a variety of in-kind services and "soft" money.

The Legislature and Tax Paid Reelections

Because incumbent legislators themselves would control any spending limits, resolving the dilemma currently facing the Commonwealth will require many steps on a long road. There are no panaceas. Instead we are faced with a gradual whittling away of a giant logjam in the free flow of our electoral process.

The unfortunate fact is that elimination of PACs, restraints on their giving, or limits on campaign spending, could actually serve to further the incumbency reelection cycle. The truth is that limits on spending would probably reduce competition by hurting the very challengers we want to help. Those who would rush to reform the PAC system must not forget the huge sums of tax money incumbents have available to promote themselves day in and day out. *The Philadelphia Inquirer* aptly described it as a "multi-million dollar propaganda machine"; a veritable army of researchers, writers, press agents, spokespersons, and techni-cal assistants never imagined by the legislators of a decade or two ago.

Today the General Assembly itself employs approximately 2000 people. The rate of growth of legislative staffs has markedly outpaced the growth rate of the Commonwealth's population whom they ostensibly serve. As opposed to the staffers of 20 years ago, today's employees are full-time professionals, many of whom command high salaries and generous state benefit packages. The burgeoning cost of the growing legislative staffs is a much larger factor in the increase of the General Assembly budget than the highly publicized legislative pay hikes.

In the past decade, the cost of running the General Assembly has risen dramatically faster than the rest of the bureaucracy. In the decade prior to the end of the 1986 fiscal year, the Penn-sylvania Senate budget doubled while the House's tripled. In the decade immediately previous to that, however, the cost of operating the General Assembly increased at the same rate as the rest of state government. According to a published report by the *Harrisburg Patriot News* in the fall of 1987, the operating expense of the General Assembly "works out to more than 1% of the state general fund budget, and nearly $450,000 for each legislative seat.[8]

Part of the reason for the heavy focus by the media on PACs is that they are an easy, obvious target, unlike the less visible institutional advantages which incumbents alone enjoy. Access to PAC money and that which it buys becomes critical to the analysis only when coupled with the dozens of other factors that perpetuate incumbency, like taxpayer funded mailings and almost instant access to the media. The result, therefore, of spending limitations would be even less money getting to deserving challengers while incumbents continued to enjoy the tremendous exposure provided by taxpayer-financed advantages.

The Ingredients of Real Campaign Reform

Many proposals put forward do not meet the criteria for real reform. Rather, they may serve to further protect incumbents and those candidates who possess great personal wealth. Clearly the electoral politics of our representative democracy would best be played on a more or less level playing field where personal wealth or incumbency is not required to seek public office. But the Supreme Court of the United States has placed one major stumbling block in the road to legislative reform that would take the process closer to the intended ideal. In *Buckley vs. Valeo*,[9] the Court held that the only permissible way to limit the use of such dollars without unconstitutionally restricting freedom of speech is to couple such limits with voluntary public financing of elections. Many conservative legal theorists and scholars believe the decision to be incorrect and predict that Congress will act, by constitutional amendment, to essentially overrule the decision. In the meantime, nearly half the states have adopted some type of public financing. Almost all of those states raise money for the programs through the tax system. Twelve states use a tax checkoff on their state income tax forms similar to the federal form. Eight use tax add-ons, which increase the taxpayers liability.

Twelve states provide public financing directly to the political parties, while eight give it directly to candidate committees. Some states require that the political parties distribute some of their public financed campaign money to candidates while others outright prohibit it. Requiring parties to use their money mostly for party operations strengthens the political parties, a laudable goal, but it does little to help candidates or to keep down the cost of political campaigns. Seven states require limits on campaign expenditures as a condition for receiving public funds. Only three states — Hawaii, Minnesota, and Wisconsin — provided funds for state legislative campaigns in the 1988 elections. The rest of the states provide public funds only for gubernatorial, or other statewide offices.[10]

Many are understandably concerned about both the philosophy and practical effects of public financing for statewide and legislative races. The idea to require taxpayers to finance political ambition is not rooted in conservative thought. Moreover, public financing would not cure many of the ills currently weakening the process because the money channels would simply shift, particularly through the independent expenditure loophole. Nevertheless, it may be that under the current restraints imposed by the courts, public financing will be a reform of last resort. In any event, it should be part of a vigorous debate in Pennsylvania that will serve to reshape the election process.

Strong campaign finance reforms are seriously needed. The question is: which ones? The aim and effect of a legitimate reform must be to make elections competitive again, to encourage voter participation, strengthen the political parties, and enhance the role of the individual while curtailing the influence of conglomerate special interests. Instead of the quick-fix remedies that are often suggested, the process, if it advances at all, will consist of slowly peeling away the layers of insulation built into the current system.

One way to begin leveling the playing field is to subtract from the actual cost of running for public office. Instead of forcing taxpayer money into the campaign kitty or artificially limiting campaign expenditures, one option would be to cut into the biggest cost in any campaign budget: advertising. Simply by reclaiming a nominal number of advertising hours of the public's airwaves from broadcasters, the budgets of most campaigns could be cut in half.

Television and radio stations, while run on a for-profit basis, are nevertheless a public trust and should be treated as such. Rather than selling air time to candidates to perform the most important exercise in the democratic process, stations might be required to offer air time to candidates, some of it in prime time. The time could be segmented for 30 second slots or even five

minute speeches on issues. This would allow challengers to at
least get their message directly to the voters. Such a proposal is
already a serious topic of debate in Washington, where Congress
is reviewing a proposal to require such a system as a prerequisite
for licensing. It makes sense to include certain state legislative
races in such a scheme. At the very least, there should be an even
lower "political rate" for candidate advertising. It's only a small
step, but it's a start.

Most important, the Pennsylvania Election Code needs to be
modified with rules that will require candidates and their committees to raise money in their own name, for their own election,
in their own district, in the year they actually stand for election.
By implementing a small package of technical reforms designed to tighten the Pennsylvania Election Code, we could
curb the common practice of safe legislators amassing excessive
sums of money to dole out to other candidates, save for a political rainy day, or simply use to ward off challengers. This package of technical changes would help restore the competitive
balance and return accountability to the voters.

Recommendations for Reform

A first step should be to limit the period during which candidates and their committees can raise funds to the year that
they are actually on the ballot. A second step could be to prohibit
the use of money raised for one office to run for another. Third, a
provision to eliminate the hoarding of leftover campaign funds
should be put into the Election Code. Candidates would be
required to use the money in the election cycle in which it was
raised, or lose it. With this reform, campaign funds left over at
the end of each election cycle would be statutorily zeroed out.

Fourthly, to eliminate the use of campaign funds for purposes
other than what were intended by the contributors, candidates
should have a limit placed on their own campaign committee's
contributions to other candidates. A cap of $2,000 would elim-
inate much of the abuse in this area under current practice.

A fifth major reform would be a requirement that candidates
raise a significant portion — a minimum of 75% — of their campaign funds from within the district in which they run. What better way to keep state lawmakers close to their districts than to
require them to garner their political funds from the con-

stituents they were elected to serve?

Sixth, a prohibition of "bundling" should be imposed. Bundling occurs when, instead of collecting and dispersing money directly in the name of a PAC, organizations ask individuals to make out their checks directly to the candidates they are supporting. The individual's checks are then stacked, or bundled, together and delivered en masse to the candidate by organization officials. Bundling is not nearly as onerous a practice where there is no campaign expenditure limit, as under current Pennsylvania law. Nevertheless, it is a practice designed to promote special interests rather than individual accountability.

A seventh area of current Pennsylvania election law crying out for correction is the use of so-called "soft" dollars. Under Pennsylvania law, corporate and unincorporated association contributions to political candidates or committees are prohibited. However, corporate dollars may legally be used for the "administrative costs" of Political Action Committees. No definition clearly setting forth what constitutes an administrative cost exists. By adding specific language that clearly defines what is and is not permitted, strict accountability for the use of soft dollars would be introduced.

Eighth, a state tax credit of up to $100 should be provided to individual voters for any contribution made to a candidate or party. This modest step would provide a strong incentive to encourage citizen involvement in the process, restore a proper balance to electoral politics, and strengthen political parties. This single step would produce a powerful reason for citizens to directly participate in the financing of political campaigns. We should also encourage the Congress to restore and increase the credit on the federal level.

Finally, a close look must be made at the length of our election season. The campaigns are simply too long. We have one of the longest primary-to-general election periods in the nation. Our April or May primary should be moved to September. Campaigns are too long in duration, too predictable in outcome, and often too irrelevant to the real issues facing Pennsylvania. There is little doubt that long campaigns contribute to complacency, apathy, and general disaffection among the public. Shortening the election season to a more reasonable length would go far in restoring public interest and involvement in the political process.

The most important need for reform applies to the hidden

advantages that incumbents hold as a result of taxpayer money used for the conduct of their offices. Given the fact that legislators themselves must make any of these badly needed changes, such reform will remain unlikely unless the public openly demands it.

Until these reforms are instituted, challengers are going to constantly be forced to dig out of a deep hole created by the hundreds of thousands of taxpayers dollars spent each year to fund constituent services. It begins with the use of the U.S. mail, a powerful means of direct communication with potential voters. Not only are there expert writers on hand to design and write direct mail pieces, there are plenty of taxpayer dollars available to send them. Just a glance at any of the "constituent services handbooks" distributed by the two party caucuses and special interest groups will reveal the fact that everyone on Capitol Hill is encouraged to exploit this advantage.

While many "constituent services" are legitimate uses of the legislative office, "services" like mailing birthday, anniversary, and graduation greetings, clippings from the local newspapers to high school athletes (the parents vote) or the recipient of the Ladies Auxiliary person of the week award raise questions. There are taxpayer funded calendars, maps, boating guides, cookbooks, and more. The centerpiece of this enterprise is the constituent newsletter, those periodic reports to the voters that extol the virtues of the Representative or Senator and which feature numerous photographs and bold print depictions of the lawmaker. Professor Larry Sabato of the University of Virginia, one of the nation's leading experts on electoral politics, portrays them more accurately: "Most...newsletters are nothing more than taxpayer subsidized reelection literature."[11] Many Pennsylvania legislators have newsletters so identical in format to their campaign literature that only reading the copy will reveal the distinction. All of these mailings, of course, are totally unsolicited by the recipient, even though that's who pays the bill.

On the federal level, estimates of the ratio of unsolicited mail to constituent letters (responses to constituent missives) run as high as 15,000 to 1. Although such data is not readily available on the state level, it is safe to say that an inordinately high number of unsolicited mail pieces go out of legislative offices each year. Earlier this year, the House Rules Committee found it necessary to double the amount of taxpayer money individual members are entitled to spend on postage for "official legislative business".

At the very least, a strict curb should be placed on mail that legislators can send which is not directly responsive to a contact initiated by a constituent. By placing a strict limit on the mailing at taxpayer expense, the practice of sending "for your information" packets to the Harrisburg lobbyists or newspaper clips to the high school swimming star would come to an end. This doesn't begin to address the issue of the transparently self-promoting newsletters sent regularly to postal patrons. Liberals and conservatives, Democrats and Republicans alike, defend this practice. "We have to inform the public about what's going on up here", they proclaim.

If legislators truly believe in the need for such newsletters, they would have little reason to quarrel with one innovative proposal. Why not have a bipartisan committee produce a newsletter detailing the issues and action before the General Assembly? No individual names would be included except to list bill sponsors, voting records, and the like. Members would then be allowed to send these generic letters to their own constituents on the same basis as they now mail. It would be an interesting study to see how loud a call for "reforming the public" existed once the photos and bold faced depictions of individual legislators was eliminated. Without these types of reforms, no challenger, short of being granted the same privilege of taxpayer funded mailing, has much of a chance of unseating a member.

The Legislature should also be called upon to limit the length of the legislative session. Clearly much of the session is not being put to productive use. Many of the days are nonvoting or ceremonial days, often put on the calendar simply to protect the legislator's $88 per diem or rights under the so-called "four day rule". The four day rule is a little known provision of the IRS code which allows state legislators only to deduct personal expenses for days within the four day cycle.

By the end of the budget debate last session, less than 175 of the more than 4000 bills introduced had actually been signed into law. It surely isn't all bad that more laws are not being written. But it is equally true that the usual explanations for the length of the session just don't comport with reality. A session limit of 120 calendar days would not only tighten up the legislative process and eliminate the abuses of token session days, it would allow legislators to spend more days in their home districts than in Harrisburg.

Reform is also needed in the strict adherence to the seniority system in parceling out committee chairmanships. The learning curve is not such that it requires today's legislators very long to understand even the long ago broke up the seniority system requiring the chairs of certain committees to be switched every four years. Dismantling an antiquated seniority system would go far to bringing new ideas and new blood to the process.

Limited Terms: An Idea Whose Time Has Come

The most bold and radical proposal has been saved for last. It is not offered as a quick fix, but simply as a guarantee of turnover in our legislature. There should be a constitutional limit placed on the number of consecutive terms any member may serve. Eight years (two terms in the Senate or four in the House) ought to be enough to provide any one person the opportunity to serve well the people who elected them and give their own special insight and input into the legislative process. There ought to be a further limit allowing an individual to serve in a leadership post no more than four years or as a presiding officer for no more than one session without relinquishing the post for at least their next term.

The Republican National Committee platform adopted in New Orleans in 1988 calls for similar restrictions on the federal level. The same rationale should undoubtedly apply to the state level.[12] The precedence for such action is strong. The state constitution limits the terms in office which the Governor, state fiscal officers, and Attorney General may serve. The members of the Judiciary must leave office on their 70th birthday. If the legislators were willing to pass a host of reforms necessary to level the playing field at election time, such a limit on terms might not be so popular among rank and file Pennsylvanians. Average citizens may not fully understand the intricacies, vagaries, and nuances of the system. But they know enough to disagree with the status quo. They want change. A recently conducted poll of 1200 Pennsylvanians by the Pennsylvania State University Data Center in conjunction with the Commonwealth Foundation indicated that 72% believe there should be a limit to the terms that state senators and representatives can serve. Furthermore, a large majority believe there is a need for a new representation in Harrisburg even if it means less experienced politicians.[13] Given the fact that Pennsylvania's "experienced" legislature has a poor record of addressing some longstanding problems in the Commonwealth — product liability reform, real reform of the unemployment compensation system, spending limitation, teachers' strikes, and equitable taxation — it is clearly time to consider ways to give new leaders the opportunity to show what they can do.

Such reforms will understandably be labeled as political pariahs. But then, so too were the reforms of two decades ago labeled at the time. If the determination of an enlightened public and public minded lawmakers is as great as we believe, then it is time to engineer an entire set of meaningful changes to create a more competitive and productive electoral system, rather than another montage of quick fix solutions, pasted together with good intentions but producing unintended consequences. In any case, a spirited and vigorous public debate of measures aimed at reshaping our electoral process into a healthier, more open and competitive system can only produce positive results. The real long-term solution does not depend on any of these reforms alone. Rather, it involves people learning how to exercise the power they have to influence legislators and to be convinced to participate fully in our free representative government. The simple Hamiltonian message — "Here, the people govern" — must not be forgotten. Pennsylvanians must be allowed to reassert control over the Commonwealth through election campaigns based on the power of ideas rather than the power of special interest money or privileges of tenure in office.

CHAPTER TWENTY-TWO

SHOULD PENNSYLVANIA BE AN INITIATIVE AND REFERENDUM STATE?

By Don E. Eberly

EDITOR'S SUMMARY

Voters in 23 states enact and rescind laws without the approval of their legislatures, a process known as Initiative and Referendum (I&R). Currently, Pennsylvanians do not enjoy this privilege, but the General Assembly is considering an Initiative and Referendum bill.

Political power is at the core of the I&R issue — how that power is currently distributed, how it is exercised, and whether it is, or could be, abused. I&R recognizes the need to both check power and provide the people a tool for spurring change when needed change is not forthcoming.

The I&R concept grew out of a desire to make sure that the powers delegated by the people were accountable to the people. I&R makes government more responsive and accountable. It would force legislators to become more attuned to the public's wishes back home in their districts as opposed to the pressures in the capitol.

I&R would open the entire legislative process for greater public scrutiny. How legislators conduct business would likely change. Legislators would be forced to give greater thought to the consequences of their actions. It would encourage them to make greater attempts to determine what the general public's sentiments are on a particular issue.

Voter involvement would be affected by I&R. Today's citizens remain eager to involve themselves in elections when they feel their efforts can produce tangible results. Studies show that voter turnout is systematically higher in states when initiative proposals are on the ballot. In 1982, a banner year for initiatives, turnout was a full one-sixth higher in states with initiatives over states without them.

Citizen involvement ensures that new ideas are brought into the political process. I&R gives ordinary people, along with the PACs, politicians, consultants, think tanks, and the media, a role in shaping the direction of policy on key issues.

The I&R process is not completely pure by any objective standard. Voters can be shortsighted and unenlightened. When people are driven by passion, they can look at issues superficially; they often look at symptoms not causes.

I&R should not be adopted on the basis that the majority is always right. Rather, I&R must be used as a tool to ensure that government is accountable, responsive, and accessible. The key is to design a system that provides the benefits that I&R offers, while minimizing the chances of misuse or overuse.

Don E. Eberly is President and Co-Founder of The Commonwealth Foundation and previously was Deputy Director of the Office of Public Liaison for The White House.

Presently, voters in 23 states may enact and rescind laws without the approval of their legislatures. In other words, millions of voters have the right to Initiative and Referendum, or I&R.

Currently, the Pennsylvania General Assembly is considering granting similar privileges to this state's voters. Before it does, it has a wealth of history and political philosophy to weigh before unleashing a civic power that can be both liberating and destructive when used in a democratic process.

By any measure, adopting I&R would be a bold stroke. Its adoption in other states has dramatically altered state-level politics, plus, of course, it has affected the way legislators carry-on the business of representative government. Its adoption, moreover, suggests that state government needs to be improved, if the voters feel the need to approve acts passed by the legislature, or if the voters feel compelled to pass acts legislators simply won't. This begs the following questions: What in state government is broken? Will Initiative and Referendum fix it?

To get to a discussion of state government's shortcomings, consider the political power the I&R proposal addresses. The original adoption and subsequent use of the I&R in the U.S. was oriented toward first structuring, then restructuring, political power arrangements. Political power, then, lies at the core of the I&R issue — how that power is currently distributed, how it is exercised, and whether it is, or could be, abused.

History of Initiative and Referendum

The first significant use of the referendum was during and immediately after the Revolutionary War, when dozens of independent states were sending the language in their constitutions directly to their citizens for approval. Later, in 1857, Congress made formal this practice by requiring that voters approve all state constitutions. In other words, the referendum concept grew out of a desire to make sure that the powers delegated by the people were accountable to the people.

The constitutional theory prevalent during the founding of our state and nation emphasized that the only legitimate government was that which originated with, and was controlled by, the people. Thomas Paine wrote, "A constitution is not the act of a government, but of a people constituting a government."

Government belonged to the people, and the most revolutionary idea of the day was that the people can and must be trusted to govern themselves.

The referendum movement reached its heyday in the late 19th century. Then, populist reformers worried about the use and abuse of power by monopolistic industry and state legislatures. As a result, many states broadened the original referendum power to include the right to initiate laws, and also to amend their constitutions. Today, besides the 23 states with I&R laws, many more states are courting similar proposals.

Many fear, however, that I&R will substitute pure democracy for the republican form of government. Yet, the Supreme Court has upheld I&R on the principle that if power belonged to the people, it was theirs to give or not to give. When the I&R issues faced its first Supreme Court challenge in 1906 in the case of Kadderly V. Portland, the court ruled:

> The initiative and referendum amendment does not abolish or destroy the republican form of government, or substitute another in its place...The people have simply reserved to themselves a larger share of legislative power.

Again, at issue was how much of their power were the people prepared to delegate.

Suspicions abounded in those early days over too much concentrated power in government, suspicions that prompted a careful attempt to check, divide, and balance the exercise of power at every level of government. In the end, elected representatives are merely delegates of the people, charged with responsibility for good government and held accountable to that through frequent elections.

But for the sake of liberty, the constitutional framers rejected pure democracy. Change must be accepted, but it must, as Edmund Burke once noted, be slow and thoughtful. For only then will it be the means for society's preservation. Reckless or hasty changes, those brought on by the momentary passions of the public, will produce the opposite results. So merely asserting rights does not safeguard liberty.

The Purpose of Initiative and Referendum

What, then, is the purpose of the I&R? Is it to place additional checks on power, or is it to remove impediments to using power for the purpose of advancing the public will? When best used, it accomplishes a bit of both. The most effective use of I&R recognizes the need to both check power and provide the people a tool for spurring change when needed change is not forth-coming.

In short, I&R makes government more responsive and ac-countable. Indeed, consider how giving the citizens the right to directly initiate legislation will circumvent the problems caused by legislators out of touch with their constituencies. A legisla-ture where 99% of incumbents routinely return to office after each election presents some problems: legislators may become more attuned to pressures in the capitol than to pressures back home, they may not properly define issues, and they might lose accountability for the way they vote.

Indeed, the very existence of I&R would encourage members of the legislature to give greater thought to the consequences of their actions, and to their inactions, and to make greater at-tempts to determine what the general public's sentiments are on a particular issue.

In many states, the filing of an initiative petition, or the mere threat of such action, provides the necessary impetus for a change in course by the legislature. With an I&R law, the entire legislative process would likely be opened to greater public scrutiny. Also, how legislators conduct business would likely change, whether it involves special interest legislation, unfair reapportionment, or the concentration of power in the hands of a relatively small group of legislative leaders. President Wood-row Wilson, an early proponent of I&R fittingly described it as a "gun behind the door" of every legislative and city council chamber.

Impact on Voter Involvement

Similarly, Initiative and Referendum would affect voter in-volvement. Many political analysts attribute the low voter turn-out in recent years to the lack of competition within the electoral process. It is very difficult to persuade busy people that waiting in line to vote for a candidate, with no opposition, is a rational use of their time.

Evidence abounds to suggest that today's citizens remain

eager to involve themselves when they feel their efforts can produce tangible results. But while election campaigns rarely produce change today, initiative campaigns often do. Forty-six percent of state-level initiative campaigns nationwide from 1985-86 succeeded, partially because they boosted voter participation.

In every election year since 1976, one half million people have circulated initiative petitions at the state and local levels across America. In a single initiative campaign in 1982, involving handgun control in California, the opposing committee recruited 30,000 volunteers.

This massive interest in initiatives boosts the turnout for candidate campaigns as well. Studies show that turnout is systematically higher in states when initiative proposals are on the ballot. In 1982, a banner year for initiatives, turnout was a full one-sixth higher in states with initiatives over states without them.

Moreover, citizen involvement ensures that new ideas are brought into the political process. Politics is increasingly funded by special interest PACs, and increasingly voters view the legislative agenda as one influenced by special interest lobbies. Consequently, many now doubt whether or not legislators are truly reflecting the people's views. The right to initiate the adoption or repeal of laws could provide the people access to change when that change isn't forthcoming from the legislature. A look at the history of I&R strongly suggests that it gives ordinary people a role, along with the PACs, politicians, consultants, think tanks, and the media, in shaping the direction of policy on key issues.

Initiative and Referendum Concerns

All change, however, begs for caution. I&R would produce change that is good and bad depending upon one's political persuasion, or one's view of the public interest.

To wit, I&R has been used effectively for and against tax limitation, for and against business interests, for and against gun control, for and against increased government spending. All this, of course, is true of the current legislative process. But I&R offers the public direct participation.

Nor is the process of Initiative and Referendum completely

pure by any objective standard. We live in a complicated society. We can't reduce many of our problems to short, simple ballot questions on which we vote up or down. Complex problems usually require complex solutions, crafted in the form of complex legislation.

We should also recognize that the voters can, at times, be shortsighted and unenlightened. Many I&R critics caution that self-interest can blind us to the need for tradeoffs and compromises. Americans want all of the benefits of a consumer society, but don't want to deal with the problems caused by consumption, such as the disposal of solid waste and hazardous materials and chemicals. No constituency exists for pollution, nor for the personal sacrifice that may be required for the siting of waste dumps in one's back yard.

Moreover, when people are driven by passion, they usually look at issues superficially; they often look at symptoms not causes. For example, consider the recent passage of a California initiative on car insurance, which mandated fixed reductions in premiums. Few Californians understood the underlying causes of insurance cost inflation. Now, many insurance companies are leaving California altogether, and drivers are finding that the alternative to high cost insurance is no insurance at all.

Conclusion

In conclusion, I&R should not be adopted on the basis of an ill-founded confidence in direct democracy, or on some overly idealized notion of "power to the people", which blindly assumes that the majority vote is always right. Broad-based direct democracy was rejected in America for good reason: electors can abuse power as deftly as elected officials. Majorities can be wrong, and the ballot can be cluttered with far more issues than most people care to, or are capable of, thinking through.

Rather, I&R must be used primarily as a tool to ensure that government is accountable, responsive and accessible. The key is to design a system that provides the benefits that I&R offers, while minimizing the chances of misuse or overuse.

When the drive for government reform reached its high water mark in the early 1900's, President Teddy Roosevelt became a strong advocate of I&R. He said then, "I believe in the Initiative and Referendum, which should be used not to destroy representative government, but to correct it whenever it becomes misrepresentative."

SECTION SEVEN:
New Initiatives to Make Government Work

CHAPTER TWENTY-THREE

GIVING THE PEOPLE THE GOVERNMENT THEY WANT
By James H. Broussard

EDITOR'S SUMMARY

**To earn the trust and cooperation of the people, tax policy must meet
four goals.** These goals are: protecting citizens against arbitrary
tax increases; raising adequate revenue for government to perform its minimal necessary obligations; preferring basic fairness for taxpayers; and encouraging economic growth. When
these goals are not met, tax policy loses legitimacy.

Pennsylvania's local tax system has failed to meet any of these goals.
Pennsylvanians have a despairing attitude toward their local tax
system. They feel they have little say in how the tax system
works. In Pennsylvania, politicians have more control over
local taxation and spending, and the people have less, than in
almost any other state.

Some state policies have made local tax problems worse. The state has
forced localities to pay for an increasing number of state-
mandated programs. The state has failed to meet their admitted
obligation to educational funding and the state refuses to help
municipalities with the burden of servicing state-owned tax-
exempt properties.

Property taxes are among the least fair methods of raising money.
These taxes are not based on ability to pay, and the assessed
value of a property often bears no relation to its market value. A
nationwide study showed that Pennsylvania ranked among the
very worst states in its assessment practices.

The local tax system hinders economic development. When one
locality levies much higher taxes than another, their future
economic development is put at risk. Taxes are second only to
labor costs in decisions about where to locate a new business.

**True tax reform must achieve three goals: protect the taxpayer; ease the
revenue pinch for local governments; and make the tax system less**

unfair. The most important is to protect the taxpayer. Ways to achieve this are: limit the tax rate but allow local voters to authorize an increase if they think it is necessary; limit the annual growth of spending of tax revenue; only increase taxes or spending by a percentage equal to the rate of inflation; require a popular vote before approval of any major bond issue; and adopt the right of initiative, referendum, and recall powers for voters.

The state must accept the responsibility of fully funding any future mandated programs. The state should also pay local governments that have more than their share of tax-exempt state property an amount equivalent to the taxes that would be due on state-owned property.

James H. Broussard is Chairman of the Department of History and Political Science at Lebanon Valley College and Director of Citizens Against Higher Taxes.

The one thing common to every government is taxation. From the most repressive dictatorship to the freest democracy, all need to raise money from those they govern. In a democratic society taxation can be effective and efficient only if those who pay taxes cooperate with the government in its effort to take money from them.

The Goals of a Good Tax Policy

To earn the trust and cooperation of the people, tax policy must meet four goals. It must offer meaningful protection against arbitrary tax increases. At the same time, it must raise adequate revenue for government to perform its minimal necessary obligations. It must be seen as fair to the taxpaying public, bearing some relation to people's ability to pay. And finally, it must encourage — or at least not hinder — economic growth.

When tax policy fails to meet those goals, it begins to lose legitimacy. This is most apparent with federal taxes today. They do not raise enough money to match the appetite of Congress for spending, so deficits rise ever higher. They provide convenient loopholes for special interest groups and even specific companies and individuals, forfeiting any claim to fairness. They penalize savings and investment, so America lags in economic growth.

Shortcomings of Pennsylvania's Local Tax System

Many Pennsylvanians have an equally despairing attitude toward their own local tax system. They are convinced that it takes more money than necessary, and from the wrong people, and in the wrong way. Experts may argue whether this popular perception of local tax policy is completely accurate, but even if it is not it still must be reckoned with.

America was founded by a generation whose political beliefs included a deep suspicion of government, based on a classical republican ideology whose roots go back to the great thinkers of ancient Greece and Rome. While a healthy skepticism toward government is doubtless beneficial in a democratic society, too much of that attitude can begin to undermine the bond between the people and their government.

The Pennsylvania tax reform campaign in the spring of 1989 uncovered a broad and deep feeling of suspicion, cynicism, and hostility toward all levels of government. It is taken for granted today that people distrust the federal government and even their state governments. But in Pennsylvania, people do not even trust their neighbor across the street who sits on the school board or the borough council. Time after time, every audience from Rotary business and professional people to liberal Democratic activists, from farmers to union members to retired couples, expressed this deep sense of alienation.

Why should this be? The blunt fact is, Pennsylvania's local tax system has failed to meet any of the four tests of good tax policy. It is neither democratic nor fair. It has achieved the brutal paradox of pinching municipalities in a revenue straitjacket while putting taxpayers in fear of relentless tax increases. And most worrisome of all when one surveys future decades, the tax system discourages business expansion and economic development.

Pennsylvania's Taxpayers Helpless To Protect Themselves

The single greatest cause of suspicion and cynicism toward local government is that people feel they have little say in how the tax system works. To a large degree, this feeling is accurate. Politicians have more control over local taxation and spending, and the people have less, than in almost any other state. Taxpayers elsewhere exercise powers that are only dreamed of in Pennsylvania.

Even a few examples reveal the forbidding depth of the chasm that separates this state from more advanced portions of the country. In New Jersey, school boards must submit their yearly budgets to a popular vote, which encourages superintendents and board members to hunt diligently for every hint of waste and inefficiency that might be trimmed out. In Ohio, increases in the property tax rate are subject to voter approval, so that every major rise in spending must be thoroughly justified.

In Virginia, notices must be mailed to all taxpayers before a local governing body votes on any substantial tax increase, forcing the public officials to make such tax decisions in well-publicized meetings under the gaze of a numerous and vigilant audience. States such as Massachusetts and California forbid local spending or tax revenues from rising more than a few percent each year unless the voters themselves allow a larger increase. Taxpayers in Texas may petition for an election to roll back any rise in taxes of more than 8%.

Beyond these specific protections that shield the public from arbitrary tax increases, many states provide even broader controls to insure that government is the servant, and not the master, of the people. In half the states, the initiative, referendum, and recall are a constant reminder to the politicians that ultimate power rests with the people.

If a governing body persistently ignores widespread public demand for action on some issue, the initiative process allows voters to place a proposed local ordinance directly on the ballot by obtaining a certain number of signatures on a petition. The referendum provides just the opposite check on government. If public officials enact an outrageous tax, pass an oppressive regulation, or make an absurd policy decision, the voters can petition to place that decision on the ballot and repeal it. And through the recall process, the public can call a special election to remove from office an arrogant, incompetent, or corrupt official.

The taxpayers have none of these protections and none of these rights in Pennsylvania. Public officials make all the tax decisions, often with little or no concern for what the public might want. The only remedy available to the people is to wait until the next election and vote the offending politicians out of office.

Of course, that is often an empty gesture. The example of just one school district outside Harrisburg exposes the empty charade that passes for democracy in Pennsylvania. The school board in that district proposed a large bond issue for construction and renovation. It became clear in public hearings that the great majority of concerned citizens opposed the bond issue. In defiance or the public will, board members approved the bond issue. So great was the public outcry that every board member up for election was swept from office by more than a two-to-one margin. The people had spoken. But the bonds had already been issued, and the people must pay increased taxes for the next two decades to service this debt. Democracy had no meaning in that district.

The next development was even more depressing for those who believe in representative government. When the voters defeated the incumbent school board, the leader of the taxpayer revolt became the new board president. For two years he had denounced the old board for ignoring the will of the people, spending money unwisely, and raising taxes. Yet within a year of taking office he deserted those who elected him, formed an alliance with the holdover members of the board, and pushed through a tax increase 600% higher than those he had complained of so loudly in previous years.

Is it any wonder that the taxpayers of Pennsylvania do not trust their local government? Is it any wonder that they feel frustrated, helpless, and cynical? Examples like this one could be multiplied endlessly. More than in any other state, the people are at the mercy of the politicians, who can push taxes ever higher with no effective popular constraint on their actions.

Local Governments Denied Adequate Revenue

Despite this well-founded complaint, it is ironic that many localities are nevertheless pinched for sufficient revenue to perform the legitimate services that their constituents require. For this problem the state legislature is chiefly culpable. It has imposed too-rigid millage limits on municipalities and counties with stagnant or declining tax bases. It has forced the localities to pay for an increasing number of state-mandated programs. It has failed to meet the state government's admitted obligation to educational funding. And it refuses to help municipalities with the burden of servicing state-owned tax-exempt properties.

Cities, unless they have a home-rule charter, cannot levy a real estate tax higher than 25 mills on each dollar of assessed value. Boroughs and first-class townships are limited to 30 mills, counties to 20-30 mills, and second-class townships to 14 mills. The local earned income tax, available to school districts and municipalities, is capped at one percent. The difficulty with such rigid limits is that they may provide insufficient tax revenue in some circumstances.

Wealthy suburban areas, those with major commercial properties to assess, or those which need to spend little on law enforcement and social services, may easily be able to live within these rigid millage limits. Unfortunately, many local officials must attempt to govern in less fortunate circumstances. The progressive deterioration of city streets and county roads in areas of heavy traffic; the growing expense of caring for the poor and homeless; and local crises in waste disposal, water quality, and other environmental problems, increasingly afflict the state's older industrial cities and some entire counties. Unable to raise property or income tax rates, these municipalities have been driven to enact increasingly onerous and even bizarre "nuisance taxes", or simply to neglect some of the necessary functions of government.

State Policies Make Local Tax Problems Even Worse

The revenue pinch is made worse in many places by the burden of servicing tax-exempt property. This type of property is not distributed equally across the state. Some places have relatively little of it, beyond the usual local schools, churches, and hospitals. Others are home to large universities, prisons, or state offices. Some unfortunate cities — Pittsburgh is a prime example — have half their property exempt from local taxes. The difficulty is that these institutions require police and fire protection, increase traffic burden on the streets, and in other ways use local government services that must be paid for by other property owners. Municipalities that suffer from a concentration of tax-exempt institutions, particularly state-owned property, quite naturally would like some compensation to relieve their financial burden.

Demands for more revenue come even more clamorously from the education establishment: the teachers' union, the local school administrators, and the state education bureaucracy. Their argument is simple: American education is in decline and the solution is to spend more money on it. This has become as predictable as an involuntary muscular reaction, direct from stimulus to response without the need for rational analysis.

But discounting the immoderate appetite of the educational establishment for bigger helpings of the taxpayers' money, it is nevertheless a fact that the obligation of educating Pennsylvania's children falls unequally on the taxpaying public. It is axiomatic that a district with many wealthy individuals or commercial properties will raise vastly more money per person than a district populated heavily by retired people and working-class families, or blighted by abandoned factories and run-down farmland. Every year, school boards in the poorer districts must make a decision that no one should ever have to face. They must decide either to shortchange their childrens' education or to bankrupt their district with sky-high tax rates.

The state government has not been entirely neglectful of this problem. It appropriates a great deal of money for the support of public education, but by the state's own admission, it falls far short of adequacy. There is a general consensus in recent years that the state should defray 50% of the cost of education. The latest calculations indicate that the actual percentage financed by state funds is barely 40%. As a result of this neglect, local taxpayers in the poorer districts — in the decaying industrial cities, in the vast rural stretches of northern and western Pennsylvania, in the worn-out coal country — see their school taxes rise beyond endurance. In wealthy districts the obligation of financing education is at least tolerable, if not irksome. In the poorer areas it is at best burdensome and in many cases has become economically unbearable.

The state government has been rightly criticized for its failure to deal adequately with the wide variation in local tax burdens necessary to support school systems and to service tax-exempt property. Unfortunately, mere neglect is the least of its offenses against local taxpayers. Legislators actually take deliberate measures every year to make the situation worse.

The current practice in Pennsylvania is for the legislature to spend nearly every penny of the state government's revenue each year. It cannot spend more because the state constitution requires a balanced budget. However, legislators long ago discovered an easy way around that restriction so that they can spend far more money than the state revenue system raises. They simply pass bills that require local governments to carry out programs but do not provide full state funding for these activities. In this sly way, legislators can spend all of "their own" state revenue and then spend millions more of local taxpayers' money. By one count there are currently more than 7,800 such mandated programs enacted by the legislature, but with the burden for implementation placed upon the counties, cities, boroughs, townships, or school districts.

This system of mandating programs is morally indefensible — it consists of spending local tax money on things that neither the local governments nor the local voters have approved. Perhaps even worse, it imposes unequal financial burdens on local taxpayers. Per capita wealth varies tremendously across the state, and any given legislative mandate might be a minor burden for some wealthy township but a heavy encumbrance for a poorer locality. Thus, every such program only tightens the revenue straitjacket in which many localities are helplessly bound.

The Unfair Property Tax System

Tax analysts have long complained that property taxes are among the least fair methods of raising money, and the citizens at large are of the same mind. A public opinion survey in mid-1989 showed that 28% of those polled thought the property tax was the "worst" or "least fair" type of tax, compared to 18% who named the sales tax and only 10% who complained about an income tax.

The two chief criticisms of the property tax are that it is not based on ability to pay, and that the assessed value of a property often bears no relation to its market value. In fact, studies have shown a reasonably close relationship between a family's income and the value of its real estate, except for two groups: the elderly and farmers. Retired people often keep the same house they had lived in when working, but their income usually drops substantially upon retirement. As property tax rates rise over the years, these families on a relatively fixed incomes find it increasingly difficult to live, and many are even forced to give up their homes.

Compounding the inequity of property taxation is the affliction of unequal and out-of-date assessments. A nationwide evaluation recently produced the embarrassing news that Pennsylvania ranked among the very worst states in its assessment practices. Some counties have not conducted a general reassessment of property values for decades. New construction is given a reasonably accurate valuation, but existing properties may be on the books at a fraction of their true worth. Two adjacent houses or commercial buildings may have the same actual market value, but the newer one will often pay several times as much in taxes as the older property. In some localities the usual procedure is at least to reassess a property when it changes hands, but other counties do not even make that concession to fairness.

Political reality — or at least political belief — dictates that reassessment is unpopular and that county commissioners who vote for reassessment are defeated for reelection. The gratitude of owners whose taxes are reduced is not nearly so strong as the wrath of those whose taxes increase because of updated valuations. Whether this is true or not, commissioners certainly believe it to be true, and even when they admit the unfairness of antiquated assessments they are rarely willing to take what they think is a major political risk by correcting the problem.

The Local Tax System Hinders Economic Development

In addition to being undemocratic and unfair, Pennsylvania's local tax system makes poor economic sense. When some cities, counties, boroughs, or school districts levy much higher taxes than other localities, their future economic development is put at risk. High property taxes, for example, drive up housing prices and rents and reduce net personal income. Why live in that place when one can live in a nearby area with lower taxes? If a business finds its tax burden significantly higher in one locality than another, or finds that high taxes make it more difficult to attract qualified employees, the company may move away or at least forego expansion. Likewise, the high-tax district or municipality is likely to find it more difficult to attract new business into the area.

A number of recent studies confirm this common sense assumption. Property taxes, in particular, are like a warning sign to business to go elsewhere. One analysis concluded that taxes were second only to labor costs in decisions about where to locate a new business or whether to expand an existing one. Although these economic studies deal with comparisons among the states, it is likely that similar conclusions could be drawn for different localities within Pennsylvania.

The problem is made worse by out-of-date assessments. When properties have not been reassessed to the market for several decades, the burden of property taxation falls upon properties that have recently been constructed or sold. This of course discourages new construction, discourages businesses from relocating or expanding in the area, reduces employment, and provides upward pressure on already-high tax rates.

The Need For Bold Tax Reform Proposals

Pennsylvania's local tax system is undemocratic, unfair, inadequate, hostile to economic growth, and almost universally despised by the taxpayers. Clearly, a bold new approach is required to prepare the Commonwealth for the 21st Century. Mere tinkering is inadequate to the demands of the modern age. Nor can "tax reform" be simply a seductively masked scheme to dig ever deeper into the taxpayer's pocket.

Why the 1989 'Tax Reform' Plan Failed

The humiliating defeat of Governor Casey's tax reform plan in the spring of 1989 shows what will happen to any effort that does not provide, as its fundamental principle, protection for taxpayers. This bill was the product of two decades of study and debate. It was graced with the attractive name of tax "reform." It passed the legislature by an overwhelming margin and had behind it the full power of the Casey administration and of three dozen powerful special interest groups. It had the editorial endorsement of almost every major newspaper and the support of most mayors and county commissioners. And yet it suffered the most stunning defeat by far of any proposed constitutional amendment in the history of Pennsylvania. Three quarters of the people voted against it; in some counties the margin was five, six, or nine to one against.

Why did the voters scorn so decisively this lavishly-publicized bill? The primary reason seemed to be that they simply did not trust their local governments and school boards with the additional taxing authority the law would provide. In debates and presentations, audiences were told in detail how the imposition of a higher local income tax would require by law a substantial immediate reduction in their real estate tax. But they focused their attention instead on the fact that, if the local governing body wished to do so, it could raise real estate taxes back up in future years while retaining the higher income tax.

An analysis of the Casey tax plan concluded that "the driving force behind" it was "the need for more money by local governments and school districts." Therefore, it provided "much more taxing authority, but no meaningful restraints on spending or future tax increases." This is precisely what the voters also thought, and that doomed the bill.

The First Essential of True Tax Reform — Taxpayer Protection

In the future, true tax reform must achieve three goals: protecting the taxpayer, easing the revenue pinch for local governments, and making the tax system less unfair. The most important of these is the first: restoring power to the people.

Pennsylvania taxpayers are the most powerless in the nation; they have almost no protection against higher local taxes. They see themselves as helpless victims, their pocketbooks open and defenseless before the eager hand of government. As long as they feel that sense of helplessness, they will be alienated, cynical, angry, and frustrated.

This need not be so. Local governments in almost every other state have been able to adjust to living with limits on their ability to tax and spend. There is no reason to believe that their ability to provide public services or public education have been impaired by the injection of democracy into the tax system. There are several ways to build a protective wall between the taxpayer and those who take his money.

The least desirable is simply to place an upper limit on the tax rate. Pennsylvania already does this in some circumstances, with disastrous effect on the ability of cities and counties to finance necessary services. Prudence will indicate that government revenue should be able to rise slowly over the years, to keep pace with the rising cost of the goods and services government must use. A rigid tax rate may actually produce declining revenue if the tax base is eroded by falling personal income or real estate values in a depressed economy.

A more sensible approach is to limit the tax rate but allow the local voters to authorize an increase if they think it is necessary. One of the frustrations public officials must contend with is that the public often demands more government services but resents tax increases. If the voters themselves were forced to make the decision between more government services or lower taxes, they might develop a more responsible attitude and be more understanding of the dilemma faced by their local officials.

Experience elsewhere has shown that voters will approve tax increases if they are convinced of the necessity. The burden is on those who want the additional taxes to present a strong case to the public. A sampling of reports from around the nation in the latter part of 1989 is instructive. Voters approved raising taxes to keep the library open in a Massachusetts town, to increase drug enforcement and treatment in a Missouri county, and to build or expand schools in several places. On the other hand, tax increases were rejected for increasing employee benefits in a Delaware town, subsidizing the St. Louis symphony orchestra, and for building a civic center in a Nebraska city and a new jail in an Oklahoma county.

Somewhat more flexible for government, but still effective in protecting taxpayers, are limits on the annual growth of spending or of tax revenue. Several possibilities exist. One is to allow a fixed percentage increase; Texas permits school districts up to 8% more in total tax revenue each year. Other plans apply a fixed percentage to the increase in spending from year to year.

Another version of the limit is less rigid. Taxes or spending could increase by a percentage equal to the rate of inflation. Thus, in "real" dollars, government budgets would remain static over the years. Funds required for new programs would have to be obtained by efficiencies that reduced the cost of existing programs, thus encouraging a prudent and businesslike approach to government operations.

Limiting the rise in local government spending to a fixed annual percentage or to the inflation rate might, however, pose difficulties for areas where population or school enrollment was increasing. Therefore, some analysts prefer a third and even more flexible limit that would tie the allowable annual increase in spending or taxes to the change in total personal income, or "gross domestic product" of the area.

Of course, there will always be occasions where spending needs may exceed the allowable limits. There may be major capital spending, or rising crime may require more for funds for law enforcement. The "safety valve" in such circumstances is the ability of the voters to approve a higher level of taxation or spending. This could be handled in two ways. One, the more usual, is "positive approval," requiring an automatic vote of the people to approve collecting or spending any tax revenue above the legal limit.

A less burdensome method is "negative approval," allowing the excess taxation or spending unless the voters veto it. Texas, for instance, has recently enacted a law limiting the rise in school district taxes 8% per year. If any school board approves a budget calling for more than an 8% tax increase, voters may petition for a "rollback election." If the required number of people sign such a petition, then a popular vote decides whether the higher taxes will stand or whether the increase will be rolled back to the 8% limit.

Another essential protection for taxpayers is to require a popular vote before approval of any major bond issue. Paying the interest and principal on bonded debt often requires increased taxes for years into the future. Recognizing this fact, almost every state forbids local governments from committing taxpayers to a bond issue merely by a vote of the governing body. In Pennsylvania, five school board members, two county commissioners, or a similar bare majority of any township, borough, or city government can incur bonded debt that may impose a backbreaking tax burden. It is essential for Pennsylvania to adopt the prudent approach of other states and require voter approval of all but the smallest bond issues.

Initiative, Referendum, and Recall

Beyond these powers directly related to taxation, the people need to be able to exercise a more general oversight of their local governments than is now possible. The initiative, referendum, and recall are the standard way of providing this popular control over government. Objections have been raised, particularly to the initiative, on the grounds that legislation by ballot may not be a wise method of making law. The usual legislative process in a city council, for instance, involves an extended period that may include public hearings, committee meetings, amendments, and compromises so that the broadest possible consensus may support the ultimate decision. In the initiative process the precise wording of an ordinance is put upon the ballot and voters must approve or reject it in an "all-or-nothing" decision with no possibility of compromise or amendment.

Even if this objection to the initiative process were to be allowed, there is little reason to fear the referendum. It does not enact positive legislation but merely allows the voters to veto a decision of their governing body. It has been used very effectively and usually quite prudently in half the states of the Union. In the national and state governments there are two legislative houses as a check against hasty decisions. But most local governments have only one decision-making body, increasing the likelihood that things will be done that are later regretted. Thus, in local governments, the referendum can provide this missing check on legislation. The people themselves become, in a sense, the "second house" of the legislature.

The power to recall elected officials from office is also an essential tool of popular government. Far too often, those who win public office forget that they are merely the representatives of the general will. They sometimes make decisions without consulting the public or even in direct violation of what they know to be majority opinion. If representative government is to have any meaning, there must be a way for the voters, at least at the most immediate local level, to cast out officials who have betrayed their trust.

In addition, the knowledge that a recall petition may always be filed acts to reduce the arrogance and improve the competence with which officials do their job. Unfortunately, local officeholders in Pennsylvania have nothing to fear from abusive and undemocratic behavior; they are secure from their masters, the people, until the last day of their term of office. Providing the recall power to local voters would be a long step toward restoring confidence in local government and convincing the voters that elected officials would in fact represent those who had elected them.

Meeting the State's Responsibilities to Local Government

Local tax reform does not consist only of limits on government and protection for taxpayers. There must also be a transformation of the existing master-slave relationship between the state and local governments. Strengthening popular control would be meaningless if school districts and municipalities are not in control of their own fiscal future. To achieve this, the state must be willing to meet its obligations to local governments and their taxpayers.

First, there must be an end to the practice of mandating programs to be financed from local resources. If legislators believe a policy is worth enacting into law, they should be courageous enough to find the money to pay for that policy. Nothing is a greater encouragement to irresponsible behavior than for the legislature to be able to pass laws and force local officials to find the money to pay for them.

The state must accept the responsibility of fully funding any future mandated programs. Those already existing should be fully paid with state money over a period of years, to avoid the need for a state tax increase.

Public education is a special case, absorbing in most areas more tax money than all other local responsibilities combined. Here, too, the state must do its duty. It would not be impossible to calculate what each district would require to provide an acceptable level of basic education for its students. There would be even less difficulty in establishing how much money each district could provide from its own resources, at a standardized level of local taxation. The state should then undertake to make up the difference, in the poorer districts, between what can reasonably be expected from the district's own taxpayers and what is necessary to pay for an adequate — not a lavish — basic education.

If legislators do not voluntarily adopt some such plan, the courts will undoubtedly force it upon them. In one state after another, challenges to unequal education funding have led to court orders for a fairer distribution of the costs of public education. Pennsylvania has very little time to work out its own solution before it also comes under a judicial mandate.

Finally, those localities burdened with more than their share of tax-exempt state property are entitled to some relief. The equitable solution is for Harrisburg simply to pay these local governments an amount equivalent to the taxes that would be due on state-owned property. The state has made occasional gestures in this direction. For instance, it has reimbursed some counties for state game lands, and it pays the city of Harrisburg for some municipal services provided to state properties.

Making the Local Tax System Less Unfair

If local governments are to continue to raise significant amounts of money from the property tax, it is important to make this levy as fair as possible. The one improvement almost everyone would agree upon is to improve the assessment process. The taxable values placed upon any two properties must be proportionate to their actual market values, and this is far from the case in most Pennsylvania counties.

Reassessing every tax parcel in a county requires a major investment; in the entire state there are about five million separate parcels of real estate. To encourage reassessments, the state could provide a revolving loan fund to defray the "up-front" costs of such a massive undertaking. It is even more vital, however, to overcome the perceived political risk that county commissioners think they will incur if they order updated assessments. The only way to eliminate this fear is for the state to require by law that all counties make a thorough and current reassessment of properties. Such a mandate would allow com-missioners to escape the wrath of owners who suffered a size-able tax increase, by pointing the finger at the state law.

There is, however, a real danger that a sudden updating of assessed values would hurt tens of thousands of retired people living on relatively fixed incomes. Many such elderly home-owners have been living in the same location for decades and since the property has been in the same hands it has often not been revalued. If these homes were suddenly to double, triple, quadruple or more in assessed value, the higher tax — even if the millage rate were sharply reduced — would devastate the living standards of such individuals.

One way to avoid this crushing and unfair burden, and to make the real estate tax more fair for everyone, is to adopt an across-the-board exemption of a fixed amount from the value of every tax parcel. If, for example, the first $10,000 of market value were exempt from taxation, the real estate levy would be more nearly comparable to a person's ability to pay. Taking $10,000 from the taxable value of a retired couple's $30,000 row home would cut their tax by one-third. The same $10,000 exemption on the $100,000 house of an upper-middle-income working couple would provide a tax break of 10%, and for the $300,000 home of a well-to-do family the tax reduction would be only 3%. For large business properties the impact of a standardized $10,000 exemption would be minimal.

Even if real estate taxation were made fairer by equalizing assessments and providing a standard property exemption, many people might prefer to reduce or eliminate their local property tax by replacing it with an increased wage tax. It would certainly be in order to allow this sort of restructuring — but only if the local taxpayers themselves wished it. If Pennsylvania is to have a more democratic tax system, there is no reason why peop-le should not be able to vote on the type, as well as the rate, of tax-ation. A large number of school districts, for instance, have imposed "nuisance taxes" such as the occupational assessment tax where each job category pays a fixed amount per year regardless of the worker's income. Voters in those districts might rather pay a somewhat higher earned income tax and do away with the nuisance taxes.

In summary, what Pennsylvania needs is a local tax system that is more democratic and more fair, and one in which the state fulfills its fiscal responsibility to local governments and their taxpayers. Impartial analysts have concluded that the state's present local taxation is among the very worst in America. The changes recommended here would bring to Pennsylvania some of the same reforms that other states have enjoyed for up to 75 years. Nothing less will do for a tax system that must soon be ready for the challenges of the 21st century.

CHAPTER TWENTY-FOUR

EASING CITY BUDGET PRESSURES: THE ROLE OF PRIVATIZATION
By W. Wilson Goode

EDITOR'S SUMMARY

Privatization is a form of creative financing that allows city officials to provide quality mandated city services at the lowest possible cost to taxpayers. The public demand for balanced budgets and no tax increases places constraints on a city's already strained dilemma. Privatization is an answer to this problem.

Privatization's workability and viability are reflected in the financial savings. In Newark, New Jersey, privatization saved the city $1 million over a three year period when it was instituted. In California, a study of 20 cities reported refuse collection by private firms cost upwards of 42% less than when the city provided the service.

In Philadelphia, many of the city's services have been privatized and the savings have been evident. The city has contracted out health services facilities and management, water department refuge, recreation facilities management, human services facilities and management, and some operations in the police and streets departments.

Privatization has brought noticeable improvements to the police department. Privatization has made it possible to increase the number of street-level police officers which has boosted morale within the force and reduced the crime rate. Privatization also enables businesses that want special police services to contract with the department for those services thereby eliminating the city's need to pay overtime.

Privatization has been effective in the operations of the streets department. Privatization has provided significant savings, easier access to high capacity compactors, and developed strong cooperation with labor unions. Trucks are able to collect 140% of what had been the collection rate due to the new capacity of collectors. Workers now operate on a "task system" whereby they are paid per task as opposed to per hour, which has improved worker incentives.

Privatization in the streets department has reduced the city's overall expenditures by $11 million. It has also resulted in a reduction of the necessary workforce by upwards of 15%. The overall cost of trash disposal, which had been increasing from 20 — 50% over the past few years, has leveled off to 5%.

Privatization, as a means of easing city budget pressures, is a viable and successful solution. As federal resources decrease and municipalities take on a greater responsibility for the delivery of services, it is essential that cities develop creative financing alternatives to ensure that they meet the mandate to provide for the needed services of the citizens.

W. Wilson Goode is Mayor of the City of Philadelphia.

The objective for every city official, elected or appointed, and for every city employee is to provide quality mandated city services at the lowest possible cost to taxpayers.

As we begin the 1990's and prepare for the 21st Century, our city governments are faced with major fiscal challenges. The detrimental effects of the 1980's, a decade of federal neglect of our cities, now plague our cities — especially our urban centers. Since 1980, subsidized housing has been cut by 79%, training and employment programs have been cut by 70%, work incentive programs have been cut by 71%, community development block grants and community service block grants have been cut by more than 33%. The January issue of *City & State* cites the fact that "in inflation-adjusted dollars, federal aid to state and local governments fell by more than a third during the 1980's."

These cuts have posed major economic and service delivery problems for cities. Municipalities are faced with the dichotomous situation of how to provide mandated city services with less federal financial support. How do cities meet the increased responsibilities with drastically decreased resources? How can cities reduce major expenditures without reducing employment opportunities?

In the midst of the "new fiscal federalism" which operates under the policy of "every community for itself", whereby each city must deal with its own social and economic problems void of federal responsibility and resources, local governments are placed in a political Catch-22 position; increased responsibilities and decreased funds.

Thus, cities are forced to consider alternative financing of mandated services. The public demand for balanced budgets and no-tax increases places further constraints on an already strained dilemma. One form of creative financing that would provide a means to retain high quality city services at the lowest rates is privatization. Although government officials have grown to regard the term "creative financing" with an aversion because of its misuse as a euphemism for admitting the impossibility of a fiscal situation, in the very real sense, the term can and should be used legitimately.

The Demand and Cost Savings of Privatization

Although some may think privatization is a new approach to

solving the old problem of providing services to citizens, it is not a new concept. From a federal government policy point of view, it has been encouraged since 1955. At the state and local level, the form of privatization known as "franchising" and "contracting out" is widespread and increasing in popularity. Thirty-five percent of municipalities across the country use some form of contracting out to deliver trash collection and disposal services alone.

In fact, lawsuits by taxpayers in several jurisdictions have required that the government provide services at the lowest cost or give taxpayers the right to choose a less costly private option. Successful efforts date back as far as 1932, when San Francisco franchised garbage collection to private companies. Today, drivers own their trucks and are responsible for collections. A 1975 study showed that San Franciscans were paying $40 a year for their service, while New Yorkers, in two comparable neighborhoods, were paying $297.

Another example can be seen in Kansas City which set the modern standard for large jurisdictions when it began contracting out trash services in 1971. Prior to that, the city collected garbage and left residents to dispose of trash. Now Kansas City collects out the balance to private haulers through a competitive bid system.

The workability and viability of privatization are reflected in the financial savings. In Newark, New Jersey, for instance, it is estimated that privatization saved the city some $1 million over a three-year period when it was instituted. In New Orleans, where trash collection occurs twice a week, first year savings of $1 million were realized when the city privatized.

The example of Phoenix can also be cited. A decade ago privatization was implemented to reduce the cost of trash collection which was estimated to be $6.50 per month per household. To establish a competitive, service-oriented climate, Phoenix City Council adopted a policy which directs the city to call for bids from private industry to ensure that city operations will be performed economically while maintaining desired service levels.

The results have been successful. The cost of trash collection and disposal over a ten-year period have actually plummeted, so that in constant dollars today it costs each person only two-thirds of what it cost ten years ago for trash collection and disposal. The savings have been calculated to be a decrease of 4%

per year. This downward spiral is counter to the trend of other city services. In fact, the sanitation services are the only ones in Phoenix where costs have been reduced so sharply. Costs in other major operating departments have, in fact, risen.

In addition, a 1984 service delivery survey was taken of twenty California cities. They all reported that trash collection by private firms cost 28 to 48% less than the provision of the same service by the municipality.

Privatization and Philadelphia's Police Department

In Philadelphia, many of the city's services have been privatized and the savings have been evident. The city has contracted out for health services facilities and management, water department refuse (sludge hauling and treatment), recreation facilities management, human services facilities and management, and some operations in the Police Department and the Streets Department.

Although reductions of programs were made in other departments due to budgetary constraints, increases were made in the staffing of the Police Department. The administration contended that one of the services that the city could not risk reducing was protection. The administration set a goal for Fiscal Year 1990 to increase the police workforce by 475 new hirings. Overall, by June 1992, the police force will have increased from 6,000 to 6,900. The implementation of this goal in the face of budgetary reductions was possible through privatization. Businesses and organizations that want special police services contract with the department for those services. This procedure eliminates the city's having to pay overtime.

Privatization of the police services has resulted in increasing the number of police officers on the streets, increasing morale within the police force because police can receive overtime pay, and reducing crime because more police are visible throughout the city. Currently, the Police Department has contracted with organizations and companies that want additional services. These include construction companies, shopping galleries, and the sports stadiums.

Privatization and Philadelphia's Streets Department

Privatization has also been effective in the operations of the

Streets Department. Negotiations for a four-year contract with renewal options were successful. Privatization has benefited this operation by providing significant savings, enabling access to high capacity compactors, and developing strong cooperation with labor unions. Trucks are able to collect 140% of what had been the collection rate due to the new capacity of containers.

In addition, transportation costs have been significantly reduced because the same trucks can collect and transport the waste to the landfills, whereas in the past, two different modes of transportation were required for the two operations. On the labor side, worker incentive increased, mostly due to the fact that workers' rates of pay are competitive and workers operate on a "task system" whereby they are paid per task as opposed to per hour.

The privatization of this service has reduced the city's overall expenditures by 10-15%, or $11 million. It has also resulted in a reduction of the necessary workforce by 12-15%. Even the overall cost of trash disposal, which had been increasing from 20-50% over the past few years, has leveled to 5% over the course of the contract.

Privatization and Philadelphia's Health Services

As in other city services, privatization can result in a reduction of costs in health services. The city operated Central Pharmacy is currently being converted to a private contractor. Although there will continue to be a Central Pharmacy with mostly different functions, the functions of procuring, warehousing, and distributing pharmaceuticals which were previously done by the Central Pharmacy will be the exclusive province of an outside vendor.

The advantages of this conversion are manifold. They would include more frequent and timely deliveries, including weekends, to user sites; greater availability of medications, particularly at the district health centers; more efficient third-party billing; less reliance on an "emergency system" to procure medications which should produce a lesser unit cost; less "expired drugs" through a more efficient inventory system which should translate into a lesser unit cost; the availability of in-service professional training; and, the implementation of a "unit-of-use" system which will reduce both pharmaceutical and nursing costs.

Conclusion

These are a few examples that give evidence that privatization, as a means of easing city budget pressures, can be a viable and successful solution. As the populations of our cities increase, as federal resources decrease, as municipalities take on a greater responsibility for the delivery of services, it is essential that cities develop creative financing alternatives to ensure that they meet the mandate, as public servants, to provide for the needed services of the citizens.

CHAPTER TWENTY-FIVE

CONTRACTING OUT: INVOLVING THE MARKET IN DELIVERING LOCAL PUBLIC SERVICES

By Anthony R. Tomazinis

EDITOR'S SUMMARY

Government has greatly expanded its functions in this century. Since the Great Depression, government at all levels has responded to perceived social needs with the creation of new programs and services. As a result of these additional responsibilities, several alternative ways of service provision must be examined.

Privatization of public sector services is a viable alternative for carrying out governmental functions. Non-governmental involvement in the provision of public services has historical precedence. In Pennsylvania, privatization began as early as 1794, when the first private road opened between Philadelphia and Lancaster.

There are seven major privatization methods to facilitate the needs of local and state government. Included are contracting out, franchise and concessions, subsidies, vouchers, volunteers, self-help, and tax incentives. These approaches are in addition to using intergovernmental agencies or consortiums.

Contracting out is the most widely used privatization approach. The main reason its use has doubled in the past two decades is the significant reduction of costs it offers for local governments. Contracting out also eliminates the need for large initial capital expenditures and introduces greater flexibility in adjustments in services.

Evaluations of contracting out local governmental services should involve several criteria. These include cost to citizens, choice to clients and feasibility of service. All variables should be evaluated in determining whether privatization can be effective in a particular situation.

Quality improvement can be enhanced through privatization. Introducing competition and reducing the monopoly of a single government agency usually leads to more effective service. Multiple providers in competitive circumstances can provide an increase in the level of quality along with providing service stability.

There is a difference between producing public services and providing public services. The government has a responsibility to provide many services, but that does not mean it must *produce* them. For example, when government contracts with the private sector for transit services, it transfers the responsibility to provide service to the private firm.

Anthony R. Tomazinis is Professor of City and Regional Planning at the University of Pennsylvania.

The question of "What is the responsibility of government in the field of service provision?" has been receiving differing answers during each historical period and each set of circumstances. The common thread in the answers given over the years is that government should provide whatever is requested from it and whatever it can indeed provide. The early "contracts" between the people and their government included only three functions; that of external defense, that of internal security, and that of dispensing justice in local disputes. In the 20th century, however, we have seen government expanding its functions according to the manifest needs of our society and in response to certain philosophical or ideological perceptions of the role of government. We have thus had various examples of total involvement of government in all aspects of human activities. These examples include the totalitarian social regimes that own all resources of production and produce all essential services, as well as those western style governments which produce a measured array of services within a framework of free markets and considerable private sector economic activity.

In practically all cases the two basic concerns remain the same however. Those concerns focus on the responsibility of providing what is requested by the government, and on the capability of producing what is decided to be provided. The first concern is usually handled within a framework of philosophical beliefs and comparative options, while the second concern is usually handled on the basis of what are the requirements of production and the comparative skill limitations within and without the government. Obviously the answers provided in each set of circumstances have been quite different and evolving. In addition, the answers have been different for each level of government. Historical traditions, personal leadership, and institutional relationships have also entered to influence the answer in each case.

Since the Great Depression of 1929-1932, the trends in the Western world have been for government to expand its responsibility in providing the essential services that society requires. The emergencies of World War II also added to these trends as did the pressures of the socialist paradigm of government that prevailed in the Soviet Union since the Revolution of 1917. During all the postwar period, government at all levels responded to perceived social needs with the creation of additional services and additional governmental programs and agencies that were needed to each case. It is this immense, in comparative terms, expansion of the responsibilities and activities of modern government that raised the question in the minds of many scholars and government practitioners as to whether government is indeed the best vehicle in actually providing and producing each additional service that was added.

Local government is by tradition and practice the level of government that provides local public services in the United States. This role was further expanded and reinforced in the early 1970's when many new government factions were transferred from the federal level to states and local government. Many of these services were indeed new in type and substance and therefore did not correspond to existing skills, or interest groups, or traditions within the government circles. As a result, many new responsibilities were handled with alternative ways of service provision, many of which involved extensive utilization of the private sector. A new trend for "privatization" of public sector services was thus created.

Methods of Privatization

Government has made use of many approaches in providing goods and services its leaders deemed necessary for a long time in history. Although privatization is currently the fashionable word, the concept of using non-governmental employees and agencies to carry out governmental functions is a long honored practice in many societies, including the United States. Private roads have been known in the United States and Pennsylvania since as early as 1794 when such a roadway opened between Philadelphia and Lancaster. Even the use of mercenaries to carry out external defense tasks and the use of private detective agencies to investigate specific cases has been known for centuries. Also, many functions which are currently considered as proper governmental services were performed for centuries by non-governmental individuals and organizations, such as voluntary charitable, educational and civic organizations. Even the extended family patterns that prevailed in so many societies and for so many centuries were devices of delivering services which modern government theory defines as proper governmental functions. Thus, examining ways of reinforcing this non-governmental involvement in public sector services is just a reasonable and traditionally honored practice in spite of what some modern government theorists might suggest, and what some entrenched vested interests of public employees may demand.

An examination of privatization practices currently in effect in the United States would reveal that many approaches are indeed applied in the field to facilitate the needs of local and state government. In the *Municipal Year Book of 1989* of the International City Managers Association, Dr. Elaine Morley of the Urban Institute presents a discussion of seven such methods of doing business by local governments. These seven methods or approaches are in addition to the typical ones of using government employees and agencies and that of using intergovernmental agencies or consortiums. The seven methods are the following:

(1) **Contracting Out:** The government contracts out to a firm (private firms for profit, or nonprofit organizations) the job of doing a specific task for the government. All the definition of the product is done by the government but the actual production and delivery is done by the private firm. Payment arrangements are established competitively and can take several forms, safeguarding the interests of both parties.

(2) **Franchise and Concessions:** The government franchises a firm to produce directly a service for a group of people and/or locality. Payments are made directly by the receivers of the service.

(3) **Subsidies:** The government provides financial support to a private organization to produce and deliver a public service at a reduced cost to some consumers. Cultural services that are produced by private for-profit or not-for-profit organizations are typical partners in such a method.

(4) **Vouchers:** The government provides coupons or tickets with a certain monetary value to a specified group of people who need (or desire) a particular service and who then can choose among a number of private providers to

purchase that service. The government thus chooses a specific subsidy that it wants to provide and/or an enhancement of the provision of a certain service that it wants to promote.

(5) **Volunteers:** The government accepts the offers of volunteer organizations and assigns to them the production and/or direct delivery of specific services to certain population groups, institutions, or operations. Volunteer services have a long history of use in both the public and private sectors of this country.

(6) **Self-Help:** The government encourages and supports citizens to carry out or contribute in the production of all or some portion of a service that they themselves need (i.e., car pooling, neighborhood watch).

(7) **Regulatory and Tax Incentives:** The government uses its regulatory and taxing authority in order to induce the provision of some desired services by the private sector or to foster the reduction of the need for such a service.

Of all the above approaches of privatization the one defined by "contracting out" is clearly the most widely practiced approach currently in the United States, and the central topic of this chapter.

Contracting Out

Although contracting out has been practiced by government for many years, considerable confusion can still be found in the field. To start with, government has reached contractual agreements with many providers that are able to purchase or produce commodities or services that the government needs to use. Typically the various governmental units proceed purchasing from vendors many types of support services, inventory material and even, on occasion, capital facilities. Most governmental units at all levels are well acquainted with these practices and are supportive of their continuous utilization. However, the modern term of contracting out includes the purchasing from vendors some or all of the primary service that the governmental agency was previously providing or is intending to provide.

In terms of quantitative measurements contracting out of governmental local services in the United States has grown from 11% in 1970 to 20% in 1982. Additional growth has also been registered since 1982. Clearly, contracting out is the most popular approach in privatization, exceeding by far in most services the mark reported in the 1982 Touche Ross Survey. There is hardly a local service that is not included in the group of local services experiencing the pressure of privatization. In some cases, many cities and counties are indeed reporting a substantial reliance on privatized services in general, and on contracting out of services in particular. Figure 1, taken from the 1988 Touche Ross Survey, indicates the extent of utilization that contracting out receives currently in the country.

Reasons For Contracting Out

"Contracting out" is not only the service delivery method most commonly used as an alternative method today, but also the one which seems to combine a high degree of flexibility, as well as a high level of productivity. In contracting out, the local government usually contracts with a private firm (a for-profit firm or a nonprofit organization) to deliver a specified set of goods or services. The contract may cover all or a portion of the services or goods that the local government desires to have available for its residents or government agencies.

The typical reason that most local governments pronounce in exploring contracting out in the delivery of goods or services is to achieve economies. In essence they see an important division between the responsibility of providing a service, and actually producing a service. They see the first one as the proper responsibility of government, an integral part of policy making, a consequence of the modern concept of local government, as it evolved after the 1920's. They see the second as a strictly production operation that is based on the optimal use of the factors of production, of managerial skills, of proper incentives, and of capitalization of unique opportunities within a framework of competitive ingenuity. As a result the selection of contracting out with competitive bids wins over as a means of achieving both service availability of a desired quality plus economy and flexibility in production.

A study[1] by the Urban Institute in 1978 singled out seven advantages that local governments see one time or another in contracting out public services:

(1) Reduced cost or better quality
(2) Provision of specialized skills
(3) Reduction in the expansion of government
(4) Elimination of large initial capital needs
(5) Greater flexibility in introducing adjustments
(6) Provision of a yardstick for further comparison
(7) Employment of most up-to-date management styles

These same advantages can also be seen as the reason of intense opposition to contracting out from several quarters from within or without the local government. Figure 2 indicates the results of the 1988 Touche Ross Survey in cost reduction possibilities of contracting out. Reducing the cost or the provision of better quality through mechanisms outside the bureaucratic structure of local government frequently invites unflattering comparisons, hence unyielding opposition to contracting out and other forms of privatization by some individuals and groups with particular vested interests or ideological commitments.

Contracting out can be singled out as the most promising alternative or option in public service delivery for three major reasons: (a) enhancement of competitive spirit, (b) opportunity for innovative applications, and (c) engagement of larger segments of the market and community in the provision of the goods and services desired for a locality (especially when non-profit institutions are included in the provision of services).

The competitive spirit can be enhanced and maintained in high levels through several devices that cities and counties have frequently been engaging. Competition in the provision of public services is highly desirable in spite of the views held by many labor union leaders and authors in public administration. Competition in both the exact methods in the provision of service and in management approaches is vital because it affects all aspects of the product; its quality; its costs; and its availability. After all, public services are products that need to be produced and distributed. There is hardly any uniqueness in the nature of most public services which places them outside the realm of good management and effective production processes. And yet we are constantly told that any typical public administrator, and routine labor union contract is sufficient to produce economical, high quality, and readily available public services and goods.

The production of services and goods is quite different from the provision of such services and goods. The production requires the skills of entrepreneuring minds, the constant commitment for improvement in the production process driven with ever present incentives and ingenuity. These are the conditions normally present in the competitive private sector and these are the attributes of individuals who are prepared to venture success or failure, who are driven by a constant desire to "beat" their competitor, to adapt to the most efficient process and to adjust their expectations constantly. The monopolistic basis upon which government is based is quite the opposite of what a productive system needs; a system that thrives in competition and excels in entrepreneurship.

The provision of services and goods is more of a public policy function; it involves the responsibility of deciding what is appropriate, what is fair, and what is desirable. It may also involve questions of who would ultimately pay for each service, and even when that payment should take place. Those are the functions which normally belong to the public sector; to the government who represents producers and consumers, the payers and the receivers; the representative government is also a better adjudicator of the ethical questions involved and of the distributional responsibilities and potentialities of resources and production. It is for these reasons why uniting provision and production is usually delimiting and restrictive for both. The technologist producer is quite a different individual from the institutional public servant who looks for continuity and balances. Competition in the public sector has very limited meaning and include connotations that are antithetical to the basic tenets of government. This realization positions many individuals who have not seen the difference between production and provision to oppose any privatization concepts of local public services.

The opportunity for innovation through contracting out has generally been recognized as a real possibility practically from all quarters. In addition it has been cited as one of the most urgent needs of the modern era of constantly expanding governmental responsibility, rapidly changing social services needs, and continuously evolving technological and management techniques and approaches. In most cases the manner in which social services are produced in the public sector has been established a generation ago and by the late 1980's and 1990's it is hopelessly obsolete and totally frozen within a complex network of labor union rules, traditions, vested interest, and obsolete hardware and software technology. It is patently clear that innovation in all aspects of social services delivery systems (on a large scale as well as on detail) is an item of first priority, and it promises to become more so with each passing year. Contracting out (with a competitive framework with multiple players in each region and with frequent new entries and exits of players) is a process that provides the best promise for continuous aggressive and effective innovation. After all, each new potential contract will provide the best incentive for resourceful individuals to apply the most up-to-date techniques to do the prescribed job economically.

Another indirect aspect of contracting out of local social services is that its widespread implementation will make possible the engagement of many more groups in the provision of public services and goods. This direct involvement of many more actors characterized by much greater variety, backgrounds and preparation is seen as an additional strength of this approach. Many more people will be knowledgeable of what is involved in providing local public services and many more ideas and sources of interest will be present in all deliberations. Comparing this system with the typical approach that prevails currently (that which relies on a large corps of permanent employees) reveals the reasons why the most stringent opposition to contracting out came from the ranks of public employee unions, and the reasons why most of the strongest support for contracting out came from most other segments of society. This is particularly so when in addition to the free market providers, the option for contracting out includes nonprofit organizations that can compete for specific services, on city-wide or neighborhood-wide basis. In cases in which the governmental departments can also compete for parts or segments of the derived services, the number of groups involved in the production of local public services increases substantially involving, in effect, elements of all parts of a city.

Evaluation of Contracting Out

It is a difficult task to evaluate all alternative approaches of service delivery in local areas and it is a topic that did not yet receive the proper scholarly and professional scrutiny. The variations of the circumstances and conditions of each local situation are enough reasons usually to introduce a certain uniqueness in each case and to permit reviewers to reject the pertinent findings as special studies. Also, a few studies reviewing the reasons of privatization to date have shown how much ideological potential and vested interest such studies may include. For instance a study sponsored by the American Federation of State, County and Municipal Employees (*Government for Sale: Contracting Out — The New Patronage*. J.D. Hanrahan, Washington, D.C. 1977) shows clearly the extent of the limitations imposed by special interests on attempts to produce balanced reviews of the record. Also another more recent study of privatization in general, demonstrates another risk that evaluative studies face from a prior ideological inclination (*The Emperor's New Clothes: Transit Privatization and Public Policy.* Economic Policy Institute; Washington, D.C. 1989).

A review published in the *1983 Municipal Year Book* of the International City Managers Association, authored by Dr. Harry Hatry of the Urban Institute, and Carl Valente of ICMA, offers some hope in reaching a more meaningful framework of evaluating such controversial and frequently emotional efforts. Hatry and Valente suggest an evaluation should include such items as:

> Cost to government
> Cost to citizens
> Choice to clients
> Quality/Effectiveness of service
> Distributional effects of service
> Service stability
> Feasibility of service
> Overall potential impact

Reviewing the record to date with regard to these eight evaluation variables it seems that while the comprehensive studies are not yet available to report conclusively, particularly with regard to contracting out, the sporadic evidence available suggest the following:

Cost to Government: Although there are indeed cases in which no cost savings to the government were reported, the vast preponderance of evidence clearly suggests that contracting out can produce substantial cost savings to the government, varying from 10% to as high as 60%. However, competitive conditions are considered a prerequisite; otherwise, costs may not be affected or even increased. The reasons associated with cost savings is usually mismanagement of various forms, and/or need for major and immediate capital investment which may not be available to a local government at a given point. However, the same conditions, and sometimes corruption, can lead to recommendations toward the reverse direction, particularly when competition cannot be achieved.

Cost to Citizens: Attention needs to be paid in all cases in order to achieve costs savings to the citizens as it would be for cost savings to the government. Otherwise the costs can be shifted and thus no actual savings are registered. Since the final payers, are in most cases, the citizens, shifts of costs from government to citizens make no sense and on occasion may promote monopolistic conditions on the private sector itself. In most cases contracting out that includes choice of the clients also produce reduction of costs to citizens.

Cost to the Clients: The optimal case in contracting out is when the choice offered to the client groups increases. Contracting out in parts and in sequence enhances the choice to the clients, reducing the monopoly of a single government agency or authority.

Quality and Effectiveness of Services: Contracting out can be well structured to guarantee a given, and desired level of quality of service, including effectiveness of service, quality of service in competitive circumstances and frequent shifts of providers can also be improved much faster and more effectively with the contracting out approach than with any other approach including the direct governmental provision. In fact, cost to the citizen, choice to the client and continuous quality improvements represent the three product dimensions that contracting out can enhance more than any other approach.

Distributional Effect of Service: Contracting out should, in most cases, be completely neutral to this dimension of quality. In fact, however, the distributional aspects of a service can be enhanced much more easily with specific contracting out agreements than with other approaches in service delivery. This is so because of the ability to tailor such services if and when such an action is decided.

Service Stability: Contracting out does introduce greater instability of service in such cases in which the entire locality is totally based on a single private sector monopolist provider. Strikes, stoppages, disputes, are as frequent in this case as in any other case. However, multiple providers, in competitive circumstances, can counter this risk. Also, contractual agreements that provide for city takeover in instances of service disruption, as well as contracts in which the city owns the capital facilities that the operator leases, tend to increase service stability. Finally, contracts in which the city retains a small portion of the operation (maintaining thus the expertise and the capability) tend to still enhance, not decrease, service stability.

Feasibility of Service: Contracting out must be legally feasible in each state, before it can be considered seriously. Also contracting out involves the presence of multiple private sector providers, as well as a public employees' union that does not dominate public decision making. In all cases in which the above factors dominate the situation, the option of contracting out is precluded, and the *decision is really made by special interests and/or inappropriate decision makers.*

Conclusion

Contracting out is neither a new approach nor an ideological option in local services delivery systems. It is a practical tool long in use by government practitioners that provides an opportunity for local governments to maintain greater flexibility in their activities, to insure always that the most economical process in service production is in use, and that the energies of government leaders, elected and appointed, are applied more on the familiar and challenging tasks of governing, than on the limiting and continuously evolving tasks of product production.

FIGURE 1

USE OF CONTRACTING-OUT IN LAST FIVE YEARS
BY U.S. CITIES AND COUNTIES

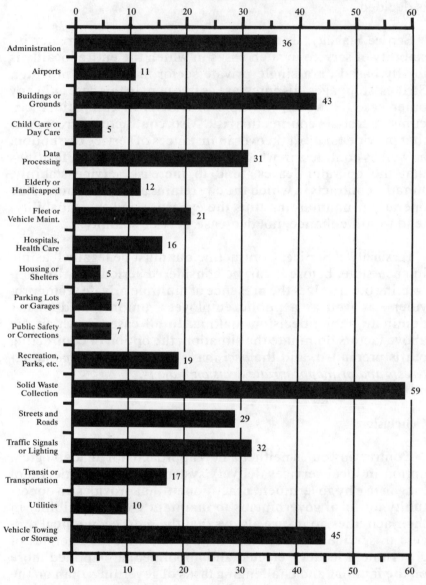

Percent of Responses to Query

Source: Adapted from Touche Ross, "Privatization in America," 1987, p. 16. and *Reason Foundation*

FIGURE 2

PERCENT OF LOCAL GOVERNMENTS REPORTING COST SAVINGS DUE TO CONTRACTING-OUT

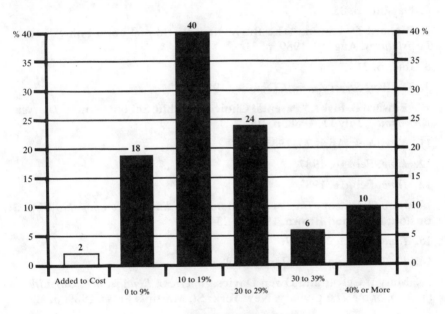

Cost Savings Reported

Source: Adapted from Touche Ross, "Privatization in America," 1987, p. 13. and *Reason Foundation*

Endnotes and References

CHAPTER ONE ENDNOTES

1. George Gallup, *Forecast 2000*, New York; William Morrow and Company, 1984, p. 11.

2. Jon Naisbitt, *Megatrends*, New York; Warner Books, 1984, p. 3.

3. David Osborne, *Laboratories of Democracy*, Boston; Harvard Press, 1988, p. 3.

4. *Forbes*, July 13, 1987.

5. Robert Reich, *The Next American Frontier*, New York; Penguin Books, 1984, p. 121.

6. Naisbitt, p. 85.

7. Richard D. Lamm, "The Brave New World of Public Policy," *State Legislatures*, Aug. 19, 1989, p. 31.

8. Ibid, p. 31.

9. *The Wall Street Journal*, October 1987.

10. Edward B. Fiske, "Parental Choice in Public School Gains," *The New York Times*, July 11, 1988, p. B6.

11. *Newsweek*, April 25, 1987.

12. *Time*, Feb. 16, 1987.

13. *Time*, Feb. 16, 1987.

14. John O. Wilson, *The Power Economy: Building an Economy that Works*, Boston; Little and Brown, 1985, p. 234.

15. *Time*, March 23, 1987.

16. *The Washington Post*, Jan. 15, 1988.

17. Marvin Cetvar and Owen Davies, *American Renaissance: Our Life at the Turn of the 21st Century*, New York; St. Martin's Press, 1989, p. 327.

CHAPTER TWO REFERENCES

1. *History of Pennsylvania*, Wayland Fuller Dunaway, Prentice-Hall, New York, 1935.

2. *A History of Pennsylvania*, Phillip S. Klein and Ari Hoogenboom, The Pennsylvania State University Press, 1980.

3. *Immigrant Destinations*, Caroline Golab, Temple University Press, Philadelphia, 1977.

4. *Pennsylvania — Keystone to Progress*, E. Willard Miller, Windsor Publications, Inc., Northridge, CA, 1986.

5. *Pennsylvania's Best*, A.H. Carstens, Pennsylvania Publications, Cresco, PA, 19609.

6. U.S. Census of Population and Housing, 1790 through 1980.

7. *U.S. Hispanics; Changing the Face of America*, Cary Davis, Carl Haub and Joanne Willette, The Population Reference Bureau, Washington, D.C., 1983.

8. *General Population Characteristics, 1980 Census of the Population and Housing*, U.S. Bureau of the Census, Washington, D.C., 1982.

9. *Pennsylvania Municipalities — 1980 General Population and Housing Characteristics*, The Pennsylvania State Data Center, Institute of State and Regional Affairs, The Pennsylvania State University at Harrisburg, 1982.

10. *Pennsylvania Migration in the 1980's*, Gordon F. DeJong and Gretchen T. Cornwell, Population Issues Research Center, The Pennsylvania State University, University Park, PA, 1989.

11. *Current Demographic Trends and State Policy: An Overview*, Gordon DeJong, Gretchen T. Cornwell and Janice Costanzo, Population Issues Research Center, The Pennsylvania State University, University Park, PA, 1987.

12. *Pennsylvania Population Projections — 1980 to 2000*, The Pennsylvania State University at Harrisburg, 1986.

13. *Pennsylvania Vital Statistics 1987*, Pennsylvania Department of Health, N. Mark Richards, M.D., Secretary, Harrisburg, PA, 1989.

CHAPTER THREE ENDNOTES

1. John E. Chubb and Terry M. Moe, "Educational Choice," Harrisburg, PA; The Commonwealth Foundation, 1989, p. 2.

2. The National Commission on Excellence in Education, *A Nation at Risk*, Washington, D.C.; Government Printing Office, 1983, p. 9.

3. Barbara Lerner, "American Education: How Are We Doing?," *The Public Interest*, Fall 1982, p. 68.

4. The College Board, National Report, *1988 Profile of SAT and Achievement Test Takers*, p. iii.

5. Lee Mitgang, "Latest SAT Results Show a Widening Racial, Gender Gap," *Sharon (PA) Herald*, Sept. 12, 1989, p. 1.

6. John I. Goodlad, *A Place Called School*, New York: McGraw-Hill Book Company, 1984, p. 13 citing Malcolm B. Scully, "Drop in Aptitude Test Scores Is Largest on Record," *The Chronicle of Higher Education*, Sept. 15, 1975, p. 15 and C.H. Edson "Why Scholastic Aptitude Test Scores Are Falling," Eugene, Oregon: School Study Council, University of Oregon, 1976, p. 9.

7. John E. Chubb and Terry E. Moe, 1989, pp. 2-3. See also B. Lerner, pp. 68-70.

8. Diane Ravitch and Chester E. Finn, Jr., *What Do Our 17-Year-Olds Know?*, New York: Harper and Row, Publishers, 1987, p. 1.

9. Ibid.

10. Ravitch and Finn, p. 70.

11. Ravitch and Finn, p. 96.

12. Ravitch and Finn, p. 89.

13. *A Nation at Risk*, pp. 5-6.

14. Lynne V. Cheney, Chairman, National Endowment for the Humanities, *American Memory*, Washington, D.C.: U.S. Government Printing Office, 1987, pp. 7, 8 and 16.

15. For a good summary of ten important education reports of the 1980's, see John W. Miller, "Ten Reform Reports That Can Change Your School," *Principal*, Vol. 66, No. 2, November 1986, pp. 26-28.

16. Stanley M. Elam and Alec M. Gallup, "21st Annual Gallup Poll of the Attitudes," *Phi Delta Kappan*, Vol. 71, No. 1, September 1989, p. 50.

17. 21st Gallup Poll, p. 42.

18. B. Lerner, pp. 78-80.

19. "3 in 4 Professors Think Their Undergraduate Students Are Seriously Unprepared," *The Chronicle of Higher Education*, August 16, 1989, p. A-13.

20. John E. Chubb and Terry E. Moe, 1989, pp. 6-7.

21. The College Board, "Pennsylvania Report, 1988 Profile of SAT and Achievement Test Takers," 1988, p. 1.

22. Lee Mitgang, p. 1.

23. Ravitch and Finn, p. 44.

24. 21st Gallup Poll, p. 53.

25. The Commonwealth Foundation, *Commonwealth Review*, Summer 1989, p. 1, 3, and 4.

26. Thomas B. Timar and David L. Kirp, "Education Reform in the 1980's: Lessons from the States," *Phi Delta Kappan*, Vol. 70, No. 7, March 1989, p. 506.

27. The term "standards approach" is one used by Tim L. Mazzoni in "State Policy Making and Public School Choice in Minnesota, from Confrontation to Compromise," *Peabody Journal of Education*, Vol. 63, No. 4, Summer 1986, p. 55.

28. Susan Fuhrman, William H. Clune, and Richard F. Elmore, "Research in Education Reform: Lessons on the Implementation of Policy," *Teachers College Record*, Vol. 90, No. 2, Winter, 1988, pp. 241-243. For particular high school curriculum changes see Chapter 5, Rules and Regulations on Curriculum, PA State Board of Education, particularly section 5.5: for professional development requirements see Act 178 of 1986, which is 24 P.S. 12-1205.1 of the PA School Code; and for teacher certification testing see chapter 49, State Board of Education and Regulations, section 49.18.

29. Section 5.5, Chapter 5, PA State Board of Education, Rules and Regulations on Curriculum.

30. A Nation at Risk, p. 24.

31. Fuhrman, Clune and Elmore, pp. 249-250.

32. Fuhrman, Clune and Elmore, pp. 249.

33. *Ibid.*

34. Fuhrman, Clune and Elmore, p. 250.

35. See Timar and Kirk, p. 506.

36. 24 P.S. 12-1205-1.

37. Fuhrman, Clune and Elmore, p. 243.

38. "The Intellectual Lives of Teachers," Edwin J. Delattre, in Chester E. Finn, Jr., Diane Ravitch and Robert T. Faucher, eds., *Against Mediocrity, The Humanities in America's High Schools*, New York: Homes and Meier, 1984.

39. Delattre, pp. 160-161.

40. Thomas E. Eissenberg and Lawrence M. Reedner, "State Testing of Teachers: A Summary," *Journal of Teacher Education*, July-August 1988, p. 21. See also State Board of Education Regulations, chapter 49, section 49.18.

41. Kevin Harley, "How 'Schools of Choice' Can Improve the Public School System," The Commonwealth Foundation, January 1989.

42. Dennis P. Doyle, "Here's Why School Choice Will Boost Student Motivation — and Learning," *The American School Board Journal*, July 1989, p. 25.

43. Tim L. Mazzoni, pp. 45-69.

44. Chubb and Moe, pp. 12-13.

45. Chubb and Moe, pp. 14-15.

46. Chubb and Moe, p. 16.

47. Chubb and Moe, p. 19.

48. 21st Gallup Poll, pp. 42-43.

49. 21st Gallup Poll, p. 43.

50. The Commonwealth Foundation Poll, p. 3.

51. Joe Nathan, "The Governor's Report: Implications for Principals," *Principal*, Vol. 66, No. 3, January 1987, p. 31.

52. Pat Ordovensky, "A Push to End School-Choice Plans," *U.S.A. Today*, July 5, 1989.

53. Patricia A. Farnan, "Parental Choice in Education," *Family Policy*, The Family Research Council, Washington, D.C., July-August 1989, p. 6.

54. Goodlad, p. 31.

55. Kathleen Sylvester, "Schools of Choice: A Path to Educational Quality for 'Tiers of Inequity'?" *Governing*, July 1989.

56. Suzanne Fields, "Choosing Education Excellence," *The Washington Times*, July 11, 1989, p. F1.

57. Dennis P. Doyle, *American School Board Journal*, July 1989, p. 25.

58. Tim L. Mazzoni, p. 66. See also Chubb and Moe, p. 24.

59. Judith Pearson, "Myths of Choice: The Governor's New Clothes?," *Phi Delta Kappan*, Vol. 70, No. 10, June 1989, p. 823.

60. Carol Innerst, "NEA Votes Against Parental Choice," *The Washington Times*, July 5, 1989.

61. Kathleen Sylvester, *Governing*, July 1982.

62. *Pennsylvania Statutes Annotated*, 24 P.S. Section 13-1327.

CHAPTER SIX REFERENCES

1. "Bush's Education Summit: Topics For Discussion," *Education Week*, 27 September 1989.

2. Doyle, Dennis P., and Kearns, David T., *Winning the Brain Race: A Bold Plan to Make Our Schools Competitive*, San Francisco: ICS Press, 1988.

3. Dornbusch, Rudiger; Krugman, Paul; Park, Yung Chul; with foreward by Chandler, Colby H., *Meeting World Challenges: U.S. Manufacturing in the 1990's*, Rochester: Eastman Kodak Company, 1989.

4. *The Forgotten Half: Pathways to Success for America's Youth and Young Families*, Washington, D.C.: Youth and America's Future: The William T. Grant Commission on Work, Family and Citizenship, 1988.

5. Koppel, Ross, *A Report to the Pennsylvania Occupational Information Coordinating Committee*, Governor's Office of Policy and The Department of Labor and Industry, Philadelphia: Social Research Corporation, 1989.

6. Murnane, Richard J., "Education and the Productivity of the Work Force: Looking Ahead." *In American Living Standards*, pp. 215-45. Edited by Robert E. Litan, Robert Z. Lawrence, and Charles Schultze, Washington, D.C.: The Brookings Institution, 1988.

7. National Alliance of Business, *The Compact Project: School-Business Partnerships for Improving Education*, Washington, D.C.: National Alliance For Business, 1989.

8. Perry, Nancy J., "How to Help America's Schools," *Fortune*, December 4, 1989, pp. 137-142.

9. Perry, Nancy J., "Saving the Schools: How Business Can Help," *Fortune Special Report*, November 7, 1988.

10. Public Education Fund Network, *Five Years: 1983-88 The Public Education Fund*, Pittsburgh: Public Education Fund Network, 1988.

CHAPTER SEVEN REFERENCES

1. *Final Report: Human Services Choices for Pennsylvanians*, Pennsylvania State Planning Board, June 1986.

2. *Pennsylvania Population Projections, 1980 to 2000*, Volume I, Pennsylvania State Data Center, January 1986.

3. *Projections of the Population of the United States, by Age, Sex, and Race: 1988 to 2000*, Current Populations Reports, Series P-25, No. 1018, U.S. Bureau of the Census, January 1989.

4. *Final Report: Human Services Choices for Pennsylvanians*, Pennsylvania State Planning Board, June 1986.

5. "The Declining Significance of Age in the United States: Trends in the Well-Being of Children and the Elderly Since 1939," by Eugene Smolensky, Sheldon Danziger, and Peter Gottschalk, in *The Vulnerable*, edited by John L. Palmer, Timothy Smedding, and Barbara Boyle Torrey, The Urban Institute Press, 1988.

6. *Caring for the Disabled Elderly: Who Will Pay?* by Alice M. Rivlin and Joshua M. Wiener, The Brookings Institution, 1988.

7. *Long Term Care for the Elderly: Issues of Need, Access, and Cost*, U.S. General Accounting Office, November 1988.

8. *Findings from Mathematica's Evaluation of the Long-Term Care Assessment and Management Program: Their Implications for Long Term Care in Pennsylvania*, Pennsylvania Department of Aging, 1989.

9. *A Briefing Book on the Status of Children*, Children's Defense Fund, 1989.

10. *Pennsylvania Population Projections, 1980 to 2000*, Volume I, Pennsylvania State Data Center, January 1986.

11. *Projections of the Population of the United States by Age, Sex, and Race: 1988 to 2000*, Current Population Reports, Series P-25, No. 1018, U.S. Bureau of the Census, January 1989.

12. *Final Report: Human Services Choices for Pennsylvanians*, Pennsylvania State Planning Board, June 1986.

13. "The Declining Significance of Age in the United States: Trends in the Well-Being of Children and the Elderly Since 1939," by Eugene Smolensky, Sheldon Danzinger, and Peter Gottschalk, in *The Vulnerable*, edited by John L. Palmer, Timothy Smedding, and Barbara Boyle Torrey, The Urban Institute Press, 1988.

14. *1988 Child Abuse Report*, Pennsylvania Department of Public Welfare, 1989.

15. *Pennsylvania Vital Statistics Annual Report, 1987*, Pennslvania State Health Data Center, July 1978.

16. Pennsylvania Natality and Mortality Statistics Annual Report, 1977, Pennsylvania Health Data Center, July 1978.

17. *The Common Good: Social Welfare and the American Future*, Ford Foundation, 1989.

18. *Injury in America: A Continuing Public Health Problem*, Committee on Trauma Research, National Academy Press, 1985.

19. "Physical Disability and Public Policy," by Gerben DeJong and Raymond Lifchez, *Scientific American*, June 1983.

20. "Late Failures of Comprehensive Rehabilitation," by Michael Alexander, M.D., in *The Care of Chronically Ill Children and Their Families*, edited by W.M. Gibson, M.D., Elizabethtown Hospital and Rehabilitation Center, 1985.

21. "Reasonable Accomodations for Disabled Employees," by George McGuire, *Bell Atlantic Quarterly*, Autumn 1986.

22. *Homelessness in Pennsylvania*, by Phyllis Ryan, Ira Goldstein, and David Bartelt, Coalition on Homelessness in Pennsylvania and Institute for Public Policy Studies of Temple University, January 1989.

23. *A Briefing Book on the Status of Children*, Children's Defense Fund, 1989.

24. *Final Report: Human Services Choices for Pennsylvanians*, Pennsylvania State Planning Board, June 1986.

25. *Human Resources in Community Human Service Programs*, Task Force on Human Resources Development, Commonwealth of Pennsylvania, February 1989.

26. *Is Prevention Better Than Cure?*, by Louise B. Russell, The Brookings Institution, 1986.

CHAPTER EIGHT ENDNOTES

1. Urie Bronfenbrenner, "Alienation and the Four Walls of Childhood," *Phi Delta Kappan*, February 1986, p. 434.

2. Reported in "Getting Tough," *Time*, February 1, 1988.

3. See my article, "Why Schools Fail: Reclaiming the Moral Dimension in Education," *The Heritage Lectures*, #172. The address was given at The Heritage Foundation, June 23, 1988.

4. Edward Banfield, *The Unheavenly City Revisited*, (Little, Brown and Co., 1986). See especially chapter three.

5. Gina Kolata, "In Cities, Poor Families are Dying of Crack," *New York Times*, August 11, 1989, p. A1.

6. See *Statistical Abstract of the U.S. 1989*, Table #28, "Projections of the Population 18 Years Old and Over, by Race and Hispanic Origin — States: 1988.

7. Ibid., Table #94, Low Birth Weight and Births to Teenage Mothers and to Unmarried Women — States: 1980 and 1986. For data on families below the poverty line see Table #733, "Persons, Families and Children Below Poverty Line — Number and percent, By State: 1979."

8. The figures for Philadelphia and Pittsburgh are reported in *1980 Census of the Population*, "Detailed Population Characteristics: Pennsylvania," Table 245, pp. 40-1522 and 40-1530. The national statistics are reported in *Current Population Reports: Population Profile of the United States 1989*, "Special Studies Report Series P-23, No. 159," pp. 34-35.

9. See the report by Jane Blotzer, "The Choice: Poor job or none," *Pittsburgh Post Gazette*, December 19, 1988, p. 6.

10. The data are from a survey reported by Jane Blotzer, "Black Teens' Outlook Grim, not Hopeless," *Pittsburgh Post-Gazette*, December 26, 1988, p. 12.

11. Barbara White Stack, "City's Black Infant Death Rate Soars," *Pittsburgh Post Gazette*, January 27, 1989, p. 5.

12. Jane Blotzer, "Blacks Face Long Road to a Better Education," *Pittsburgh Post-Gazette*, November 7, 1988, p. 10.

13. Information on both reports is published in "Cocaine Mothers Imperil Babies' Brains," *Science News*, April 1, 1989, p. 198.

14. "Fetal AIDS Mimicked in Brain-Cell Culture," *Science News*, April 1, 1989, p. 199.

15. Banfield, *The Unheavenly City Revisited*.

16. Douglas C. Glasgow, *The Black Underclass*, (New York: Random House, 1980).

17. Nicholas Lemann, "The Origins of the Underclass," *Atlantic Monthly*, June and July 1986.

18. John DeIulio, Jr., "The Impact of Inner-City Crime," *Public Interest*, Summer 1989, pp. 28-46.

19. Roger Wilkins, "The Black Poor Are Different," *New York Times*, August 22, 1989, p. 23.

20. Charles Murray, *Losing Ground* (New York: Basic Books, Inc., 1984).

21. William Julius Wilson, *The Truly Disadvantaged* (Chicago: University of Chicago Press, 1987).

22. Ken Auletta, *The Underclass* (New York: Random House, 1982).

23. Ibid., p. 28.

24. For one of the most popular works that spurned this spurious argument see William Ryand, *Blaming the Victim* (New York: Random House, 1971).

25. Lemann, "The Origins of the Underclass," *Atlantic Monthly*, July 1986, p. 56.

26. Auletta, *The Underclass*, p. 199.

27. Charles Murray, "White Welfare, Families: 'White Trash'" *National Review*, March 28, 1986, pp. 30-34.

28. For the most thorough report on the consequences of single parent families see Irwin and Sara McLanahan, *Single Mothers and Their Children: A New American Dilemma* (Washington, D.C.: Urban Institute Press, 1986). Sara McLanahan received a $600,000 grant in 1988 from the National Institutes of Health to conduct further research on this subject, the results of which should shed greater light on this problem.

29. Robert Rector and Kate Walsh O'Beirne, "Dispelling the Myth of Income Inequality," *Heritage Foundation Backgrounder*, June 6, 1989, pp. 13-14.

30. Kate Walsh O'Beirne, "U.S. Income Data: Good Numbers Hiding Excellent News," *Heritage Foundation Backgrounder*, August 19, 1988, p. 5.

31. For a detailed description of this cultural phenomenon see my *The New Freedom: Individualism and Collectivism in the Social Lives of Americans*, recently published by Transaction Press, 1989. Much of the discussion that follows is gleaned from the chapter on the family.

32. The Raspberry quote is cited by Auletta, *The Underclass*, p. 38.

33. Lawrence Mead, "Jobs for the Welfare Poor," *Policy Review*, Winter 1988, p. 66.

34. Quoted by Auletta, *The Underclass*, p. 67.

35. Robert Rector, "Fourteen Myths About Families and Child Care," *Harvard Journal on Legislation*, Summer 1989, pp. 523-25 and 538-40.

36. Much has been written about this experiment. For a good discussion of the Kenilworth-Parkside project see Stuart Butler and Anna Kondratas, *Out of the Poverty Trap* (New York: Free Press, 1987).

37. See "The Commonwealth Foundation Poll: Support for Schools, A Call for Limited Terms, and An Appeal for More Taxpayer Influence in Harrisburg," *Issue Briefs*, August 1989.

38. James S. Coleman, "Private Schools, Public Schools, and the Public Interest," *Public Interest*, Summer 1981.

39. Michael Wines, "Poll Finds Public Favors Tougher Laws Against Drug Sale and Use," *New York Times*, August 15, 1989, p. A16.

40. Kenneth Clark, *Dark Ghetto* (New York: Harper and Row, 1965), p. 102.

CHAPTER NINE ENDNOTES

1. See Gail R. Wilensky, The "Pay or Play" Insurance Gamble, Massachusetts' Plan for Universal Health Coverage, The House Wednesday Group, September 26, 1988.

2. A "deductible" defines a particular amount of initial medical expenses each year that the insured worker must pay for directly before the insurance begins to cover expenses.

3. A "co-insurance" fee defines a proportion of covered medical expenses that the insured must pay directly. For example, a co-insurance fee of 10% would require the insured to pay 10 cents of each dollar of medical bills, with the insurance company paying the other 90 cents.

4. For a comprehensive discussion of the liability problem, see Peter W. Huber, *Liability: The Legal Revolution and Its Consequences* (New York: Basic Books, 1988).

5. Peter J. Ferrara, "Medicare and the Private Sector," *Yale Law and Policy Review*, Vol. 6, No. 1, 1988. Peter J. Ferrara, "Health Care and the Elderly" in Stuart Butler and Edmund Haislmaier eds., *A National Health System for America* (Washington, D.C., Heritage Foundation, 1989).

6. For further discussion, see Ferrara, "Medicare and the Private Sector," pp. 68-70.

7. For a further discussion of these regulations and their problems, see Ferrara, "Medicare and the Private Sector," pp. 21-22; Ferrara, "Health Care and the Elderly," pp. 72-73.

8. See Aldona Robbins and William E. Hurwitz, "Catastrophic Insurance Is Bad Medicine," Institute of Research on the Economics of Taxation, *Economic Policy Bulletin* No. 26, 1987, pp. 3-4. See also *The Effects of PPS on Quality of Care for Medicare Patients*, Hearings Before the Special Committee on Aging, 99th Cong. 2nd Sess. (1985); *Quality of Care Under Medicare's Prospective Payment System*, Hearings Before the Special Senate Committee on Aging, 99th Cong., 2nd Sess. (1985); Impact of Medicare's Prospective Payment System on Quality of Care Received by

Medicare Beneficiaries, Staff of the Special Committee on Aging, 99th Cong., 2nd Sess. (1985).

9. Harvard Medicare Project, Division of Health Policy Research and Education, Center for Health Policy and Management, *Medicare: Coming of Age* (Cambridge, Mass. 1986), p. 1; Robbins and Hurwitz, op. cit., p. 5.

10. General Accounting Office, *Long-Term Care Insurance Coverage Varies in a Widely Developing Market* (Washington, D.C., 1986).

11. See Peter J. Ferrara, "Providing for Those in Need: Long Term Care Policy," *Heritage Foundation Backgrounder*, No. 646 (Washington, D.C., 1988), p. 9; Ferrara, "Health Care and the Elderly," pp. 72-73.

12. Task Force on Long Term Health Care Policies, *Report to Congress and the Secretary*, U.S. Department of Health and Human Services, September 21, 1987, pp. 19, 69.

13. Id.

14. See Ferrara, "Providing for Those in Need," p. 7.

15. Id.

16. Id.

17. For further discussion of this proposal, see Ferrara, "Medicare and the Private Sector," pp. 78-86; Ferrara, "Health Care and the Elderly," pp. 87-89.

CHAPTER TEN ENDNOTES

1. *Investment in Pennsylvania's Future: The Keystone for Economic Growth*, The Pennsylvania Economic Development Partnership (January 1988), p. 42.

2. Unlike economic projections, demographic projections are reasonably accurate and reliable.

3. The high value positions typically have national markets because the candidates are highly mobile, so there is little rationale for state government action in the higher end of the employment spectrum.

4. T.K. Glennan, Jr., "Education, Employment, and the Economy: An Examination of Work-Related Education in Greater Pittsburgh," The Rand Corporation report N-3007-OERI/HHE (September 1989), p. vi.

5. See, for example, the paper by A. Kaatz and F.J. Tannery, "Adjusting to Structural Change: A Profile of the Work Experiences and Earnings of Dislocated Workers in the Pittsburgh Region 1979-86," University of Pittsburgh (January 1988).

6. See A. Kaatz and F.J. Tannery, ibid, and L. Jacobson, "Labor Mobility and Structural Change in Pittsburgh," *American Planning Association Journal* (Autumn, 1987), 438-448.

CHAPTER ELEVEN ENDNOTES

1. If measured on the basis of the total labor force, union membership reached its highest point in the mid-1950's, with 25.5 percent of the total labor force belonging to labor unions in 1953. In terms of sustained strength, labor unions maintained their highest level of membership as a percentage of the total labor force, ranging above 24 percent, from 1951 to 1959. If measured in terms of nonagricultural employment, union membership peaked in 1945 at 35.5 percent, then remained on a plateau varying between roughly 32 and 34 percent until 1959. This information is derived from data published by the United States Department of Labor, Bureau of Labor Statistics. Data exclude members of professional and public employees associations.

2. Since the 1950's, union membership has steadily declined to 16.8 percent of all wage and salary employees in 1988, the last reported year, which is its lowest level in the last fifty years. This information was derived from data published by the United States Department of Labor, Bureau of Labor Statistics, and is based on data from the Current Population Survey: May 1977-1988; Annual Average, 1983-88.

Pennsylvania labor union membership statistics also indicate a marked decline, but with a notable difference. Although state data are not readily available, the Pennsylvania Department of Labor and Industry recently reported that union membership within the Commonwealth declined from 34.3 percent in 1975 to 27 percent in 1982. The Department's reported research also revealed that Pennsylvania ranks 5th out of the ten states that it surveyed. For reference purposes, only New York (35.8%), Michigan (33.7%), West Virginia (28.9%) and Illinois (27.5%) ranked above Pennsylvania in the study. This level of union membership is significant both in absolute terms and in relative terms in comparison to other states. These data were taken from a Pennsylvania Department of Labor and Industry briefing report, dated April 15, 1988, which used data solicited from the eleven largest states and the states surrounding Pennsylvania, with ten of the fourteen states reporting.

3. It is beyond the focus of this chapter to delve deeply into the reasons for the decline of labor union membership and strength in Pennsylvania or the United States, or to develop and explain the failings of modern liberal labor policies vis-a-vis the economy. However, a reflection on recent Pennsylvania economic history would certainly suggest a strong negative correlation between the preferential treatment given labor unions and the health of the Commonwealth's economy.

The Pennsylvania Business Roundtable, in its report entitled "Partnership for Pennsylvania's Development" (1987), noted that, since 1960, Pennsylvania lost its competitive advantage, and that this decline in Pennsylvania's competitiveness is primarily caused by our inability to compete with other states (p. 4 and p. 7). Using the methodology called shift-share analysis, the report indicated that competitive share disadvantages exist in three-quarters of Pennsylvania's industry and product groups due to factors within the Commonwealth (p. 26). Those industry sectors within the Pennsylvania economy which exhibited the most significant decline during the period studied were the primary metals sector and the apparel and textile sector (p. 7). Other major, noncompetitive sectors include mining and, to a lesser extent, transportation and public utilities. Interestingly, it is generally within the sectors noted that unions have their greatest strength. The percentage of manufacturing employees represented by labor unions in Pennsylvania as recently as 1988 was 41.8 percent (Grant Thornton's Ninth Annual Manufacturing Climates Study, 1988).

Research by Professor Michael L. Wachter, Professor of Economics, Law and Management at the University of Pennsylvania, evidences a strong correlation between declining union employment share and rising union wage premiums ("The Internal Labor Market and Labor Law: An Exploration of Rising Union Wage Premiums," 1985). To quote Professor Wachter from an article in the *Wall Street Journal* (Tuesday, February 25, 1986), "the so-called deindustrialization of America appears to be a union specific phenomenon." Unfortunately, the negative economic effects of unionization ramify through the general economy to the detriment of almost everyone.

4. U.S. General Accounting Office, *The Davis-Bacon Act Should Be Repealed* (HRD-79-18, 1979). See also *Prevailing Wage Legislation: The Davis-Bacon Act, the State "Little Davis-Bacon" Acts, The Walsh-Healey Act and the Service Contract Act* by Armand J. Thieblot, Jr., published by the University of Pennsylvania in its Labor Relations and Public Policy Series (No. 27).

5. Information was obtained from the "Unemployment Insurance Financial Data Handbook" (ET Handbook 394) of the U.S. Department of Labor for eleven major states. The calculated factor for comparison was total benefit cost as a percentage of total wages. This factor was chosen because it takes into account the economic variations between the states that otherwise have different benefit and tax structures, and different wage scales. In order to avoid possible aberrations for particular points in time, the data were analyzed for 1987 (the most recent year for which data are available), for the most recent 7 year period, the most recent 15 year period, and the most recent 20 year period. Regardless of the time frame analyzed, Pennsylvania ranks as the highest costing state. It should be noted that tax levels are a function of benefit costs. The amount of a tax levy necessary to pay for benefits is dependent upon the total cost of those benefits. Over the long term, the comparative rank order of tax levels must follow the rank order of benefit cost levels.

Historical evidence indicates that Pennsylvania's unemployment compensation program operated with overall stability until 1970. Fluctuations in reserves and solvency did occur, but over the long term the fund remained financially stable and solvent. Various enactments of benefit liberalizations during the 1970's drove Pennsylvania's benefit costs up to among the highest of the industrialized states. These costs, lacking politically sustainable taxing levels to support them, resulted in deficit spending of an enormous magnitude for well over a decade and a nearly $3 billion debt. The legislation enacted in 1983 to return the fund to solvency did include some reductions in benefits, but part of those benefits were effectively restored at the time the debt was retired. The net effect of the debt-related legislation enacted in 1983 and 1988 has been the creation of a tax structure capable of sustaining benefit levels that, prior to 1983, substantially caused the program's insolvency and its $3 billion debt. Because no meaningful benefit reform has been enacted, there is very little reason to believe that Pennsylvania's benefit cost standing will change significantly as new data are reported.

CHAPTER TWELVE ENDNOTES

1. Commonwealth of Pennsylvania, *Executive Budget 1989-90*, Harrisburg, PA, February 1989, p. E431.

2. Pennsylvania Transportation Advisory Committee, *Future Directions for PennDOT*, PA Dept. of Transportation, Harrisburg, PA, Jan. 1986.

3. *The Wall Street Journal*, Vol. LXX, No. 223, Aug. 30, 1989, p. 1.

4. Future Directions for PennDOT, op. cit.

5. Pennsylvania Intercity High Speed Rail Passenger Commission, *Final Report*, Harrisburg, PA, June 1989.

6. Transportation and Distribution Associates, *A Comprehensive Freight Rail Study for Pennsylvania*, PA Dept. of Transportation, Harrisburg, PA, Jan. 1987.

7. "The Port of the Delaware River: Rebuilding for the Future," Congressman Thomas M. Foglietta and James J. Florio, 1989.

8. Pennsylvania Public Utilities Commission, "Gas Storage in Pennsylvania," Staff Report, June 1988.

CHAPTER THIRTEEN ENDNOTES

1. George Gilder, *Microcosm: The Quantum Revolution in Economics and Technology*, Simon and Shuster, New York, N.Y. (1989): p. 21.

2. Ibid, pp. 12 and 18.

3. Robert M. Hazen, *The Break Through: The Race for the Superconductor*, Summit Books, New York, N.Y. (1989): pp. 8 and 257.

4. John Naisbitt and Patricia Aburdene, *Re-Inventing the Corporation: Transforming Your Job and Company For the New Information Society*, Warner books (1985): p. 2.

5. Pat Langiotti, "The State of Pennsylvania," an interview on Public Television (1 March, 1987).

6. John Naisbitt, *Megatrends: The New Directions Transforming Our Lives*, Warner Books (1984): p. 103.

7. Newt Gingrich, *Window of Opportunity: A Blueprint for the Future*, TOR Book, New York, N.Y. (1984): p. 74.

8. Gilder, op. cit., p. 312.

9. Bell Atlantic, *Delivering the Promise: A Vision of Tomorrow's Communications Consumer* (April 1989): pp. 70-71.

10. John Naisbitt and Patricia Aburdene, *Megatrends 2000: Ten New Directions for the 1990's*, William Morrow and Company, Inc., New York (1990): p. 24.

11. Shooshan and Jackson, Inc., *The Impact of Regulation and Public Policy on Telecommunications Infrastructure and U.S. Competitiveness*, Northeast Midwest Institute, The Center for Regional Policy, Washington, D.C. (April 1989), p. 19.

12. Ibid, p. 17.

13. David L. Wenner, "Are You Ready For Residential Broadband?," *Telephony* (May 22, 1989): p. 84.

CHAPTER SEVENTEEN ENDNOTES

1. Hazardous Waste Capacity Assurance, Commonwealth of Pennsylvania, Appendix A, Northeast States Capacity Assurance Plan, pp. 1.

CHAPTER EIGHTEEN ENDNOTES

1. *Intermediate Sanctions*, Tonry, M. and R. Will, Preliminary Report to the Department of Justice, 1988. I also am indebted to Tonry and Will for many of the points which are raised in the discussion which follows. Similarly, I have drawn heavily from the work and ideas in numerous articles by Joan Petersilia.

2. *Expanding Options For Criminal Sentencing*, J. Petersilia, Santa Monica, CA: Rand Corporation, 1987.

3. Two excellent sources for summary descriptions of these and other intermediate sanctions programs are Petersilia, *op. cit.*, and Tonry and Will, *op. cit.*.

4. "Shock Incarceration Programs in State Correctional Jurisdications: An Update," *National Institute of Justice Reports*, Vol. 214, May/June 1989.

5. Calibrating the percentage of program participants who would not have been prison-bound is inherently speculative. The internal evaluators

of the Georgia ISP program estimate that only 20% of participants were not prison-bound. Will and Tonry, however, argue that it is closer to 50%.

6. Petersilia reports that failure rates in ISP and house arrest programs range from 5% to 35%.

7. One might object that the participant who commits a new crime deserves to be incarcerated. I don't necessarily disagree but that doesn't change the fact the program may have created a prison admission that would not have otherwise occurred.

8. *Comparing Intensive and Regular Supervision for High-Risk Probationers: Early Results from an Experiment in California*, J. Petersilia and S. Turner, Santa Monica, CA: Rand Corp., 1989.

9. *Identifying Drug Users and Monitoring Them During Conditional Release*, E.P. Wish, M.A. Tobory, J.P. Bellassai, National Institute of Justice (NEJ 108560), 1988.

CHAPTER NINETEEN ENDNOTES

1. W. John Moore, "Dissenters in the Drug War," *National Journal*, November 4, 1989: p. 2693.

2. "Mission Just Possible," *The Economist*, September 30, 1989: p. 72.

3. Candace L. Romig, ed. "Combatting Substance Abuse and Its Effect Upon Families," *Family Policy: Recommendations for State Action*, National Conference of State Legislatures, Denver, Colorado, December 1989: p. 121.

4. Pennsylvania Commission on Crime and Delinquency, "Pennsylvania's Statewide Drug Law Enforcement and Violent Crime Strategy," The Commonwealth of Pennsylvania, Harrisburg, Pennsylvania, February 1989: p. 3.

5. Steven Findlay, "How to Beat Drugs," *U.S. News and World Report*, September 11, 1989: p. 74.

6. Dick Kirschten, "Taking Back the Streets," *National Journal*, September 30, 1989: p. 74.

7. Douglas J. Besharov, "Children of Crack: Will We Protect Them?" *Public Welfare*, Fall 1989: p. 7.

8. *Ibid.*, p. 11.

9. Donald C. Bacon, "Business Moves Against Drugs," *The Nation's Business*, November 1989: p. 82.

10. Eugene E.J. Maier, "Why Not Courts Just For Drug Cases?" *The Philadelphia Inquirer*, November 2, 1988: p. 17-A.

1. Moore, p. 2694.

406   ENDNOTES AND REFERENCES

12. James Cook, "The Paradox of Anti-Drug Enforcement," *Forbes*, November 13, 1989: p. 113.

CHAPTER TWENTY-ONE ENDNOTES

1. John M. Baer, "Special Interest Dough Keeps Rising," *The Philadelphia Daily News*, March 20, 1989, p. 4ff.

2. Richard Robbins, "PACs/Redistricting Help Incumbents Keep Their Jobs," *The Greensburg Tribune Review*, Sept. 4, 1988, p. A1-A8.

3. Ibid., p. A8.

4. Ibid., P. A8.

5. Brooks Jackson, "Send Most PACs Packing," *The Wall Street Journal*, Sept. 22, 1988, p. 17.

6. "Election Reform," *The Sunday Patriot News*, May 16, 1989, p. B6.

7. Jackson, p. 17.

8. Eric Conrad, "Legislators Return to Top Salary in U.S.," *The Sunday Patriot News*, September 27, 1987, p. B1.

9. *Buckley V. Valeo*.

10. Sandra Singer, "The Arms Race of Campaign Financing," *State Legislatures*, July 1988, p. 27.

11. Larry Sabato, "The Attack on PACs," *The Washington Post*, August 1, 1987, p. 14.

12. Republican National Committee, "Republican Platform, August 15, 1988, p. 39.

13. Clifford Frick, "Commonwealth Foundation Poll . . . ," *Commonwealth Review*, Summer 1989, p. 1.

CHAPTER TWENTY-FIVE REFERENCES

1. Johnson, Manuel J., *Better Government at Half the Price*, Ottawa, Illinois, Carolina House Publishing.

2. AFSCME, *Passing the Bucks*, AFSCME, Washington, D.C., 1983.

3. American Bus Association, *Optimizing Public Transit Service through Competitive Contracting*, Washington, D.C., 1987.

4. Citizens League of the Twin Cities, *Enlarging Our Capacity to Adapt*, Minneapolis, Minn., 1983.

5. Kolderie, Theodore, *What Do We Mean by "Privatization"?* in Society, September-October 1987, pp. 46-51.

6. Center for Privatization, *Privatization Matrix Database*, Washington, D.C., 1987.

7. Reason Foundation, *Second Annual Report on Privatization: 1987*, Santa Monica, CA, 1988.

8. AFSCME, *When Public Services Go Private*, AFSCME, Washington, D.C., 1987.

9. Congressional Budget Offices, *Contracting Out: Potential for Reducing Federal Costs*, A Special Study, June 1987.

10. OECD, *Managing and Financing Urban Services*, Paris, 1987.

11. Edwards, Howard W., *Successful Approaches to Privatization: A Conference Paper*.

12. Sclar, E.D., Scheaffer, K.H., and Brandwein, R., *The Emperor's New Clothes: Transit Privatization and Public Policy*, Economicy Policy Institute, Washington, D.C., 1989.

13. Touche Ross, Inc., *Privatization in America: An Opinion Survey of City and County Governments on Their Use of Privatization*, Washington, D.C., 1987.

14. Savas, E.S., *Privatization: The Key to Better Government*, Chatham House Publishing, 1987.

15. Hatry, Harry and Valente, Carl, "Alternative Service Delivery Approaches Involving Increased Use of the Private Sector," *Municipal Year Book 1983*, International City Managers Association.

16. Morley, Elaine, The Urban Institute, "Patterns in the Use of Alternative Services Delivery Approaches," *Municipal Year Book 1988*, International City Managers Association.

17. Hanrahan, J.D., *Government For Sale: Contracting Out — The New Patronage*, AFSCME, Washington, D.C., 1977.

18. Fisk, D., Keisling, H., and Muller, T., *Private Provision of Public Services: An Overview*, Washington, D.C., The Urban Institute, 1978.

19. Committee for Economic Development, *Public-Private Partnership: An Opportunity for Urban Communities*, Washington, D.C., 1982.

20. Shulman, Martha A., "Alternative Approaches for Delivering Public Services" in *Urban Data Services Report*, Vol. 14, Number 10, ICMA, Washington, D.C., 1982.

21. Mercer/Slavin, Inc., *Findings of a National Survey of Local Government Service Contracting Practices*, Mercer/Slavin, Inc., Atlanta, GA, 1987.

CHAPTER TWENTY-FIVE ENDNOTE

1. Fisk, D., Keisling, H., Muller, T. *Private Provision of Public Services: An Overview*, Washington, D.C., 1978, The Urban Institute.